DELIA'S HOW TO COOK

Photographs by Miki Duisterhof

LONDON, NEW YORK, SYDNEY, DELHI, PARIS,
MUNICH, AND JOHANNESBURG

Cookbook Editor and americanization by Sarah Randell
Publisher: Sean Moore
Editorial Director: Chuck Wills
Project Editor: Barbara Minton
Art Director: Dirk Kaufman
Jacket Design: Gus Yoo
Designer: Megan Clayton
Editorial Assistants: Tracy McCord, Jane Perlmutter

First US edition, a combined edition of the BBC Volumes 1 and 2, published in 2001 by
DK Publishing, Inc.

This book is published to accompany the PBS television series
Delia's How To Cook
which was produced for BBC Birmingham by Spire Films Ltd
Series Producer: David Willcock
Directors: John Silver and Philip Bonham Carter
Executive Producers for the BBC: Rod Natkiel and Stephanie Silk

Presented by   Sponsored by

Produced by

Delia's How To Cook Book 1, first published by BBC Worldwide Ltd. in 1998
Delia's How To Cook Book 2, first published by BBC Worldwide Ltd. in 1999
Woodlands, 80 Wood Lane, London W12 0TT

Library of Congress Cataloging-in-Publication Data

Smith, Delia.
    Delia's How To Cook.--1 st American ed.
        p. cm.
    Includes index
    ISBN 0-7894-7186-8 (alk. paper)
    1. Cookery. I Title.

TX651 .S495 2001
641.5--dc21   00-045193

Edited for BBC Worldwide Ltd by New Crane Publishing Ltd
Printed and bound in Singapore by Tien Wah Press
Color separation by Tien Wah Press
Jacket printed in Singapore

Conversion tables

All these are approximate conversions, which have either been rounded up or down. In a few recipes, it has been necessary to modify them very slightly. Both American Standard and metric measurements are given. Never mix methods of measurement in one recipe; stick to one system or the other. All spoon measurements used throughout this book are level unless specified otherwise; all butter is salted unless specified otherwise.

Weights

½ oz	10 g
¾	20
1	25
1½	40
2	50
2½	60
3	75
4	110
4½	125
5	150
6	175
7	200
8	225
9	250
10	275
12	350
1 lb	450
2	900 g
3	1.35 kg

Volume

⅛ cup	25 ml
¼ cup	50 ml
⅓ cup	75 ml
½ cup	125 ml
⅔ cup	150 ml
¾ cup	175 ml
1 cup	250 ml
2 cups	500 ml
4 cups (1 quart)	1 liter

Dimensions

⅛ inch	3 mm
¼	5 mm
½	1 cm
¾	2
1	2.5
1¼	3
1½	4
1¾	4.5
2	5
2½	6
3	7.5
3½	9
4	10
5	13
5¼	13.5
6	15
6½	16
7	18
7½	19
8	20
9	23
9½	24
10	25.5
11	28
12	30

Oven temperatures

275°F	140°C
300	150
325	170
350	180
375	190
400	200
425	220
450	230
475	240

My little corner of Suffolk, and the writer's tree house at the end of the garden, where How To Cook was written

DELIA'S
HOW TO COOK

PART ONE

Part One Contents

Part One Introduction

It's now almost 30 years since I first started writing recipes, and 25 since I first started cooking on television. As you would expect, things changed quite dramatically during the last quarter of the 20th century.

In food terms we have moved on into what I would call an era of plenty. Absolutely everything we could possibly want is available. We can now walk into any large supermarket or gourmet food market and literally shop for ingredients around the world. We can eat whatever we want whenever we want. If we don't want to cook at all we can buy take-out meals, including vegetables and salads. Every city street has any number of fast food outlets, take-outs, home deliveries, as well as all kinds of restaurants. On top of all that we can simply "graze" all day on snack foods like potato chips and chocolate bars.

It could be said that we're immensely privileged in having so much choice. Therefore, where on earth does *How To Cook* fit in? Well, it's my personal belief that the opposite could be true – that we may be in danger of losing something very precious, and that is a reverence for simple, natural ingredients and the joy and pleasure they can bring to everyday life. We are not talking about spending masses of time in the kitchen, either. We need to be reminded that after a hard day, a perfectly made moist, fluffy omelette – which is so easy to make – is not only more satisfying but quicker than picking up take-out food.

One thing we have to come to terms with is that food, perhaps more than any other subject, lends itself to pretentiousness, and the beauty of simplicity can so easily be eclipsed. Yes, we all want to experience the "highs" of eating on special occasions and celebrations, of eating a meal in a beautiful restaurant cooked by a great chef, but the sensual pleasure of eating belongs to everyday life as well, and it's not always to be found in the vast amounts of mass-produced, fast foods that we're subtly persuaded to eat.

I am hoping to achieve two things in *How To Cook*: one is to reintroduce people to the pleasure of basic, staple ingredients, and the second is to provide a first-time cookbook, a book that will provide a good grounding in the simple basics and be a springboard for a lifetime of learning – not just in how to cook but in how to experience the sheer joy and pleasure of eating good food every single day.

Delia Smith

1

All about eggs

If you want to learn how to
cook, start with eggs. That's
my advice. Eggs are, after all,
a powerful symbol of something
new happening – new life, a new
beginning. But there is another
reason. Somehow eggs have
become an equally negative
symbol. When someone says,
"Oh, I can't even boil an egg,"
what they are actually saying is,
"I can't cook anything at all."

It's the amount of air in the pocket at the wide end of the egg – which in turn depends on the egg's freshness – that will determine how best to use the egg

The inner membrane within the shell begins as a taut, stretched skin; with age, however – and the inclusion of more air – this skin slackens

That's why anyone wanting to learn to cook should begin by understanding eggs. Yes – even how to boil them. By cracking egg cooking (sorry about the pun) and simply knowing how to boil, poach, scramble, make an omelette and so on, you're going to give your cooking confidence a kick-start and make sure you will never go hungry. You'll also be able to offer your friends and loved ones a very quick and pleasurable meal. But that's not all: eggs are a supremely important ingredient in the kitchen, serving the cook in any number of ways. They can thicken soups and sauces, set liquids and baked dishes, they can provide a glorious airy foam to lighten textures, and they will also, quite miraculously, emulsify oils and butter into a rich smoothness.

What we have to do first and foremost, though, before we even begin cooking, is to try and understand what eggs are and how they work.

Understanding eggs

A hen's egg is, simply, a work of art, a masterpiece of design, construction, and brilliant packaging! It is extremely nutritious, filled with life-giving protein, vitamins, and minerals. It has a delicate yet tough outer shell which, while providing protection for the growing life inside, is at the same time porous, allowing air to penetrate and the growing chick to breathe.

It's the amount of air inside the egg that the cook needs to be concerned with. If you look at the photograph, above left, you'll see the construction of the egg includes a space for the air to collect at the wide end, and it's the amount of air in this space that determines the age and quality of the egg and how best to cook it. In newly laid eggs, the air pocket is hardly there, but as days or weeks pass, more air gets in and the air pocket grows; at the same time, the moisture content of the egg begins to evaporate. All this affects the composition of the egg, so if you want to cook it perfectly it is vital to determine how old the egg is. Now, look at the photograph at the top of the opposite page and see what the egg looks like when it is broken. What you start off with, on the left, is an egg at its freshest, with a rounded, plump yolk that sits up proudly. The white has a thicker, gelatinous layer that clings all around the yolk, and a thinner outer layer. After a week, shown in the egg on the right, the yolk is flatter and the two separate textures of white are not quite so visible.

Now, all is revealed! You can see very clearly why you may have had problems in the past and why an egg needs to be fresh if you want to fry or poach it, because what you will get is a lovely, neat, rounded shape. Alas, a stale egg will spread itself more thinly and what you will end up with if you are frying it is a very thin pancake with a yellow center. If you put it into water to poach, it would probably disintegrate, with the yolk and white parting company. Separating eggs is yet another hazard if the eggs are too old, because initially the yolk is held inside a fairly tough, transparent membrane, but this weakens with age and will break more easily.

A fresh egg, far left, is distinguished by its plump, rounded yolk and distinctive two-layer white. A week-old egg, however, is characterized by a flatter yolk and a more even-textured white, left

So far, so good. But we haven't quite cracked it yet because, just to confuse matters, a very fresh egg isn't always best. Why? Because we have another factor to take into consideration. If we get back to the presence of air, what you will see from the photograph below left is that inside the shell is an inner membrane, a sort of safety net that would have protected the chick if the egg had been fertilized. When the egg is fresh, this is like a taut, stretched skin; then, as more air penetrates the egg, this skin slackens. This explains why, if you hard-boil a really fresh egg, peeling off both the shell and the skin is absolute torture. But if the egg is a few days' or even a week old, the skin will be looser, and the egg will peel like a dream.

What all this means is, yes, you can cook perfect eggs every time, as long as you know how old they are.

How to tell how old an egg is

How to tell how old a raw egg is while it is still safely tucked away in its shell could seem a bit tricky, but not so. Remember the air pocket? There is a simple test that tells you exactly how much air there is. All you do is place the egg in a glass of cold water: if it sinks to a completely horizontal position, it is very fresh; if it tilts up slightly or to a semi-horizontal position, it could be up to a week old; if it floats into a vertical position, then it is stale. The only reason this test would not work is if the egg had a hairline crack, which would allow more air in, but a cook can do this simple test and know precisely how the egg will behave 99 percent of the time. To sum up, the simple guidelines are as follows:

1 For poaching and frying, always use eggs as spanking fresh as you possibly can.

Below, left to right: a very fresh egg will rest horizontally when placed in a glass of water; one that lies semi-horizontally is generally up to a week old; and one that floats in a vertical position is stale

2 For separating egg yolks from whites, use eggs that are as fresh as possible; up to a week old is fine.

3 For peeled hard-boiled eggs, use eggs that are about a week old but up to two weeks is okay.

4 For scrambled eggs and omelettes, the fresher the eggs the better, but up to two weeks is fine.

5 For baked dishes, such as quiches or for home baking and so on, eggs more than two weeks old can be used.

6 In my opinion, all eggs should be used within two weeks if at all possible. An extra week is okay, but three weeks is the maximum storage time.

How to buy and store eggs

Number one on the list here (unless you happen to know the hens) is to buy your eggs from a supplier who has a high turnover. Cartons of eggs from producers whose eggs are USDA inspected carry a packing date. They may also carry a "best before" date. Egg producers whose plants are not USDA inspected are guided by the laws of the state, check the egg producing rules in your state.

Unless you live in a very cool climate and have a cool room or storage area, eggs should be stored in the refrigerator. For most cooking purposes, however, eggs are better used at room temperature, so you must remember to remove them a half an hour or so before using them. I think it is best to always buy eggs in small quantities so that you don't keep them too long.

The very best way to store eggs is to keep them in their own closed, cartons. Because the shells are porous, eggs can absorb the flavors and aromas of other strong foods, so close the egg cartons and keep them fairly isolated, particularly if you're storing them in the refrigerator.

There is, however, one glorious exception to this rule. My dear friend and great chef Simon Hopkinson once came to stay in our home. He brought some new-laid eggs in a carton, which also contained a fresh black truffle. He arrived on the Thursday before Easter, and on Easter Sunday he made some softly scrambled eggs, which by now had absorbed all the fragrance and flavor of the truffle. Served with thin shavings of the truffle sprinkled over them, I have to say they were the very best Easter eggs I have ever tasted!

The porosity of eggs' shells isn't always a bad thing: here a fresh black truffle is kept with the eggs, which in turn absorb its flavor and fragrance, adding an unexpected dimension to the finished dish

What about cholesterol?

Eggs, I am very happy to report, are out of the firing line on the cholesterol front. It is now believed that the real culprits on this one are saturated fat and partially hydrogenated fat, in which eggs, thankfully, are low. There is more good news, too: even if you are on a low-fat diet, eating up to seven eggs a week is okay. Hooray!

How safe are they?

Poor old eggs; just as they recover from one slur, along comes another. Eggs, as we know, can harbor a bacterium called salmonella. Cases of food poisoning, or even death, from eating raw eggs are isolated but do occur. Therefore, the only way we can be absolutely certain of not being affected is by only eating eggs that are well cooked, with hard yolks and no trace of softness or runny yolk at all. Ugh!

What we need to do is consider this very seriously and be individually responsible for making our own decisions. Life, in the end, is full of risks. The only way I can be absolutely sure I won't be involved in a car accident (and statistically this is a far greater risk than eating an egg harboring salmonella) is to never ride in a car. But I am personally willing to take that risk – as I do when I eat a soft-boiled egg. So it's a personal decision. As a general practice, though, it is not advisable to serve these to vulnerable groups, such as very young children, pregnant women, the elderly or anyone with a weakened immune system.

Some general egg information

1 Is there any difference between brown and white shells?
   None whatsoever. The color of the shell is determined by the breed of the hen that laid it. Aesthetically speaking, white denotes a kind of purity, while brown is full of rural wholesomeness.

2 Size. Size descriptions for eggs are as follows: jumbo, extra large, large, medium, and small. Please note that in this book the eggs used in all recipes are large.

3 The eggs now available on a large scale commercially are as follows: free-range means the hens have continuous daytime access to open-air runs that contain vegetation. In the US, "free-range" is not a legal egg industry term. Farmers use it to imply a humane standard of production, but there is no regulation regarding the use of the term. Eggs labeled organic are produced in the same way as free-range, but, in this case, the hens' habitat has been certified as free from herbicides and pesticides (as is the land on which their feed has been grown). Most other eggs sold are produced by chickens kept in confined spaces or units.

4 There are, of course, other types of eggs. I have included recipes and timings for commercially produced eggs (ie, hens' and quails' eggs), but if you have access to and want to cook other types of eggs (goose, turkey, or duck), then allow extra time for size. If you are baking, the best way to measure is by comparing the eggs you are using weight for weight with hens' eggs to give you a guideline. Goose and duck' eggs are rarely found in supermarkets, but if you are able to buy them from a local farmer, they taste very good boiled.

How do you boil eggs?

A pinprick made in the rounded end of an egg will allow steam to escape while it boils, thus avoiding cracking

The answer to this is carefully. Even the simplest of cooking tasks demands a degree of care and attention. But in the end all it involves is first knowing the right way to proceed and then happily being able to boil perfect eggs for the rest of your life without even having to think about it. What we need to do first of all, though, is memorize a few very important rules.

1 Don't ever boil eggs that have come straight from the refrigerator, because very cold eggs plunged straight into hot water are likely to crack.

2 Always use a kitchen timer. Trying to guess the timing or even remembering to look at your watch can be hazardous.

3 Remember the air pocket? During the boiling, pressure can build up and cause cracking. A simple way to deal with this is to make a pinprick in the rounded end of the shell, at left, which will allow the steam to escape.

4 Always use a small saucepan. Eggs with too much space to careen about and crash into one another while they cook are, again, likely to crack.

5 Never have the water fast-boiling; a gentle simmer is all they need.

6 Never boil eggs longer than necessary (you won't if you have a timer) because the yolks will turn dark and the texture will be like rubber.

7 If the eggs are very fresh (less than four days old), allow an extra 30 seconds for each timing below.

Soft-boiled eggs – method 1

Obviously every single one of us has a personal preference for the precise way we like our eggs cooked. Over the years I have found a method that is both simple and reliable, and the various timings set out here seem to accommodate all tastes. First of all have a small saucepan filled with enough simmering water to cover the eggs by about ½ inch (1 cm). Then quickly but gently lower the eggs into the water, one at a time, using a tablespoon. Now, switch a timer on and give the eggs exactly 1 minute's simmering time. Then remove the pan from the heat, put a lid on it, and set the timer again, setting one of the following timings:

> 5 minutes will produce a soft, fairly liquid yolk and a white that is just set but still quite wobbly
>
> 6 minutes will produce a firmer, more creamy yolk with a white that is completely set

Don't boil eggs in too large a saucepan: the less room they have to move about in the simmering water, the less likely they are to crack

Soft-boiled eggs – method 2

I have found this alternative method also works very well. This time you place the eggs in the saucepan, cover them with cold water by about ½ inch (1 cm), place them on a high heat, and as soon as they reach boiling point, reduce the heat to a gentle simmer and give the following timings:

> 2 minutes if you like a really soft-boiled egg
>
> 3 minutes for a white that is just set and a yolk that is creamy
>
> 4 minutes for a white and yolk perfectly set, with only a little bit of softness in the center

Hard-boiled eggs

Some people hate soft-boiled eggs and like to eat them hard-boiled straight from the shell. All well and good, but if you want to use hard-boiled eggs in a recipe, you have to peel them, and this can be extremely tricky if the eggs are too fresh. The number one rule, therefore, is to use eggs that are at least five days old from their packing date. The method is as follows: place the eggs in a saucepan and add enough cold water to cover them by about ½ inch (1 cm). Bring the water to the simmering point, put a timer on for 5 minutes if you like them a bit of soft in the center, 6 minutes if you want them cooked through. Then, the most important part is to cool them rapidly under cold running water. Turn on the cold water tap to run over them for about 1 minute, then leave them in cold water until they're cool enough to handle – about 2 minutes. Once you've mastered the art of boiling eggs you can serve them in a variety of ways; one of my favorites is in a curry, as in the recipe on the following page.

Peeling hard-boiled eggs

The best way to peel hard-boiled eggs is to first tap them against a hard surface to crack the shells, then hold each egg under a slow trickle of running water as you peel the shell off, starting at the wide end. The water will flush off any bits of shell that hang on. Then back they go into cold water until completely cold. If you don't cool the eggs rapidly they will go on cooking and become overcooked, then you get the dark-ring problem.

Quails' eggs

Quails' eggs for boiling should, again, not be too fresh, and these are best cooked by lowering them into simmering water for 5 minutes. Then cool them rapidly and peel them as above.

Clockwise from top: a very soft-boiled egg has a liquid yolk and a white that is still wobbly; a soft-boiled egg has a creamy yolk and a white that is just set; in a medium-boiled egg, both the white and yolk are set

The distinctive coloring of quails' eggs makes them a beautiful alternative to hens' eggs, and they're just as simple to cook

Egg and Lentil Curry with Coconut and Pickled Lime

This is one of my very favorite pantry recipes. If you always keep a stock of spices and lentils handy and a can of coconut milk stashed away in the pantry, you can whip this one up in no time at all. It also happens to be inexpensive, and it's suitable for vegetarians.

Serves 2
4 large eggs
⅓ cup (75 g) green lentils
1½ teaspoons lime pickle
or other spicy pickle
juice and grated zest ½ fresh lime
1 large onion
1 small red chili (preferably bird eye)
2 fat cloves garlic
1 inch (2.5 cm) piece fresh ginger
3 cardamom pods, crushed
1 teaspoon cumin seeds
1 teaspoon fennel seeds
2 teaspoons coriander seeds
2 tablespoons peanut or other mildly flavored oil
1½ teaspoons turmeric powder
1 teaspoon fenugreek powder
2½ cups coconut milk
salt

To serve:
⅔ cup (150 ml) rice, cooked
(see page 202)
a little extra lime or other pickle

You will also need a medium frying pan with a lid.

Start off by having everything prepared and ready to go. First, peel the onion, cut it in half and then into thin slices. Next, seed and finely chop the chili, peel and chop the garlic, and measure out the lime pickle, chopping it finely. Now, peel and grate the ginger – you need 1½ teaspoonfuls.

Now, place the frying pan over a medium heat, and as soon as it gets hot, measure the whole spices (cardamom, cumin, fennel, and coriander) into it. What they need to do now is to dry-roast, and this will take 2-3 minutes. Shake the pan from time to time to toss them around a bit, and as soon as they start to jump, remove them from the heat and drop them straight into a mortar.

Place the frying pan back over the heat, turn it up high, and add the oil. As soon as it is really hot, add the onions, and keeping the heat almost at high, let them sizzle and brown and become quite dark at the edges, which will take about 4 minutes. After that, turn the heat back down to medium and add the chili, ginger, garlic, and lime pickle, along with the turmeric and fenugreek. Now, crush the roasted spices finely with a pestle, add these to the frying pan and stir everything together.

Now, stir the lentils in to join the rest of the ingredients; add the grated lime zest and the coconut milk; stir again, and as soon as the mixture reaches simmering point, turn the heat down. Put the lid on and let it simmer as gently as possible for 45 minutes, stirring it now and then (don't add any salt at this stage).

About 10 minutes before the end of the cooking time, place the eggs in a saucepan of cold water, bring them up to a gentle simmer and time them for 5-6 minutes, depending on how you like them. When they're ready, run cold water from the tap over them until they're cool enough to handle. When the sauce is ready, season it well with salt and add the lime juice. Now, peel the eggs under cold running water, slice them in half and place them on top of the sauce, giving everything a couple more minutes' cooking with the lid on. Serve the egg curry with rice, some more lime pickle, and perhaps some mango chutney for a touch of sweetness.

Open-Faced Egg, Chive, and Scallion Sandwiches

Serves 2
3 small bread rolls, warmed,
halved and buttered

For the topping:
3 large eggs, hard-boiled as
described on page 19
1½ tablespoons fresh
snipped chives
4 scallions, very finely chopped
(including most of the green as well)
½ teaspoon butter
1 tablespoon mayonnaise
salt and freshly ground black pepper

To garnish:
a little garden cress or
chopped watercress

My next-door neighbor Dot always keeps me well supplied with delightful, homemade, grainy brown rolls. Since our suppers at home on Sundays are almost always snack meals, we love to eat them warmed, halved, and buttered, then spread with one of these delicious egg toppings.

As soon as the eggs are cool enough, peel them, discard the shells, and place them in a bowl with the rest of the topping ingredients. Now, take a large fork and mash thoroughly until the eggs are thoroughly blended with the rest of the ingredients. Then pile the egg mixture onto the rolls and sprinkle each one with the cress or watercress before serving.

For an egg and bacon topping
Broil six slices of bacon until crispy, chop four of these into small pieces and add these to the egg mixture (minus the scallions and chives). Top the rolls with the mixture and garnish with the other two slices of bacon, as in the photograph, right.

For an anchovy and shallot topping
Add six drained and finely chopped anchovies to the egg mixture (minus the scallions and chives), and add a very finely chopped shallot and a tablespoon of finely chopped parsley. Pile this onto the rolls and garnish each one with another anchovy fillet wrapped around a black olive, as in the photograph, right.

*Opposite, clockwise from top:
Open-Faced Egg and Bacon Sandwich;
Open-Faced Egg, Chive, and Scallion
Sandwich; Open-Faced Egg, Anchovy,
and Shallot Sandwich*

How to poach eggs

The key to a well-poached egg is to keep the water barely simmering throughout the cooking process

Before we begin to talk about how to poach eggs, I think it is appropriate to clear up a few myths and mysteries that surround the whole subject. I met someone recently who said they had been to six leading kitchen supply stores and not one of them sold an egg poacher. My reaction was, "What a great leap for mankind." Egg poachers not only came out of the ark, but they never did the job anyway. What they did was to steam and toughen the eggs, not poach them – and did you ever try to clean one afterwards? The dried-on toughened egg white was always hell to remove.

Then came professional chefs, who passed their exams only if they created a strong whirlpool of simmering water using a whisk and then performed a sort of culinary cabaret act by swirling the poached egg back to its original shell shape. At home we can now relax, throw out our egg poachers, and poach eggs simply and easily. The method below is not at all frightening or hazardous, but bear in mind that for successful poaching the eggs have to be really fresh (see page 15). For four or even six people, you will need:

4-6 large, very fresh eggs (under four days old)
a suitably sized frying pan (according to the number of eggs)
boiling water from the kettle
a slotted spoon and a folded square of paper towel

Place the frying pan over a gentle heat and add enough boiling water from the kettle to fill it to 1 inch (2.5 cm). Keep the heat gentle; very quickly you will see a trace of tiny bubbles beginning to form over the bottom of the pan (above left). Carefully break the eggs, one at a time, into the water and let them barely simmer, without covering, for just 1 minute. A timer is essential because you cannot accurately guess how long 1 minute is.

After that, remove the pan from the heat and let the eggs rest calmly and happily in the hot water, this time setting the timer for 9 minutes. This timing will give perfect results for a beautifully translucent, perfectly set white and a soft, creamy yolk. Now, remove each egg by lifting it out of the water with the slotted spoon and then letting the spoon rest for a few seconds on the paper towel, which will absorb the excess water. As you remove the eggs, serve them immediately. (For the toast, see page 85.)

There are now dozens of ways that you can use your new-found skill in egg poaching. For someone on a strict budget, canned baked beans on toast topped with a poached egg (or two) is one of the world's cheapest but greatest nutritional combinations. If you're not on a budget, natural food stores sell baked beans that taste almost homemade, in a sauce that does not contain any sugar - more expensive but very good.

Another fast but comforting supper dish is to poach finnan haddie in a frying pan of water. Drain well and keep it warm while you slip a couple of eggs into the same water to poach. Serve the finnan haddie with the eggs on top and buttered chunks of brown Irish soda bread.

Warm Spinach Salad with Poached Eggs, Frizzled Sausage, and Bacon

This is actually a delightful combination of sausage, egg, bacon, and mushrooms. The salad greens, crisp, crunchy croutons, and the sherry dressing make this salad special.

Serves 2 as a light lunch or supper
4 oz (110 g) ready-washed baby spinach, plus a few sprigs of watercress
4 large, very fresh eggs
3 oz (75 g) smoked kabanos or chorizo sausage
4 slices smoked bacon
1 small onion, peeled
2 oz (50 g) open mushrooms, e.g. cremini
2 slices white bread, crusts removed
3 tablespoons extra virgin olive oil
3 tablespoons dry sherry
1½ tablespoons sherry vinegar
freshly ground black pepper

You need to begin this by preparing everything in advance. The onion, mushrooms, and bacon slices need to be finely chopped into ¼ inch (5 mm) pieces; the sausage should also be chopped, but fractionally larger. Then cut the bread into ¼ inch (5 mm) cubes (croutons) and arrange the spinach and watercress on two large plates, removing any large stems first.

Now, poach the eggs as described on the previous pages, and, while they're resting in the hot water, take a medium-sized, heavy-bottomed frying pan and heat 1 tablespoon of the oil in it until it's very hot and gives off a fine haze. Then fry the croutons, tossing them around in the pan, until they're crisp and golden brown, about 1-2 minutes, and after that remove them to drain on paper towels.

Now, add the rest of the oil to the pan and, again, let it get really hot before adding the prepared bacon, onion, and sausage. Toss them all around, keeping the heat high to make everything brown and toasted at the edges.

After 4 minutes, add the chopped mushrooms and toss these around, still keeping the heat high, for about 2 minutes. Finally, season with freshly ground black pepper, add the sherry and sherry vinegar to the pan giving it a few seconds to bubble and reduce. Then transfer the eggs to the top of the spinach and watercress, pour the contents of the pan over everything, and sprinkle the croutons over all.

*Can there be anybody who doesn't love the thought of Eggs Benedict?
Soft, lightly toasted bread, really crisp bacon, and perfectly poached eggs
which, when the yolks burst, flow into a cloud of buttery hollandaise
sauce. It's certainly one of the world's greatest recipes. Although originally
it was meant to be served at breakfast or brunch (and still can be), I
think it makes a great first course, particularly in winter. A light version
of this can be made using Foaming Hollandaise on pages 72-3, which
also has the advantage that it can be prepared ahead.*

Poach the eggs as described on page 24. When the pancetta is cooked,
keep it on a warm plate while you lightly toast the split muffins on both
sides. Now, butter the muffins and place them on the baking sheet; then
top each half with two slices of pancetta. Put a poached egg on top of each
muffin half and then spoon over the hollandaise, covering the egg (there
should be about 2 tablespoons of sauce for each egg).

    Now, flash the Eggs Benedict under the broiler for just 25-30 seconds,
as close to the heat as possible, but don't take your eyes off them – they
need to be tinged golden but no more. This should just glaze the surface
of the hollandaise. Serve immediately on warmed plates.

Serves 3 for brunch or 6 as an appetizer
1 recipe Hollandaise Sauce (see
page 72)
6 large, very fresh eggs
12 slices pancetta, broiled until crisp
3 English muffins, split in half
horizontally
a little butter

You will also need a broiler pan and
rack and a 10 x 14 inch (25.5 x 35 cm)
baking sheet.

Preheat the broiler to its highest
setting.

How to fry eggs

A perfectly fried egg is a glory to behold – crispy edges and a wobbly, pinkish yolk. One of my treasured memories of eating fried eggs is on the beautiful Caribbean island of Barbados, where I have been lucky enough to get to spend several holidays. For me it's the best place on earth for an early morning dip in the sea, and as you swim and look back at all that beauty, the evocative smell of bacon and eggs cooking is sheer heaven. At breakfast, there's always a happy, smiling Bajan wielding an old, blackened frying pan, enquiring how you like your eggs fried.

When considering a recipe for fried eggs, this is the pertinent question – how *do* you like them? It's very personal, but my own method, below, can be adjusted to suit most tastes. So here goes.

You will need:

2 large, very fresh eggs
2 teaspoons of fat left from frying bacon (or peanut or grapeseed oil)
1 small heavy-bottomed frying pan
1 slotted spatula
some paper towels

First, place the pan over a high heat, and as soon as the fat or oil is very hot (with a faint shimmer on the surface), carefully break the eggs into the pan. Let them settle for about 30 seconds, then turn the heat down to medium, and proceed with cooking them, tilting the pan and basting the eggs with the hot fat so that the tops of the eggs are also lightly cooked. After about 1 minute the eggs will be ready, so remove the pan from the heat, and lift the eggs out with the spatula. Let them rest on paper towels for a couple of seconds before putting them on a plate, then lightly blot up any excess fat with paper towels and serve the eggs as soon as possible.

This method will provide a fried egg with a slightly crispy, frilly edge; the white will be set and the yolk soft and runny. If you prefer not to have the crispy edge, use a medium heat from the beginning, and if you like your eggs more cooked, give them a little longer.

Note: If you would like to fry your eggs in butter, then you need to use a gentler heat and give them a bit longer so the butter doesn't brown too much.

For fried eggs and bacon: fry the bacon first and then the eggs as above. Add about a teaspoon of peanut oil to a fairly hot frying pan and fry the strips of bacon until they are crisp and golden. Transfer them to a warm plate, blotting them with paper towels, and keep them warm while you fry the eggs in the fat left from the bacon.

Basting the egg while cooking, top, will help it to cook evenly, resulting in a perfectly fried egg: crispy edges and a wobbly pinkish yolk, above

Corned Beef Hash with Fried Eggs

I love New York City and, in particular, the delis there, where I always order a hot pastrami sandwich on rye bread. My husband always orders corned-beef hash with a fried egg. Although not all of us have a place to buy New York corned beef, the humble, modest, canned version makes a mean old hash and, what's more, at an amazing price.

Start this off by cutting the corned beef in half lengthwise, then, using a sharp knife, cut each half into four ½ inch (1 cm) pieces. Now, chop these into ½ inch (1 cm) pieces, then scoop them all up into a bowl. Combine the Worcestershire sauce and mustard in a cup and pour this all over the beef, mixing it around to distribute it evenly.

Now, peel and halve the onion, cut the halves into thin slices, and then cut these slices in half. The potatoes need to be washed and cut into ½ inch (1 cm) cubes, leaving the peeling on, then place the cubes in a saucepan. Pour enough boiling water from the kettle to almost cover them, add salt and a lid, and simmer for just 5 minutes before draining them in a colander. Cover the potatoes with a clean dish towel to absorb the steam.

Now, heat 2 tablespoons of the oil in the frying pan, and when it's smoking hot, add the sliced onions and toss them around in the oil to brown for about 3 minutes altogether, keeping the heat high since they need to be very well browned at the edges.

After that, push all the onions to the edge of the pan, and keeping the heat very high, add the potatoes and toss these around, too, because they also need to be quite brown. Add a little more oil here if necessary. Now, add some seasoning, then, using a spatula, keep turning the potatoes and onions. After about 6 minutes, add the beef and continue to toss everything around to allow the beef to heat through (about 3 minutes).

After that, turn the heat down to its lowest setting, and in the smaller frying pan, fry the eggs as described left. Serve the hash divided between the two warm plates with an egg on top of each. Don't forget to have plenty of tomato ketchup on the table.

Note: Tomato ketchup with a real tomato flavor but without the sugar is now available in health food stores.

Serves 2

7 oz (200 g) canned corned beef
2 large, very fresh eggs
2 tablespoons Worcestershire sauce
1½ teaspoons grain mustard
1 large onion
10 oz (275 g) round red
or white potatoes
2-3 tablespoons peanut or other
mildly flavored oil
salt and freshly ground black pepper

You will also need a heavy-bottomed frying pan approximately 8 inches (20 cm) in diameter, a slightly smaller frying pan for the eggs and two plates warmed in a very low oven.

Chorizo Hash with Peppers and Paprika

This, if you like, is a more sophisticated version of the previous recipe, with red bell peppers as well as onion and potato. It's brilliant, but only worth making if you get genuine Spanish chorizo made in Spain, available at deli counters and gourmet food shops.

First, the onion needs to be peeled, sliced in half, and then each half sliced as thinly as possible so you end up with little half-moon shapes. Next, halve and seed the red bell pepper, slice it, then chop it into ½ inch (1 cm) pieces. After that, peel the skin off the chorizo sausage and cut into pieces roughly the same size as the pepper.

The potatoes need to be washed and cut into ½ inch (1 cm) cubes, leaving the peeling on. Then place them in a saucepan and pour enough boiling water from the kettle to almost cover them; then add salt, cover with a lid and simmer for just 5 minutes before draining them in a colander and covering with a clean dish towel to absorb the steam.

Next, heat 2 tablespoons of the oil in the frying pan, and when it's fairly hot, add the onion, pepper, and garlic and cook for about 6 minutes until softened and tinged brown at the edges. Then push these to the side of the pan, add the chorizo, and keeping the heat fairly high, cook for about 2 minutes again, until nicely browned at the edges. Next, add the paprika and stir everything together, then remove the mixture to a plate. Now, add the last tablespoon of oil to the pan, and keeping the heat high, add the potatoes and seasoning. Toss them around in the hot pan for about 3 minutes, keeping them moving, until they begin to crisp and brown at the edges, then return the chorizo, onion, and bell pepper to the pan, and using a spatula, turn the mixture over. Continue cooking the whole thing for 5-6 minutes, until it's all really brown and crispy. Then turn the heat down to its lowest setting, and in the other pan, fry the eggs as described on page 30. Serve the hash divided between the two warmed plates with an egg on top of each, as shown on page 31, and have plenty of tomato ketchup to serve at the table.

Serves 2

5 oz (150 g) chorizo sausage
1 small red bell pepper
1¼ teaspoons hot paprika
1 medium onion
10 oz (275 g) round red
or white potatoes
3 tablespoons olive oil
1 fat clove garlic, peeled and crushed
2 large, very fresh eggs
salt and freshly ground black pepper

You will also need a heavy-bottomed frying pan approximately 8 inches (20 cm) in diameter, a slightly smaller frying pan for the eggs and two plates warmed in a very low oven.

How to make softly scrambled eggs

Add the beaten eggs to the butter in the pan and scramble until three-quarters of the egg is a creamy mass. Off the heat, add the rest of the butter and finish scrambling

I learned how to make scrambled eggs for the very first time by following a recipe by the famous French chef Auguste Escoffier, and I still think his is the best version of all. During the past 20 years since the first *Cookery Course* was published, however, there has been an enormous move away from butter, which in some ways is right because at one stage we were all far too heavy-handed with it, so much that it sometimes obscured the delicate flavor of fresh vegetables and other foods. But let's never forget what a beautiful ingredient butter is and what a great affinity it has with eggs. For this reason I am sticking with Escoffier on scrambled eggs.

To begin with, there's only one rule and that is not to have the heat too high; if you do, the eggs will become flaky and dry. The trick is to remove the pan from the heat while there's still some liquid egg left, then this will disappear into a creamy mass as you take the eggs to the table to serve them.

Scrambled Eggs for One

For more people, just multiply the ingredients accordingly. The method remains the same, but more eggs will obviously take longer to cook.

2 large eggs
1 tablespoon (10 g) butter
salt and freshly ground black pepper

First of all, break the eggs into a small bowl and use a fork to lightly blend the yolks into the whites, whisking gently. Add a good seasoning of salt and freshly ground black pepper.

Now, take a small, heavy-bottomed saucepan and place it over a medium heat. Put in half the butter and swirl it around so that the bottom and about 1 inch (2.5 cm) of the sides of the pan are moistened with it. Then, when the butter has melted and is just beginning to foam, pour in the beaten eggs. Using a wooden fork or a wooden spoon with a point, start stirring briskly using backwards and forwards movements all through the liquid egg, getting into the corners of the pan to prevent it from sticking. Don't, whatever you do, turn up the heat: just be patient and keep on scrambling away until you calculate that three-quarters of the egg is now a creamy, solid mass and a quarter of it is still liquid.

At this point, remove the pan from the heat, add the rest of the butter, and continue scrambling with the fork or spoon. The eggs will continue cooking in the heat from the pan. As soon as there is no liquid egg left, serve the scrambled eggs immediately. The secret of success is removing the pan at the right stage, because overcooking makes the eggs dry and flaky. Once you've mastered the art of allowing them to finish cooking off the heat, you will never have a problem. If you like, you can add a little heavy cream or crème fraîche as well as the butter. Either way, soft clouds of perfectly scrambled eggs are one of life's special joys. Serve on buttered toast or bagels.

Dieters' Scrambled Eggs

This recipe is devised for people on a diet or for those who have to cut down on fat. Nevertheless, it's extremely good, and on diet days I like to spread it onto sesame Ryvitas. I like it best made with Quark, which is a soft skim milk cheese, but it also works well with cottage cheese.

Serves 1

2 large eggs
1 tablespoon milk
1 tablespoon Quark or cottage cheese
1 tablespoon fresh snipped chives
salt and freshly ground black pepper

You will also need a small non-stick saucepan and a wooden fork.

Begin by beating the eggs in a bowl, together with a good seasoning of salt and pepper. Now, place the saucepan over a gentle heat, then add the milk to moisten the pan, whirling it around the edges. Add the eggs, and using a wooden fork or pointed wooden spoon, briskly stir backwards and forwards through the liquid egg. Keep on scrambling until three-quarters of the egg is a creamy, solid mass and a quarter of it is still liquid. Now, add the Quark or cottage cheese and chives and continue to scramble, then remove the pan from the heat and continue scrambling until no liquid egg remains.

Scrambled Eggs with Smoked Salmon and Brioche

This has to be one of the most sublime combinations: soft, creamy scrambled eggs, together with the subtle, smoky flavor of the salmon. Some restaurants serve the scrambled eggs topped with slices of smoked salmon, but what a waste: soaking strips of salmon in cream and incorporating them into the scrambled eggs is in another league altogether.

Serves 2

4 large eggs
4½ oz (125 g) smoked salmon trimmings
4 tablespoons light cream
2 all-butter brioche buns
1 tablespoon (10 g) butter
salt and freshly ground black pepper

To garnish:
a little fresh dill

The salmon needs to be chopped fairly small for this, so if you're using trimmings you might still need to chop some of the larger pieces. I say chop here, but very often I use scissors. Either way, place all the salmon pieces in a small bowl, pour in the cream, give it all a good stir, cover the bowl and set it aside for 30 minutes.

When you are ready to make the scrambled eggs, preheat the broiler to its highest setting. Slice the top off each brioche, then carefully scoop out and discard half the bread from inside; place each one, alongside its lid, under the broiler, and lightly toast on both sides.

Now melt the butter in a medium-sized saucepan over a very gentle heat. While it's melting, break the eggs into a bowl and beat them lightly with a fork, seasoning with a little salt and freshly ground black pepper. When the butter has melted and begins to foam, swirl it around the edges of the pan and pour in the beaten eggs. Increase the heat slightly, and using a wooden fork or a wooden spoon with a point, stir continuously backwards and forwards, making sure you get into the corners of the pan.

As soon as the eggs begin to solidify – after about 1 minute – and when you have about 50 percent solid and the rest still liquid, quickly add the salmon and cream, then keep on stirring like mad until almost all the liquid has gone, which will take 3-4 minutes. Then remove the pan from the heat and continue stirring until the eggs become a soft, creamy mass. Taste to check the seasoning and spoon into the toasted brioche buns. Top with a little dill, replace the lids, and serve immediately.

Gratin of Eggs with Peppers and Chorizo

This is a variation on oeufs sur le plat, and the name means, literally, eggs cooked on a plate, and a plate can indeed be used, provided it's heatproof. Best to use, though, are shallow gratin dishes measuring 6 inches (15 cm) in diameter, which have enough space for one or two eggs. This recipe has a Basque element since the eggs are baked on a bed of onions, garlic, bell peppers, and chorizo sausage. The whole thing is topped with bubbling cheese. It makes a perfect quick to prepare lunch or supper dish.

Begin by preparing all the ingredients. Remove the skin from the chorizo and slice it into ¼ inch (5 mm) rounds. The onion needs to be peeled, sliced in half, and then each half sliced as thinly as possible so you end up with little half-moon shapes. Remove the stem from the pepper and then halve it, scooping out the seeds. Slice it first into quarters and then each quarter into thin slices. The tomatoes need to be peeled, so pour boiling water over them, leave for 30 seconds, then drain, and slip off their skins. Slice each tomato in half, squeeze each half gently to remove the seeds, then chop the flesh into small cubes. Peel and finely chop the garlic.

Next, take a large, heavy-bottomed frying pan, place it over a high heat and add the olive oil. When the oil is really hot, brown the chorizo pieces, tossing and turning them around until they turn slightly brown at the edges. Using a slotted spoon, transfer the chorizo from the pan to a plate. Next, add the onion and pepper to the pan and toss these around, keeping the heat high, until they're nicely tinged brown at the edges and softened, which will take 5-10 minutes. Now, add the tomatoes and garlic and cook for 1 minute more, then return the chorizo to join the rest of the ingredients. Finally, mix everything well and season with salt and freshly ground black pepper.

Remove the pan from the heat and divide the mixture between the two gratin dishes. Carefully break two eggs side by side on top of the mixture in each dish, season them, then sprinkle them with the grated cheese. Place the dishes on the baking sheet on the top shelf of the oven to cook for 10-13 minutes (or a little longer, depending on how you like your eggs). I think this needs some quite robust red wine and to be accompanied by some warm crusty baguette.

Serves 2

4 large eggs
1 small red or green bell pepper
3 oz (75 g) chorizo sausage
1 medium onion
3 medium tomatoes
1 fat clove garlic
1 tablespoon olive oil
2 oz (50 g) Gruyère, grated
salt and freshly ground black pepper

You will also need two round, 6 inch (15 cm) diameter gratin dishes moistened with a few drops of olive oil, and a baking sheet measuring 14 x 11 inches (35 x 28 cm).

Preheat the oven to 350°F (180°C).

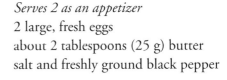

This is another special way of cooking and serving eggs. The classic French name for this type of egg dish is oeufs en cocotte, and it is named after the dishes in which the eggs are cooked, which are called ramekins and look like mini soufflé dishes with enough space for baking one egg. The following recipe will give you the basic method of baking eggs in ramekins, including several variations.

First, boil some water. Break an egg into each ramekin, season, then put a pat of butter on top of each yolk. Place the dishes in the baking pan, then place it on the center shelf of the oven and pour enough boiling water into the pan to come halfway up the sides of the dishes. Now, let the eggs bake for 10 minutes if you like them soft and runny, or 13 minutes if you like them more firmly set. Either way, bear in mind that they go on cooking in the dishes after they've been taken out of the oven and brought to the table.

There are several variations, too. Instead of a pat of butter, pour in a tablespoon of heavy cream, sour cream, crème fraîche, or for a lower-fat version, Greek yogurt. In addition, you could sprinkle a tablespoon of grated cheese on top of the cream. Other ingredients that can be included under the egg are lightly cooked asparagus tips or cooked, chopped leeks. You could also use chopped smoked salmon or lightly cooked flakes of finnan haddie.

Serves 2 as an appetizer
2 large, fresh eggs
about 2 tablespoons (25 g) butter
salt and freshly ground black pepper

You will also need two ramekins with a 3 inch (7.5 cm) diameter, 1½ inches (4 cm) deep, well buttered, and a baking pan measuring 11 x 8 inches (28 x 20 cm), 2 inches (5 cm) deep.

Preheat the oven to, 350°F (180°C).

Eggs en Cocotte with Morel or Porcini Mushrooms

I love to make this with dried morels, which are available from gourmet food markets, but dried porcini will also be excellent.

Serves 4 as an appetizer
4 large, very fresh eggs
½ oz (10 g) dried morels or porcini
⅔ cup (150 ml) boiling water
3 shallots, peeled and finely chopped
4 oz (110 g) cremini mushrooms, roughly chopped
¼ whole nutmeg, grated
2 tablespoons (25 g) butter
5 tablespoons crème fraîche or Greek yogurt
salt and freshly ground black pepper

You will also need four ramekins with a bottom diameter of 3 inches (7.5 cm), 1½ inches (4 cm) deep, well buttered, and a baking pan measuring 11 x 8 inches (28 x 20 cm), 2 inches (5 cm) deep.

Start by soaking the morels or porcini about 30 minutes ahead of time. Place them in a bowl with the boiling water and set them aside to soak. After that, strain them in a sieve and squeeze them to get rid of any surplus water. (You can reserve the soaking water, which can be frozen and is great for soups and sauces.) Set aside 4 pieces of the morels or porcini and put the rest in a food processor, along with the shallots, mushrooms, nutmeg, and salt and freshly ground black pepper. Process until finely chopped. Heat the butter in a small saucepan. When it starts to foam, add the chopped mushroom mixture, and keeping the heat low, let it cook very gently, without a lid, for 25-30 minutes; the idea is that any excess liquid will evaporate and leave a lovely, dark, concentrated mixture.

All this can be prepared in advance, but when you're ready to cook the eggs, start by preheating the oven to 350°F (180°C) and boil a kettle of water. Gently re-heat the mixture and, stirring in 1 rounded tablespoon of the crème fraîche or yogurt, divide it between the ramekins, making a small indentation where the egg will be placed. Now, break an egg into each one and season. Stir the rest of the crème fraîche or yogurt around to loosen it, divide between the dishes, then spread it gently over the eggs using the back of the spoon or a small spreading knife. Place a piece of the reserved morels or porcini on top of each ramekin, then place the ramekins in the baking pan, place the pan on the center shelf of the oven, and add enough boiling water to the pan to come halfway up the sides of the dishes. Bake for 10-13 minutes. These are lovely served with slices of whole wheat bread and butter.

2

The art of the omelette

"Egg may be dressed in a multiplicity of ways but seldom more relished in any form than in a well made, expeditiously served omelette." (Eliza Acton)

So says Eliza, and things have not changed. She has said everything I want to say. If I can teach you how to master the "well made, expeditiously served omelette" then I will have served you well, because you'll never be short of one of life's simplest, quickest and most pleasant dishes.

The art of the omelette begins not, as you might think, in the kitchen but in the kitchen supply stores. "First, catch your frying pan" is the optimum expression here. In all my years of attempting to teach cooking, buying the right frying pan has always been tricky. I was there when the non-stick revolution arrived, and the number of miserable, peeling, scratched, and worn non-stick pans that have passed through my kitchen since is legion.

The problem with these non-stick pans is that there are strict rules, and the rules have to be obeyed: thou shalt never place the pan over direct heat without anything in it; thou shalt never turn the heat higher than medium; thou shalt never, ever use metal utensils. My problem with non-stick is that I *can't* stick to the rules. I like to heat the pan before I put the butter in; I can't sear a steak unless the pan is scorching hot, and I simply cannot make an omelette without a metal spoon. Then, having made a glorious, open-faced flat omelette to be served in wedges, I'm not allowed to use a sharp knife to cut it.

Yes, I know there are special non-metal tools, but wood simply sticks to the food, and plastic is not for people with busy lives who leave it in the pan when the phone rings and then find it's melted down into the food. I am not against non-stick if carefully handled – it is a useful piece of equipment – it's just that I am not careful enough.

My last warning is beware of the "I'm only here for my looks" brigade. Stainless steel never was a good conductor of heat, and pans made only of stainless steel, however professional they look, are to be avoided.

There I'll rest my case, but the good news is that after years of testing omelette pans I have discovered a little gem: a humble, unglamorous but utterly reliable, heavy gauge aluminum pan. Yes, I know red lights are flashing, "What about the safety of aluminum?" I have done my homework and discovered that, like most health scares, this was unproven. Extensive tests have concluded that aluminum is perfectly safe for all cooking, except for very acidic fruits and vegetables, such as plums, tomatoes, and rhubarb, where the acid can attack the metal. This type of pan is also one of the cheapest quality pans on the market, and if you season it properly, it becomes virtually non-stick and will serve you for a lifetime of happy omelette-making.

Size is crucial

The size of the pan is vital: too small and the omelette will be thick, spongy, and difficult to fold; too large and the eggs will spread out like a thin pancake and become dry and tough. When you buy a pan, take a tape measure and measure the bottom (not the top), because that's where the cooking happens. I have found the pan recommended above best for either a two- or three-egg omelette, which is average for a folded omelette. The bottom measures 6 inches (15 cm) in diameter. Pans with an 8 inch (20 cm) bottom are suitable for tortillas or open-faced omelettes.

How to season a new frying pan

Please, please, whatever pan you buy, don't forget to do this. All you do is coat the bottom of the pan with about ½ inch (1 cm) of any old cooking oil (something lurking in the back of the pantry, past its use-by date would be ideal). Make really sure the sides and the whole surface of the pan are well oiled, then just put it on the lowest heat possible for about eight hours. Do keep an eye on it, don't go out and leave it, and be sure to check from time to time that the oil is barely warm. The best frying pan is a well-used one, so what this is doing is the equivalent to about six months of cooking. You can use the pan for any kind of frying; the more you use it the better it will be. After use, wash it in mildly soapy hot water with a dish cloth. Dry it and then rub a little oil round the inside surface.

Making a folded omelette

Before you begin, have everything ready: bowl, eggs, omelette pan, fork, tablespoon, salt and pepper, butter, and oil. Put the plates in a warm oven.

1 *Eggs*
   One omelette will serve one person, and because it is so quick to make, it's not worth cooking a large one for two. So, according to how hungry you are, use two or three large eggs per person. Just break the eggs carefully into a bowl, add a seasoning of salt and freshly ground black pepper, then gently combine the yolks and whites with a fork – don't overbeat them, combine is the word you need to think of here. Under-rather than overbeating the eggs seems to make a fluffier omelette.

2 *Oil or butter?*
   You can use either, but remember that butter burns very easily on a high heat. Some oil will prevent this from happening, so if you like a buttery flavor, I would recommend that you use half a teaspoon of each. For extra butteriness or creaminess you could add a teaspoon of melted butter or heavy cream to the eggs in the bowl.

3 *Heat*
   Heat is a vital element in omelette-making because the essence of success is speed. Begin by turning the heat to medium, place the pan over the heat and let it get quite hot (about half a minute). Now, add the butter and oil, and as soon as it melts, swiftly swirl it round, tilting the pan so that the bottom and the sides get coated. Turn the heat up to its highest setting now – when I first demonstrated this on television I remember saying, "hot as you dare," and that still stands.

4 *Cooking the omelette*
   When the butter is foaming, pour the eggs into the pan, tilting it to and fro to spread the eggs evenly over the bottom. Then leave it on the heat without moving it for a count of five.

5 *Working with a spoon*
   After 5 seconds a bubbly frill will appear round the edge. Now, you can

When making an omelette, heat the oil or butter on as high a heat as you dare; next, pour the eggs into the pan, tilting it so they cover the bottom; using a spoon, start to draw the edge of the omelette into the middle so the liquid egg runs into the space, continuing until almost all the liquid egg has cooked

tilt the pan to 45°, and using a tablespoon, draw the edge of the omelette into the center. The liquid egg will flow into and fill the space. Now, tip the pan the other way and do the same thing. Keep tilting it backwards and forwards, pulling the edges in with the spoon and allowing the liquid egg to travel into the space left – all this will take only half a minute. Soon there will be just a small amount of liquid left, just on the surface, so now is the time to start folding. Tilt the pan again and flip one side of the omelette into the center, then fold again. Take the pan to the warm plate, and the last fold will be when you tip the omelette out onto the plate.

6   Remember, an omelette will go on cooking, even on the plate, so serve it immediately. For this reason it is important to have some liquid egg left before you start folding, but if you have left too much, let it set on the plate before eating. The perfect omelette is one just tinged with gold on the surface and very soft and squishy on the inside.

Omelettes with fillings

Now, you have mastered the art of a plain omelette you can begin to think about fillings.

Fontina, Gruyère (pictured), and Taleggio make a great melted-cheese omelette, particularly with the addition of ham

To make a *simple cheese omelette*, add 1½ oz (40 g) of grated sharp Cheddar to the egg mixture and sprinkle some Parmesan over the finished omelette before it goes to the table.

For a *blue cheese and onion omelette*, add 1½ oz (40 g) of grated Stilton, Roquefort, or Gorgonzola, plus 2 finely chopped scallions, to the egg mixture, then cook as described.

For a *melted-cheese omelette*, first, preheat the broiler, then take 2 oz (50 g) of a good melting cheese, such as Fontina, Gruyère, or Taleggio; slice it thinly, lay the slices all over the omelette at the stage where it is almost set but still liquid (you could also add some ham), then flash the omelette pan under the preheated broiler to melt the cheese quickly. Then turn it out as described earlier. This will produce a melted cheese center that oozes out when you take your first forkful.

For a *Swiss omelette,* preheat the broiler and add ½ oz (10 g) of grated Gruyère to the egg mixture. Have ready another ½ oz (10 g) of grated Gruyère mixed with 1 tablespoon of heavy cream. After folding and turning out the omelet, spoon this mixture over the folded omelette and flash it under the hot broiler to form a cheesy, creamy glaze. Not good for the waistline but…

On a diet? Yes, you can still have a *cheese omelette.* Grated Parmesan (Parmigiano Reggiano) has a wonderful flavor and not too high a fat content. Just 2 tablespoons (10 g) – half in the egg mixture and half sprinkled over the top – will set you back only 39 calories and 2.8g of fat.

For a *mushroom omelette,* for one person use 2 cups (110 g) of chopped mushrooms. Gently stew them, uncovered, in 1 teaspoon of oil or butter for 20 minutes, until all the excess moisture has evaporated and the flavor is concentrated. Scatter them over the omelette before folding.

For a *fines herbes omelette,* combine 1 tablespoon of chopped parsley and 1 tablespoon of fresh snipped chives (or any herb combination you choose). Stir the herbs into the mixed eggs 30 minutes before making the omelette to allow the flavors to develop.

For a *smoked salmon omelette,* soak 2 oz (50 g) of smoked salmon trimmings in 1 tablespoon of light cream or milk for 30 minutes, then add this to the egg mixture before making the omelette.

Open-Faced Flat Omelettes

While the French folded omelette described earlier is probably the ultimate "fast food" in the home, it does make certain demands on the cook in that it all has to happen fairly quickly, which is great for one or two people but not so easy when you're doing a kind of production line for four or more. The open-faced omelette, on the other hand, gives you time to play with. Here, the whole thing is much more laid back – you can even place one on the stove to cook while you sip an aperitif and chat and then serve even as many as six people with absolute ease.

Tortilla (Spanish Omelette)

*I sometimes marvel how it is that three basic, very inexpensive ingredients – eggs, onions, and potatoes – can be transformed into something so utterly sublime. Yet it's simply the way the Spanish make their omelettes. A Spanish omelette, or tortilla, is not better than a French one, and it certainly takes longer to make, but in this age of complicated, overstated, fussy food, it's a joy to know that simplicity can still win the day.
A well-made tortilla served with a salad and a bottle of wine can give two or more people a luxurious meal at any time and at very little cost.*

Serves 2-3
6 large eggs
1 medium onion, about 4 oz (110 g)
10 oz (275 g) small round red potatoes
3 tablespoons olive oil
salt and freshly ground black pepper

Potatoes and onions are cooked until they are gently stewed; every now and then the edge is drawn in gently with a spreading knife, giving the tortilla a rounded edge

First, some points to note. The size of the frying pan is important: a bottom measurement of 8 inches (20 cm) diameter is about right for two to three people. If using a larger pan for more people, it should not be too heavy because you need to turn the omelette out using both hands. Use a non-stick pan if you don't have a well-seasoned frying pan. An enormous asset here is a flat saucepan lid or large plate that fits the pan.

Tortilla can be served as a main course, or because it is good served cold, it makes excellent picnic food cut into wedges and wrapped in plastic wrap. In Spain they serve it as tapas, cut into small cubes and speared with toothpicks – lovely with chilled amontillado sherry. The Spanish also serve tortilla sandwiched between chunks of crusty bread – sounds delicious but very fattening!

First of all, peel and cut the onion in half, then thinly slice each half and separate the layers into half-moon shapes. Now, thinly peel the potatoes using a potato peeler and slice them into thin rounds – you have to work pretty quickly here because you don't want the slices to darken. When they are sliced, rub them in a clean dish towel to get them as dry as possible.

Next, heat 2 tablespoons of the olive oil in the frying pan and, when it's smoking hot, add the potatoes and onions. Toss them around in the oil to get a good coating, turn the heat down to its lowest setting, add a generous sprinkling of salt and pepper, cover the frying pan, and let the onions and potatoes cook gently for 20 minutes or until tender. Turn them over halfway through and shake the pan from time to time, since they are not supposed to brown very much but just gently simmer in the oil.

Meanwhile, break the eggs into a large bowl, and using a fork, whisk them lightly – it's important not to overbeat them. Finally, add some seasoning. When the onions and potatoes are cooked, quickly transfer them to the eggs in the bowl.

Put the frying pan back on the heat, add the rest of the oil, and turn the heat back up to medium. Then mix the potato and eggs thoroughly before pouring the whole mixture into the frying pan and turning the heat down to its lowest setting immediately. Now, forget all about French omelettes and be patient, because it's going to take 20-25 minutes to cook slowly, uncovered. Every now and then draw the edge in gently with a spreading knife, since this will give it a lovely rounded edge. When there is virtually no liquid egg left on the surface of the omelette, place a flat lid or plate over the pan, invert it, turning the pan over, and put it back on the heat, using the spreading knife to gently ease the omelette back in. Give it about 2 minutes more, then turn the heat off and leave it for another 5 minutes to settle. It should then be cooked through but still moist in the center. Serve hot or cold, cut in wedges, with a salad and a glass of Rioja – it's brilliant.

How to make an Italian frittata

This is Italy's version of an open-face omelette, and while the tortilla is golden brown, the frittata is cooked even more slowly and should not be too colored on the outside. The Italian word here is *lentamente* – very slowly; the eggs cook through gradually and the finished omelette will be very moist. For this reason it is better not turned over but rather quickly flashed under a hot broiler so that the top only just sets. It then has to be served immediately, otherwise it continues to cook and loses its soft creaminess.

Melted Cheese Frittata with Four Kinds of Mushroom

Serves 4
8 large eggs
4 oz (110 g) Fontina or Gruyère
12 oz (350 g) mixed mushrooms
(3 oz/75 g of each)
1 tablespoon olive oil
salt and freshly ground black pepper

You will also need a 10 inch (25 cm) frying pan and the oven preheated to its lowest setting.

I like to use Fontina cheese for this, but Gruyère is also a good melting cheese, so you could use that instead. The mushrooms can be whatever kind are available, though I love the contrasting textures and colors of a mixture of oyster, shiitake, cremini, and the vibrant pied de mouton. None of this, however, is vital: if you use only one type of mushroom it will still be extremely good.

First of all, chop the mushrooms into roughly 1 inch (2.5 cm) chunks – it's going to look like an enormous quantity at this stage, but the mushrooms will lose approximately half their volume in the initial cooking. Now, heat a teaspoon of the olive oil in a frying pan, and when it's hot, throw in the mushrooms and toss them around by shaking the pan. Don't worry that there is so little oil, because the mushrooms give off masses of juice once the heat gets to them. Season with salt and pepper, then turn the heat down to very low, and let the mushrooms cook gently, uncovered, so that all the juice evaporates and the flavor of the mushrooms becomes more concentrated. Leave them like that for 30 minutes, stirring them around once or twice.

While they are cooking, cut two-thirds of the cheese into ¼ inch (5 mm) cubes and grate the other third on the coarse blade of the grater. When the mushrooms are ready, break the eggs into a large bowl, whisk lightly with a fork, and season. Then add three-quarters of the cooked mushrooms to the eggs, together with the cubed cheese. Place the rest of the mushrooms in a bowl covered with foil and keep them warm in the oven.

Now, wipe the pan clean with some paper towels and put it back on a medium heat, add the rest of the olive oil and, when it's hot, swirl it around the pan. Turn the heat down to its lowest setting and pour the egg mixture into the pan, scattering the grated cheese over the surface. Now, all you have to do is leave it alone and put a timer on for 15 minutes.

When 15 minutes have passed, turn the broiler onto its highest setting and see how the omelette is cooking – it will probably take about 20 minutes in total to cook, but there should still be about 10 percent of liquid egg left on the top. At that stage transfer the pan to the broiler – not too close – and cook briefly to allow the liquid egg to set. This will take 20-30 seconds. Scatter the remaining cooked mushrooms over the top of the frittata and cut it into four wedges. Transfer the wedges to warm plates and serve immediately because the egg will continue cooking even though the frittata is no longer in contact with the heat. I like to serve this with two salads – a simple lettuce salad and a tomato and basil salad.

The initial quantity of mushrooms for this frittata will seem like a lot to begin with, but they will lose about half their volume during the initial cooking

A Soufflé Omelette with Three Cheeses and Chives

Though making a soufflé proper can be a stressful experience, particularly if you've had no practice, making a soufflé omelette is a snap. It takes no more than five minutes and honestly tastes every bit as good as the oven-baked variety. This one has three cheeses, but you can make it with just one, or even four if you happen to have several kinds around.
I've included this in the omelette section, but if you are unsure of beating the egg whites, read the notes in the next chapter on page 58.

Serves 1
3 large eggs
1 oz (25 g) sharp Cheddar,
finely grated
1 oz (25 g) Parmesan (Parmigiano
Reggiano), finely grated
1 oz (25 g) Gruyère, finely grated
1½ tablespoons finely
snipped chives
1 tablespoon (10 g) butter
salt and freshly ground black pepper

You will also need a heavy medium-sized frying pan with a bottom diameter of 7 inches (18 cm).

Preheat the broiler to its highest setting for 10 minutes and have a warm plate ready.

First, separate the eggs – yolks into one small bowl and whites into a squeaky-clean large bowl; it helps if you separate the whites singly into a cup first before adding them to the bowl because if one breaks, you won't get yolk into the rest. Now, beat the egg yolks with a fork, seasoning well with salt and pepper. Next, put the pan onto a low heat to warm through.

While the pan is warming, whisk the egg whites with either a hand mixer or a balloon whisk, until they form soft peaks. Next, add the butter to the pan and turn the heat up. Then, using a large metal spoon, quickly fold the egg yolks into the egg whites, adding the Cheddar, half the Parmesan, and the chives at the same time.

Then, when the butter is foaming, pile the mixture into the pan and give it a good hefty shake to even it out. Now, let the omelette cook for 1 minute exactly. Then slide a spatula around the edges to loosen it, sprinkle the grated Gruyère all over the surface, and place the omelette under the broiler, about 4 inches (10 cm) from the heat. Let it cook for 1 more minute until the cheese is melted and tinged golden. Next, remove the pan from the heat, then slide the spatula around the edge again. Take the pan to the warmed plate, then ease one half of the omelette over the other and tilt the whole lot out onto the plate. Scatter the rest of the Parmesan on top and serve immediately.

Note: If you want to make this omelette for two, it's okay to double everything. Just use a 9 or 10 inch (23 or 25.5 cm) diameter pan and give each stage more time, then divide the omelette into two.

3
Separate ways with eggs

For me, the talent of the egg
as an ingredient seems infinite.
It could be thought of as rather
ordinary and everyday, but when
closely examined, the humble
egg becomes an absolute star of
the kitchen. Though we've
already discovered its potential
for providing endless
combinations of delightful and
nutritious meals that can be
made in moments, in addition,
eggs are essential for making
batters, baking desserts, and
cakes and for setting the fillings
of tarts and quiches.

For now, though, I want to introduce you to yet another dimension of egg cooking, namely what happens when you separate the yolk from the white. While, as whole eggs, they can make desserts, batters, cakes, and so on, once separated, they move on to being two quite unique and essential components in cooking.

If you want to separate the yolk from the white of an egg, the egg has to be as fresh as possible. The protective membrane that encloses the yolk weakens with age and breaks more easily, and this can cause problems, because if even one speck of yolk gets into the white, it won't be suitable for beating. So with eggs as fresh as possible there's much less chance of that happening.

How to separate eggs

To separate yolks from whites, all you do is hold the egg over one bowl and have another bowl beside it. Crack the egg on the side of the bowl, about at its center, then, using both hands, break it into two halves, one in each hand. Now, slip the yolk back and forth from one half-shell to the other, tilting it as you do so and letting the white trickle down into the bowl while you save the yolk. When there is no white left in the shells, drop the yolk into the other bowl.

Egg whites whipped to the soft-peak stage

Leftover whites and yolks

One query that often comes up in letters I receive is what I do with leftover whites if I'm using only the yolks, or vice versa. The good news here is that eggs freeze very well, so pack them in small containers and don't forget to label them with the amount – trying to guess how many egg whites you have is not a good idea.

Egg whites

In the *Complete Cookery Course* I wrote: "The secret of beating egg whites is knowing when to stop." Twenty years and many more egg whites under my belt, I would add another proviso – you also need to know when *not* to stop.

I have to say in all honesty that getting beaten egg whites precisely right is an acquired skill, no doubt about it. But all skills can be acquired, and it does help a) if someone (hopefully me) explains it properly so you know precisely what you're supposed to do and why, and, b) if you are prepared to practice enough, because nothing beats experience.

So let's begin with egg whites.

… and to the stiff-peak stage

Egg whites

What happens when you whisk egg whites?

First of all, the most important ingredient is not the egg white but the air, because the whisked egg white is going to provide aeration for soufflés, meringues, cakes, and the like. In whisking them, what you're actually doing is incorporating air, and as you do so, the original volume of the egg white can actually be increased by up to eight times.

As you whisk in the air, tiny air bubbles are formed. It might help to compare the process to when you blow up a balloon – too little air and the balloon will not be buoyant and bouncy, too much air and it will burst and the air will be lost. Therefore, the cook has to whisk precisely the right amount and then stop – too little and the egg white will be flabby, too much and the bubbles will burst, releasing the precious air (and it will still be flabby!).

When do you stop?

Knowing the right moment to stop is tricky. All the cook can do is follow the tried and trusted guidelines, namely, to stop when you reach the stage at which the egg white stands up in well-defined peaks. If the egg white is for a cake, mousse, or soufflé, where it needs to be folded into other ingredients, the peaks should be soft (so that when you lift the whisk the peaks drop slightly); if it is for a meringue, where sugar is going to be incorporated, it should stand up in stiff peaks. In this book I will always indicate whether stiff or soft peaks are called for (see the photographs on page 57).

Grease: the enemy

The one thing that will prevent egg whites from reaching their full-blown potential is even the tiniest presence of grease. That's why the merest trace of yolk in the white means you are done for. But I'm afraid that's not all – you also have to be scrupulously careful about the bowl and whisk, which must also be grease-free. So always wash them in soapy water, rinse in very hot water, then dry them with an absolutely clean dish towel. And to be absolutely certain, run a slice of lemon around the whisk and the bowl.

Which equipment?

A balloon whisk is said by chefs to be the best, but it is too much like hard work for me. If you're young and more energetic, by all means go for it. A free-standing mixer may be used, but I have always felt that the whites are not exposed to enough air this way. Others disagree, and you might find it best for you. An electric hand mixer is my personal favorite, because I can feel and see everything and the motor actually does all the work for me.

How to whisk egg whites

Before you begin, make sure that the mixing bowl is as large as you can get, which means as much air as possible can circulate around the egg whites as you beat them.

Separate the eggs one at a time, placing each white in a cup or small bowl before adding it to the beating bowl. This means that if an accident occurs with, say, the third egg, and you break the yolk, the other two are safe. Turn on the mixer to a slow speed, first of all, and begin whisking for about 2 minutes, until everything has become bubbly (this timing will be right for two to three egg whites; you'll need slightly more time for four, five or six). After that, switch to a medium speed for another minute, then beat at the highest speed and continue beating through the soft-peak stage until stiff peaks are formed.

Fear not

Always remember that a cake, or even a soufflé, with more or less air in it will not be a disaster. If the egg whites are not quite right, the finished dish will still taste good. If you're cooking with natural, fresh ingredients, who cares what it looks like? It's bound to taste good. I have often got egg whites wrong but still enjoyed the not-quite-so-puffy pavlova. Of course, we should always endeavor to get things right, but cooking, like life, isn't always perfect.

How to make meringue

I think one of the best ways to start practicing beating egg whites is to make meringues.

Meringue must be the most popular egg-white recipe of all, whipped with fine sugar into tall, stiff, shining peaks, then very lightly baked so that the surface is crisp and the center is soft and chewy. The tricky bit is beating the egg whites (see the method above), but the way it is cooked is important, too. My own method of baking has stood the test of time and, provided your oven temperature is correct, it will never let you down. The secret, I think, is allowing the meringue to remain in the closed oven after the heat is turned off so that it partly bakes and then slowly dries out.

Egg whites, whipped with sugar into stiff, glossy peaks, are the basis of all meringues

Petits Monts Blancs

When I first worked in a restaurant kitchen in the early 1960s, this recipe was on the menu and I became totally addicted to the sweetened chestnut purée. Chestnuts have an amazing affinity for meringue and whipped cream, but in this modern version I have replaced the cream with Mascarpone and fromage blanc; this way you get the flavor and creamy richness of the Mascarpone but lightened by the fromage blanc.

Serves 8
For the meringues:
2 large egg whites
½ cup plus 2 tablespoons (110 g) superfine sugar

For the topping:
1 cup (250 g) Mascarpone
¾ cup (200 ml) fromage blanc
1 tablespoon superfine sugar
1 teaspoon vanilla extract

To finish:
2 x 9 oz/250 g cans crème de marrons de l'Ardèche (sweetened chestnut purée), chilled
a little confectioners sugar

You will also need a 16 x 12 inch (40 x 30 cm) baking sheet lined with parchment paper.

Preheat the oven to 300°F (150°C).

To make the meringues, place the egg whites in a large bowl, and using an electric hand mixer on a low speed, begin beating. Continue for about 2 minutes, until the whites are foamy, then switch the speed to medium and continue beating for 1 more minute. Now, turn the speed to high and continue beating until the egg whites reach the stiff-peak stage. Next, beat the sugar in on fast speed, a little at a time (about a tablespoon), until you have a stiff and glossy mixture.

Now, all you do is spoon the mixture onto the prepared baking sheet, making 8 meringues, using about 2 tablespoons for each one. Space them evenly, and using the back of the spoon or a small spreading knife, hollow out the centers. Don't worry if they are not all the same shape – random and rocky is how I would describe them (see the photograph below left). Next, place them on the center shelf of the oven, immediately reduce the heat to 275°F (140°C) and leave them for 30 minutes. Then, turn the oven off and let the meringues dry out in the warmth of the oven until it is completely cold (about 4 hours) or overnight. The meringues will store well in a canister or plastic container, and will even freeze extremely well.

To assemble the Monts Blancs, spoon equal quantities of the crème de marrons into each meringue, whisk the topping ingredients together, and spoon equal amounts on top of the chestnut purée. A light dusting of confectioners sugar is good for a snowcapped-mountain image.

Meringue nests before cooking…   *and afterwards*

Meringues with Passion Fruit

This is a variation of the Petits Monts Blancs recipe on the previous page, and all you need is the same amount of meringue and Mascarpone filling, along with 6 passion fruit and a little confectioners sugar.

To assemble the 8 meringues, spoon the seeds from half a passion fruit into the bottom of each meringue nest. Then, mix the seeds from the other two passion fruit, into the Mascarpone mixture. Spoon this mixture on top of the nests, dust with confectioners sugar, and serve.

Meringues with Summer Berries

The two previous meringue fillings are perfect for the winter months, but in the summer berries make the perfect filling, since their sharp acidity contrasts beautifully with the sweetness of the meringue. For 8 meringue nests, use the same quantity of Mascarpone cream as for the Petits Monts Blancs, together with 1 lb (450 g) of strawberries, raspberries, or, my favorite, a mixture of red currants, raspberries, and strawberries. Then dust the fruit with confectioners sugar before serving – nice with a sauce made of puréed fresh raspberries sweetened with a little confectioners sugar.

The yolks of eggs fulfill three main functions in cooking. One is turning liquids into solids, as in a baked custard or quiche. The second is as a thickening agent for liquids. What happens here is that when the yolks are whisked into liquids over heat, the thickening agent in the yolk gets distributed to make a smooth, thick sauce or soup. They are also a powerful emulsifier that can bind and thicken oil- or butter-based sauces such as mayonnaise or hollandaise.

How to handle egg yolks

The problem the cook has when dealing with egg yolks is that if they are not treated properly and with care, they can "split," or curdle, a mixture. In parting company with the whites they have lost some of their stability, since egg whites are great stabilizers. This often causes problems and stress for beginners, but there is some good news here. Over the years I have spent cooking, developing recipes, and trying to help busy people cook at home without undue stress, I have developed various ways of using egg yolks in all the traditional recipes without the worry of curdling and therefore ruining a recipe. On this subject, I have to part company with the purists. I'm perfectly aware that there are people who simply don't mind standing over things for ages, nurturing them along and whisking "'til the cows come home" (as my Welsh grandmother would say), but not me – I don't want to be confined to the kitchen, missing out on a conversation.

Therefore, I am here to tell you that you need never be afraid to use egg yolks in a custard. If you add just a small amount of cornstarch there will never be any danger of it curdling, and even if it looks like it might, it will soon whip back to an amazing smoothness, because that tiny amount of cornstarch will stabilize the eggs.

No more whisking!

If you use exactly the same method making lemon curd, sabayon sauce, or zabaglione, it will mean (as with custard) that the time you spend carefully whisking will be 2 minutes instead of 20. So here's an end to boring whisking sessions over bowls of barely simmering water, because life is short enough as it is! Similarly, I have discovered that when trying to make a lighter version of hollandaise sauce (for health reasons – not quite so much butter), adding whisked egg whites not only makes it go twice as far but also stabilizes it perfectly. This means no last-minute fuss, that you can make it two days ahead if you want to re-heat it, and you can even freeze it so that if you only want a small amount, you can have some stored away.

Traditional English Custard

This is the ultimate custard, perhaps <u>the</u> traditional British sauce. I offer it here as it has been made down the centuries – with thick heavy cream, but you can, if you wish, modify this extravagance by using light cream or creamy whole milk. These last two might be better if the custard is to be used for pouring, but for preparing a trifle for a special occasion I recommend going the whole hog! It's now fashionable to split a vanilla bean and incorporate the seeds into the sauce reducing the time it takes to infuse in the hot cream. But I can also recommend pure vanilla extract, which is a wonderful pantry stand-by.

Serves 6-8
1 vanilla bean
2½ cups (570 ml) heavy cream
6 large egg yolks
2 teaspoons cornstarch
¼ cup (50 g) superfine sugar

Begin by splitting the vanilla bean lengthwise and scraping out the seeds with the end of a teaspoon. Then, place the bean and the seeds in a small saucepan, along with the cream. Now, place the pan over a gentle heat and heat it to just below simmering point. While the cream is heating, whisk the egg yolks, cornstarch, and sugar together in a medium bowl using a balloon whisk. Next, remove the vanilla bean from the hot cream. Then, constantly whisking the egg mixture with one hand, gradually pour the hot cream into the bowl. When it's all in, immediately return the whole mixture back to the saucepan using a rubber spatula. Now, back it goes on to the same gentle heat as you continue whisking until the custard is thick and smooth which will happen as soon as it reaches the simmering point. If you do overheat it and it looks grainy, don't worry, just transfer it to a large measuring cup or bowl and continue to whisk until it becomes smooth again. Pour the custard into a large measuring cup or bowl, cover the surface with plastic wrap, and let it cool. To serve it warm later, remove the plastic wrap and place the bowl over a pan of barely simmering water.

The very finest ingredients make a truly indulgent traditional custard

Though the vanilla bean is removed from the cream, its distinctive seeds remain

Whisking the custard over a low heat guarantees a smooth, creamy finish

Butterscotch and Banana Trifle with Madeira

There are endless variations on the trifle theme, and this is the latest of my versions. It's wickedly rich and quite wonderful – not for an everyday event, but perfect sometimes for those really special days.

Serves 6-8
3 medium bananas
⅔ cup (150 ml) Madeira
12 ladyfingers, e.g. Boudoir Biscuits

For the butterscotch sauce:
⅔ cup (150 ml) dark corn or
golden syrup
4 tablespoons (50 g) butter
½ cup (75 g) brown sugar
¼ cup (50 g) granulated sugar
⅔ cup (150 ml) heavy cream
a few drops vanilla extract

For the topping:
1 quantity Traditional English Custard
(see page 64)
½ cup (50 g) pecan halves
1¼ cups (275 ml) heavy cream

You will also need a 2 quart (1.75 liter) glass trifle bowl.

First of all, make the butterscotch sauce and to do this place the syrup, butter, and sugars in a small saucepan. Then place the pan over a gentle heat and allow to slowly melt and dissolve, stirring from time to time, which will take 5-7 minutes. Let it continue to cook for about 5 minutes, then gradually stir in the heavy cream and vanilla extract until well combined. After that, let it cool. While it's cooling, make the custard.

To assemble the trifle, begin by spreading one side of the ladyfingers with butterscotch sauce, then form into 6 sandwiches. Arrange the ladyfingers in the bottom of the glass bowl. Drizzle any remaining butterscotch sauce over the top and carefully pour the Maderia all over them, distributing it as evenly as you can. Set the bowl aside to allow the ladyfingers to soak it all up – about 20 minutes.

Now, peel and slice the bananas into chunks about ¼ inch (5 mm) thick, scatter these all around the biscuits, then pour the remaining butterscotch sauce as evenly as possible over all. Pour the custard in next, then cover the bowl with plastic wrap and let the dessert chill in the refrigerator to firm up.

Meanwhile, preheat the broiler, line the broiler pan with foil, and toast the pecans carefully for about 4 minutes, watching them all the time, since they burn easily. After that, whip the cream to the soft stage, spread it over the trifle, scatter the toasted nuts on top, re-cover, and chill until needed.

Note: This is best made the day you want to serve it. I used to scatter the nuts on just before serving, but forgot them so many times that I now put them on directly after the cream.

Hot Lemon Curd Soufflés

Serves 4

For the soufflés:
3 large eggs
grated zest and juice 1 medium lemon
(2 tablespoons juice)
¼ cup (50 g) superfine sugar and
2 teaspoons superfine sugar

For the quick-method lemon curd:
grated zest and juice 1 small lemon
1 large egg
3 tablespoons (40g) superfine sugar
2 tablespoons (25g) cold unsalted
butter, cut into small cubes
1 teaspoon cornstarch

To serve:
a little sifted confectioners sugar

You will also need four ramekins with
a bottom diameter of 2½ inches
(6 cm), a top diameter of 3 inches
(7.5 cm), 2 inches (5 cm) deep, lightly
buttered, and a small, heavy
baking sheet.

Preheat the oven to 325°F (170°C).

On the television series I called these "everlasting" and yes, it's true, because unlike traditional soufflés, they never collapse. They will shrink when they come out of the oven, but they will still be light and soufflé-like 15 minutes later. And just to prove my point, the soufflé in the picture below was actually a day old – not brimming up over the edge, but still a soufflé: soft, squishy, and very lemony. The quick lemon curd rounds the whole thing off making this my favorite lemon recipe to date.

First of all, make the lemon curd by lightly whisking the egg in a medium-sized saucepan, then add the rest of the lemon curd ingredients and place the saucepan over a medium heat. Now, whisk continuously using a balloon whisk until the mixture thickens; this won't take long – about 3 minutes in all. Next, lower the heat to its minimum setting and let the curd gently simmer for 1 more minute, continuing to whisk. After that, remove it from the heat and divide the curd among the bottoms of the ramekins. (This can all be done well in advance, but cover and leave at room temperature.)

When you're ready to make the soufflés, separate the eggs, putting the yolks into a medium-sized bowl and the whites into a spanking-clean larger one. Now, using an electric hand mixer, beat the whites to the stiff-peak stage, which will take 4-5 minutes – start on a slow speed, gradually increasing to medium and then high. Then add the 2 teaspoons of superfine sugar and mix on a high speed for 30 seconds more. Next, add the zest, the lemon juice, and the remaining ¼ cup (50 g) of sugar to the yolks and mix them together briefly. Now, take a tablespoon of the whites and fold them into the yolks to loosen the mixture, then fold the rest of the whites in using a light cutting and folding movement in order not to lose the precious air. Spoon the mixture into the prepared ramekins, piling it high like a pyramid, then run a finger round the inside rim of each one.

Next, place them on the baking sheet and put this in the oven on the center shelf for 15-17 minutes or until the tops are golden. Then remove them and let them settle for about 5 minutes to allow the lemon curd to cool. They will sink a little, but that's normal. Just before serving, place them on smaller plates and dust them lightly with confectioners sugar.

Twice-Baked Roquefort Soufflés

The obvious advantage of twice-baked soufflés is that they can be done and dusted the day before you need them. Then they rise up again like a dream, with a brilliantly light texture and flavor.

Serves 6
6 oz (175 g) Roquefort
1 cup (250 ml) milk
¼ inch (5 mm) onion slice
1 bay leaf
grating of nutmeg
6 whole black peppercorns
3 tablespoons (40 g) butter
¼ cup (40 g) all-purpose flour
4 large eggs, separated
6 tablespoons (100 ml) heavy cream
salt and freshly ground black pepper

To garnish:
6 sprigs watercress

You will also need six ramekins with a 3 inch (7.5 cm) diameter, 1½ inches (4 cm) deep, lightly buttered, an 11 x 8 x 2 inch (28 x 20 x 5 cm) baking pan, and a 14 x 10 inch (35 x 25.5 cm) shallow baking pan.

Preheat the oven to 350°F (180°C).

Begin by heating the milk, onion, bay leaf, nutmeg, and peppercorns in a medium-sized saucepan until the mixture reaches the simmering point, then strain the milk into a large measuring cup, discarding the rest now. Rinse out the saucepan, then melt the butter in it. Add the flour and stir to a smooth, glossy paste, and cook this for 3 minutes, still stirring, until it turns a pale straw color. Then gradually add the strained milk, whisking all the time, until the sauce is thick and cleanly leaves the sides of the pan. Then season lightly and cook the sauce on the gentlest heat possible for 2 minutes, stirring now and then.

Next, remove the pan from the heat and let it cool slightly, then beat in the egg yolks one at a time. Now, crumble 4 oz (110 g) of the cheese into the mixture and stir until most of it has melted – don't worry if some cheese is still visible. Put a kettle on to boil, and in a spanking-clean large bowl, beat the egg whites to the soft-peak stage, then fold a spoonful of egg whites into the cheese sauce to loosen it. Now, fold the sauce into the egg white using a large metal spoon and a cutting and folding motion.

Divide the mixture equally among the ramekins. Put them in the baking pan, place it on the center shelf of the oven, then pour about ½ inch (1 cm) of boiling water into the pan. Bake the soufflés for 20 minutes, then transfer them to a cooling rack (using a pancake turner) so they don't continue cooking. Don't worry if they sink a little as they cool because they will rise up again in the second cooking.

When they are almost cold, run a small spreading knife around the edge of each ramekin and carefully turn the soufflés out on to the palm of your hand, then place them the right way up on a lightly greased, shallow baking pan. They can now be stored in the refrigerator for up to 24 hours, lightly covered with plastic wrap.

When you are ready to re-heat the soufflés, preheat the oven to 350°F (180°C) and remove the soufflés from the refrigerator so they can return to room temperature. Dice the remaining Roquefort into ¼ inch (5 mm) pieces and sprinkle it on top of the soufflés, then place them in the oven, on the shelf above center, for 30 minutes.

Then, 2 or 3 minutes before serving, spoon a tablespoon of cream over each soufflé and return them to the oven while your guests seat themselves. Serve the soufflés immediately on warm plates garnished with a sprig of watercress.

Hollandaise Sauce

This great classic butter sauce from France can be tricky if it gets too much heat, so great care is necessary here. Since the advent of blenders and processors, however, the risk is not as large as it used to be. It has to be said that a blender is best, but a processor works well, too. My own problem has always been how to keep it warm, since I always like to make it in advance, and overheating will make it curdle. There are two possible answers for this: either use a wide-necked Thermos rinsed first with boiling water, or to make a lighter, more stable version, see right.

Serves 4

2 large egg yolks (reserve the whites if you want to make Foaming Hollandaise)
2 teaspoons lemon juice
2 teaspoons white wine vinegar
8 tablespoons (110g) butter
salt and freshly ground black pepper

Begin by placing the egg yolks in a small bowl and season them with a pinch of salt and pepper. Then place them in a food processor or blender and blend them thoroughly for about 1 minute. After that, heat the lemon juice and white wine vinegar in a small saucepan until the mixture starts to bubble and simmer. Turn the processor or blender on again and pour the hot liquid onto the egg yolks in a slow, steady stream. After that, turn the processor or blender off.

Now, using the same saucepan, melt the butter over a gentle heat, being very careful not to let it brown. When the butter is foaming, turn the processor or blender on once more and pour in the butter in a thin, slow, steady trickle; the slower you add it the better. (If it helps you to use a large measuring cup and not pour from the saucepan, rinse the cup with boiling water and then pour the butter mixture into it.) When all the butter has been incorporated, wipe around the sides of the processor bowl or blender with a spatula to incorporate all the sauce, then give the sauce one more quick burst and you should end up with a lovely, smooth, thick, buttery sauce.

Once the egg yolks are blended, add the hot lemon juice and white wine vinegar to the processor in a slow, steady stream

Next, melt the butter in the same pan used for the lemon juice and vinegar and add it in a thin, even stream

When the butter has been incorporated you will end up with a beautifully smooth, thick Hollandaise Sauce

Foaming Hollandaise

Foaming Hollandaise

I nearly always make this one now. What happens here is that the 2 reserved egg whites are beaten to soft peaks and folded into the sauce as soon as it's made. The advantages are great: first, it lightens the sauce, so it doesn't have quite so many calories, and you get a greater volume, so it goes further. It will never curdle because the egg whites stabilize the whole thing, which means you can happily keep it warm in a bowl fitted over simmering water. That's not all: you can also re-heat it in the same way, which means you can make it the day before. Finally, it will even freeze, allowing you to store anything leftover for a rainy day.

Either version of this supremely wonderful sauce can be used for serving with asparagus, artichokes, or with any kind of broiled or poached fish. And served with Eggs Benedict (see page 29), it's a positive star.

4
Rediscovering bread

"Wherefore do ye spend money on that which is not bread?" When the late Elizabeth David was struggling to find the words to introduce her masterpiece *English Bread And Yeast Cookery*, these words, spoken by the prophet Isaiah in 600 BC, said all she wanted to say about the state of commercially made bread. That was over 20 years ago, and I am here to say that not a lot has changed. It is a sad fact that while there has been some improvement, "that which is not bread" is still what a vast number of people consume.

Small bakeries in suburban communities and city neighborhoods struggle to produce quality, but it gets harder and harder because they can't possibly compete on price with the larger commercial bakeries, where low prices often override quality. Thus in buying cheaper bread we may well be richer by the money saved, but in truth we are infinitely poorer. If you think about it, few people could deny that having really good bread on a daily basis would instantly and inexpensively improve the quality of life.

The majority of people choose the dull, commercial option, instead. Is it perhaps because we don't value ourselves enough to feel we deserve the best – who knows? All I know is that "that which is not bread," ie, the average packaged, preserved, and sliced loaf (although there are, of course, exceptions), compared with what bread should be, is extremely dull and poor quality - a flat, tasteless kind of blotting paper. Take a close look at a slice: it will be slightly damp and clammy; if you squeeze it in your hands it will emerge looking like an elongated piece of rough dough with the indentations of your fingers all along it. Do you really want to consume it?

It's a kind of downward spiral of "how low can you go?" Millers mill their flour to provide for larger factories that bake mass-produced bread. Retailers sell it, then large supermarkets get involved in price wars. Something has to give in order for the stores to afford to cut prices, so quality is what has to give. The commercial bakeries can't afford to provide quality if the retailer can't afford to pay for it, because they have to keep their prices competitive. So quality cutting goes back to the bread factory, then to the miller, and even to the farmer. And what do we get?

I once heard modern bread given a sort of job description by a flour miller, who said that it was merely required to be a carrier. Isn't that a sad statement? In other words, it's what goes in or on the bread that's more important. If I can achieve anything at all in this whole *How To Cook* project it will be to persuade the younger generation to bake and taste some real bread, just so they know what it's really like.

That which *is* bread

That which *is* bread is both astoundingly simple (mainly flour and water), but at the same time gloriously luxurious because of its rarity. It's a strange paradox – here we are, spending a fortune on food and restaurants (you could say on the "food experience") - yet give anyone at all a slice of real homemade bread and you might as well be giving them the moon. When we were filming the bread program for the television series to accompany this book, absolutely everyone was drooling, so enthusiastic and so appreciative, and forever wanting just one more slice. So why is it that homemade bread has so much going for it?

I would put flavor as number one on the list – the real, pure, natural flavor of the wheat, which is somewhat enhanced and intensified by the yeast, which also adds its own subtle flavor. Number two on my list would be texture. In a white loaf the texture is very soft, aerated, and silky fine. Number three is the crust, which is very crisp and crunchy but at the same time light, and a well-baked crust is always fairly dark since this darkness creates extra flavor. Freshly baked white bread and good butter is one of the simplest pleasures in life. I love eating it with soft-boiled eggs (see page 18).

Whole wheat bread

This is not as delicate as white bread, but has other charms. Here we have all the flavor of whole, ripe wheat berries crushed so the germ and the bran are present. It has, therefore, a more gutsy and robust flavor. It also has a crisp and crunchy crust on the outside and is moist and mealy within.

But how can busy people find time to make bread?

I'm afraid it's a myth that breadmaking takes time. True, the bread itself needs its own time, but it will take only about 6-10 minutes of your *actual* time. I have come to the conclusion that it takes me less time than traveling to a really good baker and back. It is also a myth that breadmaking is difficult. One of the joys of making bread is that it needs so few ingredients; in fact, for a straightforward loaf, only four are required.

1 Flour

What the cook needs to know is that there are three types of wheat grain – hard, medium, and soft, and the flour they yield will contain something called gluten. In order not to get too technical, gluten can be described as somewhat like chewing gum. Soft grains produce ordinary chewing gum, which will be sticky, but hard grains produce something more like bubble gum, which means air can be incorporated and the gluten will stretch and expand into bubbles. So, when it comes to baking pastry, cookies, or cakes, what you need are very light-textured, soft grains containing the chewing-gum variety, but in bread, when the action of the yeast needs to rise the dough, you need hard wheat – the bubble-gum variety.

All-purpose flour has a fine texture, so this is the one for cakes, pastry, and so on, while the flour labeled bread flour, which has a high gluten content, is the one needed for most types of bread, although for something like a pizza dough, where you don't need the dough to rise as much, a soft ordinary all-purpose flour is, I think, better. So just think chewing gum or bubble gum and you've got your gluten sorted.

Flour milling

What happens here is the wheat grains are crushed and ground either between traditional milling stones or modern automatic rollers, but it's the human skill of the miller – not the method – that determines the quality of the flour. A grain of wheat is made up of three components: the protective layers of outer casing called bran, the white starchy endosperm, and the germ, which contains oils, vitamins, and protein.

Flours and meals

Originally, the whole wheat berries were ground into the flour, which, more correctly, should be called meal. Flour is the fine white powdery part that has had the bran layers and germ removed. Wholefood enthusiasts will say that white flour, having much of the bran removed, is a refined product and not a so-called healthy, whole one.

In my opinion, however, we need both types, and thankfully the so-called health-food era, with its heavy brown pastries, cakes, pizzas et al has moved on and given way to a more balanced view on what is or isn't healthy. Now, both refined and whole bran flours can be enjoyed equally or combined in certain recipes, producing the required flavor and texture.

Top row, from left: grains of durum wheat, hard wheat, and soft wheat
Second row: whole wheat
Third row: fine semolina and medium semolina
Fourth row: all-purpose flour, wheatgerm, and bran

Self-rising flour This is simply a term used to describe soft flour to which leavening and salt have been added by the manufacturer.

Semolina This word comes from the Italian, meaning semi milled, and it is, as you can see in the photograph, not ground to fine flour, meaning the grains are coarser. Semolina is what is used for traditionally made pasta – milled from hard wheat grain to a texture specified by the pasta maker so that the finished product will be rough-textured to enable the sauce to cling sufficiently (see page 218). Semolina from softer wheat has also played a part in other cuisines, where it has been used in puddings and cakes, and durum semolina gives a lovely texture to shortbread.

2 Liquid

This is usually water, though milk and buttermilk are sometimes used. The water should always be lukewarm, meaning you can hold your finger in it without discomfort. If the water is too hot it will kill the yeast.

3 Yeast

For beginners, working with yeast is now blissfully simple, because it's powdered into something called active dry yeast (or you can use instant yeast): no mixing, no waiting for frothy heads, and so on. All you do is sprinkle it in with the flour, and that's all. Don't forget to inspect the date stamps, though, because if it's too old it won't do its work.

4 Salt

Salt is an important ingredient in bread, but don't use too much since it slows down the rising. But if you like a little more than I have included in my recipes, then allow a little extra rising time.

Kneading

There are two schools of thought on this: one is "what a bore," because 3 minutes is a long time in a busy life. Alternatively, some people find the whole operation extremely therapeutic. I am in both camps here: resentful if I'm short of time, but it also has to be said that kneading and daydreaming are a pleasant occupation if time permits.

Kneading in a food processor

On busy days it's all perfectly simple. If you use a processor with a dough hook attached, the whole thing – mixing and kneading – is really very little trouble.

How to knead dough

For bread dough that has to be kneaded, simply place it on a flat work surface then stretch it away from you, using the heel of one hand to push from the middle and the clenched knuckles of your other hand to pull the other half of the dough towards you (both hands should move simultaneously to stretch out the dough). Then lift the edges over and back to the middle. Give it a quarter turn and repeat the process. It soon becomes a rather rhythmic operation, and the dough will then start to become very elastic. What happens here is you begin to feel the magic – the dough literally begins to spring into life as you push it away and it defiantly springs back to challenge you. When it's become very smooth, springy, and begins to appear blistery on the surface, which takes about 3 minutes, it's then ready to be set aside to rise.

Rising

We don't need to go into the science of breadmaking, but when flour, water, and yeast are introduced to each other, something magical occurs, and the mixture (which started out being a heavy lump of dough), after the correct amount of time, will stretch and expand to twice its original volume. This process can be sped up if the dough is put in a warm place, but the longer you leave it to rise naturally at room temperature, the better the bread. I now prefer to just leave it to rise naturally. One point, though: bread will also rise at a cold temperature, so if it's more convenient, place it in the lowest part of the refrigerator and let it rise overnight, ready to bake in the morning.

Bread dough, which starts off as a heavy lump, stretches over time and expands to twice its original volume

Once the dough has risen, the air is punched out (just use your fist) and then left to rise again, this time in its pan

What is punching down and proofing?

White bread dough is better if it has a second rise, giving it a more even texture. So now what happens is you punch out all the air using your fist, shape the dough, place it in a pan and give it a second rise, which will be much quicker. The word "proofing" refers to this second rise, because you're actually testing, or proofing, that the yeast is still (we hope) alive and kicking.

Bread pans and cooling racks

Good old-fashioned bread pans with pleated corners are thankfully still available (see page 74) in the sizes 8½ x 4½ x 2¾ inch (22 x 11 x 7 cm), 7½ x 3⅝ x 2¼ inch (19 x 9 x 5 cm), and 6 x 3 x 2 inch (15 x 7.5 x 5 cm), measured on top. Grease them well with butter first. Then, when the bread is baked, it's most important to remove it from the pan to cool on a wire cooling rack. If you leave it in the pan or place it on a flat surface, it will become steamy and soggy. A cooling rack allows the air to circulate and guarantees that the crust stays crisp and crunchy.

Has it finished baking?

The way to test whether the bread is done is to turn the loaf out, holding it in a cloth, then give the underneath a sharp tap with your knuckles: if it has finished baking, it will sound hollow and not dense. Remember, it's always better to overbake rather than underbake bread. Because I like an extra crunchy crust, I always put the loaf back in the oven without its pan for 5-10 minutes to crisp up the underneath and sides, so if you do this, you will be sure the loaf is cooked through.

Once this second rising, or "proofing," is done, the loaf is ready to be baked in the preheated oven

To test whether the loaf is cooked, hold it in a cloth and tap the underneath with your knuckles – it should sound hollow

Plain and Simple White Bread

A good, old-fashioned, white, crusty loaf, soft inside and lightly textured, is still hard to beat – it's my own favorite to go with softly boiled eggs, and the next day or the day after it always makes divine toast. Made either by hand or with the help of a food processor, it couldn't be easier, and the pleasure of eating it is difficult to match.

Makes 1 large or 2 small loaves
5 cups (700 g) bread flour, plus a little extra for the top of the bread
1 tablespoon salt, or less, according to taste
1 x ¼ oz (7 g) package active dry yeast
1 teaspoon superfine sugar
about 2 cups (425 ml) lukewarm water

You will also need two 7½ x 3⅝ x 2¼ inch (19 x 9 x 5 cm) loaf pans or one 8½ x 4½ x 2¾ inch (22 x 11 x 7) loaf pan, well buttered.

Preheat the oven to its lowest setting.

Begin by warming the flour in the oven for about 10 minutes, then turn the oven off. Sift the flour, salt, yeast, and sugar into a bowl, make a well in the center of the mixture, and add the water. Now, mix to a dough, starting off with a wooden spoon and using your hands in the final stages of mixing, adding a few drops more water if necessary to incorporate the dry ingredients. Wipe the bowl clean with the ball of dough and transfer it to a flat work surface (very lightly floured). Knead the dough for 3 minutes or until it develops a shiny look and blisters under the surface (it should be springy and elastic). Transfer the dough back to the bowl and cover it with plastic wrap that has been lightly oiled on the side that is facing the dough. Leave it until it looks as though it has doubled in bulk, which will be about 2 hours at room temperature.

After that, punch out the air, then knead again for 2 minutes. Divide the dough in half, pat each piece out to an oblong, then fold one end into the center and the other in on top. Put each one into a buttered pan, dust lightly with flour, then place them side by side in an oiled plastic storage bag until the dough rises above the tops of the pans – this time about an hour at room temperature. Alternatively, place all the dough in the larger pan. Meanwhile, preheat the oven to 450°F (230°C).

Bake the loaves on the center shelf for 30-40 minutes (or 35-45 minutes for the large loaf) until they sound hollow when their bottoms are tapped. Now, return them upside-down, out of their pans, to the oven to crisp the bottom and side crusts for about 5 minutes, then cool on a wire rack.

White bread using the processor

Although making bread as above is not difficult, it can be even easier if you make the whole thing in a food processor. To do this you fit the dough hook onto the processor (some also have a special bowl); then all you do is sift the dry ingredients into the bowl, put the lid on, and turn the processor on to a low speed or the one recommended in the manufacturer's handbook for use of the dough hook. Now, pour the water through the feeding tube, then leave the processor to "knead" the dough for about 3 minutes – but don't go away, because the machine can sometimes stick and slide around. Then transfer the dough to a clean bowl and cover it with plastic wrap that has been lightly oiled on the side facing the dough. Leave it until it looks as though it has doubled in bulk – about 2 hours at room temperature. You can now, return the dough to the food processor and "knead" it again for 1 minute, still at a low speed. Then simply continue to make the loaves as above.

Quick and Easy Whole Wheat Loaf

The poet Pam Ayres once said, when describing her homemade whole wheat bread, that it was like "biting into a cornfield," and that's it – the very best description I've ever come across. A crisp, crunchy crust and then all the flavor of the whole wheat grain – take a bite, close your eyes and you'll know just what she meant. Then, when you've grasped how easy whole wheat bread is to make, you'll probably never stop making it. The recipe here is adapted from Doris Grant's famous loaf in her book Your Daily Bread, *for which I continue to give thanks.*

Makes 1 large or 2 small loaves
3¾ cups (570 g) preferably organic whole wheat flour, plus a little extra for the top of the bread
2 teaspoons salt
1 teaspoon light brown sugar
1 x ¼ oz (7 g) package active dry yeast
about 1¾ cups (400 ml) lukewarm water

You will also need either a 8½ x 4½ x 2¾ inch (22 x 11 x 7 cm) loaf pan or two 7½ x 3⅜ x 2¼ inch (19 x 9 x 5 cm) loaf pans, well buttered.

Preheat the oven to its lowest setting.

Begin by warming the flour slightly in the oven for about 10 minutes, then turn the oven off for now. Next, turn the warm flour into a large mixing bowl and all you do is simply sprinkle on the salt, sugar, and the yeast; mix these together thoroughly, make a well in the center and pour in the lukewarm water. Then take a wooden spoon and begin to mix the warm liquid into the flour gradually to form a dough: the exact amount of water you'll need will depend on the flour. Finish off by mixing with your hands until you have a smooth dough that leaves the bowl clean – there should be no bits of flour or dough remaining on the sides of the bowl and, unlike pastry, it is better to have too much water than too little.

Now, transfer the dough to a flat surface and stretch it out into an oblong, then fold one edge into the center and the other over that. Now, fit the dough into the pan, pressing it firmly all round the edges so that the top will already be slightly rounded. Next, sprinkle the surface with a generous dusting of flour, then cover the pan with a damp, clean dish towel and let it rise in a warm place for 30-40 minutes or at room temperature for about an hour. If you're making two loaves, divide the dough in half before following the steps above and folding it into the two pans.

Meanwhile, preheat the oven to 400°F (200°C). When the dough has risen to the top of the bread pan or pans, bake the bread for 40 minutes for the larger loaf pan or 30 minutes for the smaller loaf pans. When the bread is baked, turn it out onto a cloth to protect your hands – it will sound hollow when rapped underneath with your knuckles. Then return the bread, out of its pan, upside-down to the oven for another 5-10 minutes to crisp the bottom and sides. Cool the bread on a wire rack, and never put it away or freeze it until it is absolutely cold.

Toast

A friend of mine invented the term "wangy," which I use to describe the cold, leathery, bendy little triangles that often arrive at breakfast when you order toast in eating establishments.

So I've been thinking, as this is a basic cooking course, why not give the world the definitive recipe for perfect toast? To begin with, I am not a disciple of electric toasters. The ones I've experienced all seem to be a bit erratic, and if you're rather inept at slicing bread (like me), then they're not very helpful at all because if the bread is cut slightly irregularly, a) it probably won't go in the toaster at all, and, b) if it does, one area ends up not being toasted at all while another bit is giving off nasty black smoke signals!

1 The key to slicing bread is to use gentle, rapid sawing movements with the knife and not to push down too hard on the loaf. For toast, cut the bread into slices of about ½ inch (1 cm) thickness. The crusts can be left on or cut off, depending on how you like them.
2 Preheat the broiler for at least 10 minutes before making the toast, turning it to its highest setting.
3 Place the bread on the broiler rack and position the baking sheet 2 inches (5 cm) from the heat source.
4 Allow the bread to toast on both sides to your own preferred degree of pale or dark golden brown.
5 While the bread is toasting, keep an eye on it and don't wander away.
6 When the toast is done, remove it immediately to a toast rack. Why a toast rack? Because they are a brilliant invention. Freshly made toast contains steam, and if you place it in a vertical position, in which the air is allowed to circulate, the steam escapes and the toast becomes crisp and crunchy. Putting it immediately onto a plate means the steam is trapped underneath, making it damp and soggy. If you don't possess a toast rack you really ought to invest in a modest one. Failing that, stand your slices of toast up against a jar or something similar for about 1 minute before serving.
7 Always eat toast as soon as possible after that, and never make it ahead of time.
8 Never ever wrap it in a napkin or cover it because the steam gets trapped and the toast gets soggy.
9 Always use good bread, because the better the bread, the better the toast. It is also preferable for the bread to be a couple of days old.

A toast rack is absolutely necessary if you want to avoid soggy toast; if you don't have one, prop the slices up against a jar for a minute or so before serving

Goat Cheese, Onion, and Potato Bread with Thyme

Don't make this if you are on a diet – it's so wonderful that it's impossible to stop eating it. It's also great for a packed lunch or a car trip because you've got the bread and cheese all in one. It must also be the quickest, easiest homemade bread on record.

Makes 1 loaf, to serve 4-6
4 oz (110 g) round firm goat cheese
4 scallions, finely sliced
1 medium round red potato weighing
approximately 6 oz (175 g)
1½ teaspoons chopped thyme leaves,
plus a few small sprigs
1¼ cups (175 g) self-rising flour, plus a
little extra for the top of the loaf
½ teaspoon salt
⅛ teaspoon or generous pinch of
cayenne pepper
1 large egg
3 tablespoons milk
1½ teaspoons grain mustard

You will also need a heavy baking
sheet, very well greased.

Preheat the oven to 375°F (190°C).

Start off by taking your sharpest knife, then pare the rind from the cheese and cut it into ½ inch (1 cm) cubes. Then sift the flour, salt, and cayenne into a big, roomy mixing bowl, holding the sifter up high to give the flour a good airing. Then thinly peel the potato using a potato peeler and grate the potato directly into the flour using the coarse side of the grater. Then add the scallions, chopped thyme, and two-thirds of the cheese. Now, take a narrow spatula and blend everything together thoroughly.

After that, beat the egg gently with the milk and mustard, then pour the mixture into the bowl, just bringing it all together to a loose, rough dough, still using the spatula. Next transfer it on to the baking sheet and pat it gently into a 6 inch (15 cm) rough round. Now, lightly press the rest of the cheese over the surface, dust with a little flour, and scatter the small sprigs of thyme over.

Bake the bread on the middle shelf of the oven for 45-50 minutes or until golden brown. Then remove it to a cooling rack and serve it still slightly warm if possible (but I have to say it's still divine a day later, warmed through in the oven).

Feta Cheese, Potato, and Rosemary Bread

This is a delicious variation on the recipe above, using a different cheese and a different herb. Simply substitute the goat cheese for the same amount of cubed Feta cheese, a quarter of a red onion, peeled and finely chopped, instead of the scallions, and use rosemary instead of thyme. Before baking, scatter a quarter of an onion, sliced into half-moon shapes, on top along with some small sprigs of rosemary and a few halved olives.

Goat Cheese, Onion, and Potato Bread with Thyme, right; Feta Cheese, Potato, and Rosemary Bread, left

Irish Oatmeal Soda Bread

This is the real thing – proper Irish soda bread. As it bakes in the oven and the aroma reaches you, close your eyes, picture the beauty of the Irish landscape, and dream you're there. It's heaven spread generously with butter and good jam, or with a chunk of Irish cheese such as Cashel Blue or Milleens along with a glass of Murphy's Irish beer. It will give you a little taste of that wonderful country, even though you're not there.

Making this bread could not be easier. Begin by placing the dry ingredients in a large, roomy bowl; mix to combine, then beat the egg and buttermilk together and add them to the dry ingredients. Start mixing, first with a fork, then finish off with your hands to form a smooth dough. All you do now is transfer the dough to the loaf pan and level the top. Alternatively, shape into a round about 6 inches (15 cm) across and make a deep cut across it three times, but don't cut all the way through. Sprinkle lightly with flour and bake in the center of the oven for 50-60 minutes, then turn it out immediately onto a wire rack to cool. This is best eaten fresh, but fear not about leftovers, because the next day or the day after, it makes wonderful toast.

Makes 1 loaf, to serve 4-6
1¼ cups (175 g) whole wheat flour
⅓ cup (50 g) all-purpose flour
¼ cup (50 g) steel-cut oatmeal
¼ cup (25 g) wheatgerm
1 teaspoon baking soda
1½ teaspoons salt
1 teaspoon sugar
1 large egg
1 cup (250 ml) buttermilk
a little extra flour for dusting

You will also need a 7½ x 3⅝ x 2¼ inch (19 x 9 x 5 cm) loaf pan, well greased.

Preheat the oven to, 375°F (190°C).

Cornmeal and Mixed-Seed Bread

This is another very quick and easy loaf, but with lots of varying textures. And don't worry if the sunflower seeds turn green during baking – it actually looks very attractive.

Makes 1 small loaf
1 cup (150 g) polenta (cornmeal)
1¼ cups (175 g) bread flour
1½ teaspoons salt
1 teaspoon baking soda
¼ cup (25 g) pumpkin seeds
¼ cup (25 g) sunflower seeds
¼ cup (25 g) poppy seeds, reserving
1 teaspoon for the top of the loaf
3 tablespoons (25 g) steel-cut oatmeal
1½ teaspoons superfine sugar
1 large egg
1 cup (250 ml) buttermilk

You will also need a 7½ x 3⅝ x 2¼ inch (19 x 9 x 5 cm) loaf pan, lightly oiled.

Preheat the oven to 375°F (190°C).

Begin by sifting the flour, salt, and baking soda together into a large bowl, then add the polenta, all the seeds, the oatmeal, and sugar and give everything a good mixing. Next, whisk the egg and buttermilk together, add this to the bowl, and gradually stir with a wooden spoon until the mixture forms a soft and slack dough, adding a little more buttermilk, if necessary. Now, transfer the dough to the prepared loaf pan, scatter the reserved poppy seeds on top, and bake the loaf on the middle shelf of the oven for 50-60 minutes. Check that the loaf is baked by turning it out and listening for the hollow sound when you tap the underside with your knuckles. Return it to the oven upside-down, without its pan, for 5 minutes to give it a final "crunch," then cool it on a wire rack.

Crostini Lazio

Italian in origin, crostini are "little crusts." In France they are called croutons, but both are little rounds or squares of bread brushed with olive oil or butter, and sometimes crushed garlic, then baked in the oven.

For the crostini, drizzle the olive oil over the baking pan, add the garlic, then, using your hands, spread the oil and garlic over the surface of the baking pan. Now, place the bread on top of the oil and turn them over so that both sides are lightly coated. Now, bake them in the oven for 10-15 minutes, until crisp and crunchy, but put a timer on since they soon overbake.

For the topping, simply peel the rind off the goat cheese using a sharp knife, then cut the cheese into four pieces. Next, place all the ingredients, including the reserved oil, into a food processor and blend until the mixture is smooth. If making this ahead, cover and chill in the refrigerator until needed, then remove it half an hour before serving and spread it on top of the crostini, topped with a caper berry (if using). Don't assemble them until the last minute, though, or the bread loses some of its crispness.

Makes 12, to serve 4-6

For the crostini:
1 small, thin French baguette cut into 12 slices about 1 inch (2.5 cm) thick, or 3 slices from a thick sliced loaf, cut into quarters
3 tablespoons olive oil
1 fat clove garlic, peeled and crushed

For the topping:
4 oz (110 g) firm goat cheese
4 oz (110 g) tuna in oil – the best quality you can buy – drained, reserving 1 tablespoon of the oil
1 tablespoon salted capers or capers in vinegar, thoroughly rinsed and drained
1 tablespoon finely grated Parmesan (Parmigiano Reggiano)
2 teaspoons lemon juice

To garnish:
12 caper berries (optional)

You will also need a shallow baking pan measuring approximately 14 x 10 inches (35 x 25.5 cm).

Preheat the oven to 350°F (180°C).

Bruschetta

Bruschetta is a very special type of toasted bread, pronounced brusketta. When I first tasted the real thing in Tuscany, it was one of the most memorable eating experiences of my life. Italian country bread is toasted on both sides over hot, fragrant coals, then slashes are made along the surface of each piece of bread, which is then rubbed with a cut clove of garlic. After that, peppery Italian extra virgin olive oil is poured over it quite generously so that it runs into the bread, making little pools all around the bottom of the plate. The pleasure and joy in its utter simplicity are indescribable.

Since few of us have hot coals handy (though don't forget bruschetta during the barbecue season), the next best thing is a cast iron ridged grill pan or an ordinary oven broiler.

First, preheat the ridged grill pan over a high heat for about 10 minutes. When it's really hot, place the slices of bread – on the diagonal – and pan-broil them for about 1 minute on each side, until they're golden and crisp and have charred strips across each side. (Alternatively, toast them under a conventional broiler.) Then, as they are ready, take a sharp knife and quickly make about three little slashes across each one, rub in the garlic, and drizzle about half a tablespoon of olive oil over each one. Serve immediately, sprinkled with a little rock salt.

Makes 12, to serve 4-6
1 ciabatta loaf, cut in 12 thin slices
1 clove garlic, peeled and rubbed in a little salt
about 6 tablespoons extra virgin olive oil
rock salt

You will also need a cast iron ridged grill pan.

Bruschetta with Tomato and Basil

Good bread, good olive oil – what more could you want? Just two things: very red, ripe plum tomatoes and basil leaves. It's perhaps the best bruschetta of all, and perfect for serving with drinks before a meal as an appetizer.

Prepare the tomatoes before toasting the bread. All you do is place them in a bowl, pour boiling water over them, and leave for exactly 1 minute before draining them and slipping off the skins (protect your hands with a cloth if the tomatoes are too hot). Then chop them finely.

When the bruschetta are made (as above), top with the tomatoes and basil leaves, season with salt and freshly ground black pepper, and sprinkle a few more drops of olive oil over before serving. It's hard to believe that something so simple can be so wonderful.

Makes 12, to serve 4-6
6 red, ripe plum tomatoes
a few torn basil leaves
a few drops extra virgin olive oil
rock salt and freshly ground black pepper

Bruschetta with Tomato and Basil

93

Croque Monsieur

Serves 1
2 large slices good-quality white bread, buttered
2 oz (50 g) Gruyère, finely grated
2-3 slices smoked cooked ham, Prosciutto or wafer-thin ham
1 tablespoon (10 g) butter, melted
2 teaspoons finely grated Parmesan (Parmigiano Reggiano)
salt and freshly ground black pepper

Preheat the broiler to its highest setting.

This is my version of the toasted cheese and ham sandwich of Paris café fame, and just thinking about it and imagining atmospheric, crowded pavement cafés makes me long to be in Paris and eat it there. But, that not being possible, it's one of the nicest snack meals for one that I know.

This could not be simpler. On one slice of the buttered bread, spread half the grated Gruyère, then cover that with the slices of ham, folding them if necessary to fit the size of the bread. Now, sprinkle the rest of the Gruyère on top of the ham, season, place the other slice of bread on top of that, and press it down very firmly. You can at this stage cut off the crusts, but I think they add extra crunchiness. Now, brush half the melted butter on the top side of the sandwich, sprinkle it with half the Parmesan, and press it in. Now, transfer the sandwich to the broiler pan and broil it for about 2 minutes, 2 inches (5 cm) from the heat. When it's golden brown, turn it over, brush the other side with the remaining melted butter, sprinkle the rest of the Parmesan on top and broil for another 2 minutes. Cut into quarters and serve while still crunchy.

Toasted Cheese and Chili Relish Sandwich

Serves 1
2 large slices white bread, buttered
3 teaspoons tomato chili relish
2 oz (50 g) Gruyère, finely grated
½ small onion, peeled and sliced into thin rings
1 tablespoon (10 g) butter, melted
1 oz (25 g) Parmesan (Parmigiano Reggiano), finely grated
salt and freshly ground black pepper

Preheat the broiler to its highest setting.

This is the vegetarian version of Croque Monsieur. Use a good-quality white bread, and a store-bought relish normally served with burgers or my own homemade version on page 190.

Start off by spreading both slices of bread with 1½ teaspoons of relish each. Now, sprinkle the Gruyère on one of the slices and the onion rings over the cheese; season with salt and pepper and then place the other piece of bread on top.

Next, brush the top of the sandwich with half the melted butter and sprinkle with half the Parmesan, lightly pressing it down. Then place the sandwich on the broiler rack and broil it 2 inches (5 cm) from the heat until the top of the sandwich is golden brown – about 2 minutes. Turn the sandwich over and brush the top with the rest of the melted butter and Parmesan, then return the sandwich to the broiler for another 2 minutes. Finally, cut it into quarters and eat it pretty quickly.

Basic Pizza Dough

Pizza dough is made in almost the same way as the white bread on page 82 – by hand or using a food processor, except that you add olive oil and a little sugar to the flour mixture and there isn't a second rising. You might consider making double the quantity and freezing half to make another pizza at a later stage. Just place the dough, after punching out the air, into a plastic storage bag, seal, and freeze.

Makes a 10 inch (25.5 cm) bottom pizza – serves 2
1¼ cups (175 g) all-purpose flour (see page 77)
1 teaspoon salt
1 teaspoon active dry yeast
½ teaspoon superfine sugar
1 tablespoon olive oil
½ cup (120 ml) lukewarm water

To roll out:
2-3 tablespoons cornmeal (polenta)

You will also need a pizza stone or solid baking sheet measuring approximately 14 x 11 inches (35 x 28 cm).

Preheat the oven to its lowest setting.

Left to right: once the dough has doubled in bulk, remove the plastic wrap; turn the dough onto the work surface and punch out the air; finally, knead briefly using the cornmeal and shape into a ball

Begin by warming the flour slightly in the oven for about 10 minutes, then turn the oven off. Sift the flour, salt, yeast, and sugar into a bowl and make a well in the center of the mixture; then add the olive oil and pour in the water. Now, mix to a dough, starting off with a wooden spoon and using your hands in the final stages of mixing. Wipe the bowl clean with the dough, adding a few more drops of water if any dry bits remain, and transfer it to a flat work surface (there shouldn't be any need to flour this). Knead the dough for 3 minutes or until it develops a shiny look and blisters under the surface (it should also be springy and elastic). You can now either leave the dough on the surface covered by the upturned bowl or transfer it to a clean bowl and cover with plastic wrap that has been lightly oiled on the side that is facing the dough. Leave it until it looks as though it has doubled in bulk, which will be about an hour at room temperature.

Having made the dough and left it to rise, preheat the oven to 450°F (230°C), along with the pizza stone or baking sheet. The next stage is to turn the dough back onto the work surface that has been sprinkled generously with cornmeal to prevent the dough from sticking. Punch all the air out of the dough and knead it for a couple of seconds to begin shaping it into a ball. Then dust your rolling pin with cornmeal and roll the dough out to a circle that is approximately 10 inches (25.5 cm) in diameter. Finish stretching it out with your hands, working from the center and using the flat of your fingers to push the dough out; it doesn't need to be a perfect round, but you want it to be a fairly thin-crusted pizza, with slightly raised edges. You can now top the pizza with one of the toppings that follow.

Four Cheese Pizza

This is the classic version of one of the most wonderful combinations of bread and cheese imaginable. You can, of course, vary the cheeses, but the ones I've chosen here are a truly magical combination.

First, make the pizza crust as described opposite. Then, using a thick oven mitt, very carefully lift the baking sheet or pizza stone out of the oven and sprinkle it with cornmeal. Now, carefully lift the pizza dough onto the stone or baking sheet and quickly arrange teaspoonfuls of Ricotta here and there all over. After that, scatter the Mozzarella and Gorgonzola pieces in-between, and, finally, scatter the Parmesan on top. Bake the whole thing on a high shelf for 10-12 minutes, until the crust is golden brown and the cheese is bubbling. You can lift the edge up slightly to check that the underside is crisp and brown. Carefully remove the baking sheet or pizza stone from the oven, again using a thick oven mitt, and immediately serve the pizza on hot plates.

Sufficient for a 10 inch (25.5 cm) bottom pizza – serves 2

1 basic pizza crust (see opposite)
⅓ cup (60 g) Ricotta
2 oz (50 g) Mozzarella, cut into 1 inch (2.5 cm) slices
2 oz (50 g) Gorgonzola Piccante, cut into 1 inch (2.5 cm) slices
1 oz (25 g) Parmesan (Parmigiano Reggiano), grated
a little cornmeal (polenta) for dusting

Preheat the oven to 450°F (230°C).

Four Seasons Pizza

Enough for a 10 inch (25.5 cm)
bottom pizza – serves 2
1 basic pizza crust (see page 96)
2 tablespoons sun-dried
tomato paste
3 oz (75 g) Prosciutto (about 4 slices)
5 oz (150 g) Mozzarella, cubed
4 oz (110 g) small tomatoes, thinly
sliced (approximately 3 tomatoes)
2 oz (50 g) small open mushrooms,
e.g. cremini, thinly sliced
1½ tablespoons salted capers or capers
in vinegar, rinsed and drained
8 pitted black olives, halved
4 anchovy fillets, drained and split in
half lengthwise
a few basil leaves, dipped in oil and
torn, plus a few extra leaves to garnish
2 tablespoons olive oil

Preheat the oven to 450°F (230°C).

*Originally, the toppings were placed on this pizza in four sections,
representing each season, but because this pizza serves two, it's better
to distribute them around more evenly.*

Begin by making the pizza crust as described on page 96, then spread the
sun-dried tomato paste up to the edges of the pizza dough. Carefully lift it
onto the hot baking sheet or pizza stone, then place, first, the slices of
Prosciutto on top, folding them, then simply scatter the cubes of
Mozzarella, the tomatoes, mushrooms, capers, and olives all over. Finally,
decorate with the anchovy fillets in a criss-cross pattern and the basil leaves.
Now, drizzle the olive oil over everything and bake on a high shelf for 10-
12 minutes, until the crust is golden brown. Scatter the whole basil leaves
on top before serving.

*Four Seasons Pizza; uncooked, above,
and cooked, right*

Puttanesca Pizza

Puttanesca has always been one of my favorite pasta sauces – strong and gutsy, with lots of flavor – then one inspired day I decided to try it on a pizza crust instead. The result is brilliant, with the added charm of pools of Mozzarella and crusty bread.

First, make the pizza crust as described on page 96. For the sauce, heat the oil in a medium saucepan, then add the garlic and chili and cook briefly until the garlic is pale gold. Then add all the other sauce ingredients, stir and season with a little pepper – but no salt because of the anchovies. Turn the heat to low and simmer the sauce very gently without a lid for 40 minutes, when it will have reduced to a lovely, thick mass with very little liquid left. Spread the filling over the pizza crust, taking it up to the raised edge, then carefully lift it onto the hot baking sheet or pizza stone. Now, scatter the Mozzarella on top, dip the basil leaves in the olive oil, and place them here and there on top. Bake the pizza on a high oven shelf for 10-12 minutes until the crust is golden brown and crusty. Use an oven mitt to remove it from the oven, then garnish with the extra basil.

Enough for a 10 inch (25.5 cm) bottom pizza – serves 2
1 basic pizza crust (see page 96)

For the sauce:
1 tablespoon olive oil
1 clove garlic, peeled and finely chopped
½ red chili, seeded and finely chopped
2 teaspoons chopped fresh basil
8 oz (225 g) fresh tomatoes, peeled and chopped
1 oz (25 g) anchovies, drained and cut in half lengthwise
3 oz (75 g) black olives, pitted and chopped small
2 teaspoons salted capers or capers in vinegar, rinsed and drained
freshly ground black pepper

For the topping:
5 oz (150 g) Mozzarella, cut into 1 inch (2.5 cm) slices
a few small whole fresh basil leaves, plus a few extra to garnish
a little olive oil

Preheat the oven to 450°F (230°C).

Puttanesca Pizza; cooked, left, and uncooked, above

Steamed Panettone Pudding with Hot Punch Sauce

Yes, this is a bread recipe. Panettone is an Italian fruit bread that's sold mostly in the fall and around Christmas time in beautifully designed boxes with ribbons for carrying it. If you would like a light but quite delectable alternative to a Christmas plum pudding, this is it. I've tried making it in advance, freezing, and then re-heating it, and it works beautifully. But don't confine it to Christmas because it's great to serve at any time, and it goes particularly well with Eliza Acton's citrus sauce.

Serves 6

For the steamed panettone pudding:

11 oz (315 g) panettone cake

1¼ cups (175 g) dried mixed fruit, soaked in 5 tablespoons rum overnight

⅓ cup (50 g) whole almonds with the skins left on

2 oz (50 g) candied citrus rind, finely chopped

grated zest 1 orange

grated zest 2 lemons

⅓ cup (50 g) dark muscovado or brown sugar

1¼ cups (275 ml) milk

¾ cup (150 ml) heavy cream

3 large eggs

For Eliza Acton's hot punch sauce:

1 large orange and 1 lemon

½ cup (110 g) superfine sugar

1¼ cups (275 ml) water

¼ cup (25 g) all-purpose flour

4 tablespoons (50 g) unsalted butter, softened

2 tablespoons rum

2 tablespoons brandy

¾ cup (175 ml) medium sherry

You will need a 1¼ quart (1.2 liter) pudding mold, 6½ x 3½ x 3⅜ inch (16.5 x 9 x 9.5 cm), or a charlotte mold with a similar capacity, well-buttered. You will also need a steamer or a saucepan with a collapsable steamer and a tight-fitting lid, foil, and string.

Begin by soaking the dried mixed fruit in the rum overnight. The next day, toast the almonds. To do this, preheat the broiler to its highest setting for 10 minutes; then place the almonds on some foil and toast them under the broiler for 2-3 minutes, but don't leave because they will burn very quickly. When they look nicely toasted on one side, turn them all over to toast the other side, then remove them from the broiler and set them aside to cool.

Next, cut the panettone into 1 inch (2.5 cm) chunks and place them in a large mixing bowl along with the candied peel, orange and lemon zests, the soaked dried mixed fruit, and any drops of rum that didn't get soaked up. Now, chop the almonds into thin slivers and add these. Give it all a really good stir to distribute everything evenly.

In another bowl, whisk together the sugar, milk, cream, and eggs and pour this all over the panettone, giving everything another good stir. Now, pour the mixture into the buttered pudding mold and press everything down to pack it in. Now, cover the top of the pudding with a double sheet of foil measuring about 10 inches (25.5 cm) square and tie it securely with the string around the top of the mold, then make a string handle by taking a length of string over the top of the pudding mold and attaching it to each side – this will help you lift the pudding in and out of the steamer. Now, boil a kettle of water and pour it into the saucepan, about half-full; place it on a medium heat, and when it comes back to a boil, fit the steamer over the top.

Now, place the pudding in, put the lid on, and steam the pudding for exactly 2 hours. After 1 hour, check the water level in the saucepan, and, if necessary, top it up with boiling water. If you are using a collapsible steamer, put in enough water to just reach the steamer, and you'll need to top it up two or three times.

Meanwhile, make the hot punch sauce. First prepare the orange and lemon zests, and to do this it's best to use a potato peeler and pare off the outer zest, leaving the white pith behind. What you need is four strips of each zest measuring approximately 2 x 1 inch (5 x 2.5 cm). Then, using a sharp knife, cut the strips into very thin, needle-like shreds. Now, drop these into a medium-sized saucepan along with the sugar and water, bring everything up to a slow simmer, and let it simmer as gently as possible for 15 minutes.

While that is happening, squeeze the juice from the orange and lemon, and in a separate bowl, mix the flour and butter together to form a paste.

When the 15 minutes is up, add the orange and lemon juice, along with the rum, brandy, and sherry, and bring it all back up to a gentle heat. Now, add the paste to the liquid in small, peanut-sized pieces, whisking as you add them, until they have dissolved and the sauce has thickened. Serve the sauce hot in a warmed serving pitcher, and if you make it in advance, re-heat it gently without letting it come to a boil.

To serve the pudding, remove the foil and string and let it stand for 5-10 minutes, then slide a narrow spatula all around to loosen it and turn it out onto a warmed plate. Pour some of the hot punch sauce over the pudding, and carry it to the table with the rest of the sauce in a pitcher to pass around separately.

5

First steps in pastry

If you can't make pastry and don't even know how to start, the very first thing you need to do is forgive yourself and not feel guilty. Please understand it isn't because you're inadequate or not born to such things; it's probably because no one's ever actually taught you how. In the age we now live in, cooking skills are rarely learned from watching our mothers because working mothers have little time for home baking. So now we have to think differently. But teaching is essential: someone had to teach you to swim, ride a bike or drive a car, things that are now second nature to you.

With pastry it is precisely the same - someone (hopefully me) has to show you how, and then, with a little practice, pastry-making will become automatic, something you do without having to think about it.

What I want to do here is show you how to make two basic types of pastry, and if you master these, you can have a lifetime of happy pastry baking without having to worry.

What is pastry?

Originally pastry was an inedible paste used to seal in juices and aromas, but there must have been a time when some clever person thought, "What a waste," added some fat to make it deliciously edible in its own right. Now, the pastry crust itself is every bit as important as what it encases or surrounds.

But what should it be like? What are the constituents of a really good pastry crust? First, it should be crisp, but the word that has been adopted to describe perfect pastry is "short" (meaning meltingly light). It should also be well baked and offer a character and flavor in its own right so that it complements whatever it is partnering.

I have a theory about how to make good pastry at home, and that's to keep it simple. Professional pâtissiers have years of training and great skills, and we can all be dazzled by what they can produce. The trouble is that if we have busy lives, we can't do the same at home, so we should enjoy their expertise whenever we can. But at home, learn to master simple pastry well. It's also important not to fall into the trap of some chefs by adding too much fat, because sometimes the pastry gets so rich that it begins to compete with and not complement the filling.

The case for shortcrust

Not fashionable, not clever, not overly-rich, but for my money, the humble shortcrust is one of the best pastries of all. What it provides is a light, crisp, melting crust, containing the important flavors of the wheat – all that you imagine homemade pastry to be. It is made, quite simply, from flour, fat and water, with nothing else added. But a well-made, thinly rolled shortcrust provides a discreet "melt in the mouth" presence, a perfect backdrop to the richness, intensity, or even delicacy of filling and ingredients. First, let's take a look at what is needed to make a good pastry.

Ingredients

Flour

The flour should always be all-purpose, made from softer wheat than bread flour. Note the date stamp when you buy it and be careful how long you store it. Flour can lurk in the back of your pantry long after its shelf life has ended, and I've found that stale flour does not make the best pastry. In my opinion, self-rising flour does not make good shortcrust, and neither does 100 percent whole wheat – witness those dense, brown creations that are offered in the name of healthy eating. A mixture of half whole wheat and half soft all-purpose flour works well and gives a nutty flavor.

Fat

The type you use is your choice, and can depend on whether or not you are a vegetarian or have anything against animal fats. Vegetable shortenings and margarines can be used, but after years of cooking and comparison tests and tastings, my opinion is that, in most cases, the very best flavor and texture I've obtained with shortcrust pastry is when equal quantities of lard and butter are used. Generally speaking, the amount of fat in shortcrust is half the amount of flour - so for ¾ cup plus 2 tablespoons (110 g) of flour you use 4 tablespoons (50 g) of fat. People sometimes add more fat because they think this will produce a "shorter" texture; I do not agree with this and feel the result is actually heavier and too rich and fatty.

The most important rule to remember is that the fat should be at room temperature and soft enough for a knife to make an indentation straight through it in a second. This is because it needs to be quickly incorporated into the flour. If it's too cold, you will have to rub it in for twice as long, making the fat oily with the warmth of your hands and the pastry difficult to roll out. One tip here: leave a note on the refrigerator the night before you want to make the pastry saying, "Don't forget to remove fat!"

"But help! I forgot!" you say. Don't worry – we all forget, but don't panic. Cut the cold fat into lumps and drop it into a food processor along with the flour, and process with the pulse button until you have a crumbly mixture (see page 108).

Salt

I've changed my mind on this over the years and now think that pastry, like bread, needs some salt, even if it is to be used in sweet dishes.

Keep cool

This means you yourself, psychologically, as well, because keeping things as cool as possible is important. If the fat, as I mentioned earlier, becomes oily because the rubbing takes longer and everything is too warm, what happens is it coats more flour grains than it should. This means the flour is unable to absorb enough water and the pastry will crumble and be difficult to roll out. I always make pastry by an open window, as a bit of a draught coming in seems to keep things nicely cool.

Liquid

In shortcrust pastry don't use milk or egg – just add plain water, and leave the tap running to get the water as cold as possible. Remember, too, that exact amounts can never be specified in recipes because the amount of water that flour absorbs varies. Start with about 1 tablespoon, sprinkling it evenly all round, then add more little by little. Too much water will make the pastry stick and it will be too difficult to roll out, and when it's baked it will be hard; too little water, on the other hand, will also make rolling out a problem, and the cooked result will be too crumbly. But don't be afraid – if you follow the precise directions given below and on page 108, it's easy to get just the right amount.

Air

Believe it or not, air is the most important ingredient in pastry. So, rule number one is to sift the flour into the bowl, holding the sifter as high up as possible, so that the flour gets a really good airing before you begin.

Rubbing in

After the flour is sifted into the bowl, add the fat, cut into small lumps. Using a knife, begin to cut the fat into the flour. Go on doing this until it looks fairly evenly blended; then, being as light and gentle as possible, begin to rub the fat into the flour using only your fingertips. Being light with your fingers is not a special gift, it's just a conscious decision, a signal the brain gives to the fingertips involving a bit of concentration.

As you lightly rub the fat into the flour, lift it up high and let it fall back into the bowl, which allows air to be incorporated all the time, and air is what makes pastry light. Speed is also what's needed here, so don't start daydreaming and go on rubbing all day, but just long enough to make the mixture crumbly with a few odd lumps here and there.

Adding the water and mixing

Sprinkle 1 tablespoon of cold water in, then, with a knife, start bringing the dough together, cutting and turning and using the knife to begin to make it cling together. Then put aside the knife, and finally, bring it all together with your fingertips. When enough liquid is added, all the bits of flour and fat should be incorporated and the pastry should leave the bowl completely clean. If this hasn't happened, then add a sprinkling of water (sometimes it really only needs your fingers dipped into water once or twice to bring it together).

Processing pastry

I have found it impossible to make shortcrust pastry in a food processor alone because you can't gauge how much water the pastry needs without feeling it. But it is possible to process the flour and fat in a processor, and the advantage is that you can take the fat straight out of the refrigerator. Be careful not to over-process - just 1-2 minutes on a low speed is enough. Then tip it into a bowl and add the water as described earlier.

Resting

All pastries must be allowed to rest before rolling out. If you're in a hurry, this can seem like an awful bore, but I promise you resting the pastry will, in fact, save you more time in the end. Why does it need to rest? Flour contains something called gluten (see page 77), and gluten reacts to water in a way which – if it's given time – makes the dough more elastic in texture, so that when you start to roll out the pastry, this elasticity makes the dough roll out like a dream. Without this resting time rolling can be a nightmare, because the pastry won't have enough stretch so it will break and crack. So, as the pastry is made, place it in a plastic storage bag and leave it in the refrigerator for 30 minutes.

Surface

A flat surface is all you need to roll out – a pastry board is not absolutely necessary – a scrubbed kitchen counter top will do. If, however, you want to frequently make pastry, you might like to invest in a piece of granite or marble. It is expensive and very heavy, but it will last a lifetime and can be purchased from a marble supplier. The ideal size is approximately 18 x 18 inches (46 x 46 cm).

Rolling out

Rolling out, as I've said, is easy if the pastry has rested. Use a rolling pin that is absolutely straight – handles can get in the way if you want to roll out large quantities. Place the dough on a lightly floured surface and place the pin, also dusted with flour, in the center of it, then place the flat of your hands lightly on each end of the pin and begin to roll, re-dusting the pin and surface lightly with flour if you need to stop the pastry from sticking.

If you want to roll it out to a round, give it quarter turns as it expands and, provided you roll backwards and forwards, it will roll out into a round shape. Don't be tempted to roll from side to side, unless for some reason you want to roll out a map of the US! If you can concentrate on only going backwards and forwards, you will end up with a better rounded shape. If you want an oblong, just punch the sides gently with the rolling pin to keep it in shape; if you want a square, give quarter turns – as for a round – and then square it up using the rolling pin to knock the edges into shape.

Storing pastry

Making pastry in advance is perfectly alright – it will keep for up to three days in a plastic storage bag in the refrigerator, but don't forget to remove it and let it come back to room temperature before rolling it out. Raw pastry also freezes extremely well for up to three months.

Basic Shortcrust Pastry

¾ cup plus 2 tablespoons (110 g)
all-purpose flour, plus a little extra for
dusting
pinch of salt
2 tablespoons (25 g) softened lard
2 tablespoons (25 g) softened butter
a little cold water

Begin by sifting the flour and salt into a large bowl, then add the soft fat; if the fat is too cold, it won't rub in effectively

Begin by sifting the flour and the pinch of salt into a large bowl, holding the sifter as high as possible, so that the ingredients get a really good airing before you begin. Now, add the lard and butter, cut into smallish lumps, then take a knife and begin to cut the fat into the flour. Continue doing this until it looks fairly evenly blended, then begin to rub the fat into the flour using your fingertips only and being as light as possible. As you gently rub the fat into the flour, lift it up high and let it fall back into the bowl, which again means that all the time air is being incorporated, but do this just long enough to make the mixture crumbly with a few odd lumps here and there.

Now, sprinkle in 1 tablespoon of water, then, with a knife, start bringing the dough together, using the knife to make it cling. Then put aside the knife, and finally, bring the pastry together with your fingertips. When enough liquid is added, the pastry should leave the bowl fairly clean. If this hasn't happened, then add a drop more water. Now, place the pastry in a plastic storage bag and leave it in the refrigerator for 30 minutes to rest.

Note: This will make 6 oz (175 g) finished weight of pastry, which will be enough to line a 7 or 8 inch (18 or 20 cm) flan or quiche pan.

Starting with a knife, cut the fat into the flour, then lightly rub it in with your fingertips until the mixture looks crumbly

Add the liquid by sprinkling it all over the mixture, then use a knife again to start bringing the dough together

The final stage is to bring the pastry together with your hands, adding a little more liquid if necessary

How to line the quiche pan

Once the pastry is rolled out to the correct size, place the rolling pin in the center, fold the pastry over and lift it onto the pin. Transfer it to the quiche pan, laying it down evenly and carefully. Using your hands, gently press the pastry into the pan to line the bottom and sides. (If the pastry stretches while you are lifting it, don't worry – as you line the pan, ease the excess back, especially round the edges.) When you've pressed it all around with your fingers, try to ease the pastry that is sticking up above the edges back down, so what you're in fact doing is reinforcing the edge, because if it gets stretched too much, it will shrink during cooking. When you've lined the pan, trim off any excess around the edges with a knife, but press the edges again so you have ¼ inch (5 mm) above the edges of the pan.

Pre-baking

Forget about ceramic pie weights – it's too much bother. If you've lined the pan correctly, as above, all you now need to do is prick the bottom all over with a fork since this will release any trapped air, which is what causes the center to rise up. Then brush the bottom and sides all over with beaten egg, which will provide a sort of waterproof coating so that the pastry stays beautifully crisp even after the filling has gone in. Normally this small amount of beaten egg can be taken from the egg used for the filling in the recipe.

The oven

At the same time you preheat the oven, you should also preheat a heavy baking sheet on the center shelf. Then place the pastry shell in to pre-bake for 20-25 minutes or until the pastry turns a golden brown. It's a good idea to take a peek halfway through – if the pastry is bubbling up a bit, just prick it with a fork and press it back down again with your hands.

To remove the quiche pan, place the tart on a can or jar, loosen the pastry all round with a small knife or skewer and ease it down

Now, place the pastry in a plastic storage bag and refrigerate for 30 minutes, which will make rolling it out far less trouble

Once rolled out, transfer the pastry to the pan by rolling it over the pin, then gently ease it into the pan using your hands

Finally, prick the bottom all over with a fork to release any trapped air, then brush the bottom and sides with the beaten egg

109

Leek and Goat Cheese Tart

This is what I call a wobbly tart – creamy and soft-centered. Leeks and goat cheese have turned out to be a wonderful combination, and the addition of goat cheese to the pastry gives it a nice flavor.

Serves 6 as an appetizer or 4 as a main course

For the pastry:
1 oz (25 g) firm goat cheese (rindless)
¾ cup plus 2 tablespoons (110 g) all-purpose flour, plus a little extra for dusting
pinch of salt
2 tablespoons (25 g) softened lard
2 tablespoons (25 g) softened butter
a little cold water

For the filling:
1 lb 6 oz (625 g) leeks, ie, 12 oz (350 g) trimmed weight (see instructions in the method)
6 oz (175 g) firm goat cheese (rindless)
1 tablespoon (10 g) butter
3 large eggs, beaten
¾ cup (200 ml) crème fraîche or heavy cream
4 scallions, trimmed and finely sliced, including the green parts
salt and freshly ground black pepper

You will also need an 8 inch (20 cm) diameter fluted quiche pan with a removable bottom, 1¼ inches (3 cm) deep, very lightly buttered, and a small, heavy baking sheet.

First, sift the flour with the pinch of salt into a large bowl, holding the sifter up high to give it a good airing. Then add the lard and butter, and using only your fingertips, lightly rub the fat into the flour, again lifting the mixture up high. When everything is crumbly, coarsely grate in the goat cheese and then sprinkle in some cold water – about 1 tablespoon. Start to mix the pastry with a knife and then finish off with your hands, adding a few more drops of water until you have a smooth dough that will leave the bowl clean. Place the pastry in a plastic storage bag and let it rest in the refrigerator for 30 minutes. Meanwhile, preheat the oven to 375°F (190°C); put the baking sheet into the oven to preheat on the center shelf.

Now, prepare the leeks. First take the tough green ends off and throw them out, then make a vertical split about halfway down the center of

each one and clean them by running them under the cold-water tap while you fan out the layers – this will rid them of any hidden dust and grit. Then slice them in half lengthwise and chop into ½ inch (1 cm) slices.

Next, in a medium-sized frying pan, melt the butter over a gentle heat and add the leeks and some salt. Give it all a good stir and let them cook gently, without a lid, for 10-15 minutes or until the juice runs out of them. Then you need to transfer them to a sifter set over a bowl to drain off the excess juice. Place a saucer with a weight on top of them to press out every last drop.

By now the pastry will have rested; remove it from the refrigerator and roll it out into a circle on a lightly floured surface. As you roll, give it quarter turns to keep the round shape and roll it as thinly as possible. Now, transfer it, rolling it over the pin, to the pan. Press it lightly and firmly over the bottom and sides of the pan, easing any overlapping pastry down to the sides; it is important not to stretch it. Now, trim the edges and press the pastry up about ¼ inch (5 mm) above the rim of the pan all around, then prick the bottom all over with a fork. After that, paint some of the beaten egg for the filling over the bottom and sides. Now, place the pan on the baking sheet and bake for 20-25 minutes until the pastry is crisp and golden. Check halfway through baking to check that the pastry isn't rising up in the center. If it is, just prick it a couple of times and press it back down.

While the pastry case is pre-baking, crumble the goat cheese and gently combine it with the leeks. Now, in a large measuring cup, mix the beaten eggs with the crème fraîche or heavy cream, seasoning with just a little salt (there is some already in the leeks) and a good grinding of freshly ground black pepper. As soon as the pastry case is ready, remove it from the oven, arrange the leeks and cheese all over the bottom, and then sprinkle the scallions over the top. Now, gradually pour half the cream and egg mixture in to join them, then put the tart back on the baking sheet with the oven shelf half pulled out, then slowly pour in the rest of the mixture. Gently slide the shelf back in and bake the tart for 30-35 minutes, until it's firm in the center and the surface has turned a lovely golden brown. Next, remove it from the oven and allow it to settle for 10 minutes before serving. This 10 minutes is important as it will be much easier to cut into portions. The best way to remove the tart from the pan is to ease the edges from the sides of the pan with a small knife, then place it on an upturned jar or pan, which will allow you to carefully ease the sides away. Next, slide a narrow spatula or wide pancake turner underneath and ease the tart onto a plate or board ready to serve, or simply cut it into portions straight from the pan.

Leek and Goat Cheese Tart; cooked, above, and uncooked, left

Smoked Fish Tart with a Parmesan Crust

This tart is not as wobbly as the previous one because it has a substantial amount of filling. The various smoked flavors of the fish are quite sensational partnered with the hint of piquancy in the cornichons and capers.

Serves 6-8 as an appetizer or 4-6 as a main course
For the pastry:
1 oz (25 g) finely grated Parmesan (Parmigiano Reggiano)
¾ cup plus 2 tablespoons (110 g) all-purpose flour, plus a little extra for dusting
pinch of salt
2 tablespoons (25 g) softened lard
2 tablespoons (25 g) softened butter
a little cold water

For the filling:
8 oz (225 g) finnan haddie fillet (skinned raw weight)
3 oz (75 g) smoked trout fillet (skinned weight)
9 oz (250 g) smoked salmon trimmings
¼ cup (55 ml) milk
1 bay leaf
pinch of ground mace
2 large eggs, plus 2 egg yolks
a little ground nutmeg
¾ cup (200 ml) crème fraîche or heavy cream
2 teaspoons salted capers or capers in vinegar, well rinsed and drained
2 mini pickles (cornichons), finely chopped
freshly ground black pepper

You will also need an 8 inch (20 cm) diameter fluted quiche pan with a removable bottom, 1¼ inches (3 cm) deep, very lightly buttered, and a small, heavy baking sheet.

First of all, sift the flour with the pinch of salt into a large bowl, holding the sifter up high to give them a good airing. Then add the lard and butter and using only your fingertips, lightly and gently rub the fat into the flour, again lifting the mixture up high all the time to give it a good airing. When everything is crumbly, add the Parmesan and then sprinkle in some cold water – about 1 tablespoon. Start mixing the pastry with a knife and finish off with your hands, adding more drops of water until you have a smooth dough that will leave the bowl clean. Then place the pastry in a plastic storage bag and let it rest in the refrigerator for 30 minutes.

Meanwhile, preheat the oven to 375°F (190°C) and put the baking sheet in to preheat on the center shelf.

After that, roll the pastry out into a circle on a surface lightly dusted with flour; as you roll, give it quarter turns to keep the round shape, rolling it as thinly as possible. Now, transfer it, rolling it over the pin, to the pan. Press it lightly and firmly all over the bottom and sides of the pan, easing any overlapping pastry back down to the sides, being careful not to stretch it too much. Now, trim the edges and press the pastry up about ¼ inch (5 mm) above the rim of the pan all around. Then prick the bottom all over with a fork, and after that, brush some of the beaten egg for the filling all over the bottom and sides. Now, place the pan on the baking sheet and bake it for 20-25 minutes or until the pastry is crisp and golden. Check halfway through the cooking time to make sure that the pastry isn't rising up in the center. If it is, just prick it again a couple of times and press it back down again with your hands. When the pastry is baked, remove it from the oven and lower the temperature to 325°F (170°C).

For the filling, put the finnan haddie and smoked trout in a medium-sized saucepan, along with the milk, bay leaf, and mace. Bring it up to simmering, cover with a lid, and poach gently for about 2 minutes, then remove the fish from the milk. Discard the bay leaf, but reserve the milk.

Then lightly whisk the eggs and egg yolks together with a seasoning of black pepper and nutmeg, but no salt, since the fish will be fairly salty. Then heat the reserved milk, whisking in the crème fraîche or heavy cream. Then, when it has come to simmering point, pour it over the beaten eggs, whisking well. Now, divide the finnan haddie and smoked trout into flakes about ½ inch (1 cm) in size and arrange them in the cooked pastry shell along with the salmon trimmings. Next, scatter the capers and cornichons over all and slowly pour in half the cream and the egg mixture, allowing the liquid to settle as you pour. Then place the baking sheet in the oven, gradually add the remainder of the filling, and bake for 30-35 minutes or until the surface is golden brown and feels firm in the center.

When you have removed it from the oven, let it rest for 10 minutes, then ease it away from the edges using a small knife and place it on a suitable-sized jar, which will allow you to carefully ease the sides away. Then slide a narrow spatula or wide pancake turner underneath and ease the tart carefully onto a plate or board ready to serve, or simply cut it into portions straight from the pan.

Smoked Fish Tart with a Parmesan Crust; cooked, left, and uncooked, below

Pumpkin Pie

This recipe uses another version of shortcrust pastry that is used for sweet open-faced flans and tarts. It's richer than shortcrust, but very crisp, and the eggs give it a shortbread quality. Nuts can sometimes be added; here there are toasted pecans, although walnuts or hazelnuts can be used, or the pastry can be made without nuts if you prefer. In the fall, I love the velvet texture of pumpkin, but this tart could be made with butternut squash.

Serves 8

For the pastry:
½ cup (40 g) pecan halves
1¼ cups (175 g) all-purpose flour, plus a little extra for dusting
½ oz (10 g) confectioners sugar
pinch of salt
6 tablespoons (75 g) softened butter
a little cold water
1 large egg yolk

For the filling:
1 lb (450 g) prepared weight pumpkin flesh, cut into 1 inch (2.5 cm) chunks
2 large eggs plus 1 yolk
(reserve the white)
1 tablespoon molasses
½ cup (75 g) dark brown sugar
1 teaspoon ground cinnamon
½ teaspoon freshly grated nutmeg
½ teaspoon ground allspice
½ teaspoon ground cloves
½ teaspoon ground ginger
1¼ cups (275 ml) heavy cream

You will also need a 9 inch (23 cm) diameter fluted flan pan, 1½ inches (4 cm) deep, with a loose bottom, lightly greased, and a medium-sized solid baking sheet.

Preheat the oven to 350°F (180°C).

To begin, you need to toast the pecans. First of all, when the oven has preheated, spread the nuts out on the baking sheet and toast them lightly for 8 minutes, using a timer so that you don't forget them. After that, remove them from the oven to a chopping board (turning the oven off for now), and let them cool a little. Then either chop them really finely by hand or pulse them in a food processor, being careful here, though, because if you overdo it the nuts will turn oily.

For the pastry, sift the flour, confectioners sugar, and the pinch of salt into a large bowl, holding the sifter up high to give them a good airing. Then add the butter and start cutting it into the flour using a knife. Using only your fingertips, lightly and gently rub the butter into the flour, again lifting the mixture up high all the time to give it a good airing.

When everything is crumbly, add the chopped nuts, then sprinkle in about 1 tablespoon of water and the egg yolk. Start to mix the pastry with a knife and then finish with your hands, lightly bringing it together (you may need to add more water) until you have a smooth dough that will leave the bowl clean. Then place it into a plastic storage bag and let it rest in the refrigerator for 30 minutes.

Meanwhile, preheat the oven to 350°F (180°C) with the baking sheet inside. Now, place a steamer over a pan of simmering water, add the pumpkin, put a lid on and steam for 15-20 minutes, until the pieces feel tender when tested with a skewer. After that, place a large, coarse sieve over a bowl and press the pumpkin through it to extract any seeds or fibers.

By this time the pastry will have rested, so now remove it from the refrigerator. Roll it out into a circle on a surface lightly dusted with flour, and as you roll, give it quarter turns to keep the round shape. Roll it into a circle approximately 12 inches (30 cm) in diameter, as thinly as possible. Now, transfer it, rolling it over the pin, to the pan. Press it lightly and firmly all over the bottom and sides of the pan, easing any overlapping pastry back down the sides, since it is important not to stretch this bit too much. Now, trim the edge, leaving ¼ inch (5 mm) above the rim of the pan all around. Then prick the bottom all over with a fork and brush it and the sides with the reserved egg white, lightly beaten. Now, place the pan on the preheated baking sheet on the center shelf of the oven and bake it for 20-25 minutes, until the pastry is crisp and golden. Check halfway through the cooking time to make sure that the pastry isn't rising up in the center. If it is, just prick it again a couple of times and press it back down again.

Now, for the filling. First lightly whisk the eggs and extra yolk together in a large bowl. Next, measure the molasses (lightly greasing the spoon first makes this easier), then just push the molasses off the spoon with a rubber spatula into a saucepan. Add the sugar, spices, and the cream and bring it up to simmering, giving it a whisk to mix everything together. Pour it over the eggs and whisk it again briefly. Now, add the pumpkin purée, still whisking to combine everything, then pour the filling into a large measuring cup. When the pastry shell is ready, remove it from the oven on the baking sheet using an oven mitt. Pour in half the filling, return it to the oven, and with the shelf half out, pour in the rest of the filling and slide the shelf back in. Bake the pie for 35-40 minutes, by which time it will puff up round the edges but still feel slightly wobbly in the center. Then remove it from the oven and place the pan on a wire cooling rack.

I prefer to serve this chilled (stored loosely covered in foil in the refrigerator) with some equally chilled crème fraîche, but warm or at room temperature would be fine. Alternatively, serve with ice cream.

Old-Fashioned English Custard Tart

This old-fashioned Custard Tart needs a thick, wobbly filling, so I've used a round pan with sloping sides and a rim, which gives a good depth. The nutmeg is very important to the flavor, so always use it freshly grated. First, grate it onto a piece of foil so that you can sprinkle it on quickly when the tart goes into the oven.

Serves 6

For the shortcrust pastry:
1 cup (150 g) all-purpose flour, plus a little extra for dusting
pinch of salt
2 tablespoons (25 g) softened lard
3 tablespoons (40 g) softened butter
a little cold water

For the filling:
2½ cups (570 ml) light cream
3 large eggs, plus 2 large egg yolks, lightly beaten
¼ cup (50 g) superfine sugar
½ teaspoon vanilla extract
1½ whole nutmegs, freshly grated
1 teaspoon softened butter

You will also need a 2 inch (5 cm) leaf-shaped cookie cutter, a pan that has a rim and sloping sides (1½ inches/4 cm deep, with a 7 inch/18 cm bottom and a ½ inch/1 cm rim), lightly greased, and a medium-sized, heavy baking sheet.

To make the pastry, sift the flour with the pinch of salt into a large bowl, holding the sifter up high to give it a good airing. Then add the lard and butter, and using only your fingertips, lightly and gently rub the fat into the flour, again lifting the mixture up high all the time to give it a good airing.

When everything is crumbly, sprinkle in about 1 tablespoon of cold water. Start to mix the pastry with a knife and then finish off with your hands, adding a few more drops of water, until you have a smooth dough that leaves the bowl clean. Then place the pastry into a plastic storage bag and let it rest in the refrigerator for 30 minutes. Meanwhile, preheat the oven to 375°F (190°C) and place the baking sheet in to preheat on the center shelf.

After that, roll the rest of the pastry out into a circle, giving it quarter turns to keep its round shape; it's a good idea at this stage to put the pan lightly on top of the pastry – the size needs to be 1 inch (2.5 cm) bigger all round. Now, transfer it, rolling it over the pin, to the pan, and press it lightly and firmly around the bottom, sides, and rim. Now, take a sharp knife and trim the overlapping pastry. Then press the rim of the pastry so that about ¼ inch (5 mm) overlaps the edge. Next, roll the trimmings and cut out about 24 leaves, making veins in them with the blunt side of the knife. Now, brush the whole surface of the pastry shell with some of the beaten eggs, arranging the leaves all around the rim, overlapping them. Brush these, too, with beaten egg. Now, prick the bottom of the tart with a fork, place it on the baking sheet, and bake on the center shelf for 20 minutes until the pastry is crisp and golden. Check after 4 minutes to make sure that the pastry isn't rising up in the center. If it is, prick it again a couple of times, pressing it back down with your hands. After 20 minutes, remove it from the oven, leaving the baking sheet there, and reduce the temperature to 325°F (170°C).

Now, place the cream in a saucepan and bring it up to a gentle simmer, then whisk the beaten egg mixture and sugar together in a large heatproof measuring cup using a balloon whisk – but not too vigorously because you don't want to make bubbles. Then pour the hot liquid over the beaten eggs, add the vanilla extract and half the nutmeg and whisk briefly again.

Now, place the pie pan back on the baking sheet with the oven shelf half out and have ready the rest of the grated nutmeg on a piece of foil. Carefully pour the filling into the pastry shell (it will be very full) and sprinkle with the rest of the nutmeg; then dot with the softened butter and bake in the oven for 30-40 minutes, until the filling is golden brown, firm in the center and slightly puffed up. Serve either warm or cold.

Mini Apple and Raisin Tarts

This is yet another version of a good old apple pie, but the great thing about this recipe is that it bakes into individual portions, making serving it much easier. Raisins are a good winter addition, but in the fall, you could replace them with 4 oz (110 g) of blackberries or blueberries in the summer.

Serves 8

For the shortcrust pastry:

2½ cups (350 g) all-purpose flour

pinch of salt

6 tablespoons (75 g) softened lard

6 tablespoons (75 g) softened butter

a little cold water

For the filling:

8 oz (225 g) Granny Smith apples (unpeeled), cored and cut into ½ inch (1 cm) dice

4 oz (110 g) McIntosh apples (unpeeled), cored and cut into ½ inch (1 cm) dice

½ cup (75 g) raisins, soaked overnight in ½ cup (120 ml) hard cider

8 teaspoons semolina

16 whole cloves

¼ cup (50 g) superfine sugar, plus an extra teaspoon for sprinkling

1 egg white, lightly beaten

You will also need a non-stick baking pan measuring 10 x 6 inches (25.5 x 15 cm) and 1 inch (2.5 cm) deep.

Start this recipe the night before by soaking the raisins in the cider. The next day, start the pastry. To do this, sift the flour with the pinch of salt into a large bowl, holding the sifter high. Add the lard and butter, and using your fingertips, lightly rub the fat into the flour, lifting the mixture up to give it a good airing. When the mixture is crumbly, add about a tablespoon of cold water. Start mixing the pastry with a knife, then finish off with your hands, adding a little more water until you have a smooth dough that leaves the bowl clean. Now, place it in a plastic storage bag and chill it for 30 minutes.

Meanwhile, preheat the oven to 400°F (200°C). Remove the pastry from the refrigerator, then divide it into four pieces. Dust your work surface lightly with flour, roll each piece into a length about 10 x 5 inches (25.5 x 13 cm), and trim each one into two 5 inch (13 cm) squares. Working with two squares at a time, scatter a teaspoon of semolina over each pastry square, then mix both varieties of apple together, and add about 3 tablespoons of chopped apples, 2 cloves, 2 teaspoons of sugar, and some drained raisins to each square. Now, brush the edges of each square with some of the beaten egg white, then loosely fold over the corners. Then, using a spatula to help you, lift each tart into the pan, tucking them neatly into the corners, and repeat with the remaining squares so that they all fit snugly in the pan. If you have any fruit left over, carefully lift the corners of each tart and add some more apples and raisins. Now, either leave the tarts open or squeeze the pastry corners together a little more (for the closed version see the photo on page 102). Next, brush the pastry with the remaining beaten egg white and sprinkle the rest of the sugar on top along with the extra teaspoon of sugar. Bake in the oven on the shelf just above center for 50 minutes, and serve the tarts warm with cream, ice cream, or Traditional English Custard (see page 64), and don't forget to warn your guests that there are a few whole cloves lurking inside the tarts.

Note: If you're using blackberries, blueberries or rhubarb, use 2 teaspoons of semolina in each tart to absorb the extra juice.

Quick and easy flaky pastry

Clever chefs and professional pâtissiers make proper puff pastry and sometimes call it *millefeuille* (meaning "thousand leaves"). It involves rolling and folding the pastry several times to trap the air, letting it rest between rollings. It is a labor of love and dedication – and can be therapeutic if you have time to lock yourself away for a few hours – but it is not something for the harried cook, trying to juggle this with the rest of life happening outside the kitchen. Yet all is not lost because there is a quick and easy version – crisp, light, and if you close your eyes, you won't know whether you are eating 50 or 1,000 leaves, because the taste will be the same.

Quick flaky pastry is really a cheater's version, because it doesn't involve the turning, rolling, resting, and all the complications that go into the real thing. The advantage is that what you get is a homemade pastry made purely with butter, giving you a texture and flavor that is quite unique and special without, at the same time, involving either a lot of time or – believe it or not – a lot of skill. The secret is grating partly frozen butter and then mixing it with flour (so no boring rubbing in). Making this flaky pastry involves the minimum of skill, but at the same time, produces spectacular results.

What should perfect flaky pastry be like? Answer: as light as possible, wafer-thin and so crisp it tastes like a whisper so that you hardly know it's there. So if you don't believe that it's incredibly easy to achieve, here are the detailed instructions. I promise you will be so pleased with the results that you will want to make four more batches to put in the freezer for a rainy day.

Flour should always be soft, all-purpose, and sifted, lifting the sifter high as you do so and letting it fall into a large, roomy bowl. I have said it before, but there is no harm in underlining that the most important ingredient in pastry is air. Sifting the flour like this gives it a good airing.

Butter Because the butter is going to be coarsely grated, it needs to be almost frozen. So measure it out, then wrap it in foil and place it in the freezer or freezing compartment of the refrigerator for 30-45 minutes. If it is too soft, it won't grate properly.

Resting Like all pastries, quick flaky pastry must be allowed to rest after it has been mixed – that means putting it in a plastic storage bag in the refrigerator and leaving it there for 30 minutes.

Baking Because this pastry has a high fat content, it's essential to have a high oven temperature, which is important if you want to achieve that lovely, light, crisp effect, so do be sure to preheat the oven before baking the pastry.

Texture Quick flaky pastry is not puff pastry, so don't expect it to rise up like a thousand leaves. It is light-textured and flaky, though, and will puff and rise somewhat when it is cooking.

Your secret weapons in this cheat's flaky pastry are frozen butter and a grater…

120

To begin the recipe, first of all remove the butter from the refrigerator, measure out 8 tablespoons (110 g), then wrap it in a piece of foil and return it to the freezer or freezing compartment of the refrigerator for 30-45 minutes.

Then, when you are ready to make the pastry, sift the flour and salt into a large, roomy bowl. Take the butter from the freezer, fold back the foil, and hold it in the foil to protect it from your warm hands. Then, using the coarse side of a grater placed in the bowl over the flour, grate the butter, dipping the edge of the butter onto the flour several times to make it easier to grate. What you will end up with is a large pile of grated butter sitting in the middle of the flour. Now, take a narrow spatula and start to distribute the gratings into the flour – don't use your hands yet, just keep trying to coat all the pieces of fat with flour. Now, sprinkle 2 tablespoons of cold water over all, continue to use the narrow spatula to bring the whole thing together, and finish off using your hands. If you need a bit more moisture, that's fine – just remember that the dough should come together in such a way that it leaves the bowl fairly clean, with no bits of loose butter or flour anywhere. Now, place it into a plastic storage bag and chill for 30 minutes before using. Remember, this pastry, like other pastries, freezes extremely well, in which case you will need to defrost it thoroughly and let it come back to room temperature before rolling it out on a lightly floured surface.

For the pastry:
8 tablespoons (110 g) butter
1¼ cups (175 g) all-purpose flour
pinch of salt
a little cold water

All you do is grate the frozen butter into the flour using the coarse side of the grater

Once the butter is distributed, add water and use a narrow spatula to combine

Finish off with your hands, adding a little more water if the pastry needs it

Tomato and goat cheese Galettes

Galettes are very thin circles of pastry which, unlike conventional tarts, have no sides. The concept is a good one because the pastry is barely there, yet it gives a light, very crisp background to all kinds of toppings, both savory and sweet. There's no limit to what you can put on top of them — the combinations are endless, and you can serve them for a light lunch, as an appetizer, on a picnic, or for a dessert. What I often do is freeze the pastry circles raw, interleaved with foil or parchment paper, so you can just whip some out for an impromptu meal in almost no time at all. If you don't have the right-sized cutter, just cut around a saucer of the same size.

The first of my recipes for galettes calls for lovely, ripe, red tomatoes for color, and the preferred cheese in our house is Crottin de Chavignol, but any firm goat cheese will do.

*Serves 3 as a light lunch
or 6 as an appetizer*
quick flaky pastry made with 1¼ cups (175 g) all-purpose flour and 8 tablespoons (110 g) butter (see page 121)
12 medium tomatoes
7 oz (200 g) firm goat cheese
18 large basil leaves, plus 6 sprigs for garnish
a little olive oil, for drizzling
salt and freshly ground black pepper

You will also need two heavy baking sheets measuring approximately 14 x 11 inches (35 x 28 cm), lightly greased, and a 6 inch (15 cm) circular cookie cutter.

Preheat the oven to 425°F (220°C).

Make the pastry as described on page 121 and chill it for 30 minutes in the refrigerator. Meanwhile, you need to peel the tomatoes, so pour boiling water over them and leave for exactly 1 minute before draining and slipping off the skins (protect your hands with a cloth if they are too hot). Next, on a lightly floured surface, roll out the pastry very thinly to ⅛ inch (3 mm), cut out six 6 inch (15 cm) disks and place these on the baking sheets.

Now, scatter the large basil leaves over the pastry, tearing them first if they're very large. Next, thinly slice the tomatoes and arrange them in circles overlapping each other on top of the basil. Peel the goat cheese and crumble it over the tomatoes, then pour some olive oil onto a saucer and dip the reserved basil leaves in it, placing one on each tart. Then season well and drizzle each one with a little extra olive oil. Now, bake the galettes in the oven, one baking sheet on a high shelf, the other on the next one down, for 10-12 minutes or until the tomatoes are tinged brown and the cheese is bubbling, swapping the baking sheets over halfway through. Serve warm directly from the oven, or since they're still excellent cold, you can cool them first on a wire rack.

This is a very Greek combination in which, authentically, the filling gets wrapped in pastry circles. I now prefer this version, though, which has less pastry and is much prettier to look at.

Make the pastry as described on page 121 and chill it for 30 minutes in the refrigerator. Meanwhile, cook the spinach by placing it in a saucepan covered with a lid, then place it over a medium heat. Let the spinach collapse down into its own juices, timing it for 2-3 minutes and turning it over halfway through. Drain the spinach in a colander, pressing it with a saucer to extract every last bit of liquid, then season the spinach with a little nutmeg. Next, roll out the pastry on a lightly floured surface to ⅛ inch (3 mm), cut out six 6 inch (15 cm) disks and place these on the baking sheets. Finely chop the spinach and divide it between the pastry circles, spreading it out towards the edges of the pastry but leaving a small uncovered rim around the edge. Next, scatter the Feta over the spinach and sprinkle with the pine nuts. Now, cook the galettes for 10-12 minutes, one baking sheet on the high shelf, the other on the next one down, until golden brown, interchanging the sheets halfway through. Remove from the oven, sprinkle with the Parmesan, and serve warm, or cool them on a cooling rack.

Serves 3 as a light lunch or 6 as a first course
quick flaky pastry made with 1¼ cups (175 g) all-purpose flour and 8 tablespoons (110 g) butter (see page 121)
4½ oz (125 g) Feta cheese, chopped into small cubes
8 oz (225 g) young leaf spinach
¼ cup (25 g) pine nuts
a little freshly grated nutmeg
1 oz (25g) Parmesan (Parmigiano Reggiano), finely grated

You will also need two heavy baking sheets measuring approximatcly 14 x 11 inches (35 x 28 cm), lightly greased, and a 6 inch (15 cm) circular cookie cutter.

Preheat the oven to 425°F (220°C).

Tomato and Goat Cheese Galette, far left; Feta Cheese, Spinach, and Pine Nut Galette, left

Apricot Galettes with Amaretto

Serves 6
quick flaky pastry made with 1¼ cups
(175 g) all-purpose flour and 8
tablespoons (110 g) butter
(see page 121)
27 soft dried apricots
6 teaspoons amaretto liqueur
18 whole blanched almonds, toasted
and cut into slivers (optional)
3 tablespoons demerara or raw brown
sugar

To serve:
a little confectioners sugar, sifted
¾ cup (200 ml) crème fraîche

You will also need two 12 x 10 inch
(30 x 25.5 cm) heavy baking sheets,
lightly greased, and a 4 inch (10 cm)
circular cookie cutter.

Dried apricots are great for this in the winter, but in summer the galettes are also good with fresh apricots, in which case you'll need the same quantity of small apricots, halved and pitted.

Make the pastry as described on page 121 and chill for 30 minutes in the refrigerator. Then roll the pastry out on a lightly floured surface to ⅛ inch (3 mm), cut out six 4 inch (10 cm) disks and place these on the baking sheets. Meanwhile, preheat the oven to 425°F (220°C).

Now, cut the apricots in half, and place nine apricot halves on each round of pastry, topped by a few almond slivers (if using). Sprinkle a teaspoon of amaretto over each one, then sprinkle them all with the demerara sugar. Bake for 10-12 minutes in the oven, one baking sheet on the highest shelf, the other on the next one down, until the pastry is crisp and brown and the apricots have browned and caramelized a little at the edges, interchanging the baking sheets over halfway through. Serve right from the oven, dusted with confectioners sugar, and with a spoonful of the chilled crème fraîche; or you could choose to let them cool to serve later.

Prune and Apple Galettes

Serves 6
quick flaky pastry made with 1¼ cups
(175 g) all-purpose flour and
8 tablespoons (110 g) butter (see
page 121)
15 pitted soft prunes,
halved lengthwise
3 small McIntosh apples (unpeeled)
a little ground cinnamon
2 tablespoons honey
cream or crème fraîche, to serve

You will also need two 12 x 10 inch
(30 x 25.5 cm) heavy baking sheets,
lightly greased, and a 4 inch (10 cm)
circular cookie cutter.

If you can get mi-cuit plums, the lovely squashy half-dried Agen prunes from France, so much the better.

Make the pastry as described on page 121 and chill for 30 minutes in the refrigerator. Then roll out the pastry on a lightly floured surface to ⅛ inch (3 mm), cut out six 4 inch (10 cm) circles and arrange them on the baking sheets. Meanwhile, preheat the oven to 425°F (220°C).

Now, cut and core each apple into quarters and then cut each quarter into two slices. Then arrange five prune halves and four slices of apple in a circle on top of each pastry round, then sprinkle over a little ground cinnamon. Now, place the baking sheets in the oven for 10-12 minutes, one baking sheet on the highest shelf, the other on the next one down, until the galettes are golden brown, interchanging them halfway through. Remove from the oven and, while they are still warm, glaze each one by brushing a little of the honey over the prunes and apples. Serve warm with cream or crème fraîche.

Poached Pear Galettes

These are exceptionally pretty to look at. I like to serve them as a sweet ending to a special meal. They're a bit more trouble than other pastries but still very easy to make and assemble.

Make the pastry as described on page 121 and chill for 30 minutes in the refrigerator. Meanwhile, find a lidded saucepan that all the pears will fit in comfortably, placing them in the pan on their sides. Now, mix the wine with the sugar and pour this over the pears, then add the cinnamon stick and ½ vanilla bean. Put the lid on the pan and gently simmer the pears for 45 minutes until tender when tested with a skewer. Turn them over halfway through the cooking time so the other half rests in the wine and they color evenly. Toward the end of the cooking time, preheat the oven to 425°F (220°C). Then roll the pastry out to ⅛ inch (3 mm) thick and cut it into six 4 inch (10 cm) circles and arrange them on the baking sheets.

Now, lift the pears from the liquid and halve them by first making a slit in the stem as you press it on to a flat surface. Then stand each pear upright and cut through the split stem, halve the pears, and remove the cores. Now, you need to slice each half into a fan, so take a sharp knife, and starting from the top of the stalk end, about ½ inch (1 cm) in, slice the pear downward and at a slight angle so you end up with the slices of pear fanning out but still attached to the stem. Now, place each half pear on to a pastry circle and fan it out. Then place the baking sheets in the oven for 10-12 minutes, one on the top shelf, the other on the next one down, interchanging them halfway through the cooking time.

Meanwhile, you need to reduce the poaching liquid, so first remove the cinnamon stick and vanilla bean, then place the saucepan over a high heat and let it bubble for about 5 minutes. Next, mix the arrowroot with a little cold water in a cup until you have a smooth paste; then add this to the saucepan, whisking with a balloon whisk all the time. This will thicken the sauce slightly. Then remove it from the heat and let it cool.

When the tarts are ready, remove them from the oven. Serve hot or cold but, just before serving, pour a little of the sauce over each tart to give them a pretty glaze.

From top: Poached Pear Galette;
Prune and Apple Galette; Apricot Galette
with Amaretto

Serves 6
quick flaky pastry made with 1¼ cups (175 g) all-purpose flour and 8 tablespoons (110 g) butter (see page 121)
3 firm unripe pears, peeled but with the stems left on
1¼ cups (275 ml) red wine
2½ tablespoons (25 g) superfine sugar
½ cinnamon stick
½ vanilla bean
1 teaspoon arrowroot

You will also need two 12 x 10 inch (30 x 25.5 cm) heavy baking sheets, lightly greased, and a 4 inch (10 cm) circular cookie cutter.

Wild Mushroom Tartlets with Poached Quails' Eggs

This is my version of one of the most delightful appetizers I've ever eaten. It was created by Michel Bourdin, head chef at London's prestigious Connaught Hotel. His version has boiled quails' eggs, but I can't bear the trouble of peeling them, so I now poach them, cutting out a great deal of time and work. I also have Michel's approval since he told me that he originally did them like this. It's still not the quickest, easiest course, but when you want something really special for a celebration, this is it.

Serves 6

quick flaky pastry made with ¾ cup
plus 2 tablespoons (110 g) flour and 6
tablespoons (75 g) butter
(see page 121)
18 quails' eggs
1 recipe Foaming Hollandaise
(see page 73)

For the mushroom filling:
10 oz (275 g) cremini mushrooms
¾ oz (20 g) dried porcini mushrooms,
soaked in boiling water and drained
5 shallots, peeled
2 tablespoons (25 g) butter
⅓ whole nutmeg, grated
sea salt and freshly ground
black pepper

You need six ½ inch (1 cm) deep
quiche pans with a bottom diameter of
3 inches (7.5 cm) and a top diameter
of 3½ inches (9 cm), greased, a
medium-sized heavy baking sheet, and
a 4 inch (10 cm) round cookie cutter.

Place the fresh and soaked mushrooms and the shallots in a food processor and process until finely chopped. Next, melt the butter in a medium-sized pan over a high heat; add the mushroom mixture, nutmeg, and seasoning; reduce the heat and gently sauté for 20-25 minutes until all the juices have evaporated. Then remove from the heat and allow the mixture to cool.

On a lightly floured surface, roll out the pastry to ⅛ inch (3 mm) thick and cut out six rounds with the cutter, re-rolling the pastry if necessary. Now, line each pan with the pastry, pushing it down from the tops so the pastry doesn't shrink during cooking. Trim the pastry around the tops to ¼ inch (5 mm) and prick the bottoms with a fork; then refrigerate for 30 minutes.

Preheat the oven to 400°F (200°C). Now, place the pans on the baking sheet and bake them on the top shelf of the oven for 15 minutes. (All this can be done well in advance. The mushroom mixture should be cooled, then covered, and stored in the refrigerator, and the pastry shells carefully removed from their pans and stored in an airtight container. The Foaming Hollandaise can also be made in advance (see page 73).

Then, in a medium-sized frying pan half-filled with boiling water from the kettle, you can begin to poach the eggs. Have a bowl of cold water ready. Place the pan over a gentle heat. Now, as soon as the pan has fine bubbles all over the bottom, make a slit in 6 quails' eggs with a small serrated knife, carefully slipping the eggs in to poach. Put a timer on for 1½ minutes, then, after this time and using a perforated spoon, remove them, starting with the first one that went in. Transfer them to the bowl of cold water, then repeat the whole process twice until all the eggs are poached.

With everything ready – the mushroom filling, the tartlet shells, the hollandaise, and the poached eggs – you can now assemble the tartlets.

When you are ready to serve the tartlets, preheat the broiler to its highest setting. Next, place the tartlet shells on a baking sheet, cover with foil, and place them under the broiler 6 inches (15 cm) from the heat to warm through for 5 minutes. Then, while this is happening, re-heat the mushroom mixture in a small saucepan and get it really hot. Then fill the pastry shells with the mushroom mixture and top each one with 3 quails' eggs, using a perforated spoon and a square of paper towel to drain off any water. Next, spoon the Foaming Hollandaise over each one, then place the tarts back under the broiler again, at least 6 inches (15 cm) from the heat, and watch them like a hawk – it should take only 30 seconds for the sauce to warm through and brown slightly. Then turn the broiler off and serve the tartlets on warm plates as quickly as possible.

This is a beautiful bite-sized version of mince pies, and I think not as much trouble. If you don't have a pastry wheel you can forgo the frilly edge and use a sharp knife to cut the pastry.

First, make the pastry as described on page 121 and chill for 30 minutes. Then remove the rested pastry from the refrigerator onto a floured surface and shape it into an oblong. Cut the oblong into two, one piece slightly larger than the other, then, on a lightly floured surface, first roll the smaller piece into a rectangle 12 x 10 inches (30 x 25.5 cm), roll it around the rolling pin, and transfer it to the baking sheet.

Next, brush the surface of the pastry with the beaten egg, then, with the oblong turned lengthwise, place 5 level teaspoons of mincemeat along one top edge and continue with another row until you end up with six rows of mincemeat blobs. Now, roll the larger piece of pastry into another oblong approximately 13 x 11 inches (32.5 x 28 cm), transfer this again by wrapping it around the rolling pin, and lay it carefully over the bottom piece of pastry, being careful not to trap too much air. Now, gently press the pastry together to seal the little squares; then trim the edges, and cut the pastry sheet into little squares using the pastry wheel. Next, with a pair of small scissors, make 2 little snips in each one to allow the air to escape. Now, bake the whole lot in the oven for 15 minutes or until golden brown.

To serve, preheat the broiler to its highest setting for at least 10 minutes, then sprinkle the ravioli liberally with the sifted confectioners sugar and place them under the broiler, very close to the heat source, for 40-60 seconds. What will happen is the confectioners sugar will caramelize to a lovely shiny glaze. Then serve dusted with a little more confectioners sugar as soon as they have cooled enough to serve, or cool and serve cold. Alternatively, re-heat and serve warm later.

Makes 30
quick flaky pastry made with 1¾ cups (225 g) all-purpose flour and 12 tablespoons (175 g) butter (see page 121)
7 oz (200 g) mincemeat
1 large egg, beaten
⅓ cup (25 g) confectioners sugar, sifted, plus extra for dusting

You will also need a heavy baking sheet measuring 16 x 12 inches (40 x 30 cm), lightly greased, and a pastry wheel.

Preheat the oven to 400°F (200°C).

6
Cakes and cookies for beginners

If you think you can't make a cake, let me tell you now that you most certainly can! Cake-making is not the minefield of possible disaster that many people imagine it to be. Basically, there are only two things you have to remember: number one is to always follow the rules, and number two is to always follow the recipe. Making a cake can never be a throw-it-all-in-and-see-what-happens affair, and people who boast about never following recipes are, I suspect, happy with a good deal of mediocrity. The perfect cake, as I've said, needs close attention to the rules, and once you know what they are, it makes the whole thing blissfully clear and simple.

When making cakes, it's vital that the butter you use is extremely soft

The all-in-one method means that all the ingredients go into the bowl together…

…then they are whipped to a smooth, soft consistency using a hand-held whisk

The case for making a cake

A homemade cake has a lot going for it on days when life seems to lack that special edge. So instead of trying to treat yourself to something bland and boring made in a factory, why not try the real thing? Home baking transports you psychologically to a world of comfort and well-being; the quality of life seems utterly assured as your home is filled with the warm, evocative aroma of something quietly, happily baking in the oven.

In my *Book Of Cakes*, published way back in 1977, I wrote: "A cake is a symbol of love and friendship – if someone actually goes to the trouble of baking a cake specially for family and friends, they can't fail to feel spoiled and cared for." I haven't changed my mind on that, but perhaps the simplest way to start venturing towards a lifetime of happy cakemaking is to take the rules on board and try to memorize them.

The top five rules of cake making

1 It is absolutely crucial to use the correct-sized pan
2 You must have a reliable recipe
3 You need to measure the ingredients correctly
4 Once you've put the cake in the oven, don't open the door
5 Make sure your oven is functioning correctly

Pan size

This is where 99 percent of cake making goes wrong. I have, over the years, struggled to encourage manufacturers to standardize pan sizes so that people like me, who write and test recipes, are able to communicate to as many people as possible that they can enjoy making cakes. Well, I'm sorry to report that until now I have failed, due, I think, to the unacceptable face of commercialism, which also seeks to undercut the competition.

Let me explain. The most popular everyday cake is probably a sponge cake. It's all quite simple: three eggs and 1¼ cups (175 g) flour mixture fits an 8 inch (20 cm) pan that's 1½ inches (4 cm) deep; two eggs and ¾ cup plus 2 tablespoons (110 g) flour mixture fits a 7 inch (18 cm) pan the same depth. But in most supply stores, you will find 7½, 8¾, 7¾ inches. Why? Because the way manufacturers undercut prices is to make pans smaller and thus cheaper. There is quite a lot of cheap garbage out there that claims to be baking equipment; my advice is to only buy the right-sized pans, which thankfully some manufacturers still make, and though quality is expensive, it *will* last a lifetime. The cheap versions, which need to be constantly replaced, work out to be a lot more expensive.

Depth of pan

This is also crucial, so a sponge cake pan has to be at least 1½ inches (4 cm) deep because depth of support at the sides encourages the cakes to rise up and be as light and airy as possible.

Larger cake pans

These seem more easily available. An 8 inch (20 cm) round cake pan is a good average size, but remember that if you use a square pan, the same mixture will fit 7 inches (18 cm); the rule is that square pans should always be 1 inch (2.5 cm) smaller than round ones.

Loaf pans

The quality of these changes like the wind and vary among manufacturers, but thankfully old-fashioned bread pans (see page 81) are always available, so I use them for loaf cakes. Sizes include 8½ x 4½ x 2¾ inch (22 x 11 x 7 cm) and 7½ x 3⅝ x 2¼ inch (19 x 9 x 5 cm), measured on top.

It's important that the bottom of the pan is lined with parchment paper

Measuring ingredients

If you have a reliable recipe and the right-sized pan, the next step is to measure everything carefully. (In the US measurements are done in volume instead of weight, so cup measurements have been given.) Weighing ingredients in cakemaking is the most accurate method, so if you want to use the metric measurements also in this book, the best scales to buy are the balance kind; they last a lifetime and never let you down.

Lining sponge pans

Whether or not you use non-stick pans, it's important to line them with non-stick parchment paper (baking parchment), which gives the cake some protection but also makes it easier to remove it from the pan. The way to line a sponge pan is shown in the photograph, above right.

Once the mixture is in the pan, level it off using the back of a spoon

Cooling racks

After cakes are baked, it's important to cool them with air circulating around them, so a wire cooling rack is a vital piece of equipment.

Please leave it alone!

One of the perennial problems of beginning to cook is curiosity. You've done it; you've made the cake, but it's now out of sight behind a closed oven door, and even if it's glass, you can't see over the rim of the pan, so you feel anxious and cut off. All you want to do is have one little peek. Please don't - it will be a disaster! Without being too technical, what happens to the cake mixture is that the heat causes the air bubbles within to push up and expand the mixture, making a light, airy cake. This only happens if the heat is constant until finally the cake has reached a point where it can't expand any more and the structure is set. If you open the oven door, cold air rushes in, diminishing the heat and interrupting the expansion process. So instead of rising to great heights, the cake collapses and sinks into heaviness. So now you know *never* to open the door of the oven until at least three-quarters of the cooking time has elapsed.

After the cake is baked, turn onto a wire rack, then peel off the bottom paper

How do I know if it has finished baking?

For years, and when I first started cooking, the rule of thumb here was to stick a skewer in the center of the cake, and if it came out clean, the center was cooked. But I have changed my mind on that particular rule, first because I never found it reliable, and second, if the cake had fruit in it, then obviously if the skewer had passed through a sticky raisin it wouldn't be coming out clean, even if the cake was baked. Now, I feel the best test is to press lightly on the center surface of the cake with your finger (doesn't matter which one), then, if the cake springs back without leaving an impression, it's done; if not, give it another 5 minutes.

Cake ingredients

Because I have attempted to simplify things and make cakemaking easily accessible to absolute beginners, I have only included recipes for cakes that are made by the all-in-one method. This means everything is mixed together in just one mixing, so a few notes on the ingredients might be useful here.

Butter and other fats

Butter must be very soft indeed (see the picture on page 130) so the flat blade of a knife can make a deep impression all the way through immediately. Therefore, I always leave the butter out of the refrigerator to stay at room temperature overnight, which works beautifully – but as I said in Chapter 5, you may need to leave a note on the refrigerator door to remind you. Other fats, such as soft margarine or whipped white vegetable shortening, need only be taken out of the refrigerator for 30 minutes; they produce excellent results but they don't, in my opinion, have the flavor of butter.

Flours and leavening agents

In most cases cakes are made with self-rising flour, which already has a raising agent, but all-in-one mixtures need a little extra help, so baking powder is also used. Always sift the flour, lifting the sifter up high to give it lots of air as it falls down into the bowl, since air is an important ingredient.

Eggs

Cakes require large eggs (as do all my recipes), and if you keep them in the refrigerator, remember to remove them one hour before you start baking; they blend more easily with the other ingredients if they're not too cold.

Ovens

As a cooking writer struggling to give people foolproof recipes, all I can say is if I could wave a magic wand so that we all had the same oven, life would be so simple, but every single oven seems to vary. We have fan ovens, fan-assisted ovens, ovens without fans, and so on. A cake is a very good test of an oven – if it browns too much on one side and not on the other, it's not your fault – it shows you need to have your oven checked. If cakes are overcooked or undercooked, the oven thermostat may be faulty. It's very simple to have it tested professionally, and it only takes about 5 minutes. What I find really useful is having my own thermometer. Place this in the oven when you preheat it and it will tell you simply and clearly if your oven temperature is true. If it isn't, then have the oven checked.

Fan ovens

Here you must follow the manufacturer's instructions. Because fan ovens vary, it's impossible for me to give correct timings. Calculate the cooking time according to your oven instruction manual; ie, in a fan oven the heat temperature will be lower and the cooking time will be slightly reduced, and no preheating will be needed.

Conventional ovens

This is my preferred choice, and here it is necessary to preheat the oven about 10-20 minutes before the cake goes in.

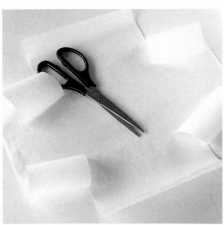

To line a round, greased cake pan, cut a strip of parchment paper slightly longer than the circumference of the pan and 3 inches (7.5 cm) higher. Fold it back about 1 inch (2.5 cm) along its length, then snip it at a slight angle at intervals up to the fold. Now, press the paper around the sides – the cut edge will overlap on the bottom of the pan for a snug fit. Finally, cut a circle out – using the pan as a template – to fit over the cut paper over the bottom

To line a square pan, cut a piece of parchment paper to size by first measuring the length and width of the pan and then adding twice its depth. Center the pan on the sheet of paper, then make four cuts from the paper's edge right up to the corners of the pan. Grease the pan and fit the parchment paper inside, folding and overlapping it at the corners. For the bottom paper, cut out a square, again using the pan as a template, and fit it in the bottom

A Classic Sponge Cake (with Passion-Fruit Filling)

This sponge cake could also be made in a 7 inch (18 cm) pan (just use two eggs and ¾ cup plus 2 tablespoons flour, ½ cup sugar, and 8 tablespoons butter). It can then be filled with jam and cream. And while the berries of summer, when they're available, are perfect for filling sponge cakes, in winter, passion fruit fulfill all the criteria needed, ie, something sharp, fragrant, and acidic to contrast with the richness of the cake and cream.

Serves 8
For an 8 inch (20 cm) cake:
1¼ cups (175 g) self-rising flour
1½ teaspoons baking powder
3 large eggs at room temperature
12 tablespoons (175 g) very soft butter
¾ cup (175 g) superfine sugar
½ teaspoon vanilla extract
a little sifted confectioners sugar,
for dusting

For the filling:
6 passion fruit
1 cup (250 g) Mascarpone
¾ cup (200 ml) fromage blanc
2 teaspoons superfine sugar
1 teaspoon vanilla extract

You will also need two 8 inch (20 cm) 1½ inch (4 cm) deep layer cake pans, lightly greased and the bottoms lined with parchment paper.

Preheat the oven to 325°F (170°C).

Take a very large mixing bowl, put the flour and baking powder in a sifter and sift it into the bowl, holding the sifter high to give it a good airing as it goes down. Now, all you do is simply add all the other cake ingredients to the bowl and provided the butter is really soft, just go in with an electric hand mixer and beat everything together until you have a smooth, well-combined mixture, which will take about 1 minute. If you don't have an electric hand mixer, you can use a wooden spoon, using a bit more effort. What you will now end up with is a mixture that drops off a spoon when you give it a tap on the side of the bowl. If it seems a little too stiff, add a little water and mix again.

Now, divide the mixture between the 2 pans, level it out and place the pans on the center shelf of the oven. The cakes will take 30-35 minutes to bake, but don't open the oven door until 30 minutes have elapsed. To test whether the cakes are baked or not, touch the center of each lightly with a finger: if it leaves no impression and the sponges spring back, they are ready.

Next, remove them from the oven, then wait about 5 minutes before turning them out onto a wire cooling rack. Carefully peel off the bottom papers, which is easier if you make a fold in the paper first, then pull it gently away without trying to lift it off. Now, leave the sponge cakes to get completely cold, then add the filling.

To make the filling, first slice the passion fruit into halves, and using a teaspoon, scoop all the flesh, juice, and seeds into a bowl. Next, in another bowl, combine the Mascarpone, fromage blanc, sugar, and vanilla extract using a balloon whisk, which is the quickest way to blend them all together. After that, fold in about two-thirds of the passion fruit. Now, place the first sponge cake on the plate or cake stand you are going to serve it on, then spread half the filling over it, drizzle the rest of the passion fruit over that, then spread the remaining filling over the passion fruit. Lastly, place the other cake on top, press it gently so that the filling oozes out at the edges, and dust the surface with a little sifted confectioners sugar.

Banana and Walnut Loaf

This is a lovely, moist cake that keeps well and is perfect for picnics or packed lunches. In the summer it's delicious served cut in thick slices and spread with whipped cream.

As soon as the oven has preheated, begin making the cake by spreading the nuts out on a baking sheet and toasting them lightly in the oven for 7-8 minutes – use a timer so that you don't forget them. After that, remove them from the oven to a chopping board, let them cool briefly, then chop them fairly roughly. Now, in a bowl, peel and mash 3 of the bananas to a purée with a fork, and peel and chop the other one into ½ inch (1 cm) chunks.

Using a large mixing bowl, sift the salt, baking powder, cinnamon, and both the flours into it, holding the sifter up high to give it a good airing, then adding the bran that's left in the sifter. Now, simply add all the remaining ingredients (except the chopped banana and nuts), and using an electric hand mixer, begin to beat the mixture, first on a slow speed for about half a minute, then increasing the speed to mix everything thoroughly and smoothly. Then lightly fold in the chopped banana and walnuts. You may need to add a drop of milk to give a mixture that drops easily off a spoon when you give it a sharp tap on the side of the bowl.

Next, pile the mixture into the pan, level the top with the back of a spoon, and sprinkle on the demerara sugar. Bake in the center of the oven for 1¼-1½ hours, until the cake feels springy in the center. After that, remove it from the oven and let it cool for about 5 minutes before turning it out onto a wire tray. Then let it get completely cold before serving or transferring it to a container.

Serves 8
4 medium bananas (approximately 12 oz/350 g)
1½ cups (175 g) walnut pieces
pinch of salt
1½ teaspoons baking powder
1 teaspoon ground cinnamon
¾ cup plus 2 tablespoons (110 g) all-purpose flour
¾ cup plus 2 tablespoons (110 g) whole wheat flour
grated zests of 1 orange and 1 lemon
8 tablespoons (110 g) butter at room temperature
1 cup (175 g) dark brown sugar
2 large eggs at room temperature

For the topping:
1 tablespoon demerara or raw sugar

You will also need a 8½ x 4½ x 2¾ (22 x 11 x 7 cm)loaf pan, lightly buttered.

Preheat the oven to 350°F (180°C).

Austrian Coffee and Walnut Cake with Coffee Cream

This is unashamedly rich and luscious. First, because coffee and walnuts have a great affinity; secondly, so do coffee and creaminess; and thirdly, since the cake is soaked in coffee syrup, it's also meltingly moist.

First of all, you need to toast all the walnuts, so spread them on a baking sheet and place in the preheated oven for 7-8 minutes. After that, reserve 10 halves to use as decoration later and finely chop the rest. Take a very large mixing bowl, put the flour and baking powder in a sifter and sift it into the bowl, holding the sifter high to give it a good airing as it goes down.

Now, all you do is simply add all the other ingredients (except the coffee and walnuts) to the bowl and, provided the butter is really soft, just go in with an electric hand mixer and beat everything together until you have a smooth, well-combined mixture, then fold in the coffee and chopped walnuts. This will take about 1 minute but, if you don't have an electric hand mixer, you can use a wooden spoon and a little bit more effort. What you should end up with is a soft mixture that drops off the spoon easily when you give it a sharp tap; if not, add a drop of water. Divide the mixture between the prepared cake pans, spreading the mixture around evenly. Then place the pans on the center shelf of the oven and bake them for 30 minutes.

While the cakes are cooking you can make up the syrup and the filling and topping. For the syrup, first place the coffee and sugar in a heatproof measuring cup, then measure the boiling water into it and stir briskly until the coffee and sugar have dissolved, which will take about 1 minute. Next, the filling and topping, and all you do here is place all the ingredients, except the reserved walnuts, in a bowl and whisk them together until thoroughly blended. Then cover the bowl with plastic wrap and chill until needed.

When the cakes are cooked, ie, feel springy in the center, remove then from the oven but leave them in their pans and prick them all over with a skewer while they are still hot. Now, spoon the syrup as evenly as possible over each one and let them soak up the liquid as they cool in their pans. When they are absolutely cold, turn them out very carefully and peel off the bottom papers – it's a good idea to turn one out onto the plate you're going to serve it on. Then spread half the filling and topping mixture over the first cake, place the other cake carefully on top, and spread with the other filling half. Finally, arrange the reserved walnut halves in a circle on top. It's a good idea to chill the cake if you're not going to serve it immediately.

Serves 8
For the sponge cake:
1½ tablespoons instant coffee mixed with 2 tablespoons boiling water
¾ cup (75 g) walnut halves
1¼ cups (175 g) self-rising flour
1½ teaspoons baking powder
12 tablespoons (175 g) softened butter
¾ cup (175 g) superfine sugar
3 large eggs at room temperature

For the syrup:
1 tablespoon instant espresso coffee powder
⅓ cup (50 g) demerara or raw sugar
⅓ cup (55 ml) boiling water

For the filling and topping:
1 tablespoon instant espresso coffee powder
1½ tablespoons superfine sugar
10 walnut halves, reserved from the sponge cake
1 cup (250 g) Mascarpone
¾ cup (200 ml) fromage blanc

You will also need two 8 inch (20 cm) layer cake pans, 1½ inches (4 cm) deep, lightly greased and the bottoms lined with parchment paper.

Preheat the oven to 325°F (170°C).

Fresh Coconut Layer Cake

Serves 8

For the cake:

1 cup (75 g) finely grated fresh coconut

1¼ cups (175 g) self-rising flour

1½ teaspoons baking powder

3 large eggs at room temperature

12 tablespoons (175 g) very soft butter

¾ cup (175 g) superfine sugar

1 teaspoon vanilla extract

For the coconut frosting:

½ cup (40 g) finely grated fresh coconut

1 cup (250 g) Mascarpone

¾ cup (200 ml) fromage blanc

1 teaspoon vanilla extract

2 teaspoons superfine sugar

For the topping and sides:

¾ cup (50 g) coarsely grated fresh coconut

You will also need two 8 inch (20 cm) layer cake pans with a depth of 1½ inches (4 cm), lightly greased and the bottoms lined with parchment paper.

Preheat the oven to 325°F (170°C).

The optimum word here is "fresh." If you've ever suffered cakes made with dry, dull flaked coconut, let me transport you to a different world. Fresh coconut is very moist and has a fragrant, slightly sour, sweet flesh that is perfect for this cake.

Before you start this cake, you'll first have to deal with the coconut. This isn't half as impenetrable as it might seem. All you do is first push a skewer into the three holes in the top of the coconut and drain out the milk. Then place the coconut in a plastic storage bag and place it on a hard surface – a stone floor or an outside paving stone. Give it a hefty whack with a hammer – it won't be that difficult to break. Now, remove the pieces from the bag, and using a cloth to protect your hands, pry the nut meat from the shell by inserting the point of a knife between the nut and the shell. You should find that you can force the whole piece out in one go. Now, discard the shell and take off the inner skin using a potato peeler. The coconut is now ready to use. The best way to grate coconut flesh is with the grating disk of a food processor, but a hand grater will do just as well.

To make the cake, sift the flour and baking powder into a large bowl, holding the sifter high to give the ingredients a good airing. Now, add all the other ingredients, except the grated coconut, to the bowl and use an electric hand mixer to combine everything until you have a smooth mixture, which will take about 1 minute. If you don't have an electric hand mixer, use a wooden spoon, which takes a little more effort. What you should now have is a mixture that drops off a spoon when you give it a tap on the side of the bowl. If it seems a little stiff, add a drop of water and mix again. Finally, stir in the finely grated coconut and divide the mixture between the pans. Now, place them on the center shelf of the oven for 30-35 minutes. To test whether the cakes are cooked, lightly touch the center of each with a finger, if it leaves no impression and the sponges spring back, they are ready.

Next, remove them from the oven, then wait about 5 minutes before turning them out onto a wire cooling rack. Carefully peel off the bottom papers, and when the cakes are absolutely cold, carefully divide each one horizontally into two halves using a very sharp serrated knife.

Now, mix up the frosting by simply whisking all the ingredients together in a bowl to combine them. Next, select the plate or stand you want to serve the cake on (you'll also need a narrow spreading knife), then simply place one cake layer on the plate or stand first, followed by a thin layer of frosting (about a fifth), followed by the next layer of cake and frosting, and so on. After that, use the rest of the frosting to coat the sides and top of the cake. Don't worry how it looks: the good thing is that it's all going to be covered with the rest of the grated coconut next. And that's it!

Low Fat Moist Carrot Cake

I have been making carrot cake for years, and each time it seems to improve with a little tinkering here and there. Last year I attempted a low fat version rather reluctantly, not believing it was possible. Now, I have to admit it's become one of my favorites. It's also one of the quickest, easiest cakes ever.

Serves 12
1 cup (175 g) dark brown sugar
2 large eggs at room temperature
⅔ cup (120 ml) sunflower oil
1½ cups (200 g) whole wheat flour
1½ teaspoons baking soda
1 teaspoon ground cinnamon
1 teaspoon freshly grated nutmeg
2 pinches ground cloves
1 pinch ground coriander
¼ teaspoon ground ginger
grated zest 1 orange
7 oz (200 g) carrots, peeled and
coarsely grated
1 cup (175 g) golden raisins

For the topping:
1 cup (250 g) Quark (skim-milk
soft cheese)
2 tablespoons (20 g) superfine sugar
2 teaspoons vanilla extract
1½ teaspoons ground cinnamon, plus
a little extra for dusting

For the syrup glaze:
juice ½ small orange
2 teaspoons lemon juice
¼ cup (40 g) dark brown sugar

You will also need a non-stick shallow baking pan measuring 10 x 6 inches (25.5 x 15 cm) and 1 inch (2.5 cm) deep, the bottom lined with parchment paper.

Preheat the oven to 325°F (170°C).

Begin by whisking the sugar, eggs, and oil together in a bowl using an electric hand mixer for 2-3 minutes. Then sift together the flour, baking soda, and the spices into the bowl, adding in all the bits of bran that are left in the sifter. Now, stir all this together, then fold in the orange zest, carrots, and golden raisins. After that, pour the mixture into the prepared pan and bake on the center shelf of the oven for 35-40 minutes until it is well risen and feels firm and springy to the touch when lightly pressed in the center.

While the cake is cooking, make the topping by mixing all the ingredients in a bowl until light and fluffy, then cover with plastic wrap and chill for 1-2 hours or until needed.

Now, you need to make the syrup glaze, and to do this whisk together the fruit juices and sugar in a bowl. Then, when the cake comes out of the oven, stab it all over with a skewer and quickly spoon the syrup over it as evenly as possible. Now, set aside the cake and let it cool in the pan during which time the syrup will be absorbed. Then, when the cake is completely cold, remove it from the pan, spread with the topping, cut it into 12 squares, and dust with a little more cinnamon.

Spiced Apple Muffin Cake with Pecan Streusel Topping

I have included this because I still get letters from people saying they can't make muffins. My message to them is don't try too hard – undermixing is the golden rule, and once mastered, this muffin mixture makes the lightest cakes in the world. In the summer, you could always substitute for the apples 12 oz (350 g) of fresh apricots, pitted and chopped, or, in the fall, 12 oz (350 g) of plums, pitted, and chopped. In both cases, though, weigh after pitting. This recipe will also make 24 mini or 12 large muffins, cooking them for 20 and 30 minutes respectively.

First of all, place the butter in a small saucepan and put it on a gentle heat to melt. Then, as with all muffin mixtures, you need to sift the dry ingredients twice, so place the flour, baking powder, salt, cinnamon, cloves, and grated nutmeg in a sifter and sift them into a bowl. Then, in another large mixing bowl, whisk the eggs, sugar, and milk together, pour the melted butter into the egg mixture, and whisk it all to combine. Now, sift the flour mixture again straight onto the egg mixture, and fold it in using as *few* folds as possible. Ignore the lumpy mixture you're now faced with and don't be tempted to overmix. I think this is where people go wrong: they can't believe that what looks like a disaster can possibly turn into something *so* light and luscious. Now, fold in the chopped apple and then spoon the mixture into the pan, leveling off the surface.

Next, make the topping; you can use the same bowl. Simply add the flour, sugar, and cinnamon and rub the butter in with your fingertips until crumbly. Finally, sprinkle in the nuts and cold water, then press the mixture loosely together. Again, it will be quite lumpy – no problem! Now, spoon the topping over the surface of the cake, and bake it on the center shelf of the oven for about 1¼ hours until it feels springy in the center. Allow the cake to cool in the pan for 30 minutes before removing the sides; then gently slide a narrow spreading knife under the bottom and transfer the cake to a wire rack to finish cooling. Serve this as fresh as possible, either on its own or warm as a dessert with whipped cream, crème fraîche, or vanilla ice cream.

Serves 10-12

12 oz (350 g) Granny Smith apples (weight after peeling and coring), chopped into ½ inch (1 cm) cubes
8 tablespoons (110 g) butter
2 cups (275 g) all-purpose flour
1 tablespoon plus 1 teaspoon baking powder
½ teaspoon salt
1½ teaspoons ground cinnamon
1 teaspoon ground cloves
½ whole nutmeg, grated
2 large eggs at room temperature
⅓ cup (75 g) superfine sugar
⅔ cup (175 ml) milk

For the pecan streusel topping:
½ cup (50 g) pecans, roughly chopped
⅔ cup (75 g) self-rising flour
⅓ cup (75 g) demerara or raw sugar
1½ teaspoons ground cinnamon
2 tablespoons (25 g) soft butter
1 tablespoon cold water

You will also need a 9 inch (23 cm) springform cake pan, lightly greased and the bottom lined with parchment paper.

Preheat the oven to 375°F (190°C).

Irish Whiskey Christmas Cakes

Makes four 4 inch (10 cm) square cakes or an 8 inch (20 cm) square cake

For the pre-soaking:

1¼ cups (275 ml) Irish whiskey

1½ teaspoons Angostura bitters

3 cups (450 g) raisins

1¾ cup (225 g) currants

¾ cup (110 g) pitted soft prunes

⅓ cup (50 g) glacé cherries

⅓ cup (50 g) unblanched almonds

4 oz (110 g) mixed candied peel

¾ teaspoon ground cinnamon

½ teaspoon freshly grated nutmeg

½ teaspoon ground cloves

1½ teaspoons vanilla extract

1 tablespoon dark muscovado or dark brown sugar

grated zest 1 orange and 1 lemon

½ teaspoon salt

For the cake:

2 cups (250 g) self-rising flour, sifted

2½ cups (250 g) demerara or raw sugar

20 tablespoons (250 g) unsalted butter, softened

5 large eggs at room temperature

1½ tablespoons apricot jam

1 tablespoon Irish whiskey

For the icing:

1lb 2 oz (500 g) marzipan (in a block)

4¾ cups (570 g) confectioners sugar, plus a little extra for rolling

1 large egg white

4 tablespoons molasses

3-4 tablespoons Irish whiskey

You will also need an 8 inch (20 cm) square cake pan, greased, the bottoms and sides lined with a double thickness of parchment paper to sit 4 inches (10 cm) deep.

If you've never made a fruit cake before, this one is extremely easy, and you won't be disappointed. I now prefer the much thinner layer of marzipan and icing; the flavor of the Irish whiskey in the icing, as well as the cake, is wonderful! The instructions here are for four small cakes; measurements for the large one are in the caption opposite. If you want to keep the cake for any length of time, let the marzipan dry out (covered with a clean dish cloth) for a week before icing it.

One week before you intend to bake the cake, measure out the whiskey, bitters, and 3 tablespoons of water into a large saucepan; then roughly chop the prunes, cherries, and almonds, and finely dice the mixed candied peel. Add these, along with the rest of the pre-soaking ingredients, to the saucepan, checking them off as you go to make sure nothing gets left out. Now, stir and bring the mixture to the simmering point. Then, keeping the heat low, simmer very gently, without a lid, for 15 minutes. After that, allow everything to cool completely, then pour the mixture into a large lidded jar or an airtight plastic container and leave it in the refrigerator for seven days, giving it a little shake from time to time.

When you're ready to bake the cake, preheat the oven to 275°F 140°C).

All you need to do is measure out the flour, sugar, and butter into a very large bowl, then add the eggs and beat with a wooden spoon until everything is evenly blended. Now, gradually fold in the fruit mixture until it is evenly distributed. Then spoon the mixture into the prepared pan, leveling the surface with the back of the spoon. Bake in the center of the oven for 3 hours without opening the door; then cover the cake with a double thickness of parchment paper and continue to bake it for another 30 minutes or until the center feels springy when lightly touched.

Cool the cake for 45 minutes in the pan; then remove it to a wire rack to finish cooling. When it's completely cold, wrap it in a double layer of parchment paper, then foil, and store it in an airtight container.

When you are ready to finish the cake, first take a sharp knife and cut the cake into quarters so you end up with four smaller 4 inch (10 cm) square cakes. Then melt the jam with the whiskey in a small saucepan and stir it a few times until all the lumps have dissolved. Now, using a brush, coat the surface of each cake generously with it. Cut off a quarter of the block of marzipan, and on a surface lightly dusted with confectioners sugar, roll the piece into an 8 inch (20 cm) square. Now, with a sharp knife, cut the square into quarters so you end up with four 4 inch (10 cm) square pieces. Gently take each square and place one on top of each cake, lightly pressing the marzipan down. Next, cut the remaining piece of marzipan in half and roll each half into a strip measuring 6 x 16 inches (15 x 40 cm), then cut each strip in half lengthwise so you are left with four strips: one for the sides of each cake. Press each strip lightly around the edges of each cake and pinch to seal where the pieces join with the top piece of marzipan.

For the icing, sift the confectioners sugar, then place the egg white and molasses in a large bowl, and using an electric hand mixer, beat together thoroughly. Now, with the mixer running, add a tablespoon of confectioners sugar at a time and keep adding it until the mixture thickens. As it begins to crumble, add a tablespoon of the Irish whiskey to combine the mixture, then carry on adding more confectioners sugar until it becomes thick. Add another tablespoon of whiskey, then the rest of the confectioners sugar and whiskey, and keep whisking until everything is blended together to reach a spreadable consistency. Add a little water if the icing is still slightly crumbly.

Now, divide the icing into four amounts, and using a narrow spatula, smooth it over the top and down the sides of each cake, dipping the knife into a small saucepan of simmering water to make it easier to spread. To give the cakes a nice finish, dip the knife in the simmering water once more and make swirls with the knife over the cakes; then leave them to dry overnight. Wrap each cake in parchment paper, then in foil, and keep in an airtight container. To decorate the cakes, you'll need four lengths of ribbon, each 4 ft (1.2 m) long and 1½ inches (4 cm) wide. When you're ready to finish the cakes, carefully place a length of ribbon around each one, tying the ends in a bow.

For the 8 inch (20 cm) cake, take the marzipan and cut off a quarter of the block, then roll this piece out to an 8 inch (20 cm) square. Cut the remaining piece in half and roll each half into a strip measuring 3 x 16 inches (7.5 x 40 cm), then use these strips to cover the sides of the cake. To decorate the cake, you will need a length of ribbon 6½ ft (2 m) long and about 1½ inches (4 cm) wide

Irish Tea Bread

It's always hard for me to believe that this simple little fruit loaf can taste so good. When we were testing recipes, this one disappeared the fastest – none of us could resist just one more little bit. It's good all by itself or spread with butter, and it's delicious toasted. The recipe makes two loaves, so you can place the other one in the freezer to keep it for a rainy day.

Begin this the evening before by placing all the fruit, including the candied peel, in a bowl, then dissolve the sugar in the hot tea, pour this over the fruit, cover the bowl, and leave it overnight so the fruits become plump and juicy.

The next day, preheat the oven to 325°F (170°C), then place the nuts on a baking sheet and place them into the oven for 6-8 minutes (use a timer because they burn easily). Then, when they're cool, roughly chop them. Next, add the beaten egg mixture to the bowl containing the fruit. Then sift in the flour, add the toasted nuts, and mix everything well. Now, divide the mixture between the prepared loaf pans and bake them in the center of the oven for 1¼-1½ hours until they feel springy in the center. Then immediately, loosen them with a narrow spatula and turn them out onto a wire rack to cool. Then have patience – it won't be long before you can taste some.

Makes 2 small loaves
1½ cups (225 g) raisins
1¾ cups (225 g) currants
1½ cups (225 g) golden raisins
4 oz (110 g) whole candied citrus peel,
cut into ¼ inch (5 mm) pieces
1¼ cups (225 g) demerara or raw sugar
1¼ cups (275 ml) Lapsang Souchong,
Earl Grey, or any other hot tea
1 cup (110 g) pecan halves
1 large egg at room temperature,
lightly beaten with 2 tablespoons milk
3 cups (450 g) self-rising flour

You will also need two 7½ x 3⅝ x 2¼ inch (19 x 9 x 5 cm) loaf pans, the bottoms lined with parchment paper.

Chocolate Almond Crunchies

Although you can buy high quality cookies, making them at home still has the edge, and because they are so easy, it's a very good place to start if you are a beginner in home baking. I've used "adult" chocolate in these, but for children, chocolate chips would do fine.

First of all, using a sharp knife, chop the chocolate into small chunks about ¼ inch (5 mm) square. Now, put the butter, sugar, and syrup in a saucepan over the gentlest heat possible and let it all dissolve, about 2-3 minutes. Meanwhile, chop the nuts into pieces about the size of the chocolate chunks. When the butter mixture has dissolved, take it off the heat. In a large mixing bowl, sift the flour and salt and add the oats and half the chocolate and nuts, giving all this a quick stir before pouring in the butter mixture. Now, using a wooden spoon, mix everything together, switching from a spoon to your hands to bring everything together to form a dough. If it seems a bit dry, add a few drops of cold water. Now, take half the dough and divide it into nine pieces the size of a large walnut; roll them into rounds using the flat of your hand. Place them on a countertop and press gently to flatten them out into rounds approximately 2½ inches (6 cm) in diameter; then scatter half the remaining chocolate and almonds on top of the cookies, pressing them down lightly. Once you have filled one baking sheet (allowing them room to spread out during baking), bake them on the middle shelf of the oven for 15 minutes while you prepare the second sheet. When they're all cooked, let them cool on the baking sheets for 10 minutes, then transfer them to a wire rack to finish cooling. You could store the cookies in a sealed container, but I doubt you'll have any left!

Crunchie variations

For *Apricot Pecan Crunchies*, use ¼ cup (50 g) of dried apricots and ⅓ cup (40 g) pecans, chopped, instead of the chocolate and almonds.
For *Cherry and Almond Crunchies*, use ½ cup (50 g) of dried sour cherries and ⅓ cup (40 g) sliced almonds.
For *Raisin Hazelnut Crunchies*, use ½ cup (50 g) of raisins and ⅓ cup (40 g) hazelnuts.

Makes 18
2 oz (50 g) bittersweet chocolate
8 tablespoons (110 g) butter
½ cup (75 g) demerara or raw sugar
2 teaspoons golden syrup or dark corn syrup
⅓ cup (40 g) whole almonds, unblanched
¾ cup plus 2 tablespoons (110 g) self-rising flour
pinch of salt
1⅓ cups (110 g) rolled oats

You will need two baking sheets measuring approximately 11 x 14 inches (35 x 28 cm), lightly greased with peanut or another mildly flavored oil.

Preheat the oven to 325°F (170°C)

From top: Chocolate Almond Crunchie, Apricot Pecan Crunchie, Cherry and Flaked-Almond Crunchie

7

Flour-based sauces and batter

Don't, whatever you do, be daunted by the subject of sauce making. How the enormous amount of fear that's attached to the subject was first generated it's hard to say, but now is the time to sweep it away, along with all those packages of strange-sounding chemicals and ingredients that masquerade under the name of sauce. So stop thinking too thin, too thick, or, worst of all, what about the lumps; instead, make your mind up to deal with it, learn how to do it once and for all, and then enjoy a lifetime of making and enjoying perfect sauces any time you want to.

Although the entire art of sauce making is a vast subject, covering many different methods and approaches (see Hollandaise Sauce on page 72 and Traditional English Custard on page 64), here we are concerned with flour-based sauces, which, when you've understood the rules and learned how to master them, will give you a good grounding in the rest of sauce making.

More power to your elbow

I'm not sure if this old cliché came into being through the subject of sauce making or not, but it does say something wise, and that is this: when flour, fat, and liquid are combined and heated, they always need extremely vigorous whisking. As I said in the chapter on pastry, it's the brain that gives out signals to the hands (or arms in this case) and commands either gentleness or forcefulness, and with sauces it's the latter, so the more vigorously you whisk the better. With all flour-based sauces, once you know this and put it into practice, everything will be within your control – because in the end it's the whisk that controls. Learning in the first place begins with a decision: I will always do what Delia says and whisk like mad!

Lumps are a thing of the past

Flour-based sauces, it has to be admitted, have suffered bad press. I remember well a few years ago watching a chef on a television program making a horrible lumpy white sauce in close-up. Yes, it was funny, because the chef at the time was saying how smooth and silky it was. Knowing the hazards of television cooking and the heat not always being right when the director says "go," I could sympathize. It's a shame in this case that he (the director) didn't think to look at the monitor. But making a sauce at home is nowhere near as hazardous as it is on television, so lumps really are within your control.

In a classic white sauce and all other flour-based sauces, there's only one rule apart from determined whisking, and that is the fat content: it's the flour blended with the fat that guarantees lump-free results, so never attempt to blend hot liquid and flour without the presence of fat, because this is what causes lumps.

It is all quite straightforward; once you understand the rules, lumps should never occur. But so what? If you do happen to slip up on the rules or get distracted, then don't forget why sifters were invented.

Now, let's first have a look at some of the rules. You need to remember the three ways to make a white sauce.

1 The roux method

Roux is the name given to the mixture of butter and flour that forms the basis of the classic white sauce called béchamel. The butter is melted in the pan, the flour is then stirred in to make a smooth, thick paste, and finally, the liquid is added a little at a time with continual whisking. This is the only way to make a sauce if the liquid is hot, because hot liquid can only be combined with flour if it's first blended with fat. So if you want to make a sauce with hot liquid, ie, fish-poaching liquid, hot vegetable stock, or infused milk, remember to use the roux method described here.

2 The all-in-one method

What happens here is that if you are using cold liquid you can simply place all the ingredients, ie, butter, flour, and liquid, in a saucepan and whisk continuously and vigorously over the heat until the heat thickens the sauce. By the time the heat penetrates, the butter will have been blended with the flour enough to prevent lumps and the finished sauce will be silky smooth and exactly the same as in the roux method above.

3 The fat-free, no-lump flour method

Yes, it's true. For the first time in history we have an utterly new and quite phenomenal way of making a white sauce, which has changed all the rules somewhat. It's with a flour called *sauce flour*, which has been invented by an extremely clever flour miller who was watching me on television emphasising the absolutely essential presence of fat to avoid lumps. We don't need to get scientific here, but what he did was figure out what it was that made the sauce get lumpy, and then develop a specific type of sauce flour that did not need the presence of fat. This flour, thankfully, is now available on the internet (see Suppliers, pages 481-2). After that, he sent me some samples to test, and the happy conclusion is that, sure enough, using the all-in-one method above with cold milk, you can now make a white sauce without any butter at all. Of course, milk does have some fat, but there's a vast difference in the total fat content, which is wonderful news for those on a low fat diet.

Obviously the richness and flavor of butter is what makes a classic creamy white sauce the star it is, but it's good to have the choice of not adding butter on occasions, and I think this is a huge step forward. You can now make a creamy, silky-smooth white sauce with skim or low fat milk and flour with no butter. Amazing.

What's the best saucepan?

A nagging question that has occupied me for years. The absolute truth is that a white sauce is probably the very best test of a saucepan. Why? Because what you want is a saucepan in which the sauce won't stick. If it does you will find that, as you whisk, little bits of scorched sauce will begin to appear. For years I have searched and searched, and at long last I've found what I can only describe as a little gem, left. Since I first started cooking, I've always known that heavy-gauge aluminium is the very best conductor of heat in cooking, and now, thankfully, it has at last been declared safe (see page 44).

This type of pan is perfect for making sauces and it's not the most expensive. Even though it's not particularly glamorous to look at, it is light-years ahead of anything else in performance.

How long should you cook a flour-based sauce?

When you use flour in a sauce, although it will thicken to a smooth creaminess very quickly, it then has to be cooked. This is because the flour can at first taste a little raw. Therefore, it's important to remember that all sauces using flour must have 5 minutes' cooking time over the gentlest possible heat, except if you're going to continue to cook the sauce in the oven, as in a lasagne, for example, which means you can cut this initial cooking to 2 or 3 minutes.

Can you make it ahead?

Yes, you certainly can, but a few things to remember first. When the sauce is made, place some plastic wrap directly over the surface to prevent a skin from forming; then either keep it warm by placing it over a pan of barely simmering water or, if you want to make it a long time ahead, re-heat it using the same method, and don't remove the plastic wrap until you are ready to serve. If you find it has thickened a little, this is easy to rectify by adding a little more liquid – milk, stock, or cream – to bring it back to the right consistency.

Opposite, clockwise from top right: fat-free white sauce, all-in-one white sauce, roux

Classic White Béchamel Sauce

This is the classic way of making a white sauce, using what the French call a roux (see page 149).

Makes about 2 cups (425 ml)
2 cups (425 ml) milk
a few parsley stems
1 bay leaf
1 blade of mace or a pinch of
powdered mace (optional)
10 whole black peppercorns
1 slice onion, ¼ inch (5 mm) thick
3 tablespoons (40 g) butter
3 tablespoons (20 g) all-purpose flour
salt and freshly ground black pepper

First, place the milk in a small saucepan and add the parsley, bay leaf, mace (if using), peppercorns, and onion. Then place it over a low heat and let it come very slowly up to simmering, which will take approximately 5 minutes. Then remove the saucepan from the heat and strain the milk into a large measuring cup, discarding the flavorings.

All this can be done ahead of time, but when you want to make the sauce, use the same washed pan and place it over a gentle heat. Begin by melting the butter gently – don't over-heat it or let it brown, since this will affect the color and flavor of the sauce. As soon as the butter melts, add the flour, and over a medium heat and using a small pointed wooden spoon, stir quite vigorously to make a smooth, glossy paste. Now, begin adding the infused milk a little at a time – about 2 tablespoons (30 ml) first of all – and stir again vigorously. Then, when this milk is incorporated, add the next amount and continue incorporating each bit of liquid before you add the next. When about half the milk is in, switch to a balloon whisk and start adding larger amounts of milk, but always whisking briskly. Your reward will be a smooth, glossy, creamy sauce.

Now, turn the heat down to its lowest setting and let the sauce cook for 5 minutes, whisking from time to time. While that's happening, taste and season with salt and freshly ground black pepper. If you wish to keep the sauce warm, all you do is pour it into a large warmed measuring cup and cover the surface with plastic wrap to stop a skin from forming; then place the measuring cup in a pan of barely simmering water.

All-In-One White Sauce

The golden rule here, as explained earlier, is to use cold milk. So if you want to infuse the milk, pour it into a bowl and let it get completely cold before you begin.

Makes about 2 cups (425 ml)
2 cups (425 ml) milk – this can be infused (see page 152) but must be cold
3 tablespoons (20 g) all-purpose flour
3 tablespoons (40 g) butter
salt and freshly ground black pepper

When you're ready to make the sauce, put the milk in a saucepan, then simply add the flour and butter and bring everything gradually up to simmering, whisking continuously with a balloon whisk, until the sauce has thickened and becomes smooth and glossy.

Then turn the heat down to its lowest possible setting and let the sauce cook very gently for 5 minutes, stirring from time to time. Meanwhile, taste and add seasoning.

Any Kind of Cheese Sauce

Yes, it's true – any kind of cheese can be used. If you want something more assertive, how about a sharp Gorgonzola? Or, instead of Cheddar and Parmesan, try Gruyère and Parmesan. Cheese sauce is also very obliging if you have bits of cheese lurking in the refrigerator, you can use a mixture.

Makes about 2½ cups (570 ml)
2½ cups (570 ml) milk
⅓ cup (40 g) all-purpose flour
3 tablespoons (40 g) butter
pinch of cayenne pepper
2 oz (50 g) sharp Cheddar, grated
1 oz (25 g) Parmesan (Parmigiano Reggiano), finely grated
a little freshly grated nutmeg
salt and freshly ground black pepper

All you do is place the milk, flour, butter, and cayenne pepper into a medium saucepan over a gentle heat. Then, using a balloon whisk, begin to whisk while bringing it to a gentle simmer. Whisk continually until you have a smooth, glossy sauce, and simmer very gently for 5 minutes. Then add the cheeses and whisk again, allowing them to melt. Then season with salt, freshly ground black pepper, and some freshly grated nutmeg.

Fat-free White Sauce

Okay, so you don't get to have the buttery flavor, but you do get a lovely creamy-smooth, milky white sauce by using sauce flour (see page 149), which is most helpful for those needing to cut the fat content of their diets.

Makes about 1¼ cups (275 ml)
1¼ cups (275 ml) milk – this can be infused (see page 152) but must be cold
3 tablespoons (20 g) sauce flour
salt and freshly ground black pepper

All you do to make this sauce is place the milk in a small saucepan, then simply add the flour, and over a medium heat, bring everything gradually up to the simmering point, whisking vigorously and continuously with a balloon whisk until the sauce has thickened to a smooth, rich creaminess. Then add seasoning and allow it to cook very gently for 5 minutes on the lowest possible heat.

Cauliflower and Broccoli Gratin with Blue Cheese

The cheese we used for the sauce in this recipe, as pictured on the following page, was Gorgonzola, but Roquefort, below is also extremely good.

Begin by heating the oil in the frying pan over a medium heat, then add the onions and let them cook for 3-4 minutes, until lightly tinged brown. Next, stir in the rice – there's no need to wash it – and turn the grains over in the pan so they become lightly coated and glistening with oil. Then add the boiling stock, along with the salt, stir once only, then cover with the lid, turn the heat to its very lowest setting, and cook for 40-45 minutes. Don't remove the lid and don't stir the rice during cooking, because this is what will break the grains and release their starch, making the rice sticky.

While the rice is cooking, make the sauce. All you do here is place the milk, butter, flour, and cayenne pepper in a saucepan and, using a balloon whisk, whisk over a medium heat, continuing until the sauce becomes thick, smooth and glossy. Then turn the heat to its lowest setting and give it 5 minutes to cook. After that, whisk in the cheese until it has melted, then season with the nutmeg, salt, and freshly ground black pepper.

Next, preheat the broiler to its highest setting, then place a saucepan on the heat, add some boiling water from the kettle, fit a steamer in it, and add the cauliflower. Cover with a lid and time it for 4 minutes. After that, put the broccoli in with the cauliflower, cover with the lid again, and time it for another 4 minutes.

Now, arrange the cooked rice in the baking dish, then top with the cauliflower and broccoli florets. Next, pour the sauce over all, then, finally, mix the Parmesan with the breadcrumbs and parsley. Sprinkle this all over the top, then place the whole thing under the broiler and cook for 2-3 minutes, until the sauce is bubbling and golden brown.

Serves 4
10 oz (275 g) cauliflower florets
10 oz (275 g) broccoli florets
1 tablespoon olive oil
2 medium onions, peeled and sliced into 8 through the root
1½ cups (275 ml) brown basmati rice
2½ cups (570 ml) boiling vegetable stock
1¼ teaspoons salt

For the blue cheese sauce:
4 oz (110 g) Roquefort, cubed
2½ cups (570 ml) milk
3 tablespoons (40 g) butter
⅓ cup (40 g) all-purpose flour
pinch of cayenne pepper
a little freshly grated nutmeg
salt and freshly ground black pepper

For the topping:
1 oz (25 g) Parmesan (Parmigiano Reggiano), finely grated
¼ cup (10 g) fresh breadcrumbs
1 tablespoon finely chopped fresh parsley

You will also need an ovenproof baking dish with a bottom measurement of 8 x 6 inches (20 x 15 cm), 2 inches (5 cm) deep, and a 10 inch (25.5 cm) frying pan with a lid.

Roasted Vegetable and Brown Rice Gratin

This, like the previous recipe, is obviously a dish for non-meat eaters, but I have served it to the most dedicated carnivores who, after initial apprehension, have loudly sung its praises.

Serves 4
For the rice:
1½ cups (275 ml) brown basmati rice
1 tablespoon olive oil
2 medium onions, peeled and finely chopped
2½ cups (570 ml) boiling vegetable stock
1¼ teaspoons salt

For the vegetables:
10 oz (275 g) peeled butternut squash
5 oz (150 g) each celery root, rutabaga, carrots, and parsnip (peeled weight)
2 medium red onions, peeled
2 tablespoons chopped mixed fresh herbs: parsley, thyme, and tarragon, for example
1 fat clove garlic, peeled and crushed
2 tablespoons olive oil
salt and freshly ground black pepper

For the cheese sauce:
2 oz (50 g) sharp Cheddar, grated
1 oz (25 g) Parmesan (Parmigiano Reggiano), finely grated
2½ cups (570 ml) milk
⅓ cup (40 g) all-purpose flour
3 tablespoons (40 g) butter
a little cayenne pepper
a little freshly grated nutmeg
salt and freshly ground black pepper

You will also need a 16 x 12 inch (40 x 30 cm) baking sheet, a 8 x 6 inch (20 x 15 cm) bottomed ovenproof dish and a 10 inch (25.5 cm) lidded frying pan.

Preheat the oven to 450°F (230°C).

For the vegetables, begin by cutting the squash, celery root, rutabaga, carrots, and parsnip into 1 inch (2.5 cm) cubes. Place them and the red onions, each cut into six through the root, in a large bowl, along with the herbs, garlic, a good seasoning of salt and pepper, and the olive oil, then toss them around so they get a good coating of oil and herbs. Now, arrange them evenly all over the baking sheet, then place this on the highest shelf of the oven to roast for about 30 minutes, or until they are nicely brown at the edges. As soon as they are ready, take them out and reduce the oven temperature to 400°F (200°C).

For the rice, begin by warming the frying pan over a medium heat, then add the oil and the onions and let them cook for 3-4 minutes, until lightly tinged brown. Next, stir in the rice – there's no need to wash it – and turn the grains over in the pan so they become lightly coated and glistening with oil. Add the boiling stock, along with the salt, stir once only; then cover with the lid, turn the heat to the very lowest setting and cook for 40-45 minutes. Don't remove the lid and don't stir the rice during cooking, because this is what will break the grains and release their starch, which makes the rice sticky.

Meanwhile, make the cheese sauce by placing the milk, flour, butter, and a pinch of the cayenne pepper into a medium-sized saucepan, then whisk it all together over a gentle heat until you have a smooth, glossy sauce. Let it cook on the lowest heat for 5 minutes, and after that add half the cheeses. Whisk again and allow them to melt into it, then season the sauce with salt, freshly ground black pepper, and freshly grated nutmeg.

When the vegetables and rice are cooked, arrange the rice in the ovenproof dish, then the vegetables on top of that, followed by the sauce, pouring it over and around the vegetables as evenly as possible. Finally, scatter with the remaining cheeses and a sprinkling of cayenne pepper, then return the dish to the oven and give it about 20 minutes or until the sauce is browned and bubbling.

Opposite, top: Roasted Vegetable and Brown Rice Gratin; bottom, Cauliflower and Broccoli Gratin with Blue Cheese

Roast Lamb with Garlic and Rosemary

Serves 6-8

1 leg of lamb weighing about 4 lb (1.8 kg)
3 large cloves garlic, peeled and thinly sliced lengthwise into about 24 slivers
2 large stems fresh rosemary, cut into about 24 small sprigs
1 small onion, peeled
salt and freshly ground black pepper

You will also need a heavy bottomed roasting pan measuring 11 x 9 inches (28 x 23 cm) and 2 inches (5 cm) deep.

Preheat the oven to 375°F (190°C).

I have included this recipe for roast lamb here in the sauce section because it is served with two sauces: Traditional Gravy on page 165 and the Rosemary and Onion Sauce below. I find that the Oven-Sautéed Potatoes Lyonnaises on page 190 make an excellent accompaniment.

Begin by making about 24 small, deep cuts in the skin of the lamb using a small, sharp knife. Then push a sliver of garlic, followed by a small sprig of rosemary, into each cut, and season the meat generously with salt and freshly ground black pepper. Next, cut the onion in half and place it in the bottom of the roasting pan, then transfer the lamb to the pan and place on top of the onion halves. Cover the pan loosely with foil, then cook in the oven on a high shelf for 1½ hours. After this, take the foil off and let it cook for another 30 minutes.

Remove the lamb from the oven, cover loosely with foil again and allow it to rest for about 20 minutes. Meanwhile, make the gravy (see page 165).

Rosemary and Onion Sauce

Makes about 2½ cups (570 ml)

1½ tablespoons rosemary leaves
1 large onion, peeled and finely chopped
2 tablespoons (25 g) butter
4 tablespoons (25 g) all-purpose flour
¾ cup (175 ml) milk
¾ cup (175 ml) vegetable stock
2 tablespoons crème fraîche
salt and freshly ground black pepper

This is good with the roast lamb, above, lamb chops, or served with sausages and mashed potatoes.

In a small saucepan, melt the butter and cook the onions over a very gentle heat for about 5 minutes – it's important not to let them color, so keep an eye on them. While that's happening, bruise the rosemary leaves with a mortar and pestle to release their oil, then chop them very, very finely and add them to the onion. Then continue to cook as gently as possible for another 15 minutes, again, without letting the onions color too much. Next, using a wooden spoon, stir the flour into the onions and their buttery juices until smooth, then gradually add the milk, a little at a time, still stirring, followed by the stock, bit by bit, while vigorously whisking with a balloon whisk. Now, taste and season the sauce with salt and pepper and let it barely simmer on the lowest possible heat for 5 minutes. Next, remove it from the heat, then blend or process half of it, then return it to the saucepan to join the other half. Then re-heat gently, add the crème fraîche, and pour it into a warmed serving pitcher.

Roast Lamb with Garlic and Rosemary served with Oven-Sautéed Potatoes Lyonnaises

English Parsley Sauce

Yes, it's traditional, old-fashioned, English childhood food, but I sometimes think that things like this need a revival. I love it with baked cod and creamy mashed potatoes, and it's also excellent with ham. Here, though, I've included my favorite recipe for Salmon Fish Cakes specially for the parsley sauce.

Place the milk and the next five ingredients in a small pan, bring everything slowly up to simmering, pour the mixture into a bowl, and set aside to get completely cold. When you're ready to make the sauce, strain the milk back into the pan, discard the flavorings; then add the flour and butter and bring everything gradually up to simmering, whisking continuously with a balloon whisk until the sauce has thickened and is smooth and glossy. Then turn the heat down to its lowest possible setting and let the sauce cook gently for 5 minutes, stirring from time to time. To serve the sauce, add the parsley, cream, and lemon juice; taste and season, then serve in a warm gravy pitcher.

Makes about 2 cups (425 ml)
2 cups (425 ml) milk
a few parsley stems
1 bay leaf
1 slice onion, ¼ inch (5 mm) thick
1 blade of mace or a pinch of powdered mace (optional)
10 whole black peppercorns
3 tablespoons (20 g) all-purpose flour
3 tablespoons (40 g) butter
6 tablespoons finely chopped fresh parsley
1 tablespoon light cream
1 teaspoon lemon juice
salt and freshly ground black pepper

Salmon Fish Cakes

The thing to remember here is that good-quality canned salmon makes better fish cakes than fresh, so don't be tempted to cook some salmon just for this.

First of all, boil the potatoes in salted water for about 25 minutes or until they're absolutely tender when tested with a skewer. (Be careful, though – if they are not tender you will get lumps.) Then drain the potatoes and mash them to a purée with the mayonnaise using an electric hand mixer, then add some seasoning.

Now, in a large mixing bowl, simply combine all the ingredients for the fish cakes. Mix really thoroughly, then taste and season again if the mixture needs it. After that, allow it to cool thoroughly, then cover the bowl and place it in the refrigerator, giving it at least 2 hours to chill and become firm.

When you are ready to cook the fish cakes, lightly flour a work surface, then turn the fish mixture onto it, and using your hands, pat and shape it into a long roll, 2-2½ inches (5-6 cm) in diameter. Now, cut the roll into 12 round fish cakes, pat each one into a neat, flat shape, and then dip them, one by one, first into the beaten egg and then into the matzo meal (or breadcrumbs), making sure they get a nice, even coating all around.

Now, in a large frying pan, heat the oil and butter over a high heat, and when it is really hot, add half the fish cakes to the pan; then turn the heat down to medium and give then 4 minutes' shallow frying on each side. Then drain the cakes on crumpled paper towels and keep warm. Repeat with the rest of the fish cakes, adding a little more oil and butter if needed. Serve immediately on hot plates with the parsley sauce, sprigs of parsley, and some lemon wedges.

Makes 12 (serves 6)
For the fish cakes:
15 oz (425 g) red salmon
10 oz (275 g) round red or white or Yukon Gold potatoes, peeled and cut into large chunks
2 tablespoons mayonnaise
3 tablespoons chopped fresh parsley
3 tablespoons salted capers or capers in vinegar, drained and chopped
6 mini pickles (cornichons), drained and chopped
2 large eggs, hard-boiled and chopped small
2 teaspoons anchovy paste or 4 anchovies, mashed up
2 tablespoons lemon juice
¼ teaspoon powdered mace
¼ teaspoon cayenne pepper
salt and freshly ground black pepper

For the coating and frying:
a little flour for dusting
1 large egg, beaten
1½ cups (75 g) matzo meal or fresh white breadcrumbs
about 2 tablespoons peanut or other mildly flavored oil
about 1 tablespoon (10 g) butter

To serve:
1 quantity English Parsley Sauce (see opposite)
a few sprigs fresh parsley
lemon wedges

Salmon Fish Cakes with
English Parsley Sauce

Moussaka with Roasted Eggplant and Ricotta

Once you've mastered the art of a perfect white sauce you can use it for any number of recipes. This one is a Greek classic, but the little hint of Italy I've added in the shape of Ricotta cheese makes the very best moussaka topping I've tasted. Also, roasting the eggplant is much less tiresome than standing over a frying pan watching them soak up masses of oil.

Serves 6

1 lb (450 g) ground lamb
2 medium-sized eggplants
2 tablespoons olive oil
2 medium onions, peeled and chopped small
2 cloves garlic, peeled and chopped
1½ tablespoons chopped fresh mint
1½ tablespoons chopped fresh parsley
1 teaspoon ground cinnamon
3 tablespoons tomato paste
⅓ cup (75 ml) red wine
salt and freshly ground black pepper

For the topping:

1 cup (250 g) Ricotta
1¼ cups (275 ml) whole milk
4 tablespoons (25 g) all-purpose flour
2 tablespoons (25 g) butter
¼ whole nutmeg, grated
1 bay leaf
1 large egg
1 tablespoon grated Parmesan (Parmigiano Reggiano)
salt and freshly ground black pepper

You will also need an ovenproof baking dish measuring 10 x 8 inches (25.5 x 20 cm), 2 inches (5 cm) deep, and a 14 x 11 inch (35 x 28 cm) baking sheet.

First of all, you need to prepare the eggplant to get rid of their high water content and concentrate their flavor. To do this, remove the stems, and leaving the skins on, cut them into approximately 1½ inch (4 cm) chunks. Then place them in a colander and sprinkle them with about 2 teaspoons of salt. Now, put a plate on top of them and weigh it down with something heavy; then put another plate underneath to catch the juices. Leave them like this for 1 hour. Then, shortly before the end of this time, preheat the oven to its highest setting. When the hour is up, squeeze out any of the excess juice from the eggplant with your hands and dry them as thoroughly as you can in a clean cloth. Next, spread them out on the baking sheet, drizzle 1 tablespoon of the olive oil over them, and toss them around to get a good coating. Now, put the baking sheet in the oven and roast the eggplant for 30 minutes or until they are tinged brown at the edges.

Meanwhile, heat the remaining olive oil in your largest frying pan and fry the onions and garlic gently for about 5 minutes. After that, turn the heat up high, add the ground lamb, and brown it for a few minutes, turning it and keeping it on the move. Now, cook the meat, stirring all the time, for 2-3 minutes. Then reduce the heat, and in a small bowl, mix the mint, parsley, cinnamon, tomato paste, and red wine. When they're thoroughly combined, pour them over the meat, season well, and cook the whole thing very gently for about 20 minutes, stirring from time to time so it doesn't stick on the bottom of the pan.

Now, remove the eggplant from the oven and reduce the temperature to 350°F (180°C). It's a good idea to leave the oven door open to cool it down a bit.

Next, make the topping by placing the milk, flour, butter, nutmeg, and bay leaf in a saucepan. Using a balloon whisk, whisk over a medium heat until everything comes to the simmering point and the sauce becomes smooth and glossy. Turn the heat down to its lowest setting and let the sauce cook gently for 5 minutes. Then taste and season, discard the bay leaf, remove the saucepan from the heat, and let it cool a little before whisking in the Ricotta and egg. Give it a good whisk to blend everything.

Finally, combine the roasted eggplant with the meat mixture and transfer it all to the baking dish. Then pour the topping over, sprinkle the surface with the Parmesan, and bake on the center shelf of the oven for 50 minutes, by which time the top will be golden brown. Let it stand for 10 minutes to settle, then serve with brown rice and a Greek-style salad of cucumber, tomatoes, olives, and crumbled Feta cheese dressed with olive oil and fresh lemon juice.

Gravy training

What is gravy?

Originally in the 14th century, this word was a bit of a typo. The French (who by no means have the last word in cooking) had the word *grane*, and someone at some stage mistakenly copied over the "n" as a "v," and for some unknown reason the English kept the "v" and added a "y." So, in a 14th-century cookbook we find that oysters, for instance, were stewed "in their own gravy," meaning with their own juices, plus wine broth, almonds, and rice flour, and similar gravies appeared from then on. So the French still, to this day, have only sauce or *jus* (juices), while the British have gravy, which is a sauce made from juices and other ingredients. So in many prestigious cookbooks, literature, food journals, and diaries throughout the centuries, gravy is prominently featured.

Gravy or jus?

It is, therefore, hardly surprising that even today, gravy remains a popular sauce. True, if you're a food snob, the word gravy does not have such a fashionable ring to it as the French *jus* that dominates restaurant menus, along with perfumed broths, essences, and other such pretensions. But it has to be said that gravy comes from a long line of careful cooks who knew how to prepare a perfectly flavored sauce by utilizing precious juices, adding thickening for creamy smoothness and other flavor-enhancing ingredients to provide a beautiful sauce.

Gravy again

Now, we can come to the crux of all this, and it is that everyone wants to enjoy proper gravy, but they are at the same time deeply afraid of attempting to make it. I have written about it and demonstrated it countless times, but still people ask, "How do you make gravy?"

Witness the horrors that line the supermarket shelves: cubes, packages, and granules with long lists of chemicals, producing alien artificial flavor and instant gelatinous gloop. But now is the time to move on, and once and for all, with the aid of this book plus the demonstration in the TV series that the book accompanies, everyone everywhere who wants to will be able to make proper gravy for ever and ever. It really isn't hard, and there's nothing to be afraid of, so here goes.

Traditional Gravy

First of all, remove the meat or poultry from the roasting pan and have a bowl ready, then tilt the pan and you will see quite clearly the fat separating from the darker juices. Now, you need to spoon off the fat into the bowl using a tablespoon, but remember, you need to leave about 2 tablespoons of fat in the pan. Then, using a wooden spoon, scrape the sides and bottom of the pan to release any crusty bits, which are very important for flavor. Next, place the pan over direct heat turned fairly low, and when the fat and juices begin to sizzle, add the flour, then quickly dive in with the wooden spoon using brisk circular movements. Speed is of the essence – gentle, faint-hearted stirring is not what's needed here: you should be mixing in the manner of a sped-up movie!

Soon you will have a smooth paste, so now begin to add the hot stock, a little at a time, whisking briskly and blending after each addition. Now, turn the heat up to medium and you will find that, as the stock is added and it reaches simmering point, the gravy will have thickened.

Now, your own preference comes into play. If the gravy is too thin, let it bubble and reduce a little; if it's too thick, add a little more liquid. Finally, taste and season with salt and freshly ground black pepper, then pour the gravy into a warmed serving pitcher ready for the table.

For *pork*, which has pale juices, add onion to the roasting pan. This will caramelize during cooking and give color to the juices. The onion may also be used with other roasts and poultry to give color.

For *lamb*, add a teaspoon of mustard powder with the flour, a tablespoon of red currant jelly to melt into the gravy, and red wine to add body.

For *duck*, add the grated zest and juice of a small orange, along with a glass of port.

For *beef*, add ½ cup of Sercial Madeira – this enriches the beef flavor magically.

For *instant gravy without a roast*, see the recipe for Roasted-Onion Gravy on page 167.

Makes about 2½ cups (570 ml)
the juices left in the roasting pan from cooking meat or poultry
2 tablespoons all-purpose flour
approximately 2½ cups (570 ml) hot stock (potato or other vegetable water, for example), but the exact amount will depend on how thick you like your gravy
salt and freshly ground black pepper

You will also need a heavy-bottomed, flameproof roasting pan.

Begin by spooning off most of the fat from the roasting pan, leaving a little behind

Now, add the flour and briskly mix it in using circular movements

Once you have a smooth paste, add the stock, a little at a time, blending as you go

Increase the heat; you will now see that the gravy will begin to thicken

165

Toad in the Hole with Roasted-Onion Gravy

I can't give this high enough accolades – it's a simply wonderful creation from the humble origins of British cooking. If only you could order it in a restaurant, though. Can I persuade anyone? It is, after all, a sort of fusion food – a fusion of light, crispy, crunchy batter and plump, meaty pork sausages, all moistened with a generous amount of roasted-onion jus.

Begin by making the batter, and to do this sift the flour into a large bowl, holding the sifter up high to give the flour a good airing. Now, with the back of a spoon, make a well in the center, break the egg into it, and add some salt and pepper. Now, measure the milk and water in a large measuring cup, then, using an hand mixer on a slow speed, begin to mix the egg into the flour – as you mix, the flour around the edges will slowly be incorporated. Then add the liquid gradually, stopping to scrape the flour into the mixture. Mix until the batter is smooth. Now, the batter is ready for use, and although it's been rumored that batter left to stand is better, I have never found this, so just make it whenever it's convenient.

Now, place the sliced onions in a bowl, add 1 teaspoon of the oil and the sugar, and toss the onions around to get the lightest coating, then spread them in the baking pan. Next, arrange the sausages in the roasting pan, then place the onions onto a high shelf in the oven, with the sausages on a lower shelf, and set a timer for 10 minutes. When the timer goes off, remove the sausages from the oven but leave the onions in for another 4-5 minutes – they need to be nicely blackened around the edges. When they are ready, remove them and leave to one side.

Now, place the roasting pan containing the sausages over direct heat turned to medium and, if the sausages haven't released much fat, add the tablespoon of oil. When the pan is really hot and the oil is beginning to shimmer – it must be searing hot – quickly pour the batter in all around the sausages. Immediately return the roasting pan to the oven, this time on the highest shelf, and cook the whole thing for 30 minutes.

Now, for the gravy. First, add the Worcestershire sauce and mustard powder to the stock, then add the onions from the baking pan to a medium-sized saucepan. Now, add the second teaspoon of oil, then using a wooden spoon, stir in the flour. Stir all this together over a medium heat and then switch to a balloon whisk, and gradually add the stock to the pan, whisking all the time, until it's all incorporated. Then bring it up to simmering and gently simmer for 5 minutes. Taste to check the seasoning, then pour into a warmed serving pitcher. When the batter is ready, it should be puffed brown and crisp and the center should look cooked and not too soft. Serve it immediately with the gravy, and it's absolutely wonderful with mashed potatoes.

Serves 2-3
6 good-quality pork sausages – about 14 oz (400 g)
1 tablespoon peanut or other mildly flavored oil (if necessary)

For the batter:
⅔ cup (75 g) all-purpose flour
1 large egg
⅓ cup (75 ml) low fat milk
¼ cup (55 ml) water
salt and freshly ground black pepper

For the onion gravy:
8 oz (225 g) onions, peeled and sliced
2 teaspoons peanut or other mildly flavored oil
1 teaspoon superfine sugar
2 teaspoons Worcestershire sauce
1 teaspoon mustard powder
1 tablespoon all-purpose flour
2 cups (425 ml) hot vegetable stock
salt and freshly ground black pepper

You will also need a heavy bottomed flameproof roasting pan with a bottom measurement of 9 x 6 inches (23 x 15 cm), 2 inches (5 cm) deep, and a shallow baking pan 14 x 10 inches (35 x 25.5 cm).

Preheat the oven to 425°F (220°C).

Canadian Buttermilk Pancakes with Maple Syrup

Northeastern America and Canada is where this profoundly unique syrup made from the sap of maple trees is made. These are the pancakes that a certain Madame Lafond made for me when I was in Quebec; delightfully easy but tasting so light and fluffy. I love the way they puff up, crinkle, and get really crisp at the edges. Serve these, as she did, straight from the pan onto warm plates. Absolutely drench them with maple syrup and add a generous dollop of crème fraîche.

Makes about 8
1 cup (150 g) all-purpose flour
½ teaspoon baking powder
pinch of salt
⅓ cup (75 ml) buttermilk
⅓ cup (75 ml) cold water
3 large eggs, beaten
2-4 tablespoons (25-50 g) lard

To serve:
lots of pure maple syrup and crème fraîche

First, sift the flour, baking powder, and salt together in a roomy bowl and make a well in the center. After that, whisk the buttermilk and water together in a large measuring cup and gradually whisk this into the bowl, slowly incorporating the flour with each new addition of liquid. Finally, add the eggs a little at a time until you have a smooth batter.

Now, place a large, heavy frying pan over a medium heat, add 2 teaspoons of the lard and heat it until the fat shimmers. Then, using 2 tablespoons of batter per pancake, cook 2 or 3 pancakes at a time.

They will take about 1 minute to turn golden brown, then turn them over using a spatula and fork, being careful not to splash yourself with the hot fat. Give them another 45 seconds on the other side, by which time they should have puffed up like little soufflés, then briefly rest them on some paper towels to absorb any excess fat.

Repeat this with the rest of the batter, adding a little more lard if necessary. They will keep warm in a low oven, but to enjoy them at their best, have everyone seated to eat them as soon as they come out of the pan.

8

Real potatoes

"Cuisine is when things taste like themselves" wrote Curnonsky, a distinguished 19th-century French food writer, and therein lies the whole truth about the art of cooking – how to make something really taste like itself. This is the real challenge that's set before anyone who wants to cook, and never was it more true than in the art of cooking potatoes. So the question is precisely this: how to make a potato really taste like a potato? The answer begins by perhaps rediscovering a healthy respect for what a potato actually is: no longer the humble "also ran" of the meat-and-two-vegetable syndrome or something used as a filler to extend the meat, but now hopefully re-emerging as a solo star on the food stage, loved and valued in its own right.

Potatoes make a comeback

Well, in a way this is true, because in my younger days potatoes were the enemy of the perfect waistline in a less nutritionally enlightened era; it was starch that made you fat, and starchy foods like bread and potatoes had to be avoided. Thankfully, bread and potatoes have now been rescued from this scenario; fat has now emerged as the number one culprit and the major cause of being overweight. This means that large portions of potatoes (without fat) are nutritious, healthy, high in energy-giving carbohydrate and low in calories – only about 70 per 4 oz (100 g), and, added to that, they are an important source of vitamin C in our diet. So potatoes are very "in" at the moment and it's therefore more important than ever to learn how to make the best of them.

The importance of flavor

Before you even think about how to cook potatoes, as with other foods, the key to flavor begins in the marketplace, or actually, in the earth. I remember well growing my first crop of new potatoes and discovering that straight from the ground into the cooking pot they were both soggy and tasteless and ended up being a huge disappointment. Why? I had simply grown the wrong variety, one with a high yield but absolutely no flavor.

This problem is a commercial one, too, and high-yield, disease-resistant, good-storage varieties do not always produce good flavor. So for the cook, choosing the right kind of potato is first on the list.

Varieties

Thankfully there are now many varieties of potatos to choose from; we could even be in danger of designer potatoes, like salad greens, as I have seen both black-fleshed and purple varieties (neither of which have great flavor). But while we hear a lot about the texture of potatoes – which is measured by two things, waxiness and fluffiness, and the suitability of either of these in certain dishes – we hear very little about flavor. I would therefore like to see potatoes catch up with tomatoes on this, ie, varieties grown specifically for flavor. But since we are learning how to cook potatoes, here is not the place to study the long lists of various varieties that appear throughout the year, but I would like to point you in the direction of a few varieties which, in my experience, are among the best available.

Round red or white

The waxy texture of these potatoes suits roasting, baking, frying, and mashing.

Russet Burbank

This reliable and widely available favorite is commonly known as the Idaho potato. It has a mealy texture which is dry and fluffy when cooked and is a reliable variety for baking and frying. It is also good for mashing.

Long White

This variety is sometimes called White Rose. Their dry, fluffy texture is good for frying, baking, and boiling, particularly if the skin is left intact.

Yukon Gold

This yellow-fleshed potato has a good flavor and its excellent texture suits baking, boiling, and frying. It makes wonderful fluffy mashed potatoes which are perfect for using in gnocchi, making them extra light.

Waxy or floury?

The above potatoes all have good flavor, but texture is a personal choice. Sometimes I want a firm, waxy, full-flavored baked potato, so I choose Round Red, and other times a more floury one, so it would be Russet Burbank. The same applies to mashed potatoes, and what I would recommend is that you experiment to find out what you personally prefer.

New Potatoes

New potatoes are at their best during the spring and summer months when you can find fresh, regionally grown ones at local farmers' markets. However, baby (new) potatoes of several varieties can be found in supermarkets from shipped-in sources throughout the year. The waxy texture of new potatoes makes them ideal for boiling or steaming and for serving hot or cold in a potato salad. If available, choose ones with the earth still clinging to them - they need to be as fresh as possible when you cook and serve them.

Baby round red and white, and Yukon Gold

Baby round red and white have a firm, waxy texture and are perfect for baking or roasting whole and unpeeled. They can be used in salads although the skins of the baby red can be a little tough. The butter-colored flesh of the very young Yukon Gold makes the variety an attractive potato to use sliced or halved in salads. These have a waxy, moist texture and a good flavor. Look for them at farmers' markets and in large supermarkets.

Fingerlings or Finger potatoes

These are a small version of long white and as their name suggests, they are long and thin but only finger-sized. Because they have a dry texture, they are not ideal for serving cold. They suit boiling, steaming, and roasting whole or unpeeled.

How to cook potatoes

To peel or not to peel?

This is a much debated question and I have given it a great deal of thought and consideration. My conclusions are these: yes, it's best to leave the skins on. I never peel new potatoes, but with larger potatoes, if you're not going to peel them, you must then have evenly sized potatoes so they all cook in the same amount of time.

The idea of leaving the skins on is to protect the flesh from the water or steam, which rob the potatoes of flavor. Once you start cutting them into even-sized pieces, that protection is lost. Also, if skins are left on for cooking, I would say that you should then serve the potatoes with their skins, since peeling hot potatoes while holding them in a cloth is okay if it's for one or two people, but for six servings it's quite awkward and hazardous. In Ireland, boiled potatoes are served with skins on and people who don't want to eat them leave them on the side of their plate; I think this is a good option for steamed or boiled potatoes. I have compared steaming without skins and boiling with and found very little difference in flavor. If you are going to peel the potatoes, then please, please use a potato peeler. All the best of the flavor is near the skin, so you need to peel it off as thinly as possible.

Water – the enemy

I have a beautiful old cookbook called *Henderson's House Keeper Instructions*, and in it potatoes are boiled thus: "…in so small a quantity of water as will be sufficient to keep the saucepan from burning. Keep them close covered and as soon as the skins crack they are enough."

Need I say more? Remember that having got hold of the perfectly flavored potatoes, it's water that's going to take away their precious flavor. I have witnessed potatoes being murdered – covered with gallons of water, put on a low heat and left for an hour or even more.

The number one rule here is, first of all, if you are peeling potatoes, don't let them wait around in water for hours before they're needed. If you peel them then try to do so just before you need them.

For cooking, the best way I have found to retain the flavor of the potatoes is not to boil them at all but to steam them. First, pour boiling water from a kettle into a pan fitted with a collapsible steamer (see the photograph, right), then place the potatoes in the steamer, sprinkle with salt (about 1 teaspoon per 1 lb/450 g), and if they're new potatoes tuck in a few sprigs of mint. Then put a tight lid on and let them steam over a lowish heat, which is just needed to keep the water gently boiling until the potatoes are tender. This will take 20-25 minutes, and the best way to test whether the potatoes are tender is to use a thin skewer inserted in the thickest part.

After that, drain off any water beneath the steamer, then place a cloth over the potatoes for 5 minutes, which will absorb some of the excess steam that tends to cling to the potatoes and make them soggy. If you prefer to boil rather than steam, then use as little water as possible, add it boiling from the kettle and put on a tight lid on. The lid keeps the heat in and they will cook more quickly with less time in the water.

Steamed or boiled potatoes – pure and simple

In the recipes that follow I have attempted to give you a good grounding in all the most popular ways of serving potatoes. But don't forget that, cooked with a little care, plain steamed or boiled potatoes can, just on their own, be quite special. And they don't need very much butter; a little is a nice addition, but don't drown them with butter as some restaurants still insist on doing. All that does is swamp the delicate natural flavor of the potatoes. Gilding the lily is a sign of insecurity in cooking, and I feel it's so important to renew our confidence in the simplicity of things.

Perfect
Baked
Potatoes

Could there possibly be anyone in the wide world who doesn't love the thought of baked potatoes with really crisp, crunchy skins and fluffy, floury insides with something lovely melted into them? I'm not speaking of the insipid microwave versions raved about for convenience sake, but the hallowed, reverenced beauty of the real thing. Life is too short, and therefore we need to savor every moment by spoiling ourselves with what is best and not some pale imitation that fails to satisfy. If you ever feel like treating yourself and want something supremely soothing and comforting that costs almost nothing (forget chocolate bars and the like), just bake yourself the biggest potato you can lay your hands on (see the method below), then cut it in half, and, as you do, listen carefully to the inviting crackle and crunch of the skin as the knife goes in. Next, with a fork, fluff the floury insides, add a generous amount of butter, and watch it melt and disappear into the clouds of fluffiness. Add rock salt and crushed black pepper, then savor it in all its humble, simple glory.

The secret of perfect baked potatoes like the one described above is not to hurry them – give them up to 2 hours to get the really crunchy skin; learn to use the time when you're out, so they will be ready when you come home, or go do something else and forget about them until they're ready. Below I have included the master recipe, and this is followed by some ideas for fillings and toppings.

Serves 2
2 large Idaho potatoes, 8-10 oz
(225-275 g) each
a little olive oil
rock salt, crushed
a little butter
salt and freshly ground black pepper

Preheat the oven to 375°F (190°C).

First, you need to wash the potatoes and dry them very thoroughly with a cloth, then put them aside to dry as much as possible. Next, prick the skins a few times with a fork, then put a few drops of olive oil over each one and rub it all over the skin. After that, rub in some crushed salt – this will draw out the moisture from the skin and, together with the oil, provide more crunchiness.

Now, place the potatoes right onto the center shelf of the oven and let them bake for 1¾-2 hours, or until the skins are really very crisp. When you are ready to serve, slit each potato in half lengthwise and top with the butter and seasoning. Serve immediately because, after you remove baked potatoes from the oven, they lose their crispness very quickly, so don't let them wait around.

Sour cream and chive topping

½ cup (150 ml) sour cream
approximately ½ oz (10 g) fresh chives
salt and freshly ground black pepper

This is a simple but great dressing for baked potatoes and it's still my number one favorite. All you do is snip the chives with some scissors into a bowl containing the sour cream. Add some seasoning and leave it for about 1 hour before serving, so that the sour cream has time to absorb the flavor of the chives.

Stuffed Baked Potatoes with Leeks, Cheddar, and Boursin

In this recipe the potato is scooped out, mixed with soft cheese, and topped with leeks and melted cheese.

To prepare the leek, slice it almost in half lengthwise, then fan it out under running water to wash away any trapped dirt. Now, slice each half into four lengthwise, then into ¼ inch (5 mm) slices. After that, put the Boursin into a medium-sized bowl and cut the potatoes in half lengthwise. Protecting your hands with a cloth, scoop out the centers of the potatoes into the bowl containing the Boursin, add the cream, and season well with salt and freshly ground black pepper. Now, quickly mash or beat everything together, then pile all of it back into the potato skins. Scatter the leeks on top, followed by the grated Cheddar – pressing it down lightly with your hand – then place on the baking sheet and bake in the oven for 20 minutes or until the leeks are golden brown at the edges and the cheese is bubbling.

Serves 2

2 large baked potatoes, 8-10 oz (225-275 g) each (see basic recipe left)
1 leek about 4 inches (10 cm) long, trimmed and cleaned
1½ oz (40 g) sharp Cheddar, coarsely grated
1 x 80 g package *Ail & Fines Herbes* Boursin
1 tablespoon light cream
salt and freshly ground black pepper

You will also need a baking sheet measuring approximately 12 x 10 inches (30 x 25.5 cm).

Preheat the oven to 350°F (180°C).

Welsh Rarebit Baked Potatoes

Serves 2
2 large baked potatoes, 8-10 oz
(225-275 g) each (see page 176)
3 oz (75 g) sharp Cheddar, grated
1 tablespoon Red Onion, Tomato, and
Chili Relish (see page 190)
2 teaspoons finely grated onion
1 large egg, lightly beaten
1 tablespoon finely snipped fresh chives

Preheat the broiler to its highest setting
for 10 minutes before the potatoes are
ready.

The same topping that goes with toasted bread goes perfectly with baked potatoes and makes a lovely lunch dish served with a salad. You can make your own relish for this (see page 190), or you could buy it ready-made.

All you do here is combine all the filling ingredients together in a bowl. Then, when the potatoes are ready, cut them in half lengthwise and make some criss-cross slits in them, being careful not to cut through the skins and using a cloth to protect your hands. Then divide the topping mixture between the potatoes, place them on the broiler pan, and broil 2 inches (5 cm) from the heat for 3-4 minutes, until the cheese has puffed up and turned golden brown on top.

Perfect Mashed Potatoes

This is now my standard all-time mashed potato recipe, adapted and revised from the Winter Collection.

Serves 4
2 lb (900 g) round red, white, or
Yukon Gold potatoes
2 teaspoons salt
4 tablespoons (50 g) butter
4 tablespoons whole milk
2 tablespoons crème fraîche
salt and freshly ground black pepper

Use a potato peeler to pare off the potato skins as thinly as possible, then cut the potatoes into even-sized chunks – not too small; if they are large, quarter them, and if they are small, halve them. Put the potato chunks in a steamer fitted over a large pan of boiling water, sprinkle the salt all over them, cover with a lid, and steam the potatoes until they are absolutely tender – they should take 20-25 minutes. The way to tell whether they are ready is to pierce them with a skewer in the thickest part: they should not be hard in the center, and you need to be careful here, because if they are slightly underdone, they will be lumpy.

When the potatoes are cooked, remove them from the steamer, drain off the water, return them to the saucepan, and cover with a clean dish cloth for about 4 minutes to absorb some of the steam; then add the butter, milk, and crème fraîche. When you first go in with the mixer, use a slow speed to break the potatoes up, then increase it to high and whip to a smooth, creamy, fluffy mass. Taste and, if they need it, season.

Note: To make low fat mashed potatoes, replace the butter, milk, and crème fraîche with ½ cup (150 g) of Quark (skim-milk soft cheese) and 2-3 tablespoons of low fat milk.

Perfect Mashed Potatoes begin with steaming the potato chunks until tender. With the addition of butter, milk, and crème fraîche, the result, once beaten, is a smooth, creamy, fluffy mass

Pork Sausages Braised in Cider with Apples and Juniper

Braised sausages seem to have turned up many times in my books over the years, and because I love them so much, here is yet another version – a lovely, comforting, warm, winter supper dish that needs copious amounts of fluffy mashed potatoes to spoon the sauce over. Crushing the juniper berries releases their lovely flavor.

Serves 3-4

6 large pork sausages, weighing about
1 lb (450 g), preferably free-range
2 cups (425 ml) hard cider
1 tablespoon cider vinegar
1 large Granny Smith apple, cored and
sliced into rings (unpeeled)
1 McIntosh apple, cored and sliced
into rings (unpeeled)
2 teaspoons juniper berries, crushed
slightly either in a mortar and pestle or
with the back of a tablespoon
2 tablespoons olive oil
1 large (8 oz) onion, peeled and sliced
into rings
1 large clove garlic, peeled and
chopped
8 oz (225 g) lean bacon, roughly
chopped
1 tablespoon all-purpose flour
a few sprigs fresh thyme
2 bay leaves
salt and freshly ground black pepper

You will also need a 2½ quart (2.25
liter) flameproof casserole dish
measuring 8 inches (20 cm) in
diameter, 3 inches (7.5 cm) deep, with
a tight-fitting lid.

Begin by taking a large, heavy-bottomed frying pan, place it on a medium heat, and add 1 tablespoon of the oil to it. As soon as it's hot, fry the sausages until they are nicely browned on all sides, then, using a slotted spoon, transfer them to a plate. Now, add the onions, garlic, and bacon to the frying pan and cook these until they have also browned at the edges – about 10 minutes.

Meanwhile, place the casserole onto another heat source, again turned to medium, add the other tablespoon of oil, then, when it's hot, add the apple rings and brown these on both sides, which will take 2-3 minutes. After that, add the sausages, followed by the bacon, onion, and garlic, then sprinkle the flour in to soak up the juices, stirring it gently with a wooden spoon. Next, add the cider and cider vinegar, a little at a time, stirring after each addition. Then add the thyme, bay leaves, and crushed juniper berries; season with salt and pepper, but not too much salt because of the bacon. After that, cover with a lid and simmer very gently on the lowest possible heat for 1 hour. Serve with mashed potatoes.

Pork Sausages Braised in Cider with
Apples and Juniper served with
Perfect Mashed Potatoes
(see page 178)

Aligot (Mashed Potatoes with Garlic and Cheese)

Serves 2
1 lb (450 g) round white or red, or
Yukon Gold potatoes
2 fat cloves garlic, peeled and
halved lengthwise
2 tablespoons (25 g) butter
8 oz (225 g) Lancashire, or firm goat
cheese, grated or crumbled
salt and freshly ground black pepper

I first ate this mashed potatoes with cheese in southwest France, in the Tarn region, and it was, quite simply, the best mashed potatoes I've ever eaten. Research on my return revealed that it involved a special, lovely cheese called Cantal, not generally available – but after many experiments I have, I think, come up with something comparable, made with either British Lancashire or goat cheese.

Begin this by placing the garlic in a small saucepan with the butter, then leave it on the gentlest heat possible to melt and infuse for 30 minutes. Meanwhile, thinly peel and discard the skins of the potatoes and cut them into even-sized chunks, or cut any large potatoes into quarters and small ones into halves. Place the potatoes in a steamer, then pour some boiling water straight from the kettle into a saucepan. Fit the steamer over the water, sprinkle the potatoes with 2 teaspoons of salt, cover with a lid, and let them steam for 20-25 minutes, until tender in the center when tested with a skewer. After this, remove them, transfer to a large bowl (preferably a warm one), and cover with a cloth to absorb some of the steam.

Now, with an electric hand mixer turned to slow, begin to break up the potatoes, then add the butter and garlic, some black pepper, and a handful of the grated cheese. Now, switch the speed to high and continue adding the cheese, a handful at a time, while you mix. There's a lot of cheese, but what will happen is that, as you mix it in, the potatoes will turn translucent and glossy and, as you lift and mix, it will form stiff, glossy peaks. When all the cheese is in, serve very quickly. The marinated steak recipe opposite is the perfect accompaniment, but it's also great with sausages.

Note: As the cheese goes in, the mixture becomes stiff, clinging to the beaters, but keep going - it will part company with them eventually. To keep the mixture warm, place the bowl over a pan of simmering water, but don't leave it too long.

After adding the butter, garlic, and seasoning, throw in a handful of cheese

Increase the mixer's speed and continue adding the cheese, a handful at a time

As you mix, the potatoes will turn into a translucent mass, forming glossy peaks

Marinated Sirloin Steak

This is oh, so simple, but oh, so good. Great if you're organized and can leave the steaks in the marinade the day before you need them, but a few hours will do. The recipe was created specially to serve with Aligot, but it needs two to eat and two to cook: one to do the steaks and one to whip the potatoes!

Put the steaks in the shallow dish or plastic container, then mix the red wine, Worcestershire sauce, and garlic together and pour this over the steaks. Cover with plastic wrap or cover with a lid, then place in the refrigerator for a few hours or, preferably, overnight. When you're ready to cook the steaks, drain and dry them carefully with paper towels, reserving the marinade.

Now, take a medium frying pan, place it on a high heat, and heat the oil until it's very hot. Then sear the steaks for 4 minutes on each side, and 2 minutes before the time is up, add the reserved marinade to the pan and let it bubble and reduce by about half. When the steaks are cooked, remove them from the pan to warm serving plates; then, using your sharpest knife, cut them into slices diagonally (see below) and spoon the sauce over them. Garnish with the watercress and serve immediately with the Aligot.

Serves 2
2 x 7-8 oz (200-225 g) sirloin or
rump steaks
⅓ cup (75 ml) red wine
⅓ cup (75 ml) Worcestershire sauce
1 large clove garlic, peeled and crushed
1 teaspoon peanut or other mildly
flavored oil

To garnish:
a few sprigs fresh watercress

You will also need a shallow dish or
lidded plastic container large enough
to hold the steaks closely and
comfortably.

*Marinated Sirloin Steak served
with Aligot*

183

Mashed Potatoes with Three Mustards

This is the perfect accompaniment to ham steaks, rich beef casseroles, or spicy meat casseroles, and, as always, is great with sausages.

Serves 4

2 lb (900 g) round white or red, or Yukon Gold potatoes, peeled and steamed as for the Perfect Mashed Potatoes recipe (see page 178)

1½ tablespoons coarse grain mustard

2 tablespoons French's American mustard

1 tablespoon hot mustard powder

3 tablespoons crème fraîche

4 tablespoons (50 g) butter

3-4 tablespoons light cream

salt and freshly ground black pepper

While the potatoes are cooking, mix the crème fraîche with the three mustards in a small bowl. Drain the potatoes and return them to the hot pan, cover with a clean dish cloth for 4 minutes to absorb some of the steam, then add the mustard mixture, butter, and some freshly ground black pepper. Then, using an electric hand mixer on a slow speed, break the potatoes up, then increase the speed and mix them to a light, fluffy puree, adding the light cream. Taste to check seasoning before serving.

Green Parsley Mashed Potatoes

This has an intense color and the flavor of the parsley has an amazing affinity with potatoes. It is the perfect puree to serve with fish recipes, but it's also very good with boiled ham or broiled ham steaks.

Serves 4

2 lb (900 g) round red or white, or Yukon gold potatoes, peeled and steamed as for the Perfect Mashed Potatoes recipe (see page 178)

1 small bunch (50 g) fresh curly parsley

⅔ cup (150 ml) milk

salt and freshly ground black pepper

While the potatoes are cooking, place the parsley, with the stems, into a small saucepan, add the milk, and bring very slowly up to the gentlest simmer possible for 5 minutes or until the parsley is wilted and tender. Then place the whole contents into a blender or processor and process on a high speed until the parsley is blended into the milk and has turned it a bright green color – 2-3 minutes – then strain it through a sieve to remove any bits of stems and return to the pan to keep warm. When the potatoes are tender, drain them and cover with a clean dish cloth and leave for 4 minutes. Then, using an electric hand mixer on a slow speed, start to mash the potatoes; then increase the speed of the mixer and gradually add the parsley milk and a good seasoning of salt and freshly ground black pepper. Beat until the puree is light and fluffy.

Watercress and Caper Mashed Potato

This is another recipe for mashed potatoes that's great served with fish. I love it with some freshly broiled mackerel or herring, and it's also extremely good with smoked fish.

When the potatoes are tender, drain them and cover with a clean dish cloth and leave for 4 minutes; then add the butter, milk, and crème fraîche. Now, using an electric hand mixer, begin to mix slowly to break them up, then add the watercress, increase the speed of the mixer, and continue mixing until the potatoes are smooth and fluffy. Next, stir in the lemon juice and capers and add the seasoning, though you may not need much salt if you are using salted capers.

Serves 4
2 lb (900 g) round white or red, or Yukon Gold potatoes, peeled and steamed as for the Perfect Mashed Potatoes recipe (see page 178)
1 large bunch (150 g) watercress, stems removed
2 tablespoons salted capers or capers in vinegar, washed and drained
4 tablespoons (50 g) butter
2 tablespoons milk
2 tablespoons crème fraîche
2 tablespoons lemon juice
salt and freshly ground black pepper

Clockwise from top: Aligot, Mashed Potatoes with Three Mustards, Watercress and Caper Mashed Potatoes, Green Parsley Mashed Potatoes

Crunchy Roast Potatoes with Saffron

This is my old favorite recipe for roast potatoes but with a new twist, and that's a flavoring of saffron – not too much, just a hint – and with the added dimension of a deep saffron color, which makes this look even more irresistible.

Serves 4
2 lb (900 g) round white or red potatoes, peeled and cut into approximately 1½ inch (4 cm) pieces
1 teaspoon saffron
1 tablespoon olive oil
salt

You will also need a shallow baking pan measuring approximately 16 x 11 inches (40 x 28 cm).

Preheat the oven to 425°F (220°C) and place the baking pan with 2 tablespoons of oil in it to preheat as well.

First of all, crush the saffron to a powder with a mortar and pestle. Then place the potatoes in a saucepan with sufficient boiling water to almost cover them, add 2 teaspoons of salt and half the saffron powder, cover with a lid, and simmer gently for 6 minutes. Use a timer, since it's important not to overcook them at this stage.

When the time is up, lift a potato out using a skewer to see if the outer edge is fluffy. You can test this by running the point of a skewer along the surface – if it stays smooth, give the potatoes 2 or 3 more minutes. Then drain off the water, place the lid back on the pan, and, holding the lid firmly and protecting your hand with a cloth, shake the saucepan vigorously. This is to create a fluffy surface so the finished potatoes will be really crunchy.

Now, mix the oil with the rest of the saffron powder, then remove the pan from the oven and place it over a direct medium heat. Next, using a long-handled spoon, carefully but quickly lift the potatoes into the hot fat, tilt the pan and baste them well; then, using a small brush, quickly paint the potatoes with the saffron oil, making sure they are well coated. Return the sheet to the highest shelf of the oven for 40-50 minutes, until the potatoes are golden and crunchy. Sprinkle with a little salt before serving with meat or fish or with the marinated chicken recipe on the next page.

Note: Classic plain roasted potatoes are cooked in exactly the same way, without the saffron, and don't forget, it's always important to serve them immediately, before they lose their crunchiness.

Marinated Chicken with Honey and Ginger served with Mango and Golden Raisin Salsa

This is another quick and easy recipe that's helpful for busy people because it needs to be prepared ahead and can then be cooked alongside the Crunchy Roast Potatoes with Saffron on page 186 at the same temperature. So, in theory, you could come home from work and have dinner for four ready in about an hour.

Begin this by making two cuts in each chicken breast, about ¼ inch (5 mm) deep, then place the chicken breasts neatly in the ovenproof dish. Combine all the marinade ingredients in a bowl, whisking them together, then pour this over the chicken breasts, turning them around in the marinade to get them well coated. You now need to cover the dish with plastic wrap and leave it in the refrigerator overnight.

Next, place the golden raisins for the salsa with the lime zest and juice in a small bowl so they can plump up overnight. Cover them with plastic wrap and store in the refrigerator.

When you are ready to cook the chicken, preheat the oven to 425°F (220°C). Remove the plastic wrap from the chicken and baste each breast with the marinade. Bake on the top shelf of the oven (or the next one down from the potatoes) for 20-30 minutes.

While the chicken is cooking, remove the skin from the mango using a potato peeler or sharp knife. Then slice all the flesh away from the pit and chop it into small pieces – about ¼ inch (5 mm) dice. Add it to the golden raisins, along with the remaining salsa ingredients, and garnish just before serving with the cilantro. Serve the cooked chicken with some of the salsa spooned over it and the rest served separately, along with a bowl of the saffron-roasted potatoes.

Serves 4
4 x 6 oz (175 g) bone-in chicken
breast halves, skin on
salt and freshly ground black pepper

For the marinade:
2 tablespoons honey
1 inch (2.5 cm) piece ginger, peeled
and finely grated
1 teaspoon ground ginger
2 cloves garlic, peeled and crushed
zest and juice ½ lime
salt and freshly ground black pepper

For the salsa:
1 medium or ½ large mango
⅓ cup (50 g) golden raisins
zest and juice 1 lime
½ red bell pepper, seeded and chopped
½ medium red onion, peeled and
finely chopped
1 medium green chili, seeded and
finely chopped

To garnish:
¾ cup (10 g) cilantro

You will also need an ovenproof dish
measuring approximately 8 x 6 inches
(20 x 15 cm) and 1¾ inches
(4.5 cm) deep.

Marinated Chicken with Honey and Ginger served with Mango and Golden raisin Salsa and Crunchy Roast Potatoes with Saffron

Potatoes Boulangères with Rosemary

These potatoes are so named because in France they were given to the local baker to place in a bread oven to cook slowly. The nice thing is that you can place them in your oven and simply forget about them until you are ready to serve, and, unlike other potato dishes, they don't mind being kept warm.

Begin by preparing the rosemary, which should be stripped from the stems then bruised in a mortar and pestle. After that, take two-thirds of the leaves and chop them finely. Now, cut the onions in half and then the halves into the thinnest slices possible; the potatoes should be sliced, but not too thinly. All you do is arrange a layer of potatoes, then onions, in the dish, followed by a scattering of rosemary, then season. Continue layering in this way, alternating the potatoes and onions and finishing with a layer of potatoes that slightly overlap. Now, mix the stock and milk together and pour it over the potatoes. Season the top layer, then scatter over the whole rosemary leaves. Now, put little flecks of the butter all over the potatoes and place the dish on the highest shelf of the oven for 50-60 minutes, until the top is crisp and golden and the underneath is creamy and tender.

Serves 6
2 lb 8 oz (1.15 kg) Idaho or round red or white potatoes, peeled
½ oz (10 g) fresh rosemary
2 medium onions, peeled
1¼ cup (275 ml) vegetable stock
⅔ cup (150 ml) milk
3 tablespoons (40 g) butter
sea salt and freshly ground black pepper

You will also need an ovenproof dish measuring 11 x 8 x 2 inches (28 x 20 x 5 cm), lightly buttered.

Preheat the oven to 350°F (180°C).

Oven-Sautéed Potatoes Lyonnaises

Let's face it, though sautéed potatoes are much loved, they are a bother – someone has to stand there and cook them, and for four to six people you'll need, at best, four frying pans. The kitchen gets all greasy, too. Until now, that is, because I've discovered you can just place them in the oven and forget about them until they're ready. They're particularly good alongside the Roast Lamb with Garlic and Rosemary on page 158.

Serves 4-6

2 lb (900 g) round red or white
potatoes, peeled and, if large, halved
2 teaspoons salt
3 tablespoons olive oil
1 medium onion, peeled, halved, then
cut into ¼ inch (5 mm) slices
rock salt

You will also need a flameproof
shallow baking pan measuring
approximately 16 x 11 inches
(40 x 28 cm).

Preheat the oven to 425°F (220°C).

Place the potatoes in a steamer over boiling water and sprinkle them with the 2 teaspoons of salt, cover with a lid, and let them steam for 10 minutes using a timer. When the time is up, remove the steamer, cover the potatoes with a clean dish cloth and allow them to cool slightly. Meanwhile, place the baking pan plus 2 tablespoons of the oil into a high shelf of the oven to preheat for 10 minutes. Then, when the potatoes are cool enough to handle, slice them into rounds about ⅓ inch (7 mm) thick.

Next, remove the baking pan from the oven and place it over a medium direct heat. Now, spoon the potatoes onto the pan and turn and baste them well so they get a good coating of oil, then place them back in the oven, high shelf again, for 10 minutes. While that's happening, toss the onion slices with the remaining tablespoon of oil in a bowl. When the 10 minutes are up, remove the baking pan from the oven and scatter the onion among the potato slices, then return them to the same shelf of the oven for another 10 minutes. Take a look after this time to make sure they are not becoming too brown, but give them another 5 minutes if they are not quite brown enough. Then, when they're ready, sprinkle with rock salt and serve immediately.

Red Onion, Tomato, and Chili Relish

This is a recipe I devised especially for the potato wedges opposite, which I feel are even better with some kind of dipping sauce.

Serves 4

1 small red onion, peeled and
finely chopped
8 oz (225 g) ripe red tomatoes
½ small red chili, seeded and
finely chopped
1 clove garlic, peeled and crushed
1 tablespoon dark brown sugar
½ cup (120 ml) balsamic vinegar
salt and freshly ground black pepper

First, you need to peel the tomatoes, so pour boiling water over them and leave for exactly 1 minute before draining them and slipping off the skins (protect your hands with a cloth if they are too hot). Put the onion, chili, garlic, and tomatoes in a food processor and blend until finely chopped, then place the mixture in a saucepan and add the sugar and vinegar. Place the pan over a gentle heat and simmer very gently, without a lid, for 2 hours, by which time the mixture will have reduced to a thick sauce. Toward the end of the cooking time, stir frequently so the sauce doesn't stick to the bottom of the pan. Then taste to check the seasoning and serve hot or cold. Covered in the refrigerator, the relish will keep for several days.

Oven-Roasted Potato Wedges

These are, believe it or not, low fat – just two teaspoons of oil between four to six people, so not quite as wicked as it would first seem.

First, wash the potatoes very thoroughly, then dry in a dish cloth – they need to be as dry as possible; if they're already washed, just wipe them with paper towel. Leaving the peel on, slice them in half lengthwise and then cut them again lengthwise into chunky wedges approximately 1 inch (2.5 cm) thick. Dry them again in a cloth, then place them in a large bowl with the oil and a sprinkling of salt. Now, toss them around a few times to get them well covered with the oil, then spread them out in the baking pan and place in the oven on a high shelf to roast for about 30 minutes. They should be golden brown and crisp after this time; if not, give them a few more minutes. Finely sprinkle with a little more salt, then serve absolutely immediately.

Serves 4-6
2 lb (900 g) round red or
white potatoes
2 teaspoons olive oil
salt

You will also need a heavy bottomed shallow baking pan measuring approximately 16 x 11 inches (40 x 28 cm).

Preheat the oven to 450°F (230°C).

For Oven-Roasted Potato Wedges with Garlic and Rosemary (add to the basic recipe above):
2 cloves garlic, peeled and crushed
2 tablespoons bruised and chopped rosemary leaves

Oven-Roasted Potato Wedges served with Red Onion, Tomato, and Chili Relish

191

Gnocchi with Sage, Butter, and Parmesan

Once again it's the Italians who are so clever at inventing such simple things out of what seem to be fairly ordinary ingredients which then become something quite outstanding. This happens with gnocchi – little dumplings made from potatoes, flour, and egg. Not very exciting, you might think, but like real pasta made the old-fashioned way, gnocchi have a texture and flavor of their own which can absorb and complement other flavors. This recipe is simple, served with butter, sage, and Parmesan (but is also great with four cheeses, as overleaf). Always make the gnocchi the day you are going to serve them because they discolor if left overnight.

Serves 2-3
10 oz (275 g) round red or white, or Yukon Gold potatoes (about 2 medium-sized potatoes)
¾ cup (95 g) all-purpose flour, sifted, plus a little extra for rolling
1 large egg, lightly beaten
salt and freshly ground black pepper

For the sauce:
4 tablespoons (50 g) butter
1 large clove garlic, peeled and crushed
8 fresh sage leaves

To serve:
3-4 tablespoons freshly grated Parmesan (Parmigiano Reggiano)

You will also need a shallow ovenproof serving dish measuring about 10 x 7 inches (25.5 x 18 cm).

First, place the unpeeled potatoes in a suitably sized saucepan, almost cover with boiling water, add some salt, then cover with a lid and simmer for 20-25 minutes, until tender. Then drain well, and holding them in your hand with a dish cloth, quickly pare off the skins using a potato peeler. Then place the potatoes in a large bowl, and using an electric hand mixer on a slow speed, start to break the potatoes up, then increase the speed and gradually mix until smooth and fluffy. Now, let them cool.

Next, add the sifted flour to the potatoes, along with half the beaten egg, season lightly and, using a fork, bring the mixture together. Then, using your hands, knead the mixture lightly to a soft dough – you may need to add a teaspoonful or so more of the egg if it is a little dry. Transfer the mixture to a lightly floured surface, flour your hands, and divide it into quarters. Now, roll each quarter into a sausage shape approximately ½ inch (1 cm) in diameter; then cut it, on the diagonal, into 1 inch (2.5 cm) pieces, placing them on a pan or plate as they are cut. Cover with plastic wrap and chill for at least 30 minutes, but longer won't matter.

After that, using a fork with the prongs facing upward, press the fork down onto one side of each gnocchi so that it leaves a row of ridges on each one; at the same time, ease them into crescent shapes. The ridges are there to absorb the sauce effectively. Now, cover and chill the gnocchi again until you are ready to cook them.

To cook the gnocchi, first bring a large, shallow pan of approximately 4 quarts (3.5 liters) of water to a simmer and put the serving dish in a low oven to warm through. Then drop the gnocchi into the water and cook for about 3 minutes; they will start to float to the surface after about 2 minutes, but they need 3 altogether. When they are ready, remove the gnocchi with a slotted spoon and transfer them to the warm serving dish. To serve, melt the butter with the garlic over a gentle heat until the garlic turns nut brown in color – about 1 minute. Next, add the sage leaves and allow the butter to froth while the sage leaves turn crisp – about 30 seconds – then spoon the butter mixture over the warm gnocchi. Sprinkle half the Parmesan over and serve the rest separately.

Spinach Gnocchi with Four Cheeses

I dream about eating this recipe on a warm, sunny summer's day outside, but in winter it's still an excellent lunch for two people or as an appetizer for four. For a variation, instead of using all cheese, halve the amount and add 6 oz (175 g) of crisp, crumbled bacon or pancetta.

Serves 2-3

1 medium round red or white, or
Yukon Gold potato – 6 oz (175 g)
8 oz (225 g) baby spinach
¾ cup (175 g) Ricotta
a little freshly grated nutmeg
4 tablespoons (25 g) all-purpose flour,
plus a little extra for rolling
1 large egg
⅓ cup (50 g) Mascarpone
1 tablespoon freshly
snipped chives
2 oz (50 g) creamy Gorgonzola,
roughly cubed
2 oz (50 g) Fontina, cut into
small cubes
2 oz (50 g) Pecorino Romano,
finely grated
salt and freshly ground black pepper

You will also need a shallow ovenproof
serving dish measuring about 10 x 7
inches (25.5 x 18 cm).

First, boil the unpeeled potato which will take about 25 minutes. Meanwhile, pick over the spinach, remove the stems, then rinse the leaves. Place them in a large saucepan over a medium heat and cook briefly covered with a lid for 1-2 minutes, until wilted and collapsed down. Then drain in a colander, and when they are cool enough to handle, squeeze all the moisture out and chop finely.

When the potato is cooked, drain it, and holding it in a dish cloth, peel off the skin and force the potato through a sieve into a bowl. Next, add the spinach, ricotta, nutmeg, and flour to join the potato, then beat the egg and add half, along with some seasoning. Now, gently and lightly using a fork, stir the mixture together. Finish off with your hands, kneading the mixture lightly into a soft dough and adding a teaspoonful or more of the beaten egg if it is a little dry. Then transfer the mixture to a floured surface and divide it into four. Roll each quarter into a sausage shape approximately ½ inch (1 cm) in diameter, then cut it on the diagonal into 1 inch (2.5 cm) pieces, placing them on a pan or plate as they are cut. Cover with plastic wrap and chill for at least 30 minutes, but longer won't matter.

After that, using a fork with the prongs facing upward, press the fork down onto each gnocchi, easing it into a crescent shape, so that it leaves a row of ridges on each one. Cover and chill the gnocchi again until you are ready to cook them.

To cook the gnocchi, have all the cheeses ready. Preheat the broiler to its highest setting, then bring a large, shallow pan of approximately 4 quarts (3.5 liters) of water up to simmering and put the serving dish near the broiler to warm through. Now, drop the gnocchi into the water and cook them for 3 minutes; they will start to float to the surface after about 2 minutes, but they need an extra minute. When they are ready, remove them with a slotted spoon and transfer them directly to the serving dish. When they are all in, quickly stir in first the Mascarpone and chives, then sprinkle in the Gorgonzola and Fontina, then add some seasoning and cover the whole lot with the grated Pecorino. Now, place it under the broiler for 3-4 minutes until it is golden brown and bubbling. Serve absolutely immediately on hot plates.

Note: The plain gnocchi on page 192 can also be served with four cheeses, as above.

Potato Salad with Roquefort

This potato salad, with creamy, piquant Roquefort and the added crunch of celery and shallots, is good to eat all by itself, but I also like to serve it with cold cuts at a buffet lunch. It's therefore a very good recipe to have around the holidays.

Place the potatoes in a steamer over boiling water and sprinkle them with a tablespoon of salt, then cover with a lid, and let them steam for 20-25 minutes.

Meanwhile, make the dressing. To do this, place the garlic, along with the teaspoon of salt, into a mortar and crush it to a creamy mass, then add the mustard and work that in. Next, add the lemon juice, vinegar, and, after that, the oil, then whisk everything together thoroughly. Now, in a medium-sized bowl, first combine the crème fraîche and mayonnaise, then gradually whisk in the dressing. When it's thoroughly blended, add the cheese and season with freshly ground black pepper.

When the potatoes are cooked, remove the steamer and place a cloth over them for about 4 minutes to absorb the steam. Then cut any larger potatoes in half, transfer them to a large bowl, and while they are still warm, pour the dressing over them, along with the shallots and celery. Mix everything gently, then, just before serving, crumble the rest of the Roquefort and the scallions over the salad.

Serves 6-8

2 lb (900 g) small new potatoes
1 oz (25 g) Roquefort, crumbled
4 shallots, peeled and finely chopped
2 celery sticks, trimmed and chopped into ¼ inch (5 mm) pieces
4 scallions, trimmed and finely chopped
salt

For the dressing:
1½ oz (40 g) Roquefort, crumbled
1 clove garlic, peeled
1 teaspoon salt
1½ teaspoons coarse grain mustard
1 tablespoon lemon juice
2 tablespoons balsamic vinegar
2 tablespoons olive oil
⅔ cup (150 ml) crème fraîche
2 tablespoons mayonnaise
freshly ground black pepper

9

All kinds of rice

If you want to cook perfect rice
– the kind that always stays light
and fluffy, with absolutely every
grain remaining separate – then
I can teach you. But first you
will have to make a promise,
and that is to memorize three
simple little words: *leave it
alone!* If you can do this you
will always be able to cook
long-grain rice perfectly, and
never have to worry about it.

The enemy

The number one enemy of fluffy, separate rice is the wooden spoon or, more specifically, the anxious cook who wields it. It is nervous prodding, poking, and constant stirring that ruins rice. So there it is – that's the basic principle for the most common type of rice you'll have to cook, long-grain rice, but, of course, there are other kinds of rice that need different kinds of cooking. So for the beginner it's crucial to know your rice before you attempt to buy or cook it.

Know your rice

The simplest approach to rice cooking is to think in terms of four types of eating categories: first there's the fluffy, separate kind we've talked about; second there's the creamy, soupy kind used in risottos; then the clingy, sticky kind used in the Far East; and finally what I'd call specialty rices, which have a distinctive characteristic of their own and are, therefore, not really in any of the categories already mentioned.

Brown or white?

Grains of rice, like wheat grains, are usually milled, which means the germ and the outer bran layer are removed in the process, revealing the inner grain, which comes in different shades of creamy white to pure white, depending on the variety. If the bran and germ are left intact, the color of the grain is a rather appealing greeny-brown – hence the name brown rice. Here the flavor is more pronounced, slightly nutty, and the texture is less soft, with more bite than white rice.

The advantage is that this rice contains (as you'd expect) more fiber, vitamins, and minerals, but it takes longer to cook: 40 minutes as opposed to 15. But it's good to use both; there are times when I personally prefer brown to white rice for serving with certain dishes – with chili, for instance, or in a rice salad. On the other hand, if I'm serving curry, I always prefer white rice, but it's good to experiment to find out what your own preferences are.

The long and short of it

What usually determines the "eating" categories is the shape of the grain (although there is the occasional exception, as you will see later).

Long-grain rice is precisely that, and the longer and thinner the grain is, the better the quality. So the grains should be mega-slim, with needle-sharp points at each end: this is the type of rice needed for separate, fluffy grains, and the best quality is called *basmati*. This is more expensive than others, but since cooking is about flavor, basmati is the one to buy because it has a far superior taste. Although you will see dozens of varieties of long-grain rice, I believe it's well worth paying that little bit extra for it. Whether you are using the brown or the white, it's quite certainly the best.

Medium- and short-grain rice

Here the grains are not long and thin, but rounder and plumper. This group comes in the creamy and sticky eating category described earlier. There are, however, various qualities and national preferences.

Italian risotto rice, sometimes called *arborio* rice, is superb, or for the finest-quality risotto rice of all, look for the names *carnaroli* or *vialone nano*. In creamy, almost soupy risottos the rice is stirred, which releases some of the starch, and it is this that creates the lovely, smooth, creamy mass. The same kind of plump grain is used in Spain, and one of the finest varieties comes from the Valencia region and is called *calasparra*, which is used to make paella, though here the grains are not stirred, so they remain firm and distinct but with a moist, creamy edge.

In Japan there are several varieties of short-grain rice, ranging from the mildly sticky to the very sticky rice used to make sushi (it makes absolute sense that in the countries where chopsticks are used, rice with a stickier, more clinging consistency is far more manageable). This is sometimes called "glutinous" rice, but it does not, as its name might suggest, contain any gluten and I prefer to describe it as *sticky rice*, which is more accurate.

In Thailand and Southeast Asia the rice grown and preferred is sometimes called *jasmine* or *fragrant rice*, but again I think the title is a little misleading, because it isn't actually any more fragrant than other types of rice. However, the quality is very good, and though it's actually a long-grain rice, the grains have a firm texture and a good bite when cooked, they have a faint stickiness and tend to adhere to each other. I would say in this case the rice is both fluffy and sticky, and this is how it should be.

Specialty rices

These are rice varieties with their own individual characteristics. The first is *red rice*. Red rices are grown in both America and in France (Camargue). Red rice is an unmilled short-grain rice with a brownish-red color, and I would describe its character as earthy and gutsy, with a firm, slightly chewy texture and a nutty flavor. It is excellent in salads and combined with other strong flavors. Because it is a short-grain rice it is very slightly sticky when cooked and it is not a rice meant to be separate and fluffy.

Black rice, well, it's reddish black, is an Asian rice used for sweet dishes and desserts and turns purple when cooked. It's become popular in Australia, where practically every fashionable restaurant has a special dessert made with cooked black rice dressed with a mixture of palm sugar, coconut milk, and lime. If you manage to get some, follow the instructions on the package, which vary.

Wild rice is not actually a rice grain at all but the seed of a special type of grass grown in the swamps of North America. However, it's called rice, so I've put it on my list because it is cooked and served in exactly the same

Top row, left to right: black rice, Thai fragrant rice, Japanese rice
Center, left to right: red rice, brown basmati rice, risotto rice
Bottom row, left to right: wild rice, white basmati rice, short-grain rice

way, but needs about 50 minutes. The seeds are very long and very attractive, with a shiny ebony color, and have a subtle, smoky, nutty flavor. It's good in salads and with gutsy foods with strong flavors. When cooked, the seeds tend to burst and split slightly, but this is quite normal and not some failure in the cooking – though, as with rice grains, it's important not to overcook them.

The "also rans"

There are, of course, a million and one types of rice, and the list I've given you has what I believe to be the best in quality. The "also rans," in a way, perpetuate the myth that cooking rice is difficult, and people usually buy them out of fear. Hopefully, *How To Cook* will dispel the myth and we can all enjoy the best quality of flavor when we're cooking rice. Pre-cooked or par-boiled rice is actually cooked before milling: this means the grains are tougher, requiring more water and a much longer cooking time. This is to help the grains stay more separate, but in my opinion there is a loss of flavor and I would never choose it. Quick-cooking rice has been partially cooked after milling and then dried, so all it has to do is re-absorb water. It is quicker to cook, only 8-10 minutes instead of 12-15, but the loss of character and flavor puts this in the "white bread" category, ie, dull and flat.

Dessert rice

Since I was a small child – a long time ago – we have always had in Britain a variety of short-grain rice called "pudding rice" which is used in sweet dishes. Risotto rice makes a good substitute to use in recipes such as good Old-Fashioned Rice Pudding (see page 214). It is very sticky when cooked and, simmered in milk, becomes deliciously soft and creamy.

Always measure your rice by volume, using double the amount of water to rice

First cook the onions, then add the rice, turning the grains to coat them in the oil

The next stage is to add the boiling water and salt to the rice in the pan

To wash or not to wash?

I have never washed rice since I discovered that it is possible to wash away some of the nutrients in the process, and in any case, modern rice is thoroughly cleaned in the milling. What's more, the water it's cooked in will be boiling, and that, of course, will purify it. I think some of the traditional methods of cooking rice, which require long rinsing and washing, belong to past times, when the rice was not as clean as it is today.

The ten rules for cooking perfect rice

1 Always measure rice by volume and not by weight.

2 Coating the grains of rice in a little oil before adding the water can help to keep them separate, and adding a little onion (see the recipe that follows) can provide extra flavor. But this is not a necessity – rice can be cooked quite simply in water.

3 The quantity of liquid you will need is roughly double the volume of rice, so ½ cup (100ml) needs 1 cup (250ml) of water or stock. Always add hot water or stock.

4 Don't forget to add salt, about 1 teaspoon to every cup (200ml) of rice.

5 The very best utensil for cooking fluffy, separate rice is a frying pan with a lid. Over the years I have found that the shallower the rice is spread out during cooking the better. Buying a 10 inch (25.5 cm) pan with a lid would be a good lifetime investment for rice cooking. Other than that, try to find a large saucepan lid that will fit your normal frying pan.

Stir once only – more will break the delicate grains, resulting in sticky rice

Cover with a lid, turn the heat to its lowest setting and leave for 15 minutes

Once ready, remove the pan from the heat and cover with a cloth for 5-10 minutes

6 After the hot liquid has been added, stir once only, cover with the lid and turn the heat down to its lowest setting, Give white rice 15 minutes and brown rice 40.

7 Leave it alone! Once the lid is on, set the timer and go away. If you lift the lid and let the steam out you can slow down the cooking process, and rice should always be cooked as briefly as possible. Even worse, if you stir it you will break the delicate grains and release the starch, and then it will end up sticky.

8 Use a timer – overcooking is what ruins rice. The best way to test if it is cooked is simply to bite a grain. Another way is to tilt the pan, and if liquid collects at the edge, it will need a couple more minutes' cooking.

9 When the rice is cooked, remove the lid, turn the heat off, and place a clean dish cloth over the pan for 5-10 minutes. This will absorb the steam and help keep the grains dry and separate.

10 Just before serving, use the tip of a skewer or a fork to lightly fluff up the grains.

Perfect Rice

Serves 4

1½ cups (275 ml) white basmati rice
1½ teaspoons peanut or other mildly flavored oil
1 small onion, peeled and finely chopped
2½ cups (570 ml) boiling water
1 teaspoon salt

You will also need a frying pan with a 10 inch (25.5 cm) bottom and a tight-fitting lid.

Begin by warming the frying pan over a medium heat, then add the oil and the onions and let them cook for 3-4 minutes until lightly tinged brown. Next, stir in the rice – there's no need to wash it – and turn the grains over in the pan so they become lightly coated and glistening with oil. Then add the boiling water, along with the salt, stir once only, then cover with the lid. Turn the heat to its very lowest setting and let the rice cook gently for exactly 15 minutes. Don't remove the lid and don't stir the rice during cooking, because this is what will break the grains and release their starch, which makes the rice sticky.

After 15 minutes, tilt the pan to check that no liquid is left; if there is, place it back on the heat for another minute. When there is no water left in the pan, take the pan off the heat, remove the lid and cover with a clean dish cloth for 5-10 minutes before serving, then transfer the rice to a warm serving dish and fluff it lightly with a fork before it goes to the table.

Oven-Baked Risotto Carbonara

I love pasta with carbonara sauce so much that one day I thought I'd try it with a risotto – same ingredients: pancetta (a strong-flavored Italian bacon) eggs, and sharp Pecorino cheese. The result is amazingly good and got one of the highest votes from the crew when we were filming.

First of all, place a large frying pan over medium heat, and when it is hot fry the pancetta or bacon in its own fat for 4-5 minutes, until it's crisp and golden, then remove it to a plate. Next, add the butter to the pan, then the onion; turn the heat down to low and let the onion soften in the butter for about 5 minutes. Meanwhile, heat the stock in a small saucepan. Then return the pancetta or bacon to the frying pan and stir in the rice, moving it around until all the grains are coated with the buttery juices. Now, add the hot stock to the rice along with some salt and freshly ground black pepper. Let it all come up to a gentle simmer, then transfer the rice mixture to the warmed ovenproof dish. Stir it once and then bake, without covering, on the center shelf of the oven and set a timer for 20 minutes.

When the time is up, gently stir in the Pecorino, folding and turning the rice grains over; then set the timer for another 15 minutes. Meanwhile, whisk the egg, egg yolks, and crème fraîche together, then remove the risotto from the oven and gently stir in this mixture, making sure it is well mixed. Leave the risotto for about 2 minutes by which time the eggs and crème fraîche will have thickened – but no longer or it will get too thick. Serve on warm plates with some more Pecorino Romano sprinkled on top.

Note: This recipe contains raw eggs.

Serves 2

1¼ cups (225 ml) carnaroli rice
¾ cup (125 g) chopped bacon
or pancetta
2 tablespoons (25 g) butter
1 medium onion, peeled and
finely chopped
3 cups (725 ml) chicken or
vegetable stock
3 oz (75 g) finely grated Pecorino
Romano, plus some extra
for sprinkling
1 large egg
2 large egg yolks
2 tablespoons crème fraîche
salt and freshly ground black pepper

You will also need a round ovenproof dish with a diameter of 9 inches (23 cm), 2 inches (5 cm) deep, placed in the oven when it's preheated.

Preheat the oven to 300°F (150°C).

Chinese Stir-Fried Rice

The most important point to remember if you want to fry rice successfully is that it must be cooked but cold. I have used authentic Chinese ingredients here, which are easily obtainable if you live near specialty Chinese suppliers; if not, you can use fresh shrimp instead of dried shrimp and fresh shiitake mushrooms instead of dried ones.

Begin by putting the shrimp and mushrooms in a small bowl, pour the boiling water over them and let them soak for 30 minutes. Then squeeze the liquid from them, discard the mushroom stems, and slice the mushrooms finely. Then heat half the oil in the wok or pan, and when it's really hot, quickly fry the onions and bacon for 3 minutes, moving them around in the pan until the bacon is crispy. Then add the shrimp, peas, and mushrooms and stir-fry these for about 1 minute. Now, add the remaining oil to the pan, and when it's smoking hot, add the rice and stir-fry, this time for about 30 seconds. Now, spread the ingredients out in the pan and pour in the beaten eggs. It won't look very good now, but keep on stir-frying, turning the mixture over, and the eggs will soon cook into little shreds that mingle with the other ingredients. Finally, add the scallions and soy sauce, give it one more good stir and serve.

Serves 4

1¼ cups (225 ml) white basmati rice, cooked as for Perfect Rice (see page 202, but using 2 cups/450 ml
boiling water, cooled
⅓ cup (25 g) Chinese dried shrimp
3 to 4 (5 g) Chinese dried mushrooms
2 cups (450 ml) boiling water
1½ tablespoons peanut or other mildly flavored oil
1 small onion, peeled and finely chopped
4 bacon strips, chopped into ¼ inch (5 mm) pieces
⅓ cup (50 g) peas, fresh if possible, defrosted if frozen
2 large eggs, lightly beaten
2 scallions, split lengthwise and finely chopped
1 tablespoon Japanese soy sauce

You will also need a wok or frying pan with a 10 inch (25.5 cm) bottom.

Chinese Stir-Fried Rice served with Asian Steamed Fish with Ginger, Soy, and Sesame

Asian Steamed Fish with Ginger, Soy, and Sesame

This can be a quick dinner dish for the family or it's exotic enough for entertaining: all you need is a collapsible steamer – bamboo or the old-fashioned metal kind.

You need to begin this by having a little chopping session. First the ginger, which should be thinly sliced then cut into very fine shreds. The garlic needs to be chopped small, as do the scallions, making sure you include the green parts as well.

Now, place a medium frying pan over a medium heat and, when it's hot, add the sesame seeds and toast them in the dry pan, shaking it from time to time until they're a golden brown color – this takes only 1-2 minutes. Now, transfer the seeds to a bowl.

Next, add the oils to the pan, and over a medium heat, gently fry the chopped garlic and ginger – they need to be pale gold but not too brown, so be careful not to have the heat too high. After that, add these to the toasted seeds, along with any oil left in the pan, then mix in the lemon juice, soy sauce, and chopped scallions.

Now, season the fish, spread three-quarters of the mixture over the surface of each skinned side, roll them up quite firmly into little rolls, then spoon the rest of the mixture on top of each roll. All this can be prepared in advance, as long as the fish is kept covered in the refrigerator.

Then, when you're ready to cook the fish, line the bottom of the steamer with the lettuce leaves (or foil if you don't have any). Now, place the fish on top, cover with a lid, and steam over boiling water for 8-10 minutes. Serve with the Chinese Stir-Fried Rice, left.

Serves 4

1 lb 8 oz (700 g) lemon sole or flounder fillets, skinned and cut lengthwise down the natural dividing line (ask the fishseller to do this)
2½ inch (6 cm) piece ginger, peeled
1 tablespoon Japanese soy sauce
1½ tablespoons sesame seeds
2 teaspoons sesame oil
3 cloves garlic, peeled
2 scallions
2 teaspoons peanut or other mildly flavored oil
juice 1 lemon
a few outside lettuce leaves, for lining the steamer
salt and freshly ground black pepper

You will also need a collapsible or bamboo steamer.

Very Red Rice

This was a recipe created for the charity Comic Relief. It is good with any barbecue dishes or with the pork chops opposite.

Serves 4
1½ cups (275 ml) red (Camargue, if possible) or black japonica rice
1 tablespoon oil
1 tablespoon (10 g) butter
1 small red bell pepper, seeded and finely chopped
1 small red onion, peeled and finely chopped
2 cups (425 ml) boiling water
1 teaspoon salt

To serve:
2 scallions, trimmed and finely sliced
a few sprigs watercress

You will also need a 10 inch (25.5 cm) frying pan with a lid.

First, heat the oil and butter in the pan over a medium heat. Then turn it up to high and stir-fry the chopped bell pepper and onion until they are softened and slightly blackened at the edges – 6-7 minutes. After that, turn the heat right down, add the red rice to the pan, and stir it around to get a good coating of oil. Now, pour in the boiling water and salt and stir again. When it reaches the simmering point, put the lid on and let it cook very gently for 40 minutes. After that, don't remove the lid, just turn the heat off and leave it for another 15 minutes to finish off. Garnish the rice with the sliced scallions and the watercress. Serve with the Oven-Baked Pork Chops in Maple Barbecue Sauce, opposite.

Very Red Rice served with Oven-Baked Pork Chops in Maple Barbecue Sauce

Oven-Baked Pork Chops in Maple Barbecue Sauce

Sorry about the long list of ingredients in this sauce, but it really does take only 5 minutes to make, then cooks into a heavenly, sticky, spicy goo.

First of all mix the olive oil with the lemon juice, then place the pork chops in the roasting pan with the chopped onion tucked among them. Season with a little salt and freshly ground black pepper, then brush the chops with the oil and lemon juice. You can, if you like, do this well in advance, just cover with a cloth and leave in a cool place.

Then, when you're ready to cook the pork chops, preheat the oven to 400°F (200°C), then place them in on a high shelf and cook for 25 minutes exactly. Meanwhile, combine all the sauce ingredients in a bowl and, using a small whisk, blend everything thoroughly. Then, when the 25 minutes are up, remove the roasting pan from the oven, pour off any surplus fat from the corner of the pan, and pour the sauce over the pork chops, giving everything a good coating.

Now, back it goes into the oven for about another 25 minutes; you will need to baste it twice during this time. After that, remove the roasting pan from the oven and place it over direct heat turned to medium. Then pour in the red wine, stir it into the sauce and let it bubble for about 1 minute. Then serve the pork chops on a bed of Very Red Rice with the sauce spooned over and garnish with the sprigs of watercress.

Serves 4

4 pork chops
1 tablespoon olive oil
2 teaspoons lemon juice
1 medium onion, peeled and finely chopped
salt and freshly ground black pepper

For the sauce:

2 tablespoons pure maple syrup
⅓ cup (75 ml) red wine
4 tablespoons Japanese soy sauce
2 tablespoons red wine vinegar
2 tablespoons tomato paste
1½ teaspoons ground ginger
1½ teaspoons mustard powder
2 cloves garlic, peeled and crushed
1½ teaspoons Tabasco sauce

To finish:

¼ cup (55 ml) red wine
a few sprigs watercress

You will also need a flameproof shallow roasting pan measuring 12 x 8 x 1¾ inches (30 x 20 x 4.5 cm).

Red Rice Salad with Feta Cheese

This is a lovely salad for outdoor eating on a warm, sunny summer's day.

Serves 4

1½ cups (275 ml) red (Camargue, if possible) or black japonica rice
7 oz (200 g) Feta cheese
1 teaspoon salt
2½ cups (570 ml) boiling water
2 shallots, peeled and finely chopped
1 bunch (50 g) fresh arugula, finely shredded
3 scallions, trimmed and finely chopped, including the green ends
salt and freshly ground black pepper

For the dressing:
1 small clove garlic, crushed
½ teaspoon salt
1 teaspoon coarse grain mustard
1 tablespoon balsamic vinegar
2 tablespoons extra virgin olive oil
salt and freshly ground black pepper

You will also need a 10 inch (25.5 cm) frying pan with a lid.

First, put the rice in the frying pan with the teaspoon of salt, then pour in the boiling water, bring it back up to simmering, then cover with a lid and let it cook very gently for 40 minutes. After that, don't remove the lid, just turn the heat off and leave it for another 15 minutes to finish off.

Meanwhile, make the dressing by crushing the garlic and salt in a mortar and pestle, then when it becomes a purée, add the mustard and work that in, followed by the vinegar and some freshly ground black pepper. Now, add the oil, and using a small whisk, whisk everything thoroughly to combine it. Then transfer the warm rice to a serving dish, pour the dressing over it, and mix thoroughly. Taste to check the seasoning and set aside until cold. Then add the shallots, the arugula, and the scallions. Finally, just before serving, crumble the Feta cheese over all.

Shrimp Jambalaya

This is one of the easiest and nicest rice dishes, and its origins are in traditional Cajun cooking. It's very easy to adapt it to whatever you have handy – fish, chicken, or even pork.

Begin by bringing a pan with 2½ cups (570 ml) of water to the simmering point. If using raw shrimp, drop them into the water for 3 minutes. After that, remove them with a slotted spoon, reserving the cooking liquid. (Cooked shrimp will not need this pre-cooking.) Now, set aside two whole shrimp and shell the rest. To do this, just remove the heads (if necessary), by giving them a sharp tug, then simply peel off the rest – which comes away very easily – but leave the tails intact since this makes them look nicer. Now, remove the black vein from the back of each shrimp, which will come away easily using the point of a sharp knife. Next, place the shells in the pan of water and simmer for 30 minutes, without a lid, to make a nice shrimp-flavored stock, then drain and discard the shells. Pour the hot stock into a bowl and cover with a plate to keep warm.

Now, heat the frying pan over a high heat and brown the pieces of chorizo, without adding any fat, then remove them from the pan to a plate and set aside. Then add a tablespoon of the oil, and when it's hot, fry the onions for 2-3 minutes to brown them a little at the edges; then return the chorizo to the pan and add the garlic, celery, chili, and sliced bell pepper. Continue to fry for 4-5 minutes, until the celery and bell pepper are also softened and lightly tinged brown at the edges, adding a little more oil if you need to. Now, stir in the rice to get a good coating of oil, then measure out 1½ cups (340 ml) of the reserved stock and add the Tabasco to it. Next, add the chopped tomatoes and bay leaf to the pan, then pour in the stock. Season with salt and freshly ground black pepper, give it all one stir, and push the rice down into the liquid. Now, turn the heat to low, cover with a lid and let it barely simmer for 20 minutes. Then, check the rice is cooked and return the shelled and the two reserved shell-on shrimp to the pan, adding a little more stock if necessary. Cover with a lid for 5 more minutes, then serve garnished with the chopped parsley and scallions.

Serves 2-3

8 shrimp, shell on, fresh, or frozen and thoroughly defrosted, or you could use cooked jumbo shrimp in their shells
4 oz (110 g) chorizo sausage, peeled and cut into ¾ inch (2 cm) pieces
1-2 tablespoons olive oil
1 medium onion, peeled and cut into ½ inch (1 cm) slices
2 cloves garlic, peeled and crushed
2 sticks celery, trimmed and sliced into ½ inch (1 cm) pieces on the diagonal
1 green chili, seeded and finely chopped
1 yellow bell pepper, seeded and cut into ½ inch (1 cm) slices
1 cup (175 ml) white basmati rice
1 teaspoon Tabasco sauce
3 medium tomatoes, dropped into boiling water for 1 minute, then peeled and chopped
1 bay leaf
1 tablespoon roughly chopped flat-leaf parsley, to garnish
2 scallions, trimmed and finely sliced, to garnish
salt and freshly ground black pepper

You will also need a 10 inch (25.5 cm) frying pan with a lid.

Spiced Pilau Rice with Nuts

I've always loved the fragrant flavor of spiced pilau rice, and could easily eat it on its own, adding nuts to give it some crunch. However, it's also an excellent accompaniment to any spiced or curried dish, particularly the chicken recipe that follows.

Serves 4

1½ cups (275 ml) white basmati rice
¼ cup (25 g) unsalted cashew nuts
¼ cup (25 g) unsalted shelled pistachio nuts
¼ cup (25 g) pine nuts
2 cardamom pods
¾ teaspoon cumin seeds
½ teaspoon coriander seeds
1½ tablespoons peanut or other mildly flavored oil
1 small onion, peeled and finely chopped
2½ cups (570 ml) boiling water
1 inch (2.5 cm) piece cinnamon stick
1 bay leaf
1¼ teaspoons salt

You will also need a lidded frying pan with a 10 inch (25.5 cm) bottom.

First of all, in the mortar and pestle, crush the cardamom pods and the cumin and coriander seeds. Then, warm the frying pan over a medium heat, add the crushed spices (the pods as well as the seeds of the cardamom), turn the heat up high, and toss them around in the heat to dry-roast them and draw out the flavor – this will take about 1 minute. After that, turn the heat back to medium and add the oil, onion, and nuts and fry until everything is lightly tinged brown. Next, stir in the rice and turn the grains over in the pan until they are nicely coated and glistening with oil, then pour in the boiling water. Add the cinnamon, bay leaf, and a good seasoning of salt; stir once only, then cover with a lid, turn the heat down to its lowest setting, and let the rice cook for exactly 15 minutes. After this time, take the pan off the heat, remove the lid, and cover with a clean dish cloth for 5 minutes. Then empty the rice into a warm serving dish and fluff up lightly with a fork before it goes to the table.

Marinated Chicken Kebabs with Whole Spices served with Spiced Rice Pilau with Nuts

This is a heavenly combination of textures and fragrant, spicy flavors, and has the added advantage of not being too high in fat. The cilantro chutney, pictured below, is a perfect accompaniment, but this dish also goes well with mango chutney if cilantro isn't available.

Begin by dry-roasting the cumin and coriander seeds and the cardamom pods over a medium heat for 1 minute until the seeds begin to jump. Remove from the heat, and once cool, remove the seeds from the cardamom pods and crush them with the cumin and coriander seeds using a mortar and pestle. Next, add the ginger, turmeric, garlic, and salt and mix everything well.

Now, cut each chicken breast into five pieces, place them in a bowl and toss them first in the peanut oil, then in the spice mixture, mixing everything around so they get an even coating. Next, add the yogurt, give everything a good stir, and press the chicken down well into the marinade. Cover with plastic wrap and refrigerate for a few hours or, preferably, overnight.

To make the chutney, simply blend everything together in a blender, then pour into a bowl and set aside for 2-3 hours so the flavors develop.

When you are almost ready to serve, soak the skewers in water for 20 minutes to prevent them from burning, then light the barbecue or preheat the broiler to its highest setting. Next, thread half a bay leaf onto each skewer, then a piece of chicken, a piece of onion, and half a chili. Continue alternating the chicken, onion, and chili until you have used five pieces of chicken per kebab, then finish with half a bay leaf on each. Make sure you pack everything as tightly as possible, then season, place the kebabs on the broiler rack or barbecue, and sprinkle with a little olive oil. If you're broiling, put a heatproof dish lined with foil under the rack and broil the kebabs for 10 minutes on each side, about 4 inches (10 cm) from the heat source, or simply cook over the barbecue.

Now, slip the chicken and vegetables from the skewers, using a fork to ease them off, and serve with the Spiced Pilau Rice with Nuts, garnished with lime quarters, and the chutney passed around separately.

Serves 4
4 x 6 oz (175 g) boneless chicken breast halves, skin on
4 bay leaves, cut in half
½ red onion, peeled, halved through the root and separated into layers
8 fresh green chilies, halved and seeded
a little olive oil
salt and freshly ground black pepper

For the marinade:
1 teaspoon whole cumin seeds
1½ teaspoons whole coriander seeds
12 cardamom pods
1½ tablespoons peeled and grated ginger
1½ tablespoons turmeric
3 cloves garlic, peeled and crushed
½ teaspoon sea salt or rock salt
1 tablespoon peanut or other mildly flavored oil
1¼ cups (275 ml) plain yogurt

For the cilantro chutney:
3 cups (25 g) cilantro
2 tablespoons lime juice
1 fresh green chili, halved and seeded
1 clove garlic, peeled
3 tablespoons plain yogurt
½ teaspoon superfine sugar
salt and freshly ground black pepper

To garnish:
2 limes, quartered

You will also need four wooden skewers about 10 inches (25.5 cm) long.

Thai Creamed Coconut Chicken

Serves 4

1 cooked chicken weighing about
2 lb 4 oz (1 kg), off the bone, or 5
cooked chicken breast halves
2 cups (400 ml) coconut milk
1 teaspoon coriander seeds
½ teaspoon cumin seeds
2 cardamom pods, lightly crushed
2 tablespoons peanut or other mildly
flavored oil
2 medium onions, peeled
and finely sliced
2 cloves garlic, peeled and crushed
½ oz (10 g) cilantro
1 teaspoon turmeric
4 red chilies, seeded and
finely chopped
2 teaspooons finely chopped fresh
lemon grass
2 tablespoons lime juice
salt and freshly ground black pepper

The very good news about this fantastic recipe for busy people is that it's made with pre-cooked chicken. You can, of course, cook the chicken yourself, but either way it's a quick but excellent dinner party dish for four people, and it's extra special served with the Thai Green Rice.

To prepare the chicken, remove the skin and cut the flesh into strips about 2½ inches (6 cm) long. Next, the spices will need roasting, so heat a large frying pan or wok – without any fat in it – and, when it's really hot, add the coriander, cumin, and cardamom pods. Allow the spices to roast briefly – about 45 seconds – shaking the pan from time to time, then tip them into a mortar, removing the seeds from the cardamom pods and discarding the husks, and crush them all fairly finely.

Now, add the oil to the frying pan or wok. When it's really hot, fry the onions and garlic over a medium heat for 8-9 minutes, until they're nicely softened. Meanwhile, strip the leaves from the cilantro stems, reserve these, then chop the stems finely.

When the onions are ready, add the turmeric, chili, crushed spices, and cilantro stems, along with the lemon grass, to the pan. Stir these thoroughly together, then pour in the coconut milk and lime juice. Add some seasoning, then simmer everything gently for about 10 minutes, uncovered, by which time the sauce should have reduced and thickened.

Now, add the chicken to the sauce and simmer gently for 10 minutes or so to heat it through completely. Serve the chicken on a bed of Thai Green Rice, garnished with the cilantro leaves.

Thai Green Rice

This, thankfully, is a Thai recipe that doesn't require all the speciality ingredients that are sometimes so elusive. The list of ingredients, again, seems rather long, but it is made in moments and has a lovely fragrant flavor.

Serves 4

1½ cups (340 ml) basmati rice
2 cups (400 ml) coconut milk
4 cloves garlic, peeled
3 large or 2 medium-sized fresh green
chilies, seeded

Begin by placing the coconut milk in a food processor with the garlic, chilies, ginger, and cilantro stems, mixing until everything is finely chopped.

Set this aside while you heat the oil over a gentle heat in the frying pan, then add the cinnamon sticks, cloves, peppercorns, and cashew nuts to the pan and sauté everything gently for about 1 minute. Next, add the onions and continue to cook over a medium heat until they become softened and pale gold in color, which will take 8-10 minutes. Next, add the rice, then stir once and cook for another 2-3 minutes. After that, add the coconut mixture, give everything a stir, and cook for another 2-3 minutes. Now, add the peas, salt, and hot water, bring it up to a gentle simmer, then cover with the lid. Turn the heat to low and let everything cook very gently for 8 minutes; use a timer here, and don't lift the lid.

Then remove the pan from the heat, take the lid off, and cover the pan with a cloth for 10 minutes before serving. Finally, remove the pieces of cinnamon, sprinkle in the lime juice and the finely chopped cilantro leaves; then fork the rice gently to separate the grains. Garnish with the reserved whole cilantro leaves and serve with the Thai Creamed Coconut Chicken.

1½-inch (4 cm) cube ginger, peeled
¾ oz (20 g) cilantro, leaves removed and finely chopped, the stems reserved, with a few whole leaves reserved for the garnish
1½ tablespoons peanut or other mildly flavored oil
3 x 2 inch (5 cm) pieces cinnamon stick
6 whole cloves
15 black peppercorns
⅓ cup (40 g) unsalted cashew nuts, halved
2 medium onions, peeled and finely sliced
¾ cup (110 g) fresh peas, or frozen and defrosted
1½ teaspoons salt, or to taste
2 cups (425 ml) hot water
2 tablespoons lime juice

You will also need a 9 inch (23 cm) frying pan with a close-fitting lid.

Thai Creamed Coconut Chicken served with Thai Green Rice

213

Old-Fashioned Rice Pudding

This is the real thing – a mass of creamy rice and a thick brown speckled nutmeg skin. Don't forget to take a sharp knife and scrape off all the bits of caramelized skin that stick to the edges – my grandmother always did that and served everyone an equal amount.

This is simplicity itself, because all you do is mix the evaporated milk and whole milk together in a bowl, then place the rice and sugar in the ovenproof dish, pour in the liquid, and give it all a good stir. Grate the whole nutmeg all over the surface (it may seem a lot but it needs it), then, finally, dot the butter on top in little flecks.

Next, just carefully place the dish in the oven on the center shelf and leave it there for 30 minutes, then slide the shelf out and give everything a good stir. Repeat the stirring after another 30 minutes, then place the dish back in the oven to cook for another hour, this time without stirring. At the end of this time the rice grains will have become swollen, with pools of creamy liquid all around them, and, of course, all that lovely skin! This is wonderful served warm with the Plums in Marsala, opposite.

Serves 4-6

½ cup plus 1 tablespoon (110 g) arborio rice

1½ cups (350 ml) evaporated milk

2½ cups (570 ml) whole milk

3 tablespoons (40 g) granulated or superfine sugar

1 whole nutmeg

2 tablespoons (25 g) butter

You will also need a round ovenproof dish with a diameter of 9 inches (23 cm), 2 inches (5 cm) deep, lightly buttered.

Preheat the oven to 300°F (150°C).

Plums in Marsala

The mellow but distinctive flavor of Marsala wine, when simmered together with fruit, is something I am particularly fond of. It works well with plums, which, I think, are very good served chilled along with the warm rice pudding opposite.

First, place the plums, vanilla bean, and cinnamon sticks in the baking dish, then mix the Marsala with the sugar and pour it over the plums. Now, place the dish on the center shelf of the oven and cook for 40 minutes, uncovered, turning the plums over in the Marsala halfway through the cooking time. Then remove the baking dish from the oven and strain the plums, discarding the vanilla bean and cinnamon sticks, and pour the sauce into a medium-sized saucepan. Bring it up to simmering point, then let it bubble and reduce for 5 minutes. Now, mix the arrowroot with a little water in a cup to make a paste, then whisk this into the liquid. Bring the sauce back to the simmering point, whisking all the time, until it has thickened slightly and is glossy – about 5 minutes. Then pour it back over the plums and serve them hot or cold.

Serves 6
3 lb (1.35 kg) fresh firm plums
2½ cups (570 ml) Marsala
1 vanilla bean
2 cinnamon sticks
½ cup (75 g) superfine sugar
2 teaspoons arrowroot

You will also need a 10 x 8 inch (25.5 x 20 cm) baking dish, 2 inches (5 cm) deep.

Preheat the oven to 350°F (180°C).

10
Pasta revisited

I think it's about time we gave pasta a radical rethinking. In the 1960s only two kinds of pasta were known to most people: spaghetti, which often came in cans, and macaroni, which was often served in a cheese sauce. Yet, 30 years later, pasta has exploded into our lives with such force that it's now become almost a staple. The trouble is that a lot of pasta we eat today is not, in the strictest sense, real pasta; not in the way it was originally and brilliantly conceived to be. And now many modern pasta makers have, I feel, completely lost the point.

What is real pasta?

Originally, pasta in Italy was a conception of sheer genius. It began with growing the highest-quality hard wheat, and the name given to this specific type of wheat was durum, from the Latin, meaning hard. After the pasta maker had purchased exactly the right grain, the next important stage was finding the right miller to mill the grain to a certain precise specification – and not to a fine, powdery flour but to something called semolina, which is derived from the Italian for "semi milled" and is quite unlike flour, since semolina is made up of tiny, coarse, corn-colored granules with sharp edges.

The skill of the pasta maker was to then carefully mix the semolina with cold water. Then, after the mixing came the shaping, and the pasta was forced through special bronze dies, which gave it a specific texture. After that the pasta was dried in open-windowed lofts where either the mountain air or sea breezes – or both, depending on the region – could circulate. This carefully monitored drying process could take up to two days. It was this natural drying process, along with the specifications above, that produced a quality of pasta that had captured within it all the nuttiness and flavor of the wheat grain but also a special texture. The semolina and the effect of the bronze dies produced a roughness at the edges which, in its grand design, would provide, when cooked, the right kind of surface on which the sauce being served with it would adhere and cling and not slide off. So simple, so subtle, and so wonderful.

Modern pasta (and clones)

What happened next was that, soon, everybody outside Italy wanted to eat pasta, too, and once this kind of mass production was under way, corners were cut, profit margins came into play, soft flour was added, hot instead of cold water, there were nylon dies, speeded-up hot-air quick-drying, and the whole process underwent a shift from quality to competitive price wars and then it was the "quality-downward-spiral" all over again.

But something else has crept into the picture at the same time and that is the misguided and false conception that fresh pasta is better than dried. Yes, Italians do make and eat a very small amount of *pasta fresca*, but it is a different concept; one that more usually involves a filling, as in ravioli or tortellini. But in Britian and the US – *pasta fresca* has gone crazy. It's now a far cry from the original described above and it's a strange paradox to clone a product that has a natural shelf life of two years, then make it and sell it as fresh, then add something that will give it a longer shelf life and at the same time call the resulting slithery, slimy gloop made with soft flour and eggs "pasta."

The other modern misconception is to serve more sauce than pasta. Good pasta should be enjoyed for itself, with a small amount of concentrated sauce used to merely dress it.

The case for good-quality dried pasta

If you want to enjoy cooking and eating pasta at its best, then my advice is to buy good-quality dried pasta. Yes, it does cost more, but we're not talking about great luxury here; we're talking about a main dish for two people that might cost $4 instead of $2.

There are a few artisanal pasta makers in Italy who still make the real thing; check local specialty food stores. The only fresh pastas I ever buy are ravioli, stuffed pasta shapes, or lasagne sheets, which are, I think, of a far better quality than most of the dried packages. Once you taste quality dried pasta, it will be very hard for you to return to the industrially produced alternatives. It's not just the flavor – the firm, rough texture not only puts it way out in front but actually helps you to achieve that *al dente* "firm to the teeth" texture that is the mark of well-cooked pasta. Poor quality often ends up sticky and soggy. So when you buy your pasta, make sure it says *pasta di semola di grano duro* – durum wheat semolina pasta.

There are certain dried pastas that contain eggs – *pasta all' uovo* – which add richness, but I now prefer the original semolina and water version keeping the richness confined to the sauce.

Below, from top: dried spaghetti, penne, macaroni, and rigatoni pastas

How to cook perfect pasta

The easiest way to communicate this is to give you a list of what is absolutely essential.

1. Always use a very large cooking pot.
2. Always make absolutely sure you have at least 2½ quarts (2.25 liters) of water to every 8 oz (225 g) of pasta, with 1 tablespoon of salt added.
3. Make sure the water comes up to a good fierce boil before the pasta goes in.
4. Add the pasta as quickly as possible and stir it around just once to separate it. If you're cooking long pasta, like spaghetti, push it against the bottom of the pan, and as you feel it give, keep pushing until it all collapses down into the water.
5. You don't need to put a lid on the pan; if it's really boiling briskly it will come back to a boil in seconds, and if you cover it, it will boil over.
6. Put a timer on and give it 10-12 minutes for top-quality pasta, but because this timing varies according to the shape and quality of the pasta, the only real way to tell is to taste it. So do this after 8 minutes, then 9, and 10, and so on. This only applies when you cook a particular brand for the first time. After that, you will know how long it takes. Sometimes you can give it 1 minute's less boiling and then allow an extra minute's cooking while you combine it with the sauce.
7. Have a colander ready in the sink, then, as you are draining the water, swirl it around the colander, warming it for the hot pasta.

8 Don't drain it too thoroughly; it's good to have a few drops of moisture still clinging since this prevents the pasta from becoming dry. Place the colander back over the saucepan to catch any drips.

9 Always serve it on deep, warmed plates to keep the pasta as hot as possible as it goes to the table.

10 For spaghetti, the very best way to serve it is to use pasta tongs (see the photograph opposite), and always lift it high to quickly separate each portion from the rest.

11 If the pasta is going to be cooked again, in a baked dish like macaroni and cheese, for example, give it half the usual cooking time to allow for further cooking time in the oven.

12 *Presto pronto!* In Italian this means soon and quickly. Always work quickly, as pasta won't hang around – if it cools it becomes sticky and gluey, so drain it quickly, serve it quickly, and eat it quickly.

How to eat spaghetti and other long pastas

This is how I describe this in the *Cookery Course*. "The big mistake here is trying to wind too much onto the fork at once. Select just two or three strands with your fork and coax them over the rim of the plate. Then, holding the fork at a right angle to the plate, simply wind the fork round and round, so that those few strands extricate themselves from the rest and are twisted round the fork in a little bite-sized bundle. Easier said than done, you're thinking? But remember – practice makes perfect."

Spaghetti with Olive Oil, Garlic, and Chili

This one is pure pasta eaten and savored for its own sake with the minimum amount of adornment – just a hint of garlic, chili, and olive oil.

Serves 2
8 oz (225 g) spaghetti or linguine
4 tablespoons Italian extra virgin olive oil
2 fat cloves garlic, peeled and finely chopped
1 fat red chili, seeded and finely chopped
freshly ground black pepper

Begin by putting the pasta on to cook. Then, just heat the olive oil in a small frying pan and, when it is hot, add the garlic, chili, and some freshly ground black pepper. Cook these very gently for about 2 minutes, which will be enough time for the flavorings to infuse the oil.

When the pasta is cooked, return it to the saucepan after draining, then pour in the hot oil. Mix well, then serve immediately on warmed pasta plates.

Linguine with Gorgonzola, Pancetta, and Wilted Arugula

This is a lovely combination of assertive flavors that harmonize perfectly.

Serves 2

8 oz (225 g) linguine
4 oz (110 g) Gorgonzola Piccante
4½ oz (125 g) cubetti (cubed) pancetta or chopped bacon
1 bunch (50 g) fresh arugula
¾ cup (200 ml) crème fraîche
1 clove garlic, peeled and crushed
4 oz (110 g) Mozzarella, cut into little cubes
a little freshly grated Parmesan (Parmigiano Reggiano), to serve
salt and freshly ground black pepper

Begin by putting the pasta on to cook and give it 1 minute less cooking time than normal; then place the Gorgonzola Piccante and the crème fraîche in a food processor and process to blend together. Next, place a large, heavy frying pan over direct heat, and as soon as you think it is really hot, add the cubes of pancetta or chopped bacon and sauté them in their own fat for 3-4 minutes, moving them to brown all the edges evenly. Then add the garlic to the pan and toss that around for about 1 minute. Next, remove the pan from the heat and add the arugula leaves which, when you have given them a stir, will wilt in the heat of the pan.

When the pasta is ready, drain it immediately and return it to the saucepan. Now, add the Gorgonzola mixture, Mozzarella, and the contents of the frying pan; then return the pan to a low heat and toss everything together very thoroughly for about 1 minute. Season it well with freshly ground black pepper, and if it needs it, a touch of salt, then serve very quickly in hot pasta bowls with some Parmesan sprinkled on top.

Classic Fresh Tomato Sauce

It was once said that the greatest wines of Montrachet should be drunk kneeling with the head bowed as a sign of reverence. Well, this is how I feel about this very simple, classic sauce which is made with red, ripe, flavorful tomatoes and served with pasta. The pasta absorbs the very essence of the tomatoes' concentrated flavor. It's still the best pasta sauce of all, and it can be made ahead and re-heated (it even freezes well).

First, peel the tomatoes. To do this, pour boiling water over them and leave them for exactly 1 minute or, if the tomatoes are small, 15-30 seconds, before draining and slipping off their skins (protect your hands with a cloth if they are too hot). Now, reserve 3 of the tomatoes for later and roughly chop the rest.

Next, heat the oil in a medium saucepan; then add the onions and garlic and let them gently cook for 5-6 minutes until they are softened and pale gold in color. Now, add the chopped tomatoes with about a third of the basil, torn into pieces. Add some salt and freshly ground black pepper, then all you do is let the tomatoes simmer on a very low heat, without a lid, for approximately 1½ hours or until almost all the liquid has evaporated and the tomatoes are reduced to a thick, jam-like consistency, stirring now and then. Roughly chop the reserved fresh tomatoes and stir them in, along with the rest of the torn basil leaves, and serve on pasta with a hint of Parmesan – not too much, though, because it will detract from the wonderful tomato flavor.

Note: When serving this sauce, it is a good idea to give the pasta 1 minute less cooking time than you usually would, then return it to the pan after draining and give 1 more minute while you mix in the sauce.

Serves 2 -3 (enough for 12 oz/350 g pasta)
2 lbs 8 oz (1.15 kg) fresh, red, ripe tomatoes
1 tablespoon olive oil
1 medium onion weighing about 4 oz (110 g), peeled and finely chopped
1 fat clove garlic, peeled and crushed
approximately 12 large leaves fresh basil
a little Parmesan (Parmigiano Reggiano), to serve
salt and freshly ground black pepper

To peel the tomatoes, pour boiling water over them and leave for 1 minute

Now, drain the water from the pan and slip off the tomatoes' skins

Add the ingredients to the pan and simmer on a low heat for 1½ hours

After this time, the tomatoes will have reduced to a thick, jam-like consistency

223

Pasta Vialli

This recipe is my adaptation of one I ate in the famous San Lorenzo Italian restaurant in London, which is apparently a favorite with the Chelsea Football Club players. This particular dish is named after the famous Italian one-time star player and manager, Gianluca Vialli.

Serves 2-3
12 oz (350 g) penne rigate
1 recipe Classic Fresh Tomato Sauce
(see page 223)
5 oz (150 g) Mozzarella, chopped into
¾ inch (2 cm) cubes
a little finely grated Parmesan
(Parmigiano Reggiano), to serve
a few whole basil leaves, to garnish

Start this by gently re-heating the tomato sauce and putting the pasta on to cook. When you are almost ready to eat, stir the cubes of Mozzarella into the warm sauce and let it simmer gently for 2-3 minutes, by which time the cheese will have softened and begun to melt but still retain its identity. Serve the sauce spooned over the drained pasta, sprinkle with the Parmesan, and add a few fresh basil leaves as a garnish.

Penne with Wild Mushrooms and Crème Fraîche

In the Winter Collection, *the Oven-Baked Wild Mushroom Risotto was a huge hit, but all the lovely concentrated mushroom flavor works superbly well with pasta, too. Because the pasta will be returned to the pan for 1 minute, don't forget to give it 1 minute less on the initial cooking time.*

First, place the porcini in a small bowl; then heat the milk, pour it over the mushrooms and let them soak for 30 minutes. Heat the butter in a medium frying pan over a gentle heat, stir in the shallots and let them cook gently for 5 minutes. Next, strain the porcini into a sieve lined with a paper towel, reserving the soaking liquid, and squeeze the porcini dry. Then chop them finely and add them to the pan, along with the fresh mushrooms and the balsamic vinegar. Next, season with salt, pepper, and nutmeg. Give it all a good stir, then cook gently, uncovered, for 30-40 minutes, until all the liquid has evaporated.

About 15 minutes before the mushrooms are ready, put the pasta on to cook. Then, 2 minutes before the pasta is cooked, mix the crème fraîche into the mushrooms. Add the mushroom soaking liquid, and warm through.

Drain the pasta in a colander, return it to the hot pan, and quickly mix in the mushroom mixture; then place the pasta back on a gentle heat so it continues to cook for 1 more minute while it absorbs the sauce. Take it to the table in a hot serving bowl and pass the Parmesan around separately.

Serves 4-6
1 lb 2 oz (500 g) penne rigate
1 lb (450 g) mixed fresh mushrooms (cremini, shiitake, or mixed wild mushrooms, for example), finely chopped
½ oz (10 g) dried porcini mushrooms
1 cup (250 ml) crème fraîche
3 tablespoons milk
4 tablespoons (50 g) butter
4 large shallots, peeled and finely chopped
2 tablespoons balsamic vinegar
¼ whole nutmeg, grated
lots of freshly grated Parmesan (Parmigiano Reggiano), to serve
salt and freshly ground black pepper

Spaghetti with Meatballs and Fresh Tomato Sauce

Americans invented meatballs to go with spaghetti, and there are lots of ground rules, but the main criteria for any meatball is that it should have a kind of melt-in-the-mouth lightness and not be heavy and bouncy. These, I think, are just right.

Serves 4 (makes 24 meatballs)
For the meatballs:
8 oz (225 g) ground pork
2 teaspoons chopped sage leaves
3½ oz (95 g) mortadella or
unsmoked bacon
2 tablespoons freshly grated Parmesan
(Parmigiano Reggiano)
2 tablespoons chopped fresh
parsley leaves
3 oz (75 g) white bread without crusts,
soaked in 2 tablespoons milk
1 large egg
a little nutmeg
salt and freshly ground black pepper

To cook and serve:
1-2 tablespoons peanut or other
mildly flavored oil, for frying
1 lb (450 g) spaghetti
1 quantity Classic Fresh Tomato Sauce
(see page 223)
a little Parmesan (Parmigiano Reggiano)
a few fresh basil leaves

To make the meatballs, all you do is place all the ingredients into the bowl of a food processor and blend everything on a low speed until thoroughly blended. If you don't have a processor, chop everything as finely as possible with a sharp knife and blend it with a fork. Now, take walnut-sized pieces of the mixture and shape them into rounds – you should end up with 24 meatballs. Then put them in a large dish or in a pan, cover with plastic wrap, and chill for about 30 minutes to firm up.

Meanwhile, preheat the oven to a low setting. Then, when you are ready to cook the meatballs, heat 1 tablespoon of the oil in a large frying pan, and over a fairly high heat, add 12 meatballs at a time and cook them until they are crispy and brown all over, adding a little more oil as necessary. This will take 4-5 minutes per batch, so as they are cooked, remove them to a plate and keep them warm, covered with foil, in the oven.

Meanwhile, cook the pasta and gently warm the tomato sauce. Then drain the pasta, return it to the pan, and toss in the tomato sauce; quickly mix well and then pile it onto plates. Top with the meatballs, sprinkle with some freshly grated Parmesan, and finish with a few basil leaves.

Gratin of Rigatoni with Roasted Vegetables

This recipe is another good choice for a meatless dinner dish. Oven-roasted vegetables have a magical, toasted, concentrated flavor, and they keep all their dazzling colors intact. For strict vegetarians, exclude the anchovies.

Start off by preparing the zucchini and eggplant an hour ahead of time: chop them into 1½ inch (4 cm) chunks, leaving them unpeeled, and layer them in a colander with a sprinkling of salt between each layer. Then put a plate on top and weight it down with something heavy, which will draw out any excess moisture from the vegetables. After an hour, squeeze them dry them in a clean dish cloth, then preheat the oven to its highest setting.

Now, quarter the tomatoes and chop the onion and bell peppers into 1½ inch (4 cm) chunks. Next, arrange all the vegetables on the shallow baking pan and sprinkle with the olive oil and chopped garlic. Give everything a good mix to coat all the pieces with the oil, then spread them out as much as possible. Season with salt and freshly ground black pepper, then roast on a high shelf in the oven for 30-40 minutes, until browned and charred at the edges. Meanwhile, put a large pan of water on to boil for the pasta.

About 5 minutes before the vegetables are ready, cook the rigatoni in the boiling water for exactly 6 minutes – no longer. Drain the pasta in a colander, transfer it to a large mixing bowl, and combine it with the roasted vegetables, olives, anchovies, capers, and the sauce. At this point turn the heat down to 400°F (200°C), leaving the door open to let it cool down a bit quicker. Now, layer the mixture into the gratin dish, a third at a time, sprinkling the Mozzarella over each layer and finishing with Mozzarella. Finally, sprinkle the mixture with the 2 tablespoons of Parmesan. Bake in the oven for another 6 minutes, and serve very hot with just a leafy salad and a sharp dressing to accompany it.

If you want to make this ahead of time, it will need 35-40 minutes in the oven at 400°F (200°C) to heat it from its cold state.

Serves 4

6 oz (175 g) rigatoni
2 tablespoons grated Parmesan (Parmigiano Reggiano), for the topping
2½ cups (570 ml) cheese sauce (as on page 154, omitting the Cheddar and using 2 oz (50 g) of Parmesan

For the roasted vegetables:
2 medium zucchini
1 small eggplant
1 lb (450 g) tomatoes, skinned
1 medium onion, peeled
1 small red bell pepper, seeded
1 small yellow bell pepper, seeded
3 tablespoons extra virgin olive oil
2 cloves garlic, peeled and chopped
½ cup (50 g) pitted black olives, chopped
4 anchovy fillets, drained and chopped
1½ tablespoons salted capers or capers in vinegar, rinsed and drained
2 oz (50 g) Mozzarella, grated
salt and freshly ground black pepper

You will also need an ovenproof baking dish measuring 10 x 8 x 2 inches (25.5 x 20 x 5 cm), and a shallow baking pan measuring approximately 16 x 11 inches (40 x 28 cm).

Spinach and Ricotta Lasagne with Pine Nuts

This recipe is an absolute hit with everyone who eats it – even my husband, who professes not to like spinach! The combination of the four cheeses is its secret, and it is always on my top-10 list if I'm entertaining people who don't eat meat.

Serves 4-6
For the sauce:
3¾ cups (850 ml) milk
4 tablespoons (50 g) butter
½ cup (50 g) all-purpose flour
1 bay leaf
2½ oz (60 g) Parmesan (Parmigiano Reggiano), freshly grated
salt and freshly ground black pepper

For the lasagne:
12 fresh lasagne sheets (weighing about 9 oz/250 g)
1 lb 5 oz (600 g) baby spinach
1 cup (225 g) Ricotta
½ cup (50 g) pine nuts
pat of butter
¼ whole nutmeg, grated
7 oz (200 g) Gorgonzola Piccante, crumbled
7 oz (200 g) Mozzarella, coarsely grated
salt and freshly ground black pepper

You will also need an ovenproof dish measuring about 9 x 9 inches (23 x 23 cm), 2½ inches (6 cm) deep, well buttered.

Preheat the oven to 350°F (180°C).

Begin this by making the sauce, which can be done using the all-in-one method. This means placing the milk, butter, flour, and bay leaf together in a saucepan, giving it a good seasoning, then, over a medium heat, whisking it all together continually until it comes to simmering point and has thickened. Turn the heat down to its lowest possible setting and allow the sauce to cook gently for 5 minutes. After that, stir in ¾ cup (50 g) of the Parmesan, then remove it from the heat, discard the bay leaf, and place some plastic wrap over the surface to prevent a skin from forming.

Now, you need to deal with the spinach. First of all, remove and discard the stems, then wash the leaves really thoroughly in two or three changes of cold water and shake them dry. Next, take your largest saucepan, place the pat of butter in it, then pile the spinach leaves in on top, sprinkling them with a little salt as you go. Now, place the pan over a medium heat, cover with a lid, and cook the spinach for about 2 minutes, turning the leaves over halfway through. After that, the leaves will have collapsed and become tender.

Next, drain the spinach in a colander, and when it's cool enough to handle, squeeze it in your hands to get rid of every last drop of liquid. Then place it on a chopping board and chop it finely. Now, put it into a bowl, add the Ricotta, then approximately ⅔ cup (150 ml) of the sauce. Give it a good seasoning of salt and pepper and add the grated nutmeg. Then mix everything together really thoroughly, and finally, fold in the crumbled Gorgonzola.

Now, you need to place a small frying pan over a medium heat, add the pine nuts and dry-fry them for about 1 minute, tossing them around to get them nicely toasted but being careful that they don't burn. Then remove the pan from the heat and assemble the lasagne. To do this, spread a quarter of the sauce into the bottom of the dish, and on top of that, a third of the spinach mixture, followed by a scattering of toasted pine nuts. Now, place sheets of pasta on top of this – you may need to tear some of them in half with your hands to make them fit. Now, repeat the whole process, this time adding a third of the grated Mozzarella along with the pine nuts, then the lasagne sheets. Repeat again, finishing with a layer of pasta, the rest of the sauce and the remaining Parmesan and Mozzarella. When you are ready to cook the lasagne, place it on the middle shelf of the preheated oven and bake for 50-60 minutes, until the top is golden and bubbling. Then remove it from the oven and let it settle for about 10 minutes before serving.

Sicilian Pasta with Roasted Tomatoes and Eggplant

Eggplant, tomatoes, and Mozzarella are the classic ingredients of any classic Sicilian sauce for pasta, and roasting the tomatoes and eggplant to get them slightly charred adds an extra flavor dimension.

Serves 2

8 oz (225 g) spaghetti
12 large tomatoes (roughly 2 lb/900 g)
1 large eggplant, cut into 1 inch
(2.5 cm) cubes
2 large cloves garlic, peeled and
finely chopped
about 4 tablespoons olive oil
12 large basil leaves, torn in half,
plus a few extra for garnish
5 oz (150 g) Mozzarella, cut into
½ inch (1 cm) cubes
salt and freshly ground black pepper

You will also need two shallow baking pans measuring approximately 14 x 10 inches (35 x 25.5 cm).

Preheat the oven to 400°F (200°C).

First of all, place the eggplant cubes in a colander, sprinkle them with salt, and let them stand for half an hour, weighed down with something heavy to squeeze out the excess juices.

Meanwhile, skin the tomatoes by pouring boiling water over them and leaving them for 1 minute; then drain off the water, and as soon as they are cool enough to handle, slip off the skins. Cut each tomato in half and place the halves on one of the baking pans (cut-side up), then season with salt and freshly ground black pepper. Sprinkle over the chopped garlic, distributing it evenly between the tomatoes, and follow this with a few drops of olive oil in each one. Top each tomato half with half a basil leaf, turning each piece of leaf over to give it a good coating of oil. Now, place the baking sheet on the middle shelf of the oven and roast the tomatoes for 50-60 minutes or until the edges are slightly blackened.

Meanwhile, drain the eggplant and squeeze out as much excess juice as possible, then dry them thoroughly with a clean cloth and place them in the other baking sheet. Then drizzle 1 tablespoon of the olive oil all over them and place them on the top shelf of the oven, above the tomatoes, giving them half an hour.

Toward the end of the cooking time, cook the pasta. When the tomatoes and eggplant are ready, scrape them, along with all their lovely cooking juices, into a saucepan and place the pan over a low heat; then add the cubed Mozzarella and stir gently. Now, drain the pasta, pile it into a warm bowl, spoon the tomato and eggplant mixture over the top, and scatter with a few basil leaves.

Souffléd Macaroni and Cheese

I've made many a macaroni and cheese in my time, but this, I promise you, is the best ever.

Begin by having all your ingredients measured out and the cheeses grated. Fill a large saucepan with 2½ quarts (2.25 liters) of water containing 2 teaspoons of salt and put it on the heat to bring it up to a boil. Then, in a small saucepan, melt the butter over a gentle heat, add the onions, and let them soften, without browning and uncovered, for 5 minutes. Then add the flour to the pan, stir it in to make a smooth paste; then gradually add the milk, a little at a time, stirring vigorously with a wooden spoon. Switch to a balloon whisk and keep whisking so you have a smooth sauce. Then add some salt and freshly ground black pepper, as well as the nutmeg, and let the sauce cook gently for 5 minutes. After that, turn off the heat and whisk in the Mascarpone and egg yolks, followed by the Gruyère and half the Parmesan.

Next, place the baking dish in the oven to warm it. Drop the macaroni into the boiling water, and as soon as the water returns to a simmer, cook it 4–6 minutes until *al dente* (it's going to get a second cooking in the oven). When it has about 1 minute's cooking time left, whisk the egg whites to soft peaks. Drain the pasta, giving it a quick shake to get rid of any water, then tip it back into the pan and stir in the cheese sauce, turning the pasta over in it so it is evenly coated. Then lightly fold in the egg whites, using a cutting and folding movement to retain as much air as possible.

Remove the warm dish from the oven, pour the pasta mixture into it shaking it gently to even the top, and then sprinkle with the reserved Parmesan. Return the dish to the oven on a high shelf for 12 minutes or until the top is puffy and lightly browned. Serve it, as they say in Italy, *presto pronto*.

Note: To make this to serve four people, double the ingredients using a 10 x 8 x 2 inch (25.5 x 20 x 5 cm) dish, and increase the cooking time by 3–5 minutes.

Serves 2 generously
6 oz (175 g) macaroni
2 tablespoons (25 g) butter
1 medium onion (about 4 oz/110 g), peeled and finely chopped
¼ cup (25 g) all-purpose flour
1¼ cups (275 ml) milk
¼ whole nutmeg, freshly grated
⅓ cup (75 g) Mascarpone
2 large egg yolks, lightly beaten
2 oz (50 g) Gruyère, finely grated
2 oz (50 g) Parmesan (Parmigiano Reggiano), finely grated
2 large egg whites
salt and freshly ground black pepper

You will also need a shallow ovenproof baking dish with a bottom measurement of 8 x 6 inches (20 x 15 cm), 2 inches (5 cm) deep, lightly buttered.

Preheat the oven to 400°F (200°C).

Baked Cannelloni

I have discovered that the best way to make this excellent dinner dish is to buy fresh sheets of lasagne that don't need pre-cooking, which are now quite widely available. The filling, conveniently, is the meatball mixture on page 226.

Serves 4

For the filling:

8 fresh lasagne sheets (weighing about 6 oz/175 g)

1 quantity meatball mixture (see page 226)

5 oz (150 g) Mozzarella, diced

1½ oz (40 g) finely grated Parmesan (Parmigiano Reggiano), plus a little extra to serve

For the béchamel sauce:

2½ cups (570 ml) milk

4 tablespoons (50 g) butter

⅓ cup (35 g) all-purpose flour

1 bay leaf

good grating of whole nutmeg

⅓ cup (65 ml) heavy cream

salt and freshly ground black pepper

You will also need a baking dish with a bottom measurement of 7 x 9 inches (18 x 23 cm), 2 inches (5 cm) deep, buttered.

Make the sauce first by placing the milk, butter, flour, bay leaf, nutmeg, and seasonings into a medium-sized saucepan over a medium heat, then, whisking all the time, slowly bring it up to simmering point until the sauce has thickened. Then turn the heat down to its lowest setting and let the sauce simmer for about 5 minutes, then remove the bay leaf, stir in the cream, taste to check the seasoning, cover, and set it aside.

Now, preheat the oven to 350°F (180°C), then cut the lasagne sheets in half so that you have 16 pieces. Next, divide the meatball mixture in half and then each half into eight, then lightly roll each of these into a sausage shape about 3 inches (7.5 cm) long. Place each one onto a piece of lasagne and roll it up, starting from one of the shorter edges. As you do this, arrange them in the baking dish with the seam underneath – what you should have is two rows neatly fitting together lengthwise in the dish. Now, pour the sauce over all and scatter the Mozzarella cubes here and there. Finally, scatter the Parmesan over the top and place the dish on the center shelf of the oven to bake for 40 minutes, by which time it should be golden brown and bubbling. Then remove it from the oven and let it settle for about 10 minutes before serving. Finally, sprinkle with a little extra Parmesan.

My year in East Anglia: harvests, photographic sessions, football, and writing in the tree house, with a little help from Beau

DELIA'S
HOW TO COOK

PART TWO

Part Two Contents

Part Two Introduction

When Part One of *How To Cook* was completed and sent off to the publisher, there was, I suppose, a huge question mark hanging over the whole project, including the television programs. Would a new look at basic cooking still be a useful thing for the 21st century? Given that there are now so many cooking books and television programs, would going back to the beginning just seem boring?

Thankfully, by the time Part Two was published a year later, there were no question marks. I am happy to report there is a *great* deal of interest in the basic everyday skills of cooking, particularly among the young, whose letters, comments, and general enthusiasm are very encouraging. Here in Part Two we move on from the staple ingredients to see how beginners can approach the subjects of meat, fish, poultry, and cheese. We examine how to come to terms with the rapidly increasing range of dairy products; we learn about preparing salads and dressings, cooking vegetables, and fruits, and understanding how to deal with chocolate. Above all,

the well-stocked pantry is, I feel, a mark of getting
serious about wanting to enjoy a lifetime of cooking and
good food.

   I am as passionate as ever about wanting to communicate
the techniques of good cooking to all who want to learn,
and hopefully share with them the same lifetime of joy
and pleasure that learning to cook has given – and still is –
giving me.

Delia Smith

11

The serious cook's cupboard

(or capers in the pantry)

Why the curious sub-title, you're thinking. Nostalgia, really, because it dates back to the late-1970s, when I was a very coy, shy TV cook hardly daring to look up at the camera. I was trying to expound the virtues of capers as a useful cooking ingredient, and what I said was, "I always have capers in my pantry." To which I received a very humorous letter from a gentleman curious to know just what kinds of capers I got up to in my pantry!

What do I mean when I use the word serious? I suppose what I'm trying to say is that some people like to flirt with the subject of cooking – dip in and out, try a recipe here and there – but everyone knows the difference between a flirtation and a serious relationship: at some point flirtation stops and some kind of commitment begins. Cooking is absolutely like that. If I really, truly want to know how to cook well, then I certainly can, but somewhere along the way a decision has to be made – yes, I am now going to get serious, not just flirt with the idea, but really make a commitment to doing it correctly so I can get the best out of cooking and eating for the rest of my life.

What does getting serious mean?

If you want to know how to cook then you need to begin by making life as easy as possible, and this means giving some time and investment to, first, the right utensils and cooking equipment (something that is emphasised throughout the two parts of *How To Cook*), and secondly, you need to have a well-stocked pantry.

Because I'm at the receiving end of a great deal of letters and comments, there is a familiar complaint that surfaces regularly among people who only flirt with cooking. "Why do I have to go out and buy all those expensive ingredients just for one recipe?" Or, "Can't I use curry paste in your recipe instead of all that tedious roasting and grinding?" But, if your kitchen cupboard is well stocked, you won't have to frequently rush out to buy a missing ingredient. Secondly, most pantry ingredients come in cans, bottles, or jars and have a long shelf life, and they cost very little over a period of time. And thirdly, dry-roasting and grinding spices in a mortar and pestle can all be done in 4 minutes at the most, and you will receive twice or three times the depth of flavor.

Flavor is the most important word in cooking

If you're going to bother to cook, you need to get the very best flavor from all the ingredients you use. This doesn't mean that convenience ingredients don't have their place – obviously they do because there are always going to be days when we're simply not able to do much cooking. But on the days when we can, it's wonderful to have a stock of spices and flavoring ingredients within reach – a pinch of this, a splash of that – whenever we need them.

What about the cost?

For some reason, spending money on recipe ingredients and kitchen equipment is sometimes difficult and many people simply muddle along and make do. But think of it this way: if you want to learn to drive you have to pay for lessons, then you can enjoy a lifetime of driving, which will improve your quality of life. Same with cooking: a little investment at the beginning and you'll have years of pleasure in cooking and eating very well.

The well-stocked pantry

In the photograph on page 240, you'll see an example of what a serious cook might have on stand-by. You can use the list of ingredients that follows in this chapter for an annual check, which I always try to do in January. It's then that I throw out all stale ingredients and do one shopping trip to replace them. I have learned the hard way, having been caught so often in the past – just about to make a cake that needs a certain spice combination, ground ginger for instance - finding to my horror that mine is a year out of date and very un-spicy.

What you don't need

Certainly not all those fancy gourmet ingredients that you receive as gifts or buy in an unguarded moment. Be ruthless – you're never going to use that obscure fruit liqueur that your aunt brought back from Yalta, the pickled plums that date back to the 1980s, or the gaudy-colored fruit vinegar that looks like bath essence. They're like clothes you never wear, taking up valuable space. So pack them off to the church bazaar and make room for something really useful.

The basics

What follows is what I think is a good basic list of ingredients and some suggestions of the best brands to look for – not everything you're ever going to need, but what you should always have available.

Salt

I like to use English sea salt from Maldon, in Essex. It's not a powdery pouring salt that contains chemicals to stop it getting damp and make it pour freely, but an absolutely pure salt that tastes of the sea. If you do a comparison tasting you'll find it is less sharp but somehow saltier (so you need to use less). Maldon salt consists of very pretty, small white crystalline flakes that crush very easily between your fingers for cooking with. For the table, use it either in a good-quality salt mill or a small salt dish. (See Suppliers, pages 481-2, for a source for Maldon.)
Crushed sea salt gives baked potatoes a really crispy skin, and it's wonderful coarsely crushed over French fries (or anything fried). Once, while sitting at a restaurant table, I discovered by accident that a fat, potato wedge wrapped in an arugula leaf, then dipped first in mayonnaise, then in sea salt, is a wickedly brilliant combination!

Peppercorns

You might be amused to know that when I first started writing a column for London's *Evening Standard* in 1972, I used to be unmercifully teased about my constant references to "freshly ground black pepper." Although I don't recall any stores actually selling out of black peppercorns, I quite definitely had a campaign going to encourage people to use them. I said I would always refer to pepper as freshly ground and black until I saw no more of the gray, musty, dusty stuff that people sprinkle on their food. I'm still campaigning strongly because, even now, unbelievably, it continues to turn up in restaurants.

Black pepper

Black peppercorns are whole immature berries that are harvested while still green and dried in the sun until they turn black. The berries contain a white inner kernel – the hottest part of the berry, which is quite fiery when used on its own – and a black outer husk, which has all the aromatic fragrance that enhances the flavor of food. Thus if you use the whole berries you get a little bit of fire and a lot of aromatic fragrance.

White pepper

Here the berries have been allowed to mature before harvesting; the husks are discarded and the white kernels dried to become white peppercorns. The dried peppercorns, stored whole, will keep their aroma for a long time, but once they have been powdered to dust in a factory, left stored on a cupboard shelf, and allowed to stagnate in a pepper shaker, there is no surprise that the result is a million miles from the fragrance you can keep locked up in your pepper grinder.

Sichuan pepper

Despite its name, this is not actually from the same family as black, white, and green peppercorns, but comes from a type of ash tree. It's used in Asian cooking and is an ingredient of Chinese five-spice powder.

Cayenne pepper

This is an absolute must in the kitchen. It's hot and fiery and needs to be used with extreme caution, but it is brilliant for that little sprinkling of piquancy. It's made from one of the hottest types of chili, which is dried, then crushed to a powder, including the seeds. I'm forever using a pinch here and there, and I love it sprinkled on smoked fish or shrimp cocktail. Although spices, once ground, do not have a long shelf life, cayenne does seem to go on longer than most but still needs replacing fairly regularly.

Mustard

Mustard, the home-grown English spice, is the one of the best of all spices. I admit this is a personal thing: I like the ferocious kick of English mustard that makes its presence felt even when only very little is used. Although it comes in powdered form, it does have a good shelf life and can be made up whenever you need it.

How to make mustard

The oils in mustard are what give it its pungency, but these are not developed in the whole seed or the dry milled powder. What is needed to release their flavor is the chemical reaction brought on by the addition of cold water (not hot, which causes a different reaction), just enough to make a thickish paste. Always make up your mustard in advance, since it needs at least 10-15 minutes for the flavor to develop fully. Mustard is a good emulsifier: it can help to stabilise something like mayonnaise, and can provide a slight thickening to vinaigrette or Cumberland sauce.

Made-up mustards

There are three of these I would recommend, but first it should be noted that once they are exposed to the air, they deteriorate rapidly and lose much of their kick. This means the lid must be replaced firmly and quickly each time the mustard is used.

Dijon mustard

From Burgundy, France, tempered by the mixture of unripe grape juice (verjuice) or wine vinegar, is not as fiery as English mustard. It is extremely good but after it has been opened, it's difficult to retain the fragrance.

Wholegrain mustard

This is a mixture of mustard seeds, spices, and wine vinegar, milder than freshly made mustard but very good for the pantry since it not only adds flavor to dressings and sauces but also a lovely seedy texture. It keeps better than Dijon, but be sure to replace the lid quickly to prevent the air from affecting it.

American mustard

You can't really have a barbecue without some of this famous mustard, which comes in squeezy bottles and is a mixture of mustard, turmeric, paprika, and other spices. No decent frankfurter or sausage in a hot dog should ever be without it drizzled back and forth over the surface.

Mustard mayhem…

Like olive oils and wine vinegars, mustard suffers greatly from the designer effect, with every flavor, color, and texture under the sun creeping into the mustard jar. My advice is, don't bother. Even if you like the flavor of dill mustard or similar, after being opened it will deteriorate very quickly. So don't make the mistakes I've made: one spoonful of some exotic mustard today and the whole jar thrown out several weeks later. If you want dill or tarragon or anything else in your mustard, it's best to add it yourself.

Clockwise from top: English mustard powder, Dijon mustard, and wholegrain mustard

Bottled sauces

Worcestershire sauce

The very best-loved of English bottled sauces. I know an American gourmet who has crates of Worcestershire sent over from England because it tastes so good. It's such a clever sauce because if you were asked (and didn't know) what the main ingredient was, you would never guess. It's anchovies, but only the finest anchovies from the Basque region of Spain, blended with shallots, onions, and garlic and matured for three years. Worcestershire sauce is a flavor provider and enhancer, great for jazzing up stocks, gravies, and sauces, and for enlivening dull ready-made meals. Even outside the kitchen it has another pride of place, and that's at every glitzy bar from Teesside to Thailand – because no Bloody Mary anywhere in the world could not include it.

Soy sauce

Soy sauce is an ancient and crucially important ingredient in the Far East, used not just for seasoning but also for dipping, marinating, tenderising, and at the same time purifying. What we need to concern ourselves with for the purposes of cooking is the enormous range in quality, and for cooks who care about quality the best soy sauce is made in Japan, where it is naturally fermented from wheat, soy beans, salt, and water (the only ingredients that should appear on the label). Short-cut unnaturally fermented soy sauces are not in the same league, so if you stick to Japanese you'll be sure you're using the best.

Fish sauce (nam pla)

Fish sauce used to be found only at specialty Asian food markets but now it is much more widely available and carried in supermarkets at last. You could almost say this is an Eastern version of Worcestershire sauce, not so much in flavor but in the way it gives the same lift to other ingredients. As its name suggests, it is a fermentation of small, whole fish (sometimes shrimp) and is quite salty, so a little goes a long way. It's an essential ingredient in Vietnamese and Thai cooking, and because of the growing popularity of these cuisines (which I personally love), it has become a staple pantry ingredient.

Tabasco sauce

Hot liquid chilies in a bottle. Perfect if you want to perk something up with just a dash of heat, and also useful when you've added fresh chilies to a recipe and they haven't quite provided the heat you wanted – a few drops will supplement it beautifully. There are lots of chili sauces around, but I find Tabasco has the best chili flavor.

Organic tomato ketchup

Try to find an organic tomato ketchup - it is simply in a different league than other tomato ketchups, being true to the tomatoes it's made from. Because the flavor of the tomatoes has not been eclipsed by sugar or artificial sweeteners, it's useful in cooking where you want to add true tomato flavor; it's also great with fish and French fries.

Red currant jelly

Red currant jelly is an invaluable ingredient for sauces, gravies, or simply to serve with lamb or game. Make sure it's a good-quality one with a high fruit content, the Tiptree brand, for example; cheaper versions are far too sweet, which obliterates the real flavor of the red currants.

Cranberry jelly

I always keep cranberry jelly in my cupboard, too – it's good as an instant accompaniment to chicken or game, or it can be used in sauces.

Mayonnaise

Homemade is preferable, but, since making it is not always practical, a good-quality store-bought mayonnaise should always be on hand. I find I don't use it often enough to buy it in large jars, and because it stores better unopened, I find a couple of smaller jars are a better bet than having a third of a large jar lurking in the refrigerator waiting to be used.

Pure vanilla extract

As you'd expect, this is extracted from pure vanilla beans and not made synthetically (extract is the key word; essence is not the same thing). It's very useful for sauces, custards, and a million and one sweet dishes or wherever a touch of vanilla flavor is required.

Honey

Personal preference reigns here. Try to find Greek mountain honey, available in some gourmet food stores. I prefer it because it never seems too sweet, but full of fragrance with caramel overtones. Whatever honey you prefer, it's essential for the pantry. For a quick snack, spread on top of a buttered slice of freshly baked bread or spoon over thick Greek yogurt. For recipes see pages 438 and 462.

Maple syrup

Once you get into the habit of pouring maple syrup over cereal or Greek yogurt and using it in place of sugar to sweeten all kinds of things, you're sure to get addicted. And because Buttermilk Pancakes (page 168) are so quick and easy to make, having some maple syrup on hand means you're never short of an almost-instant dessert. Note: after it's opened it needs to be stored in the refrigerator and used within 3 months.

Gravy browning

Although, if I'm roasting meat (particularly beef), I often put an onion in to caramelize and color the gravy, at other times it's useful to be able to add a spot of rich color if a gravy looks too pale. Gravy browning is just dark caramelized sugar, so a couple of drops won't affect the flavor but will enrich the color.

Canned and bottled ingredients

Anchovies

Probably one of the most significant ingredients of all. Not only are they supremely good and highly prized in their own right, they are also very effective in enhancing the flavor of other ingredients. From my studies of 18th-century cooking in England I know that a barrel of anchovies was indispensable in many kitchens to enliven all sorts of recipes. "But I don't like anchovies," some of you are thinking. True, they are strong and gutsy – an acquired taste, you could say – but they do grow on you. So keep

trying a little here and a little there until you acquire it, and don't forget that most people who say they don't like anchovies do like Worcestershire sauce, in which anchovies are the main ingredient.

Anchovy essence

This is also a great flavor enhancer and is the equivalent of the fish sauce of the Far East. As such, it can be used in Asian recipes when fish sauce is not available.

Pantry tomatoes

We are very fortunate to have tomatoes any time we want them – perhaps they are the most widely used pantry ingredient of all. First there's the canned – chopped or whole – and sometimes in the winter months their flavor in cooking is superior to fresh, provided, of course, they're Italian because these are by far the best. Regular tomato paste and sun-dried tomato paste are also very useful, as are sun-dried tomatoes preserved in oil. But one new ingredient you can sometimes find is mi-cuit tomatoes, which are half dried. The tomato flavor is concentrated but the tomatoes not as chewy as those that are totally dried.

Capers

These little Mediterranean berries – sometimes tiny, sometimes fat and squashy – are another acquired taste, but do persevere. Capers add a lively piquancy to all kinds of dishes, especially sauces and fish. Nobody likes their first alcoholic drink, but we've all experienced how soon *that* catches on, and it's the same with capers. You can buy them either preserved in salt (which I prefer) or in vinegar. Either way, you need to place them in a sieve and rinse them under cold water first. Capers in vinegar will keep well once opened, provided the vinegar covers them completely. If it doesn't you'll need to pour in vinegar to cover.

Cornichons (mini pickles)

What we used to get were midget gherkins bottled in malt vinegar that seared your throat, but now, thankfully, we get the real thing, crunchy and fragrant. They are another must in the pantry, not just for eating with pâtés or served with drinks but as an important ingredient in tartare sauce (see page 280) and fish recipes.

Horseradish and wasabi

Horseradish is not just a good ingredient for accompanying roast beef or smoked fish, but also for adding flavor to sauces. Finding a good creamed horseradish can be difficult – the tear-inducing prickle of freshly grated horseradish seems to disappear once it's creamed and bottled. Try to find English Provender or Wiltshire Tracklements; they are the best. Now we can also buy Japanese wasabi. Ground from the cousin of our horseradish and called wasabi root in Japan, it is mixed with cold water like mustard. Although its main use is as a condiment for sushi (delicious), it is also good mixed into creamed horseradish to give it back its kick. Just use a ¼ teaspoon of wasabi powder to 2 tablespoons of creamed horseradish.

Opposite page, left to right: salted capers, caper berries, and capers preserved in vinegar. Above: anchovy fillets

Below, from left: dried shrimp, rice noodles, Thai fish sauce, and shrimp paste. Bottom: dried kaffir lime leaves

Olives

A requirement for every pantry. Although you can buy loose olives at deli counters (and it's good to buy small amounts to find which varieties you like), always have them tucked away in the cupboard in jars or cans as well. That allows you to be spontaneous whenever you want to use olives in cooking. I like to have two kinds available: the quite large Greek calamata olives and the tiny purple-brown Provençal ones, which are good for garnishes. Buy the best quality olives, avoiding the pitted ones, which aren't the best. An olive pitter, *left*, will make removing the pits fairly easy.

Stem ginger in syrup

I always have a jar of this handy because it's lovely in cakes and it does wonders for rhubarb (see page 406). It can be used chopped as a garnish and sprinkled with its syrup over ice cream. It keeps for ages, so it doesn't matter if you're not using it frequently. My favorite ginger cake is made with stem ginger (see page 268).

Coconut milk

This is made from freshly grated coconut, soaked in water and squeezed to extract a creamy substance. You can buy it in cans for instant use. One of the wonderful things about Thai cooking is that it can be spontaneous and quick, provided you have all the necessary ingredients in the pantry.

Dried coconut powder

A great pantry stand-by, this is particularly good in Thai fishcakes (see the recipe on page 284).

Kaffir lime leaves

Fresh kaffir lime leaves are very hard to find, but now they come freeze-dried rather like bay leaves. They have that unmistakable Asian-Thai flavor. Pound them in a mortar or soak them in a little hot water, and they're almost as good as new. If you need to store the fresh leaves, keep them in the freezer.

Shrimp paste

Another Thai ingredient, this is made from fermented salted shrimp that are pounded into a concentrated paste and sold in jars. It must be cooked and not used in its raw state. After the jar has been opened, you need to store it in the refrigerator with a tight lid on and placed in a plastic storage bag since it has quite a strong aroma. Use it to give a wonderfully authentic flavor to Thai recipes.

Dried shrimp

These have lots of concentrated shrimp flavor, unlike tired and tasteless frozen shrimp, which have no value at all. They are available in Asian markets, but have only a short shelf life – about 4 weeks – so buy them in small quantities and, again, keep them refrigerated. Soak them in hot water for 15 minutes before using.

Dried mushrooms

Without a doubt, dried mushrooms are among the best ingredients to become available at markets in the past decade. No matter how much we value and are grateful for them, cultivated mushrooms will never have the flavor of mushrooms grown in the wild. Now, we can buy many varieties of dried and fresh wild mushrooms, and all of us can enjoy that special flavor simply by ordering on the Internet (see Suppliers, pages 481-2). Both the French and the Italians produce excellent dried mushrooms; their native varieties, including ceps and morels in France and porcini in Italy, are best of all. This means you can always add a touch of luxurious concentrated mushroom flavor whenever you cook with mushrooms.

Marigold Swiss vegetable bouillon powder

This is, without a doubt, an ingredient that can revolutionize modern cooking. Before such a product, you had to make your own stock or resort to the over-salty, chemically flavored stock cube. Fresh or frozen stock is sometimes available in stores but usually difficult to find, and it is often expensive. Marigold powder is made from vegetables and has a pure vegetable flavor, allowing you to have instant stock at any time. If there were good ingredient awards, Marigold would win first prize. (See Suppliers, pages 481-2.)

Gelatin

I always try to keep a stock of both powdered and leaf gelatin on hand, and I use both regularly. The powdered form is the most widely available and is added and used in several different ways, which I explain fully in the recipes. Leaf gelatin is always used in the same way, and instructions and photographs are on page 416.

All-natural sugars

These are made from pure all-natural sugar cane, and some examples are pictured, *right*. This means the color and flavor that is naturally present in sugar cane has not been refined out to make the sugar pure white. I use all-natural sugars for the majority of my recipes now. I love their rich flavor and pale-caramel color, and I believe after you've tasted it, you'll much prefer it to white.

All-natural sugars, clockwise from top right: molasses, golden granulated, dark muscovado (on spoon), light brown, confectioners' sugar, dark brown, demerara, light muscovado, and golden caster (milled golden cane)

Golden syrup

This is very good for sauces, puddings and custards, butterscotch or toffee sauces, steamed puddings, or simply spread thickly on homemade bread with a generous amount of butter. If you have trouble finding it, dark corn syrup can be substituted.

Molasses

This is the dark-ebony syrup that's left over in the sugar refining process. Molasses is included in different degrees in all-natural sugars. Light and dark varieties can be found in stores. Molasses is very concentrated, so only a little is needed, particularly when using the darker version. Use it frequently for its rich, luscious flavor.

Alcohol for cooking

This one is a most important section because a splash of wine or other alcohol added to a wide variety of dishes in any shape or form makes a significant difference: to a sauce or used to deglaze a pan, or as a component in cakes, desserts, and casseroles. The list is endless.

Beer and stout

These are good in slowly braised casseroles, particularly with beef or venison when they are subject to long, slow cooking. All the bitterness of the beer or stout is cooked away, leaving a rich, mellow, dark sauce.

Hard cider

I always have this available in my kitchen. It keeps longer than wine and can be used in any recipe that requires wine (making it less expensive). In some cases it is even better than wine, particularly with pork and apples (see page 316). If you have cooked some pork sausages, remove them from the pan and keep them warm, then deglaze by adding ⅔ cup (150 ml) of cider and a teaspoon of cider vinegar to the pan; let it bubble and reduce, scraping the bottom of the pan until it becomes syrupy. Then pour the cider over the sausages before serving.

Wine

Using wine in cooking can transform a quite ordinary dish into something extremely special. Now that you can buy quarter bottles with screw-tops you can always have some handy. If you have browned some pork chops or a steak, deglaze the pan with either white for the former or red for the latter (see above), to provide a concentrated sauce to spoon over the meat.

Fortified wines

These are absolute stars, both for drinking and for use in the kitchen. Over the 30 years I have been cooking I have used them in recipes time and time again. Basically, the ones I use most are dry manzanilla sherry, dry sercial Madeira, Marsala, and, lastly, port, which seems to be used around Christmas time a lot. All of them will keep well if sealed properly after use.

Spirits

When I first started writing recipes I was always terribly aware of the cost, and when a certain dish called for spirits I would always add the phrase "available in miniatures." Now I don't, because I have realized it is actually cheaper to buy a large bottle, the contents of which can be kept almost indefinitely. Here I would choose brandy, whisky, Calvados, and rum as the four spirits most likely to be included in recipes.

Shaosing brown rice wine

Rice wine always adds that wonderfully authentic flavor and aroma to Chinese cooking. Dry sherry can be used instead, but it's worth hunting around Asian food markets for the real thing if you can.

Armagnac

This is the first cousin of Cognac but with its own special, distinctive flavor. It has a great affinity for prunes, so I have used it both in the brownies and the cake recipe on pages 473 and 474 respectively.

Spices

Spices are always a tricky subject. People complain about the cost of spices, saying they "don't want to spend a fortune on one recipe." I would suggest, however, that although the initial expense may seem large, if you think about them teaspoon by teaspoon in recipes over the course of a year, they represent only a fraction of the overall cost. Having said that, though, what price is it worth for my very ordinary kitchen to be transformed by the alluring aromas of far-away, exotic places? Once the spices are roasted and ground, I can close my eyes and be transported instantly to a Turkish bazaar, a Moroccan market, to India or the Caribbean, to Africa, and the Far East – all are encapsulated in even the humblest collection of spices.

The case for whole spices

For home cooks, there's no doubt that, in most cases, buying spices whole is best. First, and most importantly, spices, after they have been ground, quickly lose much of their original pungency, while whole spices keep their exotic flavor and fragrance locked in far longer. Then, when the spices are dry-roasted and subjected to heat, all those sublime flavors and aromas are drawn out in a matter of moments.

Pre-ground spices

Without detracting from what I've just said about whole spices, there are one or two exceptions: it is difficult, for example, to grind cloves or cinnamon; paprika is already ground from dried sweet peppers, cayenne from chili peppers, and for baking it is often easier to use pre-ground spices. There is also a case for ground ginger because it has different uses from fresh ginger. But I would repeat, these spices do not have a long shelf life, so replace them frequently. The best way to buy them is in small amounts in refill packs, which are less expensive than the jars.

The *How To Cook* spice collection

Obviously whole books have been written about spices, but I will confine myself here to what I believe to be the essential list for every cook. It is hard to communicate in words their individual fragrances and flavors, but here is a little information about each one.

Allspice

This looks like a smooth peppercorn but larger, and it is so called because it is supposed to resemble in flavor a mixture of cloves, nutmeg, and cinnamon. It is not really like any one of them, however, but has a unique flavor of its own. It is sometimes called Jamaican pepper or pimento, and is used in marinades and pickles – you'll see the whole berries used in jars of commercial pickled herrings, and you can catch some of its flavor in the recipe for Tunisian Eggplant Salad on page 366.

Cardamom

This is an Eastern spice that comes encased in its own sun-dried pods, which are pale green or gray. Inside there is a treasure of tiny black, highly aromatic seeds. This is an important spice in curries, but it also turns up in sweet dishes – I once tasted a cardamom cake in which the flavor of the cardamom had permeated and mingled with the sweetness beautifully. I almost always throw in the pods as well to get every bit of flavor.

Cinnamon (whole and ground)

This is a popular spice that comes from the inner bark of a tree belonging to the laurel family. When whole, its design is exquisite: reddish-brown, brittle-layered curls that are hollow inside. Ground, it is used in home-baked desserts and whole in fruit compotes, mulled wines, and curries. In Greek cooking a little cinnamon finds its way into savoury dishes, such as the moussaka recipe on page 162. There is something evocative in the smell of home baking when cinnamon is involved, as it reminds me of the small bakeries I knew as a child.

Cloves

Cloves are like little dark-wooden nails, and can be used almost as such pressed into onions (for bread sauce) or oranges (mulled wine) or studded all over a sugar-and-mustard-glazed ham. They do have a very pungent aroma and flavor – people who were subjected to oil of cloves as a cure for toothache can't stand them, so strong was their impact – but used subtly cloves are one of my favorite spices and I still love them in apple pies and crumbles.

Coriander (whole, never ground)

The leaves of coriander, known as cilantro, became one of my enthusiasms (as did fresh limes) in the early 1990s. I'm unrepentant about encouraging its use because attention was drawn to two very important ingredients. Here we are concerned not with the leaves but with the tiny beige-brown seeds, a magical spice that is said to have the flavor of roasted orange peel. Since I first began using the leaves, I have come to discern the connection between the two, even though they're at the same time different. Coriander seeds are important in Indian curries, Middle Eastern, and Greek dishes.

Cumin (whole)

These are tiny elongated brown-gray seeds, essential to curries, but also widely used in Mexican, Middle Eastern and Moroccan cooking. Roasted and ground, they have a warm, earthy flavor that is intensely fragrant. The combination of cumin and allspice in the Tunisian Eggplant Salad recipe on page 366 is a fine example of the role of spices in cooking.

Opposite page, clockwise from top: cumin seeds, cardamom pods, juniper berries, coriander seeds, star anise, nutmeg, and (center) Sichuan peppercorns

Fenugreek (whole)

I was introduced to these tiny, pale-colored seeds when a friend gave me a recipe for a curry (*Summer Collection*) from Sri Lanka, a country where they are used widely, as in much Indian cooking. I have also used them in my Egg and Lentil Curry on page 20. Their flavor is strong, so few of them are needed; use them blended with other spices.

Juniper

A beautifully fragrant spice that is used to make gin, so think of gin and you've got juniper. The berries are purple-black, slightly wrinkled and grown wild in hill country. They ripen in the fall, so perhaps that is why juniper is often served with game and pork, wild boar and other autumnal recipes. They are quite pungent and a little goes a long way. When you place them in a mortar and begin to crush them, their deep fragrance and the anticipation of their flavor cannot fail to please.

Nutmeg and mace (whole)

Nutmeg is one of my favorite spices; Europeans have included it in recipes throughout their history – think of a speckled brown custard tart, or the shiny nutmeg skin on a rice pudding (see page 214). It's curious how the French have ignored nutmeg, but the Italians and Spanish adore it, using it in cheese dishes, pasta sauces and fillings, creamy béchamel, and spinach. But a warning: don't even think of buying nutmeg already ground because it quickly loses all its charm. Instead, always use whole nutmeg and grate it whenever you need it. Mace, see the photograph on page 241, is the outer casing of the nutmeg, resembling a thick meshed cage which is dried and becomes brittle. It is sold in pieces (blades) and can be used in infusions, such as flavoring milk for a white sauce (see page 152). Ground mace can be used in recipes for potted meats, shrimp, and pâtés. It is impossible to grind it at home, so this is one spice that has to be bought pre-ground and the date carefully watched.

Paprika (ground)

This is a spice that's ground from dried sweet red peppers – both mild and hot – and comes labeled as such. In this case hot does not really mean chili-hot, but simply piquant, so have no fear. It is made in Hungary and used extensively in Hungarian and Austrian dishes (in wonderful pepper-scented stews such as goulash or chicken paprika). The Spanish also produce paprika and it turns up in many of their recipes – the famous chorizo sausage is made with it. Recently Spain has been producing smoked paprika from dried smoked peppers, and this has added a whole new dimension to this particular spice. Once again, remember the rule: buy in small quantities and replace frequently.

Saffron

This is made from the dried stamens of a variety of purple crocus. It is therefore very expensive, but the good news is you need only very little – the flavor and color are powerful (see Crunchy Roast Potatoes with

Saffron on page 186). You can buy it pre-ground, but I find it best to buy the stamens whole and then pound them to a powder with a mortar and pestle. Mix it with a little water before adding to a recipe, or you can add the powder directly. If, like me, you worry that your paella (see page 336) doesn't look quite as colorful as the one you had in Spain, fear not: you don't need more saffron – in Spain they sometimes add food coloring!

Star anise
Open a jar of star anise and you're immediately transported to the heart of Chinatown, where the markets seem to be permeated with its exotic aroma. The star shape is the pod and the tiny seeds nestle inside each star petal. It is usually used whole, like cardamom pods, and always looks very pretty. Its flavor faintly resembles aniseed but with warm, spicy overtones.

Turmeric
This is a root that belongs to the ginger family and in some Asian markets can be bought fresh, but the powdered version has been dried and pounded. It has a very fragrant aroma and a brilliant yellow ocher color, which is what makes Indian pilau rice that lovely pale yellow. It is also a major ingredient in piccalilli. I always use a little in every curry mixture, as much for its fragrance as for its color. Because it comes pre-ground, it doesn't have a long shelf life, so note the date of purchase.

Pantry extras
Obviously you'll need flour, pasta, rice, and all the staples covered in Part One, but here is a list of other useful pantry ingredients that – as you begin to cook more and more – you might want to include. This, however, will depend very much on your own tastes and what you cook most often. Because the shelf life of these products is sometimes short, you might like to buy them whenever you need them since a two-year-old half-used bag of almonds is only fit for the birdfeeder, as I've discovered.

Dried fruits: sour cherries, apricots, prunes, and vine fruits – currants, black raisins, golden raisins, and so on.

Nuts: unsalted pistachios (these actually keep well in the freezer), unblanched almonds, roasted unsalted peanuts, walnuts, pecans, brazil nuts, and pine nuts.

Coarse semolina for gnocchi (page 460).

Sweet oat cookies and Grape-Nuts for cheesecake crusts (page 462).

Chocolate and cocoa powder: unlike the items above, these should *always* be included, and notes on these are on pages 466 and 467.

The extended pantry
In this chapter what I have included is by no means an exhaustive list: there are hundreds of fascinating and useful pantry ingredients that I have not listed but which you may want to use. What I have done is to try to include what I use the most and what I feel is a good start for beginners.

Pad Thai Noodles with Shrimp

There's a story attached to this recipe. I first ate it in a small street café in Ko Samui, an island off Thailand. It was so supremely good that my husband videoed it in close-up so that I could recreate the whole thing at home. I did, and here it is – every bit as good, I'm glad to say.

Serves 2 as a main course
4 oz (110 g) rice noodles (medium width, about ⅛ inch/3 mm thick)
2 tablespoons dried shrimp
6 oz (175 g) medium sized shrimp (if frozen, thoroughly defrosted)
3 tablespoons peanut or other mildly flavored oil
2 cloves garlic, peeled and crushed
2 medium red chilies, seeded and finely chopped
½ medium red onion, thinly sliced into half-moon shapes
2 tablespoons Thai fish sauce
juice 1 large lime (about 2 tablespoons)
2 large eggs, lightly beaten

For the garnish:
3 tablespoons cilantro
⅓ cup (50 g) natural roasted unsalted peanuts, coarsely chopped or crushed in a mortar and pestle
2 scallions, chopped, including the green parts

You will also need a deep frying pan with a diameter of 10 inches (25.5 cm), or a wok.

The way to tackle this is by having all the ingredients on the list prepared and assembled in front of you. First of all, place the dried shrimp in a small bowl, cover with some boiling water, and soak for 10 minutes. Do the same with the noodles, placing them in a bowl and making sure they're totally submerged in boiling water. After this time, drain the noodles in a colander and rinse them in cold water; then drain the shrimp. Now, to prepare the shrimp, peel off and discard the shells and devein them. To do this, make a slit all along their backs using a small, sharp knife and remove any brownish-black thread, using the tip of the knife to lift it out. Now, chop each shrimp into thirds.

When you're ready to start cooking, heat the oil in the frying pan or wok over high heat until it is really hot. Then, first add the garlic, chili, and red onion and fry for 1-1½ minutes, or until the onion is tender. Then, keeping the heat high, add the soaked dried shrimp and the raw shrimp and fry for another 2 minutes, or until the shrimp have turned pink and are cooked. After that, add the fish sauce and the lime juice, then stir this around for just a few seconds before adding the noodles. Now, toss the noodles around for 1-2 minutes, or until they are heated through. Next, add the beaten eggs by pouring them slowly and evenly all over the noodle-shrimp mixture. Let the eggs begin to set for about 1 minute, then stir briefly once more until the eggs begin to form little shreds. Then mix in half the garnish and give one final stir before serving absolutely immediately in hot bowls with the rest of the garnish passed around to be sprinkled on top.

Anchoïade with Toasted Goat Cheese Croutons

I have recently discovered semi-dried tomatoes, called mi-cuit or sun blush, which are more soft and succulent than dried tomatoes, with lots of concentrated tomato flavor. But if you can't find them in your area, use sun-dried tomatoes in oil and drain off the oil.

This is literally made in moments: all you do is place the ingredients in a food processor and briefly process until the mixture is roughly chopped. Store it covered with plastic wrap at room temperature until needed.

For the croutons, cut the small baguette into 12 slices on the diagonal (about ½ inch/1 cm thick), then spread very thinly with the goat cheese and season with salt and pepper. Place on the baking sheet and bake on the center shelf of the oven for 20 minutes, until crisp and golden.

To serve, spread the anchoïade generously onto the baked croutons, garnish with the basil leaves and olives, and serve with something like a well-chilled Provençal rosé.

Instead of the croutons you could use the goat cheese, onion, and potato bread on page 86, toasted under the broiler, as pictured below.

Serves 4
2 oz (50 g) anchovy fillets, drained
2 mi-cuit or sun-dried tomatoes in oil, drained
1 ripe tomato, peeled
1 tablespoon tomato paste
2 shallots, peeled
8 black olives, pitted
2 cloves garlic, peeled
1 teaspoon fresh oregano
1 tablespoon coarsely chopped fresh basil
1 teaspoon white wine vinegar
freshly ground black pepper

For the croutons (makes 12):
1 oz (25 g) soft goat cheese
1 small baguette
salt and freshly ground black pepper

To garnish:
basil leaves
black olives (preferably small Provençal ones)

You will also need a baking sheet measuring approximately 10 x 14 inches (25.5 x 35 cm).

Preheat the oven to 350°F (180°C).

Linguine with Sardines, Chili, and Capers

Canned sardines are now becoming fashionable again and are an ideal pantry ingredient, great for serving on toast sprinkled with a little balsamic vinegar and lots of seasoning. This is also the perfect pantry meal for two, made in moments and great for anyone on a tight budget. I love the shape of linguine, but any pasta can be used.

Serves 2

8 oz (225 g) dried linguine

a 4½ oz (120 g) can sardines in olive oil, well drained and flaked into bite-sized pieces

1 tablespoon sardine oil, reserved from the can

1 red chili, seeded and finely chopped

1 tablespoon salted capers, rinsed and drained

1 clove garlic, peeled and chopped

1 x 7 oz (200 g) can Italian chopped tomatoes, well drained, or 4 ripe, medium-sized tomatoes, peeled and diced

a few fresh basil leaves, roughly torn, to garnish

salt and freshly ground black pepper

First of all, you need to cook the pasta. Always use a large cooking pot and make sure you have at least 2½ quarts (2.25 liters) of water and 1 level tablespoon of salt for every ½ lb (225 g) of pasta. Bring the water up to a fierce boil before the pasta goes in and cook it for 8-12 minutes without a lid, until *al dente*.

Meanwhile, heat the tablespoon of the sardine oil in a small frying pan, fry the garlic and chili for about 4 minutes until softened, and add the tomatoes, sardines, and capers, gently heating them through while stirring occasionally. Taste and season with salt and freshly ground black pepper.

When the pasta is ready, drain it in a colander, then quickly return it to the saucepan. Add the sauce, toss it around thoroughly for 30 seconds or so, then serve in hot pasta bowls with the torn basil sprinkled on top.

Mexican Guacamole

The first time I used Tabasco (hot chili sauce) was when I made my first guacamole. This spicy Mexican purée, made with fresh avocados, chilies, and ripe tomatoes, is still a great favorite. Serve it as an appetizer with good crusty bread or as a dip with raw vegetable strips. Don't make guacamole more than 3 hours ahead, though, or it will darken.

First, it's important to have ripe avocados. All you do is halve them and remove the pits, then cut them into quarters, remove the flesh from the inside of the peeling, and place it in the bowl of a food processor. Now, using a teaspoon, scrape away any green part of the avocado flesh that has adhered to the peeling and add this, too, because it gives lots of green color. Now peel the tomatoes by pouring boiling water over them, then leave them for exactly 1 minute before draining, and slipping off their skins (protect your hands with a cloth). Then halve them and pop them in to join the avocado, followed by the garlic, onion, and chilies; then add the lime juice, a few drops of Tabasco, and some salt and pepper. Now, process it all to a smooth purée, pile it into a serving bowl, and cover with plastic wrap. Chill until you need it and serve it sprinkled with the cilantro.

Serves 4
2 ripe avocados
2 large, red, ripe tomatoes
2 small cloves garlic, peeled and sliced
½ red onion, cut into quarters
2 small red chilies, halved and seeded
juice 2 limes
a few drops Tabasco
2 tablespoons cilantro, to garnish
salt and freshly ground black pepper

Marinated Pork with Jerk Seasoning and Broiled Pineapple Salsa

In the Caribbean, jerk seasoning comes either wet or dry. The latter is made with dried herbs, which I don't usually have available, so this is the wet version – great for a barbecue or just plain oven broiling.

Serves 6

6 large pork chops
1 large red chili, seeded
½ small red onion
½ tablespoon chopped fresh
flat-leaf parsley
1 clove garlic, peeled
¾ inch (2 cm) piece fresh ginger,
peeled and sliced
½ teaspoon sea salt
½ teaspoon allspice berries, ground
¼ fresh nutmeg, grated
⅛ teaspoon ground cinnamon
⅛ teaspoon ground cloves
juice 1 lime
1 tablespoon Japanese soy sauce
1 tablespoon peanut or other mildly
flavored oil
1 tablespoon dark muscovado or dark
brown sugar
1¼ cups (275 ml) dry white wine
salt and freshly ground black pepper

For the pineapple salsa:

1 medium pineapple
1 tablespoon peanut or other mildly
flavored oil
1 tablespoon honey
1 small red onion, peeled and very
finely chopped
½ medium red chili, seeded and diced
juice 1 lime
2 tablespoons chopped fresh cilantro
salt and freshly ground black pepper

You will need a shallow baking pan measuring approximately 11 x 16 inches (28 x 40 cm).

Start this way ahead of time: trim the fat off the chops and season them with salt and pepper. Place all the other ingredients, except the wine, in a food processor and mix to a thick paste. Next, spread half the paste over the bottom of a shallow dish and place the pork chops on top; then spread the rest of the paste over the surface of each chop. Now, cover the dish with plastic wrap and leave for a few hours so the flavors can develop.

Meanwhile, make the salsa. To do this you need to first preheat the broiler to its highest setting, then mix the oil and honey with a generous sprinkling of salt and black pepper. Then, using a sharp knife, cut the top and bottom off the pineapple, and, standing it upright on a chopping board, remove the peeling using a large serrated knife. Dig out the "eyes" using the tip of a potato peeler. Now, cut the pineapple in half lengthwise, and lay each half, cut-side-down, on the chopping board and slice each into 6 long wedges. After that, trim off the inner core. (See the photographs on page 427.) Next, brush each wedge with the honey mixture and place them in the baking pan; then place them under the broiler about 1½ inches (4 cm) from the heat and broil for 10-15 minutes until they become nicely charred; you'll need to turn them halfway through the cooking time. After that, remove them from the broiler and allow them to cool slightly before chopping roughly into ½ inch (1 cm) pieces and mixing them with the remaining salsa ingredients. Then set aside until needed.

When you're ready to cook the pork chops, preheat the broiler to its highest setting for at least 10 minutes. Place the chops in the same baking pan, making sure their surface is completely covered with the marinade (reserve the marinade left in the dish), then broil them 3 inches (7.5 cm) from the heat for about 15 minutes. After that, turn them over, spread the surface with the rest of the marinade, and broil for another 15 minutes until the chops are cooked and the surface is crisp. Remove the pork chops to a serving dish, and scrape any crusty bits and remaining marinade from the baking pan into a small saucepan. Add the dry white wine; let it bubble to reduce it by about a third, and pour it over the pork before seasoning. Serve with the salsa.

Beef Curry Dopiaza

The word dopiaza means "double onion," and because I really love thick, spicy onions, it's what I always order in Indian restaurants. My recipe is not authentic, but I feel it is as good as any I've had.

Serves 4
2 lb (900 g) chuck steak, chopped into
1-inch (2.5 cm) pieces
1½ teaspoons cumin seeds
1½ teaspoons coriander seeds
3 cardamom pods (whole)
1 teaspoon fennel seeds
1 teaspoon whole fenugreek
(alternatively, use powder)
3 tablespoons peanut or other mildly
flavored oil
1 lb (450 g) onions, peeled and
sliced into half-moon shapes about
½ inch (1 cm) thick
3 cloves garlic, peeled and crushed
3 green chilies, seeded and
finely chopped
1 tablespoon ground turmeric
1 tablespoon freshly grated
peeled ginger
2 medium tomatoes, peeled
and chopped
1½ cups (375 ml) coconut milk
½ cup (150 ml) plain yogurt
salt and freshly ground black pepper

To serve:
juice 1 lime
1 tablespoon chopped cilantro

You will also need an ovenproof
casserole with a lid holding 2 1/2
quarts (2.25 liters).

First of all you need to roast the whole spices. To do this place them in a small frying pan or saucepan over medium heat and toss them around for 1-2 minutes, or until they begin to look toasted and start to jump in the pan. Now transfer them to a mortar and pestle and crush them to a powder.

Next, place 2 tablespoons of the oil in the casserole over high heat and, when it is really hot, brown the pieces of meat a few at a time. Remove them to a plate, then add the rest of the oil, and, when that's really hot, fry the onions until well browned – about 10 minutes. Add the garlic and chili and cook for a further 2 minutes.

Next, return the meat to the pan, add the crushed spices, fenugreek (the powdered form if you were unable to buy it whole), turmeric, ginger, and tomatoes and stir everything around. Pour the coconut milk into the casserole, followed by the yogurt and some seasoning. Now bring the mixture up to a slow simmer, put the lid on the casserole, and simmer very gently for 2 hours. Just before serving, add the lime juice and sprinkle the chopped fresh coriander on top. Serve with spiced basmati rice and Coriander Chutney (see page 211).

Beef Curry Dopiaza served with Basmati Rice, Coriander Chutney, and Mango Chutney

Lamb Kidneys with Two Mustards

This is a lovely, light recipe for summer. I like to keep the mustard flavor subtle, but if you like it more pronounced, simply add a little more.

Serves 2-3

1 lb (450 g) lamb kidneys

1½ teaspoons mustard powder

3 teaspoons hot or regular wholegrain mustard

1 tablespoon (10 g) butter

2 teaspoons peanut or other mildly flavored oil

1 small onion, peeled, halved, and thinly sliced into half-moons

4 oz (110 g) small open-cup mushrooms, e.g. cremini, cut into ¼ inch (5 mm) slices

⅓ cup (75 ml) dry white wine

¾ cup (200 ml) crème fraîche

salt and freshly ground black pepper

You will also need a frying pan with a diameter of 10 inches (25.5 cm).

First prepare the kidneys by cutting them in half horizontally and snipping out the white cores with scissors – if you don't the kidneys will be tough. Peel off and discard the skins. Next, place the frying pan over high heat and heat the butter and oil together. When it's hot and foaming, add the kidneys and cook for 3 minutes, turning them over halfway through. Remove them to a plate; add the onion to the pan, and, keeping the heat high, cook for 3-4 minutes until softened and brown at the edges. Add the mushrooms and cook for another 1-2 minutes until the juices start to run out, then add the white wine and let it bubble and reduce to half its volume. Finally, add the crème fraîche and mustards. Give everything a good seasoning, stir well, and carry on with reducing the liquid for 2-3 minutes. Finally, return the kidneys and their juices to the sauce and heat through for about 1 minute. Serve right away with plain basmati rice.

Asian Pork Casserole with Stir-Fried Vegetables

This is quite an exotic recipe, a wonderful combination of flavors that develop and permeate the pork while it cooks very slowly. The pork casserole takes only 6 minutes or so of actual preparation time from start to finish. Serve it with Thai fragrant rice.

All you need to do is arrange the pork in a single layer in the bottom of a lidded heatproof casserole that will hold 2½ quarts (2.25 liters). Then simply whisk all the other ingredients (except the cinnamon and star anise) together and pour over the pork. Now, tuck in the cinnamon sticks and star anise, place the casserole on a burner, and bring everything to a very gentle simmer. Put the lid on and simmer over the gentlest-possible heat for 45 minutes. At that point turn the pieces of pork over, replace the lid, and simmer for 45 minutes more.

For the stir-fry, first prepare the vegetables: the cauliflower should be separated and cut into tiny florets, and do the same with the broccoli. Wash and trim the leeks, then halve and thinly slice them; the scallions should be sliced into matchsticks, as should the ginger. Finally, cut each head of pak choi into 6 wedges through the root.

When you're ready to cook, heat the oil over high heat in a wok. Add the ginger and garlic and fry for 10 seconds; then add the cauliflower and broccoli and stir-fry for 1 minute. Next, add the leeks and stir-fry for another minute. Add the scallions and pak choi, toss everything together, and mix in the liquid and sugar. Reduce the heat to medium; put a lid on the wok and cook for 4 minutes, stirring occasionally. Serve the pork and stir-fried greens with the scallions and chili sprinkled over each portion, remembering to remove the cinnamon sticks and star anise first.

Note: if you like, spinach leaves can be used instead of pak choi.

Serves 4-6
2 lb (900 g) shoulder of pork, chopped into 1 inch (2.5 cm) cubes
½ cup (120 ml) Japanese soy sauce
1½ tablespoons freshly grated peeled ginger
2 teaspoons dark muscovado or dark brown sugar
1 small onion, peeled and finely chopped
2 cloves garlic, peeled and crushed
2 medium red chilies, seeded and finely chopped
½ cup (120 ml) Shaosing brown rice wine or dry sherry
2 x 3 inch (7.5 cm) cinnamon sticks
2 whole star anise

For the stir-fried vegetables:
4 oz (110 g) cauliflower
6 oz (175 g) broccoli
2 medium leeks
4 scallions
2 inch (5 cm) piece ginger, peeled
10 oz (275 g) pak choi
2 tablespoons peanut or other mildly flavored oil
2 cloves garlic, peeled and thinly sliced
3 tablespoons Japanese soy sauce
⅓ cup (75 ml) Shaosing brown rice wine or dry sherry
⅓ cup (75 ml) water
2 teaspoons superfine sugar

To garnish:
2 scallions, cut into fine shreds
1 inch (2.5 cm) long
½ medium red chili, seeded and cut into fine shreds

Preserved Ginger Cake with Lemon Icing

In all my years of cooking, this is, quite simply, my favorite cake. It's simple but absolute heaven. The spiciness of the ginger within the moist cake, coupled with the sharpness of the lemon icing, is such that it never fails to please all who eat it.

Makes 15 squares

5 pieces (3 oz/75 g) preserved stem ginger in syrup, chopped
2 tablespoons ginger syrup (from jar of stem ginger in syrup)
1½ teaspoons ground ginger
1½ teaspoons grated fresh ginger
12 tablespoons (175 g) butter, at room temperature, plus a little extra for greasing
¾ cup plus 3 tablespoons (175 g) superfine sugar
3 large eggs, at room temperature
1 tablespoon molasses
1½ cups (225 g) self-rising flour
¼ oz whole blanched almonds, finely ground in a food processor
2 tablespoons milk

For the topping:
juice 1 lemon
2 cups (225 g) confectioners sugar
2 extra pieces (2 oz/50 g) preserved stem ginger in syrup

You will also need a non-stick cake pan measuring approximately 6 x 10 inches (15 x 25.5 cm), 1 inch (2.5 cm) deep, and some parchment paper measuring 10 x 14 inches (25.5 x 35 cm).

Preheat the oven to 325°F (170°C).

First, prepare the cake pan, greasing it lightly and lining it with parchment paper: Press the paper into the pan, folding the corners to make a neat fit (see page 133) and allowing it to come 1 inch (2.5 cm) above the edge.

To make the cake, cream the butter and sugar together in a large mixing bowl until light and fluffy. Next, break the eggs into a small bowl and beat them with a fork until fluffy, then gradually beat them into the butter and sugar mixture, a little at a time until all the eggs are incorporated. Next, fold in the ginger syrup and molasses (the best way to add the molasses is to lightly grease a tablespoon, then take a tablespoon of molasses and just push it off the spoon with a rubber spatula into the mixture). Now, sift the flour and ground ginger onto a plate, then gradually fold these in, about a tablespoon at a time. Next, fold in the almonds, followed by the milk, and lastly the grated ginger and pieces of stem ginger. Spread the cake mixture evenly in the cake pan, then bake on the middle shelf of the oven for 45-50 minutes, or until the cake is risen, springy, and firm to touch in the center. Let the cake cool in the pan for 10 minutes, then turn it out onto a wire rack and make sure it is absolutely cold before you attempt to ice it.

For the icing, sift the confectioners sugar into a bowl and mix with enough of the lemon juice to make the consistency of thick cream – you might not need all the lemon juice. Spread the icing over the top of the cake - don't worry if it dribbles down the sides in places since this serves to decorate the cake. Cut the remaining ginger into 15 chunks and place these in rows across the cake so that when you cut it you will have 15 squares, each with a piece of ginger in the center. The cake is absolute heaven. You can freeze one or two of these cakes, uniced, for a rainy day.

12

Fish without fear

Why is it that people are afraid to cook fish? Is it fear of the unknown, the unfamiliar, or is it that there are now just too many varieties to choose from, making it difficult for a beginner to know where to start? Given that so many people love eating fish but so few want to cook it, I feel my task here is to reassure those of you who are afraid and try to provide a sort of simple introduction to the whole subject of cooking fish, which will hopefully persuade you to try.

It's now established that fish is in the premier food group as far as the 21st-century diet is concerned. Perhaps the most important reason for this is speed – because for people who lead busy, pressured lives fish is one of the few ingredients that can provide a main-course supper dish that's not only elegant, stylish, and up-to-the minute, but at the same time takes as little as 10 minutes and rarely more than 30 to cook from start to finish.

But there's more. Nutritionally fish is not only rich in first-class protein, an essential part of our daily diet, but at the same time it happens to be, conveniently, low in fat (for the most part). Then, by some extra miracle of nature, the group known as oily fish (a bad description, because they actually contain a very small amount of fat) contains substances known as omega-3 fatty acids that are beneficial in preventing clogged arteries, which cause heart diseases and certain skin conditions. We should therefore all be eating, and more importantly, enjoying more fish. So here goes – I am going to take a crack at persuading you. Let's first examine what the pitfalls might be.

The fear factor

Here, familiarity is the key – getting to know about fish and understanding it will automatically make you much more comfortable, so read on.

"I don't know how to handle it."

There's a bit of hand-me-down mythology here. Who says fish necessarily needs handling? This is merely a throw back to the days when cooks had to deal with freshly caught fish that needed scaling, gutting, filleting, and so on. With modern fish markets, supermarket fish counters, and freezer units, all this work is done for you. If you want to, you can now buy fish skinned, boned, and ready to cook, which probably means less handling and trimming than the average steak. Sometimes, as with cutting up a chicken, some handling is needed, but only for those who choose it. Anyway, here all the hands-on information you will ever need to know about fish will be explained to remove the fear.

"What about the bones?"

First, as explained above, there don't have to be any bones at all. However, if you really enjoy eating a wide variety of fish that's not always filleted, there's no bones about it (excuse the pun). Provided you know how to handle and deal with them. This includes a few basic lessons, not just on preparation for cooking but also on how to actually eat the fish once it arrives on the plate (see the next point).

"And the skin?"

I used to be absolutely terrified of skinning a piece of fish because I simply didn't know how to do it, then I was taught and I've never looked back.

So, if I can teach you how to do it (see page 275), you, too, will no longer have any fears. But let me say that as a fish lover, I feel that leaving the skin on is sometimes preferable because it can give extra flavor to the dish (in which case it can simply be left on the side of the plate). It's now become fashionable in restaurants, however, to sear the de-scaled skin of certain fish at very high temperatures so that it becomes so crisp that it resembles crackling, and this is, I have to say, quite delicious!

"What about the smell?"

There actually shouldn't be any smell. If you have a reliable fish market and you buy fresh fish, it should not smell at all unpleasant; in fact the opposite is true – the smell of fresh fish sizzling in the pan can be quite inviting. As with all cooking, however, kitchens need to be well ventilated, with a window open or an exhaust fan on. Some smoked fish are perhaps the exception to this no-smell rule, but keep the window wide open as you cook. If you get the chance, try cooking smoked fish outside on a barbecue grill - no smells linger, and it tastes wonderful broiled over charcoal.

"Where have all the fish markets gone?"

It has to be said that if you want to cook and enjoy eating fish, then your source is vital. Sadly, main-street food shops are victims of parking restrictions and I imagine we can put much of the blame for the demise of our fish markets on those horrid no-parking signs, making the free-parking offer of the supermarkets much more practical. However, there are still good fish markets which need our support. What happens in supermarkets is that some fish counters, together with the pre-packed fish they sell, are of superb quality, others not so, but because this does vary enormously from store to store, the best guide is your nose. If, as you walk towards the fish counter, you can smell fish, don't approach it.

"How much do I need?"

I would say 7-8 oz (200-225 g) per person for boned white fish; on the bone (whole trout, flounder, mackerel), 10-12 oz (275-350 g) each; and for richer fish, such as salmon or tuna, 6-8 oz (175-225 g) would be right.

"What kind of fish?"

For a beginner I feel the best way forward is to get to know just a few varieties of fish and what to expect from them, so what I've tried to do here is, first, put them into groups to give you an initial guide.

Firm and flaky

This is essentially the cod family, which includes cod, haddock, hake, and whiting. If you want a fairly firm, flaky flesh that is moist and succulent with a delicate flavor, this is what you'll get from this group.

Firm and meaty

This group, as these words imply, has more bite to it, and because it's more robust in texture, it can stand up to more vigorous cooking. Turbot and halibut are in this league, as are monkfish tails, and all have a fine flavor.

Delicate

This includes most of the group we call flat fish, and their texture varies. Skate, *left*, has sweet white flesh and an excellent texture; Dover sole has a fairly firm flesh with a fine flavor; lemon sole has a more delicate flesh and not such a good flavor; flounder has a very fragile flesh and a lovely fragrant flavor of the sea.

Lots of gutsy flavor

The oily fish group are for those who like real flavor, and herring, mackerel, sardines, sprats, and whitebait all belong to this family – juicy and succulent, with tons of flavor. Here you are going to have to negotiate with bones, but it's worth it for the taste alone.

The king of fish

The salmon is definitely the crowned king of fish. Wild salmon leaves the sea to enter the rivers, and freshly caught wild salmon has just about everything: firm, delicate flesh combined with all the flavor of the sea. Farmed, it can be excellent or very poor. Thankfully, it's easy to tell by looking (*see left*) – too many white fat layers mean poor quality. The reason for this, believe it or not, is lack of exercise. The wild salmon negotiates strong currents, giving it a kind of "aerobic" existence; good farmed salmon comes from lakes and areas where strong currents exist.

Trout

Sea trout – or salmon trout, as it's sometimes called – looks like a small salmon, but, though it has the appearance of salmon, it's less fatty and the flesh is more delicate. Trout proper is its small freshwater cousin that lives in lakes, rivers, and streams. Wild it's called brown trout, is exceptionally special and only available if you know someone who goes fishing, but farmed it's called rainbow trout and is not so flavorful.

Smoked fish

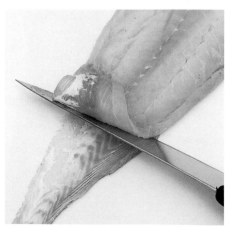

All the fish just mentioned can be purchased in smoked form, and the flavor of the smoke and fish is an inspired combination. Finnan haddie is smoked on the bone, but it is also sold in fillet form, as is smoked trout. Some fish, such as trout, are smoked by a method which actually cooks them, so they only need re-heating. Alternately, you can serve them at room temperature.

There's nothing to be afraid of

Now you are embarking on a journey of learning how to cook fish, but although I have said everything can be prepared for you, I am including instructions on how to bone and skin fish – just in case you want to learn, or perhaps find yourself the lucky recipient of some freshly caught fish.

How to skin a fillet of fish

All you need is a flat surface and a sharp knife. First of all, angle the knife at the thinner or tail end of the fillet, or if it's all the same thickness, just start at one end. Cut a little of the flesh away from the skin – enough to get the knife angled in. Now, using your fingertips, hang onto the skin, clasping it as firmly as possible, then push the knife with your other hand, keeping the blade at an angle, *opposite, bottom left*. Push at the skin, not the flesh, remembering the skin is tough and the knife won't go through it. What's happening is the knife blade, as it slides between the skin and the flesh, is cutting the skin away. If you're not experienced, don't worry if you're left with a few patches of skin; you can just gently cut these away. Practice is all you need; you'll soon be able to feel when the angle of the knife is right.

How to bone a whole fish

This method applies to herring, mackerel, and trout. First, ask the fish market counter person to scale, trim, and bone the fish for you, or, it really is very simple to bone the fish yourself. All you do is cut along the belly of the fish with scissors, snipping off the head, fins, and the tail, then place it flesh-side down on a flat surface. Now, using a rolling pin, give the fish a few sharp taps to flatten it out. Next, press very firmly with your thumbs or the handle of a wooden spoon (see *top right*) all along the back bone of the fish which will loosen it. Now, turn the fish skin-side down, and using a sharp knife, start at the head end to gently ease the back bone away (see *center*): as it comes away, almost all the little bones will come away with it. Any that don't can be removed afterwards; tweezers are helpful here. Finally, cut away the dark belly flaps using scissors, *bottom*.

How to cook fish

Set out over the next few pages are simple guidelines for various methods of cooking fish. When you have tried the recipes, each describing in detail how to cook the fish, you will have a fairly broad knowledge, and, I hope, you will feel comfortable with cooking fish for the rest of your life. The timings that follow are guidelines - just remember that thicker pieces of fish will need the longer times, thinner pieces the shorter.

Poaching

Poached finnan haddie, topped with a couple of fresh, lightly poached eggs and served with some brown bread and butter, is one of the quickest and best tasting comfort meals I know. Poaching is fast and easy. If you want to serve a sauce with the fish, using the poaching liquid introduces the flavor of the fish itself. Thus, the liquid from white fish poached in a mixture of half milk and half water can be used for a parsley sauce, and the cooking liquid from smoked fish fillets poached in the same way can be used to make a basic white sauce to which chopped hard-boiled eggs and chives can be added. Either sauce can be finished off beautifully with a tablespoon of light cream or crème fraîche.

Rolled fish fillets, ie flounder or sole, can be poached in white wine or cider, which again will make a lovely sauce. Trout can be poached in a pan of water to which a glass of dry white wine or cider has been added, along with a few sprigs of fresh herbs, a couple of bay leaves, slices of lemon, thin onion slices, and a few black peppercorns. Don't bother with fish poachers, which take up far too much storage space, since large, whole fish are better oven-baked in foil.

Poaching guidelines

Rolled fillets of sole and flounder will take 4-5 minutes, and the cooking liquid – dry white wine or cider – can be used to make a sauce. White or smoked fish fillets and fish steaks weighing 6-7 oz (175-200 g) will take 6-8 minutes, depending on their thickness. Whole trout weighing 10-12 oz (275-350 g) each will take 8-10 minutes – less for small fish. Use enough liquid to half-cover the fish and make sure the pan has a well-fitting lid.

Steaming

Steaming, like poaching, is great for people who count calories since no fat is needed, so if you are cutting the fat in your diet, steaming fish is definitely for you. You can use either a traditional steamer or a bamboo one. As Asian cooks have discovered, steaming is particularly good for rolled fillets of flounder, sole, or trout because they retain their shape perfectly and stay beautifully moist. Add about 2 inches (5 cm) of boiling water to the saucepan; then fit the steamer on top, making sure it doesn't come into contact with the water, and cover with a tight-fitting lid.

Steaming guidelines

Whole Dover sole, lemon sole, or flounder weighing 10-12 oz (275-350 g) will take 7-8 minutes; rolled fillets of the above, 7-8 minutes; trout fillets, rolled, will take 7-8 minutes; white or smoked fish, steaks, and fillets weighing 6-7 oz (175-200 g), 8-10 minutes.

Shallow-frying

I have evocative memories of my grandmother shallow-frying skate wings, her favorite fish, which she first dipped in seasoned flour – they were golden and crisp at the edges, and there were always special Victorian bone-handled fish knives and forks on the table. I think shallow-fried fish makes a simple but very tempting supper dish, but you need to follow a few basic rules to get it absolutely right. First, the fish must be dried thoroughly with paper towels, and because the flesh of white fish is so delicate, there needs to be some kind of coating – seasoned flour, white or whole wheat, beaten eggs, and breadcrumbs.

The second rule is that you must have the fat hot enough – olive oil or a mixture of peanut or other mildly flavored oil and butter are my favorites. There should be enough oil to cover the pan and give a depth of about ⅛ inch (3 mm), and the most vital point is that it must be really hot. Watch the oil while it's heating and you will see a shimmering haze that will cue you as to when to add the fish. If in doubt, add a small cube of bread, which should sizzle fiercely; if it doesn't, the oil is not hot enough. The idea is to seal the fish in the hot fat on both sides – it is only when the fat isn't hot enough that fried fish tastes oily. Always drain shallow-fried fish on crumpled paper towels before serving.

Shallow-frying guidelines
Whole Dover sole, lemon sole, or flounder weighing 10-12 oz (275-350g) each, 4-6 minutes each side; fillets of the above, 2-3 minutes each side; fish steaks and fillets weighing 6-7 oz (175-200 g), 5-6 minutes each side; skate wings, 4-5 minutes each side; whole herring or mackerel weighing 8-10 oz (225-275 g), 5-6 minutes each side; sprats, 2-3 minutes each side.

Down with deep-frying
I have, I'm afraid, eliminated deep-frying from my own cooking repertoire. I think times have changed and we've all moved on from not only the bother of it but the "write your name in it" layer of grease it leaves on the kitchen walls. Yes, there are deep-frying machines, but they're a bother to clean and take up too much space. I now prefer to use a high temperature oven-roasting for oven-roasted potato wedges (see page 191), and fish I feel can be very successfully shallow-fried. Meanwhile, I can still enjoy it from my local take-out and other deep-fried foods in restaurants and let *them* have the bother of cleaning the ceiling and walls.

Oven-baking
This and foil cooking (on the following page) are trouble-free ways of cooking certain fish because if you put on a timer, you can place the dish in the oven and forget all about it. But, having said that, there are one or two things to be wary of. White fish, steaks, and fillets on their own could end up being dry, so these are best brushed liberally with melted butter and protected with a buttered piece of foil lightly placed over them. If you use a topping which will keep the moisture in the fish, the foil is not needed.

Whole fish oven-bake beautifully if brushed liberally with butter or oil, and if a stuffing is added to the body cavity, this will help keep the fish moist.

Oven-baking guidelines

Preheat the oven to 400°F (200°C). For white fish or smoked fish fillets and steaks, brushed with butter and wrapped in buttered foil and weighing 6-7 oz (175-200 g), allow 15-20 minutes; whole mackerel, trout, or herring weighing 10-12 oz (275-350 g) each, 25-30 minutes; tilapia weighing 12-14 oz (350-400 g), 15 minutes.

Oven-roasting

This is, in all the years I have been cooking, a breakthrough for me, since it cuts out a lot of shallow-frying and broiling. What happens is the oven is preheated to its highest setting (about 450°F, 230°C), the fish then gets a real blast of heat, which cooks it quickly, retaining all its moist juices. I hate standing watching the broiler, or, equally, getting greasy from deep-frying; oven-roasting cuts time and effort, and also, used instead of frying, cuts down the fat, which is always a good thing.

Foil-wrapped fish

You can, if you wish, foil-wrap fish and then cook it in a steamer, under the broiler, on a barbecue grill, or in the oven. The advantage is that all the flavors and juices are retained inside the sealed package. It's best to follow individual recipes for timings, but I have found that foil-wrapping is the best way to cook either a whole or large piece of salmon or a sea trout. If, in the summertime, you want to serve the fish cold, you can leave it inside the foil package until you're ready to serve it, which will keep it moist and juicy.

To cook salmon, I like the slow method, which very gently cooks the fish to absolute perfection. If you want to cook a whole salmon for a party, the fish can be cut in half, wrapped in two foil packages, then, after baking and cooling, the two halves can be put back together once the skin has been removed and the join hidden by a band of cucumber slices. The oven temperature for this is 250°F (120°C). Add 2-3 bay leaves to the body cavity and some sprigs of fresh tarragon, season with salt and pepper, and tuck in 2-4 tablespoons (25-50 g) of butter. Then wrap the whole thing in a double sheet of foil, loosely but sealing it tightly, place on a baking sheet and bake in the preheated oven for the following cooking times. For a 1 lb 8 oz (700 g) salmon, 1 hour 10 minutes; 2 lb (900 g), 1 hour 30 minutes; 3 lb (1.35 kg), 2 hours; 4 lb (1.8 kg), 2 hours 30 minutes; 5 lb (2.25 kg), 3 hours.

Whole salmon or sea trout can be prepared as above and cooked with the same timings according to the weight. Salmon steaks weighing up to 8 oz (225 g) each need to be baked at a higher temperature than this:

350°F (180°C). Wrap them – either individually or 4-6 at a time – in well-buttered foil, but first season them, adding torn bay leaves, sprigs of tarragon, and 1 tablespoon of white wine per steak. Seal the edges of the foil securely and bake on a high shelf of the oven for 20 minutes. Salmon fillets weighing 5-6 oz (150-175 g) each will take 15-20 minutes.

Broiling and barbecuing

This is something of a minefield to give timings for because domestic oven broilers vary so much, as do shelf distances from the source of the heat, so bear this in mind when following these guidelines, especially with barbecue grills, where accurate degrees of heat cannot be measured. First, remember to always line your broil pan with buttered foil, since this makes it easier to clean it and prevents any fishy flavors from lingering in the pan. White fish needs to be brushed generously with melted butter and basted with more melted butter while cooking to prevent any dryness.

When using a barbecue grill, have some melted butter handy to brush on the fish; it's best to use one of the special fish grill-racks - this keeps the fish neatly intact without it breaking or sticking. Trout, mackerel, and other small, whole fish all respond well to this cooking method, and you can add herbs and seasoning. For domestic oven broilers always preheat them to their highest setting at least 10 minutes in advance.

Approximate broiling times

Whole Dover sole, lemon sole, or flounder weighing 10-12 oz (275-350 g), 4-6 minutes each side; fillets of sole or flounder, 2-3 minutes each side; fish fillets and steaks weighing 6-8 oz (175-225 g), allow 5-6 minutes each side, fleshy-side first (have extra butter ready for basting during cooking); whole mackerel weighing 8-10 oz (225-275 g), make 3 diagonal scores on each side, and, if you wish, tuck in a slice of lemon or lime, brush with melted butter, and broil for 6-7 minutes each side. Whole herring weighing 6-8 oz (175-225 g), score and butter as above and allow 4-5 minutes' broiling time each side.

Microwaving

This is a tricky subject, and one that causes a great dilemma for the cook book writer. Since microwave ovens are not standard and the power levels vary, it's difficult to give any kind of standard guidelines. The best course if you want to cook fish in the microwave is to follow the instructions in the individual manufacturer's handbook. But the danger with cooking fish in this way is that a few seconds more than it actually needs will render it overcooked and sometimes dry. For this reason I think cooking fish in a microwave is not a good idea for beginners. Conventional cooking is quick and easy anyway, so I would begin with this.

Fried Skate Wings with Very Quick Homemade Tartare Sauce

Serves 2

1 lb (450 g) skate wings (2 small, or 1 large and cut in half)
1½ tablespoons seasoned flour
2 tablespoons light olive oil

For the tartare sauce:

1 large egg
½ teaspoon sea salt
1 small clove garlic, peeled
½ teaspoon mustard powder
¾ cup (175 ml) light olive oil
2 teaspoons lemon juice
1 tablespoon fresh flat-leaf parsley leaves
1½ tablespoons salted capers, rinsed and drained
4 cornichons (mini pickles)
freshly milled black pepper

To serve:

a few sprigs fresh flat-leaf parsley
1 lemon, sliced into wedges

You will also need a frying pan with a diameter of 10 inches (25.5 cm).

People are scared of this, one of the finest and most delicious fish of all. But don't be: the flesh slides away from those ribby, gelatinous bones with simplicity and ease (see the photograph on page 274), so do give it a try. I love it simply plain with lemon squeezed over or with tartare sauce. This sauce has a mayonnaise base, which in this case is made by the quick method: that is, using a whole egg and a food processor or blender. This sauce will keep in a clean screw-top jar in the refrigerator for up to a week. It can also be served with any plain-broiled fish or with fishcakes.

Begin by making the tartare sauce. Break the egg into the bowl of the processor, add the salt, garlic, and mustard powder, then turn the motor on and add the oil through the feeder tube in a thin, steady trickle, pouring it as slowly as you can (which will take you about 2 minutes). When the oil has been added and the sauce has thickened, add some pepper and all the other ingredients. Now, turn on the pulse button and process until the ingredients are chopped – as coarsely or as finely as you like. Lastly, taste to check the seasoning, then transfer to a serving bowl.

When you are ready to cook the skate wings, set the frying pan over a gentle heat to warm it up while you wipe the fish with paper towels and coat them with a light dusting of the seasoned flour. Now, turn the heat up to high, add the oil to the pan, and as soon as it's very hot, add the skate wings. Reduce the heat to medium and fry them for 4-5 minutes on each side, depending on their size and thickness. To test if they are cooked, slide the tip of a sharp knife in and push to see if the flesh parts from the bone easily and looks creamy-white. When the fish is ready, remove it to warm serving plates, garnish with the parsley, and serve with the tartare sauce and lemon wedges to squeeze over all.

Note: for a change to the tartare sauce, replace lemon juice and parsley with lime juice and cilantro.

To make tartare sauce, simply place the egg, salt, garlic, and mustard powder in a food processor, then add the oil in a thin, steady stream through the feeder tube. Once the sauce has thickened, add the remaining ingredients and pulse to the desired consistency, then season and transfer to a serving bowl

Roasted Fish with a Parmesan Crust

This works superbly well with flounder fillets, but sole would be excellent, or thicker fish fillets such as cod or haddock, in which case allow 5 minutes extra cooking time. I don't feel it needs a sauce, but a green salad with a lemony dressing would be a good accompaniment.

Serves 2

1 lb (450 g) flounder fillets (4 fillets)
3 oz (75 g) freshly grated Parmesan (Parmigiano Reggiano)
4 oz (110 g) white bread, slightly stale, cut into cubes
a handful of fresh curly parsley leaves
4 tablespoons (50 g) melted butter, plus a little extra for brushing
salt and freshly ground black pepper

To garnish:
1 lemon, cut into quarters
a little fresh curly parsley

You will also need a shallow baking pan measuring approximately 11 x 16 inches (28 x 40 cm) and some aluminum foil.

Preheat the oven to 450°F (230°C).

First of all, prepare the baking pan by lining it with foil and brushing the foil generously with melted butter. Now, wipe the fish with paper towels, and place the fillets on the foil, seasoning them with salt and black pepper. Next, place the cubes of bread and parsley leaves in a food processor and turn on the motor to process it all into fine crumbs; then add the Parmesan, melted butter, ½ a teaspoon of salt, and some pepper and pulse again to combine them. Now, spread the crumb mixture over the fish fillets, drizzle a little more melted butter over them, and then place the baking pan on a high shelf in the oven for 7-8 minutes, or until the crumbs have turned a golden brown. Serve with the lemon quarters and a sprig of parsley as a garnish.

Fried Herrings with Oatmeal and a Beet Relish

Why is it that fresh sardines are so highly thought of and yet herrings are largely ignored? First, they're very closely related, so their taste is similar; second, herrings, being larger, have more flavorful, juicy flesh. Any leftover beet relish can be kept in the refrigerator for a couple of days.

Begin by making the beet relish. To do this simply mix all the ingredients together and sprinkle them with the chopped parsley.

Now, wipe the herrings with paper towels, then place them, flesh-side up, on a plate and season well. Dip both sides into the seasoned flour; then dip the flesh-side only into first the beaten egg followed by the oatmeal, pressing it down firmly into their flesh. Now, heat the lard or oil in the frying pan over high heat until it's shimmering hot. Fry the herrings flesh-side (oatmeal-side) down for 2-3 minutes, or until they look golden and crusty when you lift a little with a spatula. Now, flip them over using a spatula and fork and let them cook for another 1-2 minutes, transfering them to crumpled paper towels to drain. Serve them with the relish and some waxy potatoes and garnish with parsley and lime wedges.

Serves 2

2 medium-sized herrings weighing 10-12 oz (275-350 g) each when whole, boned (see page 275)
½ cup (75 g) steel-cut oatmeal (coarse oatmeal)
3 tablespoons seasoned all-purpose flour
1 large egg, beaten
2 tablespoons lard or peanut oil
salt and freshly ground black pepper

For the beet relish:
6 oz (175 g) cooked beets, chopped into ¼ inch (5 mm) dice
2 shallots, peeled and finely chopped
4 cornichons (mini pickles), finely chopped
1½ tablespoons salted capers, rinsed and drained
2 teaspoons red wine vinegar
2 teaspoons good-quality mayonnaise
a little chopped fresh parsley, to serve
salt and freshly ground black pepper

To garnish:
a few sprigs fresh flat-leaf parsley
a few lime wedges

You will also need a frying pan with a diameter of 10 inches (25.5 cm).

Thai Fish Cakes with Sesame and Lime Dipping Sauce

The ingredients list for these noble little Thai-inspired fish cakes looks very long, but the good thing is the fishcakes can be made and cooked with incredible speed. Serve them as a first or main course, or as appetizers to serve with drinks, in which case make them smaller.

Serves 4 as a main course, 8 as an appetizer

1 lb (450 g) any white fish fillets, skinned and cut into chunks
1 stem lemon grass, roughly chopped
1 fat clove garlic, peeled
½ inch (1 cm) piece fresh ginger, peeled and roughly chopped
3 tablespoons cilantro leaves, plus a few sprigs to garnish
2 kaffir lime leaves, roughly chopped (if unavailable leave them out)
zest 1 lime (the juice goes in the sauce)
1 medium red chili, seeded
½ small red bell pepper (use only ¼ if it's a large one), seeded and roughly chopped
¾ cup (75 g) dried coconut powder
2 tablespoons lightly seasoned all-purpose flour
2-3 tablespoons peanut or other mildly flavored oil, for frying
salt and freshly ground black pepper

For the dipping sauce:
1 teaspoon sesame seeds
1 tablespoon sesame oil
1 tablespoon lime juice
2 teaspoons Thai fish sauce
1 tablespoon Japanese soy sauce
1 medium red chili, seeded and very finely chopped

You will also need a frying pan with a diameter of 10 inches (25.5 cm).

To make the fish cakes, you first of all need to put the lemon grass, garlic, ginger, cilantro leaves, kaffir lime leaves, lime zest, chili, and red bell pepper into a food processor, then turn the motor on and blend everything fairly finely. After that, add the cubes of fish, process again briefly until the fish is blended in, then finally pour in the coconut powder through the feeder tube. Switch on the motor again but be careful at this stage not to overprocess – all you need to do is briefly blend it all for 2-3 seconds.

Then tip the mixture into a bowl, add some seasoning, and shape the fishcakes into 24 small, thin, flattish, round shapes about 2 inches (5 cm) in diameter. If you like, you can make them ahead up to this stage and then spread them out in a single layer, cover them with plastic wrap, and keep them in the refrigerator until needed.

Meanwhile, make the dipping sauce. To do this, first of all begin by toasting the sesame seeds. Using a small, solid frying pan, preheat it over medium heat, then add the sesame seeds and toast them, moving them around in the pan to brown them evenly. As soon as they begin to splutter and pop and turn golden, they're ready – this will take 1-2 minutes. Remove them from the frying pan to a serving bowl and simply stir in the rest of the ingredients.

When you're ready to cook the fishcakes, first coat them in the seasoned flour, then heat 2 tablespoons of the oil in the frying pan over high heat, and when it's very hot, turn the heat down to medium and fry the fishcakes briefly for about 30 seconds on each side to a pale golden color. You will need to cook them in several batches, adding a little more oil if necessary. As they cook, transfer to a warm plate and keep warm. Serve with the dipping sauce, garnished with the remaining cilantro.

Luxurious Smoked-Fish Pie

I've transformed what is usually a family supper dish into something deliciously suitable for entertaining. Garnish this luxurious pie with sprigs of watercress. Serve it with freshly shelled peas, which I always think are delicious with fish pie.

Serves 6

12 oz (340 g) finnan haddie fillet
10 oz (280 g) smoked trout fillet
8 oz (225 g) smoked salmon or smoked salmon trimmings
2 cups (425 ml) whole milk
1 bay leaf
6 black peppercorns
a few stalks fresh parsley
4 tablespoons (50 g) butter
⅓ cup (50 g) all-purpose flour
⅔ cup (150 ml) light cream
3 tablespoons chopped fresh parsley
2 large eggs, hard-boiled and chopped
1½ tablespoons salted capers, rinsed and drained
4 cornichons (mini pickles), chopped
1 tablespoon lemon juice
a few sprigs fresh watercress, to garnish
salt and freshly ground black pepper

For the topping:

2 lb (900 g) round red or white, or Yukon Gold potatoes
4 tablespoons (50 g) butter
2 tablespoons crème fraîche
1 oz (25 g) Gruyère, finely grated
1 tablespoon finely grated Parmesan (Parmigiano Reggiano)
salt and freshly ground black pepper

You will also need an ovenproof baking dish measuring 9 inches (23 cm) square and 2 inches (5 cm) deep, buttered.

Preheat the oven to 400°F (200°C).

First of all, arrange the finnan haddie in a baking pan, pour in the milk, and add the bay leaf, peppercorns, and parsley stems; then bake, uncovered, on a high shelf of the oven for 10 minutes. Meanwhile, remove the skin from the smoked trout – the flesh will come off very easily. Then chop the trout into 2 inch (5 cm) pieces, along with the smoked salmon, if the slices are whole, then place all the prepared fish in a mixing bowl. Next, when the finnan haddie is cooked, strain off the liquid and reserve it, discarding the bay leaf, parsley stems, and peppercorns. Then, when the finnan haddie is cool enough to handle, remove the skin and flake the flesh into largish pieces, adding it to the bowl to join the rest of the fish.

Next, make the sauce, and do this by melting the butter in the saucepan, stir in the flour, and gradually add the fish liquid bit by bit, stirring continuously. When all the liquid is in, finish the sauce by gradually adding the light cream, then some seasoning, and simmer for 3-4 minutes; then stir in the chopped parsley. Now, add the hard-boiled eggs, capers and cornichons to the fish, followed by the lemon juice and, finally, the sauce. Mix it all together gently and carefully so as not to break up the fish too much, then taste and check the seasoning and pour the mixture into the baking dish.

Now, to make the topping, peel and quarter the potatoes, put in a steamer fitted over a large saucepan of boiling water, sprinkle with 2 teaspoons of salt, put a lid on and steam until they are absolutely tender – about 25 minutes. Then remove the potatoes from the steamer, drain off the water, return them to the saucepan and cover with a clean dish towel to absorb some of the steam for about 5 minutes. Now, add the butter and crème fraîche. Using an electric hand mixer set at the lowest speed, break up the potatoes; then increase the speed to high and whip them up to a smooth, creamy, fluffy mass. Taste, season well, then spread the potatoes over the fish, making a ridged pattern with a spatula. Now, finally sprinkle the grated cheeses on top and bake on a high shelf in the oven for 30-40 minutes, or until the top is nicely tinged with brown. Serve each portion garnished with the watercress.

Roasted Butterflied Shrimp in Garlic Butter

This is an amazingly good appetizer for garlic lovers and needs lots of really crusty baguette to mop up all the delicious juices. It is also delightfully simple and can be prepared well in advance.

Serves 4
20 large shrimp (about 1lb 8 oz/700 g), raw, thoroughly defrosted if frozen
4 cloves garlic, peeled and crushed
6 tablespoons (75 g) butter, softened
1½ tablespoons chopped fresh parsley
grated zest and juice ½ lemon
salt and freshly ground black pepper

To serve:
1 tablespoon chopped fresh parsley
1 lemon, quartered

You will also need 4 individual gratin dishes with a bottom diameter of 5 inches (13 cm), buttered, or a shallow baking pan measuring 11 x 16 inches (28 x 40 cm), also buttered.

To butterfly the shrimp, first of all, pull off the heads and legs with your fingers and then, with your fingers, simply peel away the shells which will come away very easily. Leave the tails still attached because this makes them look prettier. Now, turn each shrimp on its back, and, using the point of a sharp knife, make a cut down the center of each shrimp (see *below left*) but do not cut through. With your thumb, ease the shrimp open like a book and remove the brownish-black thread (see *below center*) scraping it away with the point of the knife – it should also come away easily. Next, rinse the shrimp and pat them dry with paper towels, then place them in the buttered gratin dishes or in the baking pan.

Next, make the garlic butter by taking a large fork and combining the rest of the ingredients together in a small bowl. Now, spread equal quantities of the garlic butter over the shrimp. You can now cover the gratin dishes or pan with plastic wrap and chill them in the refrigerator until needed.

To cook the shrimp, preheat the oven to 450°F (230°C), remove the plastic wrap if you've prepared the shrimp in advance, and then place the dishes on the highest shelf of the oven; let them cook for 6-7 minutes (they will need only 5 minutes if you've used a baking pan). Serve sprinkled with the parsley and garnished with the lemon quarters.

Char-Broiled Tuna with Warm Cilantro and Caper Vinaigrette

Because oven broilers are so variable in their efficiency, I think an iron ridged grill pan (see page 304) is a very good investment. It's particularly good for thick tuna steaks and gives those lovely charred stripes that look so attractive.

First of all, brush the grill pan with a little of the olive oil, then place it over a very high heat and let it preheat until very hot – about 10 minutes. Meanwhile, wipe the fish steaks with paper towels, then place them on a plate, brush them with the remaining olive oil, and season both sides with salt and pepper. When the grill pan is ready, place the tuna steaks on it and grill them about 2 minutes on each side.

Meanwhile, make the vinaigrette by placing all the ingredients into a small saucepan and whisk them together over a gentle heat – no actual cooking is needed here; this only needs is to be warmed.

When the tuna steaks are ready, place them onto warm serving plates, pour the vinaigrette over them, and serve with steamed new potatoes.

Serves 2
2 tuna steaks weighing about 8 oz (225 g) each
1 tablespoon extra virgin olive oil
salt and freshly ground black pepper

For the vinaigrette:
1½ tablespoons roughly chopped cilantro leaves
1½ tablespoons salted capers, rinsed and drained
grated zest and juice 1 lime
1 tablespoon white wine vinegar
1 clove garlic, peeled and finely chopped
1 shallot, peeled and finely chopped
1½ teaspoons wholegrain mustard
2 tablespoons extra virgin olive oil
salt and freshly ground black pepper

You will also need a ridged grill pan.

Oven-Roasted Fish with Potatoes and Salsa Verde

This recipe, served with perhaps a simple green salad with a lemony dressing as an accompaniment, is delightfully different and makes a complete meal for two to three people. Here, I've recommended skinless cod fillets, but any firm, thick white fish could be used – chunks of monkfish tail would be particularly good for a special occasion.

Serves 2-3
1 lb (450 g) cod fillet, skinned
(see page 275)
1 lb 4 oz (570 g) Idaho, or round red
potatoes
1 tablespoon olive oil
1½ tablespoons finely grated Parmesan
(Parmigiano Reggiano)
salt and freshly ground black pepper

For the salsa verde:
1 clove garlic, peeled
1 teaspoon sea salt
2 anchovy fillets, drained and chopped
1 teaspoon wholegrain mustard
1 tablespoon salted capers, rinsed,
drained and roughly chopped
1½ tablespoons finely chopped
fresh basil
1½ tablespoons finely chopped
fresh parsley
2 tablespoons olive oil
1½ tablespoons lemon juice
freshly ground black pepper

You will also need an ovenproof baking
dish measuring 8 inches (20 cm)
square and 2 inches (5 cm) deep,
lightly buttered.

To begin this recipe you need to set to work preparing the salsa verde ingredients and have them lined up ready. Now, crush the garlic with the salt using a mortar and pestle, and when it becomes a purée, simply add the rest of the salsa ingredients and whisk well to blend them thoroughly.

Turn the oven on to 400°F (200°C). Next, to prepare the potatoes: put a kettle of water on to boil, then peel and chop the potatoes into ¼ inch (5 mm) slices. Place them in a shallow saucepan, add salt and just enough boiling water to barely cover them. Simmer, covered with a lid, for 7-8 minutes; they need to be almost cooked but not quite. Then drain off the water and cover them with a cloth for 2-3 minutes to absorb the steam.

Now, arrange half the potatoes over the bottom of the baking dish and season well. Wipe the fish fillets with paper towels, cut them into 1½ inch (4 cm) chunks, and arrange the pieces over the potatoes, seasoning again. Next, spoon the salsa verde on top of the fish and arrange the rest of the potato slices, slightly overlapping them, on top of the salsa. Then brush them lightly with the olive oil, season once more, and sprinkle with the cheese. Now, place the baking dish on a high shelf of the oven for about 30 minutes, by which time the fish will be cooked and the potatoes golden brown.

Shrimp Risotto with Lobster Sauce

Sounds rather fancy, doesn't it? But it's not, because this in some ways is a misleadingly simple recipe since it's baked in the oven, which means no tedious stirring, and the sauce is a ready-made lobster bisque – or you could use a French fish soup – laced with dry sherry, then sprinkled with Gruyère cheese to bubble under the broiler.

First of all, place the baking dish in the oven to preheat. Meanwhile, in the frying pan, melt the butter, and sauté the onion over a medium heat for 7-8 minutes, until soft. Now, stir the rice into the buttery juices so it gets a good coating, then pour in the lobster bisque (or soup) and sherry, and season. Give the mixture a good stir and bring it up to simmering point, then pour it into the baking dish and return it to the oven, uncovered, for 35 minutes.

Toward the end of the cooking time, preheat the broiler to its highest setting. Take the risotto from the oven, taste to check the seasoning, then add the shrimp. Next, scatter the cheese over the top and drizzle with the cream. Now, place the dish under the broiler for 2-3 minutes until the cheese is brown and bubbling. Serve immediately, garnished with the watercress and sprinkled with extra cheese.

Serves 2

6 oz (175 g) cooked, peeled medium-sized shrimp, defrosted if frozen
1⅓ cups (175 g) risotto (arborio) rice
3¼ cups (780 g) ready-made lobster bisque or French fish soup
3 tablespoons (40 g) butter
1 medium onion, peeled and finely chopped
⅓ cup (75 ml) dry sherry
2 oz (50 g) Gruyère, finely grated, plus a little extra to serve
2 tablespoons heavy cream
a few sprigs fresh watercress, to garnish
salt and freshly ground black pepper

You will also need an ovenproof baking dish measuring 9 inches (23 cm) square and 2 inches (5 cm) deep, and a large frying pan.

Preheat the oven to 300°F (150°C).

Roasted Salmon Fillets with a Crusted Pecorino and Pesto Topping

This recipe, invented by my good friend Lin Cooper, started life under the broiler, but now, in my attempt to more or less eliminate using the broiler, I'm happy to say that it cooks very happily and easily in an oven set on high. One word of warning, though: it works much better with fresh pesto sauce than it does with pesto purchased in jars.

Serves 2

2 x 5-6 oz (150-175 g) salmon fillets, about ¾ inch (2 cm) thick, skinned (see page 275)
1½ tablespoons finely grated Pecorino cheese
2 tablespoons fresh pesto sauce
squeeze lemon juice
2 tablespoons fresh breadcrumbs
salt and freshly ground black pepper

You will also need a shallow baking pan measuring approximately 10 x 14 inches (25.5 x 35 cm), covered in foil and lightly oiled.

Preheat the oven to 450°F (230°C).

Begin by trimming the fillets, if needed, and run your hand over the surface of the fish to check that there aren't any stray bones. Now, place the fillets in the prepared baking pan and give each one a good squeeze of lemon juice and a seasoning of salt and pepper.

Next, stir the pesto and measure 2 tablespoons of it into a small bowl, mix a third of the breadcrumbs with it to form a paste, and spread this combination over both fish fillets. Then, mix half the cheese with the remaining breadcrumbs and scatter this over the pesto; finish off with the remaining cheese.

Now, place the baking pan on the middle shelf of the oven and cook for 10 minutes, by which time the top should be golden brown and crispy and the salmon just cooked and moist. Serve with steamed new potatoes.

13
How to cook meat

"Oh dear, oh dear, oh dear"
was the frequently heard lament
of Tony Hancock, a truly great
comedian of whom some of you
may have heard. No matter –
those words for me are always
so applicable when things go
badly wrong, as, it has to be
said, they did for the British
meat industry. Hopefully, we
are now recovering; lessons have
been learned.

I am personally a great lover of both fish and vegetarian food, but I am also a dedicated meat-lover.

I've always been a meat person. Pure and simple. I come from a long line of meat-loving people. I well remember how my grandparents ate meat every day of their lives and at the same time enjoyed perfect health. And how my mother recovering from an operation and with a low blood count was prescribed lots and lots of red meat by her doctor.

There's absolutely no doubt in my mind that high quality meat is good for you. Everyone who lives and breathes needs protein, and meat provides what is called first-class protein all by itself. Eating just 8 oz (225 g) in any one day gives an adult all they need without having to think about it.

Knowing how to cook meat properly every time is something that can easily be learned and mastered once you know a few guidelines and have a few tips to follow. There is, after all, little point in spending money on a superb piece of tender steak if you then use an inappropriate cooking method and overcook it, making it tough. William Cobbett, the 19th-century chronicler, gave this advice to a young man looking for a wife: "Never mind if she can embroider continents into a piece of cloth, watch carefully how she deals with a lamb chop!"

So the purpose of this chapter is to encourage you to enjoy eating and cooking good meat. We don't have to eat meat every day, and a healthy, interesting diet should be varied and include fish or vegetarian meals, but when we do cook meat what we need to know is how to get the very best out of it.

Roasting

Originally what the term roasting described was meat being placed near a fire, usually on a spit, with air circulating around it. Then, as the spit was turned, all sides of the meat were exposed to the fire and the whole was gradually and evenly cooked.

Nowadays we're not technically roasting in the true sense of the word any more. Thankfully, we don't have to fan flames and rake coals to get the required heat; all we have to do is simply switch on a domestic oven to any heat we require making oven-roasting simple, efficient, and very easy.

The only thing we need to learn from our hard-working ancestors is to take care. If we want the best results possible, it's well worth reading and absorbing some of the following notes. Then, once they're understood fully, and so long as the right kind of care is taken, roasting meat will always be successful and enjoyable.

What about the fat?

If you never learn any other lesson about meat cooking, please learn this one. If you want to enjoy meat at its most succulent and best you need to understand that fat is absolutely necessary. It doesn't have to be eaten (my husband never eats it), but it does need to be there. The fat in the meat contains a lot of the flavor and provides natural basting juices both from without and within. So don't choose meat that is too lean - let the fat do its wondrous work of enhancing flavor and succulence during cooking.

Ten guidelines when roasting meat

1) The cut

If you want to serve roasted meat for a special occasion, it's best to get as large a cut as possible. The perfect roast includes a lovely crusty outside and lots of tender, succulent, juicy meat within. And while you're dreaming about that, consider how delicious it will be served cold or made into other dishes the next day. A large cut, if you have some left over for other meals, can be quite economical, too.

The loin or the thick end of a leg of pork, the prime rib (three ribs) of beef or a leg of lamb will serve a large family, and these cuts are all excellent for simple roasting at a high temperature. But what you also need to remember is that there are other cuts that are more suitable for lower-temperature roasting, which can be bought in smaller cuts. If you try to cook a cut that's meant for slow-roasting at a high temperature, it will end up tough and dry.

2) Bone in or out?

When you roast meat on the bone, the bone serves as an excellent conductor of heat; this means that the meat will be cooked more evenly with less loss of juices. I always prefer to cook meat on the bone because it has more flavor, and I think the meat cooked nearest the bone is the best part. The bones can be removed, however, and the cut rolled neatly, making it much easier to carve, so it's just a matter of personal taste.

3) Heat

For simple roasting of a prime cut of meat, it is important to preheat the oven to a very high temperature. This gives the meat a very quick and efficient blast of heat so that the edges seize up and the precious juices inside are less likely to escape.

4) Added ingredients for roasting

I find that when roasting a cut of beef or pork, if you tuck a small halved onion underneath it at the edges, it caramelizes during the roasting and provides both flavor and color to the juices for the gravy. When cooking lamb, if you insert little slivers of garlic and rosemary leaves into the flesh, this imparts a lovely flavor and fragrance whilst roasting. You can insert garlic slivers and rosemary into a pork cut, too, if you want to give it a slightly different flavor.

Another tip: if you want to give an extra-crisp finish to the surface fat of a cut, lightly coat it with some flour, and for beef use some dry mustard along with the flour. Unless you're slow-roasting you won't need to add any fat to a cut specifically meant for roasting, as there will be sufficient natural fat within the cut itself.

5) Basting

In the past, wise old cooks knew that to keep a cut really succulent while it was roasting it was important to baste it two or three times using a long-handled spoon. Use an oven mitt to slide the roasting pan halfway out of the oven (or, if it's easier, take it out completely – but close the oven door to keep the heat in), then tilt the pan and thoroughly baste the cut with the fat and juices. The exception to this is pork, first, because it has enough fat within it to provide a kind of internal basting and, secondly, if you spoon fat over the skin, you won't get good crackling.

6) When is it cooked?

If your oven is checked regularly and not faulty, the cooking times given in this chapter should serve you well. But the only way to really know if the meat is cooked to your liking is to first insert a flat skewer into the thickest part of the meat, then remove it, and press the surface hard with the flat of the skewer and watch the color of the juices that run out. If you like your meat rare (as in beef), the juices will still be faintly red; for medium the juices will still be faintly pink, and if you like it cooked all the way through, then the juices should run completely clear and not pink.

Remember, though, that meat continues to cook a little while it's relaxing, so if you like your beef rare, you'll need to take this into account.

7) All those precious juices

The reason roasting meat needs care and attention is that if it's badly cooked, it ends up dry. Careful cooking means doing all you can to keep those precious juices intact. The number-one rule is not to overcook; number two is to baste (see point 5); and number three is to always allow time for the meat to relax before you start to carve it.

What happens to meat during the cooking process is that it shrinks slightly, and juices, as they heat up, begin to bubble up to the surface. Some do escape (but not entirely, if you're making gravy). If you then carve the meat straight from the oven, all those surface juices will be lost, but if you allow the meat to relax for 30 minutes before carving, the surface juices will have time to gradually seep back down into the meat. There will still be a little coming out as you carve, so it's good to have a carving board with a little channel around the edge – then even these juices can be incorporated into the gravy.

8) Gravy

I never put meat on a roasting rack as I think the part that sits directly in the roasting pan provides lots of crusty sediment that improves the gravy. Gravy made with the meat juices ensures that every last drop of flavor and juice enhances the meat itself (see page 165).

9) Carving

A lot of people hate to carve meat, imagining that they can't do the job very well, but the truth is probably that the knife they are using simply isn't sharp enough. What you really need to do is buy a good-quality carving knife and a sharpening steel and simply practise. I was taught by a butcher, who said knives should be sharpened little and often. I have also found the following advice good for anyone who wants to learn: hold the steel horizontally in front of you and the knife vertically, *right*, then slide the blade of the knife down, allowing the tip to touch the steel, first on one side of the steel and then on the other. If you really can't face it, there are knife sharpeners available.

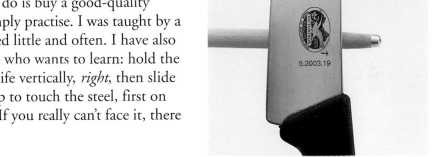

10) Serving suggestions

Most of the traditional accompaniments to roast meat are already well known: horseradish or mustard with beef, savory stuffing and apple sauce with pork, and mint sauce and red currant jelly with lamb.

How to roast beef

Choose sirloin or prime rib (three ribs) on the bone weighing about 6 lb (2.7 kg). Preheat the oven to 450°F (230°C), season with salt and pepper, and rub the fat with a dusting of flour and dry mustard. Roast at this temperature for 20 minutes, then reduce the temperature to 375°F (190°C) and continue to roast – basting at least three times – for 15 minutes per lb (450 g) for rare, plus 15 minutes more for medium, and another 30 minutes for well done. Rest for 20-30 minutes before carving.

How to roast pork with crackling

Use a 5 lb (2.25 kg) loin of pork, on the bone but chined (this means the bone is loosened), and preheat the oven to 450°F (230°C). Make sure the surface skin is really dry, then rub in sea salt (preferably Maldon) and roast for 25 minutes, then lower the temperature to 375°F (190°C) and allow 35 minutes per lb (450 g). Don't baste the pork, or the crackling won't be crisp. Relax for 20-30 minutes before carving.

How to roast lamb

For instructions on roasting lamb, turn to page 320.

Braising and pot-roasting

There's something about meat slowly braising in a casserole in the oven, filling the kitchen with sublime aromas and invoking pangs of hunger and anticipation of what's to come. I call it "feel-good food" – comforting and soothing. It can rarely be done properly in busy restaurants that are short of oven space, so if you want to really spoil your friends as well as your family, choose something from this section for entertaining.

Fast food is all very well and has its place in busy lives, but slow cooking has in a way become a luxury, simply because of its rarity. "But I don't have time for it," you might be thinking. But I'm saying, yes, you do – just read on.

Ten guidelines when braising and pot-roasting

1) Dispelling the myth

The myth is that slow cooking is a lot of bother and takes too much time. The truth is that it doesn't in fact take any more time than other cooking; the only time taken up is while it sits happily all by itself in the oven, leaving the cook blissfully free to get on with other things.

2) Think slow

The principle to grasp here is that slow cooking really should be just that – too much bubble and boil always impairs the flavor and texture of the meat. What you want to aim for is this: the barest shimmer of movement with the occasional bubble just breaking the surface. Using a heavy flameproof casserole, you need to bring the mixture up to a gentle simmer, then put a close-fitting lid on, and place it on the lowest shelf of a preheated oven at 275°F (140°C). This gives just the right amount of heat and thus allows the very best flavors of the ingredients to be drawn out and married together.

3) Choosing the right cut

Without getting too technical, I think it's worth noting that in most cases forequarter meat (which comes from the front half of the animal) is best for slow cooking because this is the bit that works harder, stretching and pulling the rest along all the time (examples for beef include brisket cut, and braising and stewing beef). Muscle and tissue begin to build up as the animal matures, and this, together with a marbling of fat in-between the meat fibers, seems happily to be tailor-made for slow cooking.

What happens when the meat is subjected to a gentle heat over a long period of time is that this is all slowly rendered down and does a splendid job of permeating the meat fibers, keeping them succulent and at the same time adding body, substance, and most important of all, flavor. So for this reason, cuts such as rump, sirloin, or filet mignon should never be cooked slowly since they do not contain the magic ingredients above!

4) What kind of cooking pot?

Old-fashioned cooks used earthenware cooking pots and sometimes, in order to seal them tightly, put a paste of flour and water on before the lid to give a perfect seal. Nowadays we have attractive flameproof casseroles so we can cook in them on top of the stove, in the oven, and even bring them to the table. This would be my choice, because I think it's important to bring the ingredients up to simmering point on the burner before they go into a slow oven. If you prefer an earthenware cooking pot, then you must preheat it and make sure the ingredients are well up to simmering point before they're poured quickly into the pot and then put in the oven. Without this precaution the ingredients won't come up to simmering point for a very long time in a slow oven.

I have found that an approximately 2½ quarts (2.25 liter) capacity flameproof casserole is a good all-round family size and that a 4 quarts (3.5 liter) casserole is a very useful size for entertaining. The modern way to seal the lid tightly is to use a double sheet of foil placed under the lid.

5) Browning meat

This is where care is really needed – and just a little patience. If the meat is seared around the edges, two things happen. First, the crusty, rather charred surface provides flavor and color and, secondly, as the edges of the meat seize up, this helps keep the juices in. What you need to remember is to only brown a few pieces of meat at a time. It's tempting to shove the whole lot in and cut corners, but if you crowd the pan, too much steam will be created and you will never, ever brown the meat.

Use a good, solid frying pan, get it really hot before adding oil or fat, then, as soon as the oil is smoking hot, add about six cubes (or one steak) at a time, browning them well on all sides and removing them before adding the next batch.

6) Adding liquid

Liquid has a very important role in slow meat cooking, because not only does it provide moisture, but as it mingles with the meat juices, it's what provides the finished sauce. Lamb and beef stock will help to enhance the flavor of both the meat and sauce. Another liquid that suits meat cooking very well is beer: both pale ale and stout are transformed into rich, fragrant sauces when subjected to long, slow cooking.

Wine – both red and white – is superb for sauces, and for a very special occasion Madeira wine makes one of the greatest sauces of all. If you want to add a touch of luxury that's really economical, the best thing to use is hard cider, either dry or medium – every kitchen should have some handy.

Fresh tomatoes, peeled and chopped, or even canned chopped tomatoes, will also respond well to slow cooking and provide body and rich flavor to the sauce.

7) How much meat?

This depends largely on appetite. I found it very difficult when I did a book of recipes to balance portions that would suit a hungry student and a not-so-hungry elderly person. However, I think 6-8 oz (175-225 g) per person is a good guide. If a recipe says "serves 4-6," it gives you the chance to size up the appetites and make your own judgement.

8) Skimming

Although meat can be trimmed of excess fat, the presence of some fat in braising cuts of meat is vital for flavor and succulence. In some cases, say with neck of lamb or oxtail, the excess fat will escape and bubble up to the surface, so if you're intending to serve this straight from the oven, tilt the casserole slightly and spoon off the fat, which will clearly separate from the juice. Any that you can't actually skim off with a spoon can be soaked up by lightly placing folded sheets of absorbent paper towels on the surface.

Finally, since most slow-cooked recipes taste better re-heated the next day, leaving the dish overnight means that the fat will completely solidify and can then be lifted off very easily before re-heating.

9) Thickening

If you're making a casserole, the easiest way to thicken the sauce is to add some flour to the ready-browned meat, onions, and so on, stir it in to soak up all the excess juice, then gradually add all the liquid, a little at a time, stirring and mixing well after each addition. With pot-roasting it's best to add the thickening later. This can be done by straining the liquid into a saucepan, then reducing it slightly by fast-boiling, which concentrates the flavor, and adding a mixture of butter and flour or olive oil and flour (1½ tablespoons of flour to 2 tablespoons/25 g of butter or 1 tablespoon of olive oil to thicken about 2 cups/425 ml of liquid). Arrowroot is another thickening agent that gives a fine glaze and a smooth-textured sauce, and it's very easy to use – just blend with a little cold water before adding to the liquid.

10) Freezing and re-heating

Casseroles and braised dishes often improve in flavor if they're made a day ahead, cooled, refrigerated, and re-heated, in which case preheat the oven to 350°F (180°C) and give it 35-45 minutes altogether. It's very important that the casserole reaches a gentle simmer. Casseroles and braised dishes also freeze very well in foil containers, but make sure they're thoroughly defrosted before re-heating. Discard the cardboard lids, cover with a double sheet of foil, and re-heat as above.

In contrast to cuts of meat for braising, the meat that comes from the hind quarter of the animal is, for the most part, more tender, and for this reason has the advantage of being more suitable for fast cooking. If you're looking for a meal in a hurry, the quick-cooking broiling or frying cuts are the ones to go for. Some of these can also be used for oven-baking with other ingredients or with a sauce.

Ten guidelines when broiling, frying, and baking

1) Choosing the right cuts for broiling or frying

Beef steaks, pork steaks, pork scallops (good for frying), lamb cutlets, and chops are ideal – and if you're in a real hurry there are "minute" steaks, which cook in 1 minute flat. Most of these can now be bought trimmed and cut into strips for the fastest of all cooking – stir-frying.

2) The healthy option

If you want – or have been told – to cut the fat in your diet, broiling is for you, since it enables you to enjoy lean meat with the minimum of fat. If you place the meat on a broiler rack with a pan underneath, you'll find a percentage of fat within the meat will run out during the cooking. The secret here is not to overcook, otherwise the meat will be dry.

3) Broiling meat

What broiling should achieve is a lovely seared, faintly charred outside edge with the rest of the meat very tender and juicy within – this is the closest thing to cooking on an open fire, because, when the meat is placed on a rack, the air circulates and this gives the broiled meat its unique flavor.

If you're using a domestic broiler, what you need to do is preheat it to its highest setting at least 10 minutes before you want to start cooking, and remember to try and position the meat 2-3 inches (5-7.5 cm) from the heat, turning the meat over halfway through to broil the other side. Timings vary because the thickness of meat differs, so you need to use a skewer or the blade of a small knife inserted in the thickest part to test if the juices are the right color. Approximate timings are as follows.

For a steak 1 inch (2.5 cm) thick (ie sirloin or rump), 1½-2 minutes on each side for rare; medium, 3 minutes on each side; and well done, about 4 minutes on each side.

For a filet mignon 1½ inches (4 cm) thick, give it 5 minutes on each side for medium; 1 minute less each side for rare; and 1 minute more for well done.

Pork chops will need approximately 10 minutes on each side, and pork steaks slightly less. Lamb chops would need about 10 minutes each side, and cutlets about 5 minutes each side.

Never season meat before broiling, frying, or browning because salt draws out the precious juices you're trying to keep in (but do remember to season before serving).

A ridged grill pan, *left*, is a very efficient way of pan-broiling meat, as well as other foods – just smear the pan with very little oil, preheat it for about 10 minutes, and use the timings just listed.

4) Frying meat

Whether you choose to broil or fry meat is, to a certain extent, personal choice. Broiling, as we've already discussed, gives special flavor to meat, but you do lose some of the juices. Frying, on the other hand, means that all the escaped juices are there in the frying pan and can be spooned over the meat or used with reduced wine to make a sauce.

5) Hot as you dare

It's very important when you're frying meat to have the heat as high as possible, so the frying pan has to be one with a thick, solid bottom to conduct the heat properly. What you need to do is place the pan over direct heat turned to high and let the pan become very hot before you add the smallest amount of oil or fat, just to cover the pan surface. Then, as soon as the fat itself is smoking hot, hold the piece of meat in both hands and drop it directly down so that the whole of the surface hits the heat at the same moment. What this does is sear the meat, sealing the edges and encouraging the juices to stay inside.

For steaks (rump and sirloin), give them 1 minute's searing on each side, then turn the heat down to medium and cook them for no more time at all if you like them really rare; otherwise, for medium-rare give them 2-3 more minutes on each side; medium, 3-4 more minutes on each side; and well done, 4-5 more minutes on each side.

For filet mignon 1½ inches (4 cm) thick, after the initial searing you'll need another 6 minutes' cooking time, turning the steak over halfway through; give it 2 minutes less for rare and 2 minutes more for well done. Once again, all these timings are approximate because the thickness of the meat will vary.

6) Adding fats and oils

If you're cutting down on fat, then broil without fat or oil; however, if that is not your priority, it is better to brush very lean meat such as pork steaks with a little melted butter and filet mignon with a little oil before broiling. If you're frying steaks, then use a little oil or a small piece of beef dripping, which will withstand the very high temperatures.

If you're frying pork, the best thing to use is a little butter and oil, mixed, so that you get the flavor of the butter, and the oil stops it from burning.

7) Marinating

This really does enhance the flavor of meat for broiling. If you marinate cubed lamb (from leg steaks), use the juice of a lemon and 6 tablespoons of oil to 1 lb 8 oz (700 g) of meat, adding 2 teaspoons of chopped oregano and some slivers of onion. Leave them in the marinade overnight, turning a couple of times, then thread the cubes of meat and slivers of onion on to flat skewers. You can make delicious kebabs and broil them for 15-20 minutes, basting with some of the marinade as you cook them. You can also do exactly the same with cubed pork, only this time using 2 teaspoons of crushed rosemary leaves and giving them 5 minutes' more broiling time.

8) Glazing

One interesting way of broiling meat is to add a glaze to it before it goes under the broiler. The best and probably the simplest one I've come across is to spread a thin layer of English mustard over the meat and then dip it in demerara or raw sugar. Once this coating hits the heat, it gives a lovely shiny barbecue-flavored crust. I like it best with lamb cutlets, but you could always use it with pork ribs. Either way, give them 5 minutes' broiling on each side.

9) Stir-frying

If you cook with gas, then a classic rounded wok is perfect for a stir-fry, but if you're using electricity you need to have a wok with a special flat bottom. If you don't have a wok, don't worry – you can still stir-fry with a large, roomy frying pan. Either way, remember that speed is what it's all about. Heat the wok or pan until it's very hot indeed, then add oil, and as it sizzles, add the meat and constantly stir it around so that it comes into constant contact with the heat on all sides (the meat should be half-cooked before the vegetables are added).

10) Oven-baking

There is a method of cooking meat that comes somewhere in-between fast- and slow-cooking, and that is oven-baking. One of the best things about it is that it leaves you free to do other things.

You can oven-bake pork or lamb chops in a shallow pan by seasoning them and tucking chopped onion in around them and baking them at 400°F (200°C) for 30-40 minutes, depending on the size and thickness of the chops. After that, you can deglaze the roasting pan with wine, hard cider, or stock to make a gravy with the juices.

Shepherd's Pie with Cheese-Crusted Leeks

This recipe can be made either with fresh ground lamb (shepherd's pie), fresh ground beef (cottage pie), or ground leftover beef or lamb from a cooked roast (in which case cut the initial cooking time to 15 minutes). In the following recipe we're using fresh ground lamb, and what puts this dish in the five-star category is the delicious crust of cheese and leeks.

Serves 4

1 lb (450 g) ground lamb
1 tablespoon olive oil
2 medium onions, peeled
and chopped
3 oz (75 g) carrot, peeled and
chopped very small
3 oz (75 g) rutabaga, peeled and
chopped very small
½ teaspoon ground cinnamon
1 teaspoon chopped fresh thyme
1 tablespoon chopped fresh parsley
1 tablespoon all-purpose flour
1¼ cups (275 ml) lamb stock
1 tablespoon tomato paste
salt and freshly ground black pepper

For the topping:

2 oz (50 g) sharp Cheddar,
coarsely grated
2 medium leeks, cleaned and cut
into ½ inch (1 cm) slices
2 lb (900 g) round red or white, or
Yukon Gold potatoes
4 tablespoons (50 g) butter
salt and freshly ground black pepper

You will also need a large lidded frying pan or saucepan, and a 8 inch (20 cm) square baking dish, 2 inches (5 cm) deep, well buttered.

Begin by placing the frying pan or saucepan over a medium flame to gently heat the olive oil. Now, fry the onions in the hot oil until they are tinged with brown at the edges – about 5 minutes. Add the chopped carrot and rutabaga and cook for 5 minutes or so, then remove the vegetables and put them to one side. Now, turn the heat up and brown the meat in batches, tossing it around to get it all nicely browned. You may find a wooden fork helpful here to help break up the ground meat. After that, give the meat a good seasoning of salt and pepper, then add the cooked vegetables, cinnamon, thyme, and parsley. Next, stir in the flour, which will soak up the juices; then gradually add the stock to the meat mixture until it is all incorporated. Finally, stir in the tomato paste. Now, turn the heat down, put the lid on the pan, and let it cook gently for about 30 minutes.

While the meat is cooking you can make the topping. Peel the potatoes, cut them into even-sized pieces, and place them in a steamer fitted over a large pan of boiling water, sprinkled with some salt. Put a lid on and steam until the potatoes are completely tender – about 25 minutes. While they are cooking, preheat the oven to 400°F (200°C).

When the potatoes are done, drain off the water, return them to the saucepan, cover with a clean dish towel to absorb the steam, and leave them for about 5 minutes. Next, add the butter and mash them to a purée – the best way to do this is with an electric hand mixer. Don't be tempted to add any milk here because the mashed potatoes on top of the pie need to be firm. Taste and add more salt and pepper if necessary. When the meat is ready, spoon it into the baking dish and level it out with the back of the spoon. After that, spread the mashed potatoes evenly all over. Now, sprinkle the leeks on top, scatter the cheese over the leeks, and bake the whole thing on a high shelf of the oven for about 25 minutes, or until the top is crusty and golden.

Sirloin Steak
Hongroise

As I've said before, I prefer to cook steak in a frying pan because the precious juices that are bound to escape can be easily incorporated into the sauce to give extra body and flavor.

Serves 2
2 sirloin steaks weighing about 8 oz (225 g) each, removed from the refrigerator about 1 hour before you need them
1 tablespoon light olive oil
3 shallots, peeled and finely chopped
1 small red bell pepper, seeded and finely diced
¾ cup (175 ml) red wine
1 tablespoon crème fraîche
¼ teaspoon paprika
a few sprigs fresh watercress, to garnish
salt and freshly ground black pepper

You will also need a heavy frying pan with a diameter of 10 inches (25.5 cm).

First of all, heat half the oil in the frying pan over a high heat, then fry the chopped shallots and pepper until they're softened and tinged dark brown at the edges, about 6 minutes, and transfer them to a plate. Now, add the remaining oil to the pan, and keeping the heat very high, season the steaks with coarsely ground black pepper - but don't add salt yet since this encourages the juices to come out. Now, add the steaks to the hot pan and press them gently with a spoon so that the underside is seared and becomes crusty. Cook the steaks for about 3 minutes each side for medium, 2 for rare, and 4 for well done. About 2 minutes before the end of the cooking time, return the shallots and peppers to the pan, pour the wine around the steaks, and, still keeping the heat high, boil until the liquid is reduced and syrupy. Then add the crème fraîche and stir it into the sauce, seasoning with salt and sprinkling in the paprika. Serve the steaks on hot plates with the sauce spooned over them and garnish with watercress. They're lovely served with baked potatoes and a salad.

Sirloin Steak Marchand de Vin

This classic French recipe has the simplest-possible sauce for a pan-fried steak. The red wine bubbles down and deglazes the pan so that all the lovely flavors of the meat are incorporated into the sauce.

First of all, heat half the oil in the frying pan over a high heat, then fry the chopped onion until it's softened and tinged dark brown at the edges, about 6 minutes, and transfer them to a plate. Now, add the remaining oil to the pan, and, keeping the heat very high, season the steaks with coarsely ground black pepper but don't salt them since that encourages the juices to come out. Now, add the steaks to the hot pan and press them gently with a spoon so that the underside is seared and becomes crusty. Cook the steaks for about 3 minutes each side for medium, 2 for rare, and 4 for well done. About 2 minutes before the end of the cooking time, return the onion to the pan, pour the wine around the steaks, and with the heat until high, boil until reduced and syrupy. Serve the steaks on hot plates with the sauce spooned on top. Oven-Roasted Potato Wedges (page 191) and a green salad would be very good with this.

Serves 2
2 sirloin steaks weighing about 8 oz (225 g) each, removed from the refrigerator about 1 hour before you need them
1 tablespoon light olive oil
1 small onion, peeled and finely chopped
¾ cup (175 ml) red wine
freshly ground black pepper

You will also need a heavy frying pan with a diameter of 10 inches (25.5 cm).

309

Individual Steak, Mushroom, and Kidney Pies

Serves 6
2 lb (900 g) chuck or blade steak, cut into 1 inch (2.5 cm) cubes
8 oz (225 g) cremini mushrooms, quartered
8 oz (225 g) ox kidney, trimmed and cut into very small cubes
2 tablespoons beef drippings or lard
8 oz (225 g) onions, peeled and thickly sliced
2 tablespoons all-purpose flour
2 tablespoons Worcestershire sauce
½ teaspoon finely chopped fresh thyme
2½ cups (570 ml) beef stock
salt and freshly ground black pepper

For the pastry:
2½ cups (350 g) all-purpose flour, plus a little extra for rolling
pinch of salt
6 tablespoons (75 g) lard, at room temperature
6 tablespoons (75 g) butter, at room temperature
about 1½ tablespoons cold water
a little beaten egg, to glaze

You will need 6 individual pie dishes holding 2 cups (425 ml) or ovenproof soup bowls, with top diameters of 5 in (13 cm) or an ovenproof pie dish with a 9 in (23 cm) diameter, and a lidded flameproof casserole with a capacity of 4 quarts (3.5 liters).

Preheat the oven to 275°F (140°C).

Steak and kidney is one of the most wonderful combinations of flavors I know, provided ox kidney and no other is used. If it's cut really small, most people who think they don't like kidney will enjoy the rich, luscious flavor without even noticing it's there.

I think the flavor of steak and kidney is improved enormously if you take a bit of time and trouble over initially browning the meat. What you need to do is melt 1 tablespoon of the beef dripping in a large, heavy frying pan. Pat the cubes of meat dry with paper towels, and when the fat in the pan is very hot, add the meat cubes a few at a time. Be sure not to crowd the pan; putting too much in at once creates a steamy atmosphere and the meat won't brown. Brown the pieces on all sides in batches, adding them to the casserole as you go.

After the meat has browned, add the rest of the dripping to the frying pan and do exactly the same with the kidney cubes. When these have been added to the casserole with the meat, brown the onions in the same frying pan over high heat, turning and moving them until they are nicely browned at the edges, about 6-7 minutes. Then, using a perforated spoon for draining, transfer the onions to the casserole. Place the casserole over a direct heat for 2 minutes before seasoning; then add the flour and stir with a wooden spoon until it's been absorbed into the meat juices. It doesn't look very nice at this stage, but that's not a problem. All you do next is add the Worcestershire sauce, thyme, and mushrooms, followed by the stock and seasoning. Stir well, bring everything up to a gentle simmer, put the lid on the casserole, and place in the preheated oven, on the center shelf, and let it cook for about 2 hours until the meat is tender.

Meanwhile, make the pastry. First of all, sift the flour with the pinch of salt into a large bowl, holding the sifter up high to give it a good airing. Then add the lard and butter, and using only your fingertips, lightly and gently rub the fat into the flour, again lifting the mixture up high all the time to give it a good airing. When everything is crumbly, sprinkle in the cold water. Begin mixing the pastry with a knife and then finish off with your hands, adding more drops of water until you have a smooth dough that doesn't stick to the bowl. Then place the pastry in a plastic storage bag and let it rest in the refrigerator for 30 minutes.

When the meat is ready, transfer it and its gravy to the individual dishes (or to one large dish) and allow it to cool.

When you are ready to make the pies, preheat the oven to 425°F (220°C), then roll out the pastry on a floured surface. Using a small saucer (about 5½ in/14 cm in diameter), cut out 6 rounds – you may have to re-roll the pastry to get all 6. Using the trimmings, roll out a strip about 3 x 14 in (7.5 x 35 cm) and cut it into 6 to make borders for the pies. First dampen the edges of each dish with water and place a strip of pastry dish around the rim of each one, pressing down well. Next, dampen the pastry strips, place one pastry round on top of each, and seal carefully. Now, use the blunt side of a knife to crimp the edges, fluting them using your thumb to push out and your forefinger to pull in again (see the photos). If you are making one large pie, cut out a 10 in (25.5 cm) circle of pastry, using the trimmings for the border. Make a hole in the center of each pastry lid to let the steam out during baking, and brush the surface with the beaten egg. Place on a large baking sheet and cook in the oven on the center shelf for 25-30 minutes for the small pies, or 35-40 minutes for the large one, at which time the pastry should be golden brown and crusty.

Note: the pies can be filled and topped the day before, covered and chilled, then brushed with egg and placed in the oven when you need them.

Latin American Beef Stew with Marinated Red Onion Salad

This is very colorful and has lots of great flavors and textures – ideal for entertaining because all the vegetables are already in it, so all it needs is some plain rice.

Serves 4-6

2 lb (900 g) braising steak, cut into
1 inch (2.5 cm) cubes
1½ tablespoons cumin seeds
1½ tablespoons coriander seeds
2 tablespoons olive oil
2 medium red onions, peeled and
roughly chopped
3 medium red chilies, seeded and
finely chopped
6 cloves garlic, peeled and crushed
1½ tablespoons all-purpose flour
1 cup (220 g) canned
chopped tomatoes
2 cups (450 ml) brown ale
⅔ cup (150 ml) red wine
12 oz (350 g) butternut squash,
peeled, seeded and cut into 1 inch
(2.5 cm) cubes
8 oz (225 g) fresh corn (cut from
about 2 ears), or frozen and
thoroughly defrosted
1 red bell pepper, seeded and roughly
chopped into 1½ in (4 cm) pieces
salt and freshly ground black pepper

For the red onion salad:
1 medium red onion, peeled and
thinly sliced into half-moon shapes
grated zest 1 lime and juice 2 limes
3 tablespoons chopped cilantro

You will also need a lidded flameproof
casserole with capacity of 4 quarts
(3.5 liters).

Preheat the oven to 300°F (150°C).

First of all, you need to roast the spices, and to do this place them in a small frying pan or saucepan over a medium heat and stir and toss them around for 1-2 minutes, or until they begin to look toasted and start to jump in the pan. Now, transfer them to a mortar and pestle and crush them to a powder.

Next, pat the cubed meat with paper towels, then place the casserole over a high heat. Add 1 tablespoon of the oil, and as soon as it's really hot, cook the meat about 6 cubes at a time, until it's well browned and crusty. As the cubes cook, remove them to a plate and brown the rest in batches. Then heat the other tablespoon of oil and fry the onions, chili, and garlic until they're nicely tinged brown at the edges. Now, add the flour and stir it in to soak up the juices. Next, add the spices and return the meat to the casserole; then add the tomatoes, ale, and wine. Season and stir well, then bring it up to simmering point, put the lid on the casserole, and place in the center of the oven for 2 hours.

After that, add the squash, corn, and red bell pepper; stir again and return the casserole to the oven for a further 40-45 minutes. Meanwhile, to make the salad, mix the red onion with the lime zest, juice, and cilantro in a small bowl and set aside to marinate for at least 15 minutes before serving. Pass the salad around separately as a garnish.

Mini Boeufs
en Croûte

If you want luxury, think filet mignon, and if you want to turn a 6 oz (175 g) filet into a man-sized portion, encase it with a wild-mushroom stuffing in the very thinnest-possible layer of puff pastry. What you'll then have is a delectable combination of juicy steak, concentrated mushrooms, and a very crisp crust. Good news, too, if you're entertaining: these can be prepared several hours ahead and just popped in the oven when you're ready for them.

Serves 4

4 x 6 oz (175 g) filet mignon, cut from the middle of the filet so they're nice and thick
9 oz (250 g) bought puff pastry
1 teaspoon beef dripping or lard
a little brandy
1 large egg, beaten
¾ cup (175 ml) red wine
salt and freshly ground black pepper

For the filling:
½ oz (10 g) dried porcini mushrooms
1 large onion, peeled
8 oz (225 g) cremini mushrooms
2 tablespoons (25 g) butter
freshly grated nutmeg
salt and freshly ground black pepper

You will also need a solid baking sheet, well buttered, and a solid frying pan.

Begin by making the filling well ahead, as it needs to be chilled before you use it. Start off by soaking the porcini in boiling water for 20 minutes, and while that's happening the onion and cremini mushrooms will need to be chopped as finely as possible. If you have a food processor you can do this in moments; if not, use a very sharp knife and chop them minutely small. When the porcini have had 20 minutes, squeeze out all the excess liquid, then chop them small as well. Now, in a medium saucepan, melt the butter and stir in the onions and mushrooms to get a good buttery coating, then season well with salt, pepper and a few gratings of fresh nutmeg.

Now, you need to turn the heat to its lowest setting and cook, uncovered, allowing the juices from the mushrooms to evaporate slowly; this will take about 35 minutes altogether. Stir it from time to time; you should end up with is a lovely concentrated mixture with no liquid left. Spoon the mixture into a bowl, cool, and chill in the refrigerator.

A few hours before you want to serve the steaks, heat the beef dripping in the frying pan until it's smoking hot, or, as the chef who taught me to cook said, "Hot as you dare!" Now, place the steaks 2 at a time in the pan and give them 30 seconds on each side – what you're trying to achieve here is a dark, seared surface without cooking the steaks – then remove them to a plate. Turn the heat off under the pan, but don't wash it, because you're going to need it again later.

While the steaks are cooling, cut the pastry into 4 pieces and roll each one out thinly to about a 7½ inch (19 cm) square; trim the edges to get a neat square and reserve the trimmings. As soon as the steaks are cold, brush them with a little brandy, season with salt and pepper, then lightly brush the surface of each pastry square with the beaten egg. Reserve 1 tablespoon of the mushroom mixture for the sauce, then place about an eighth of the remaining mixture in the middle of each square of pastry, then top with a steak. Now, place the same amount of mushroom mixture on top of each steak, then bring 2 opposite corners of pastry up to overlap in the center, tucking in the sides as if you were wrapping a gift, brush the pastry all over with more beaten egg and bring the 2 remaining corners up to overlap each other. Be careful to seal the pastry only gently, because if you wrap it too tightly it tends to burst open in the oven. If you like you can use the reserved trimmings to make leaves for decoration.

Then, using a spatula, gently lift the packages onto the baking sheet, cover with a clean dish towel and chill for at least 30 minutes, or until you're ready to cook them. When you are, preheat the oven to 425°F (220°C), place them in the oven on a high shelf, and cook for 25 minutes, which will give you medium-rare steaks. If you want them well done, give them 5 minutes more; if you want them rare, give them 5 minutes less.

While they're cooking, pour the wine and reserved mushroom mixture into the frying pan. Let it all bubble and reduce by about a third – this will deglaze the pan and you can then spoon a little of the reduction around each portion before it goes to the table. One word of warning: you must have your guests seated and ready before this is served because if the steaks wait around, they continue cooking inside the pastry.

Fast-Roast Pork with Rosemary and Caramelized Apples

It's hard to believe that you can serve a roast for six people in about 40 minutes flat from start to finish, but you can, and here it is. It's extremely simple, outstandingly good, and can be prepared in advance. Once you try it, I'm sure you'll want to make it again and again.

Serves 6

2 thick pork tenderloins (weighing 12 oz/350 g each after trimming)

1½ tablespoons fresh rosemary leaves

3 Granny Smith apples, peelings left on, cored and cut into 6 wedges each

2 cloves garlic, peeled and cut into thin slices

3 tablespoons (40 g) butter

1½ tablespoons cider vinegar

1 small onion, peeled and finely chopped

1 tablespoon demerara or raw sugar

1 cup (250 ml) hard cider

3 tablespoons crème fraîche

salt and freshly ground black pepper

You will also need a shallow baking pan measuring approximately 11 x 16 inches (28 x 40 cm), lightly buttered.

Preheat the oven to 450°F (230°C).

First of all, using a small, sharp knife, make little slits all over the pork and push the slivers of garlic into them, turning the fillet over so the garlic goes in on both sides. Next, place the rosemary leaves in a mortar and bruise them with the pestle to release their fragrant oil, then chop them very finely.

Now, melt the butter and combine it with the cider vinegar, then brush the meat with some of this mixture, sprinkle with half the rosemary, and season with salt and pepper. Scatter the onions over the bottom of the buttered baking pan and place the pork on top. All this can be done in advance, then covered with plastic wrap.

When you want to cook the roast, prepare the apples by tossing them with the remaining cider vinegar and butter mixture; arrange them all around the roast in the baking pan and sprinkle them with the sugar and the rest of the rosemary. Place the baking pan in the oven on a high shelf and roast for 25-30 minutes (this will depend on the thickness of the pork), until the pork is cooked and there are no pink juices.

After that, remove the baking pan from the oven and transfer the pork and apples to a hot serving dish, cover with foil, and keep warm. Meanwhile, pour a little of the cider into the pan, over the heat, to loosen the onions and juices from it, then pour into a saucepan over medium heat, add the rest of the cider, and let it bubble and reduce by about a third – this will take about 5 minutes. Then whisk in the crème fraîche, let it bubble a bit more, and add some seasoning.

After the pork has rested for about 10 minutes, transfer it to a board and carve it into thick slices. Transfer the slices back to the serving dish along with the apples. Pour the sauce over all and serve as soon as possible. Roast potatoes and braised red cabbage are particularly good with this.

Spanish Braised Pork with Potatoes and Olives

This is a brand new version of a recipe originally published in the Cookery Course – the pork slowly braises in tomatoes and red wine, absorbing the flavor of the olives. Because I now cook potatoes in with it, all it needs is a green vegetable or a salad for a complete meal. I started off pitting the olives, but I now prefer them whole, as they look far nicer.

Serves 4-6

2 lb (900 g) pork shoulder trimmed and cut into bite-sized pieces
1 lb (450 g) new potatoes, halved if large
1½ oz (40 g) black olives
1½ oz (40 g) green olives
1 lb (450 g) ripe red tomatoes
2 tablespoons olive oil
2 medium onions, peeled and sliced into half-moon shapes
1 large red bell pepper, seeded and sliced into 1¼ inch (3 cm) strips
2 cloves garlic, peeled and chopped
1½ teaspoons chopped fresh thyme, plus a few small sprigs
1¼ cups (275 ml) red wine
2 bay leaves
salt and freshly ground black pepper

You will also need a lidded flameproof casserole with a capacity of 4 quart (3.5 liters).

Preheat the oven to 275°F (140°C).

First, skin the tomatoes: pour boiling water over them and leave them for exactly 1 minute before draining and slipping off their skins, then roughly chop them. Now, heat 1 tablespoon of the oil in the casserole over a high heat, pat the cubes of pork with paper towels and brown them on all sides, about 6 pieces at a time, removing them to a plate as they're browned. Then, keeping the heat high, add the rest of the oil, then the onions and pepper, and brown them a little at the edges – about 6 minutes.

Now, add the garlic, stir that around for about 1 minute, then return the browned meat to the casserole and add all the thyme, tomatoes, red wine, olives, and bay leaves. Bring everything up to a gentle simmer, seasoning well, put on the lid, and transfer the casserole to the middle shelf of the oven for 1¼ hours. After that add the potatoes, cover the pan again and cook for a further 45 minutes, or until the potatoes are tender.

Pork Chops with a Confit of Prunes, Apples, and Shallots

This is a delicious recipe. The confit goes equally well with crispy roast duck, and is brilliant served with a rough pork-based pâté.

You can make the confit at any time – the day before, even. All you do is cut the apple into quarters, remove the core, then cut the quarters into ½ inch (1 cm) slices, leaving the apple unpeeled. Then simply place all the ingredients together in a medium-sized saucepan, bring everything up to a gentle simmer, then let it cook as gently as possible, without a lid, for 45 minutes to an hour – you'll need to stir it from time to time – until all the liquid has reduced to a smooth sticky glaze.

When you're ready to cook the pork chops, dip them lightly in the seasoned flour, shaking off any surplus. Now, heat the oil in the frying pan and when it's really hot, add the butter. As soon as it foams, add the pork chops and brown them on both sides, keeping the heat fairly high. Then lower the heat and continue to cook them gently for about 25 minutes in total, turning them once. While they are cooking, warm the confit, either in a saucepan or in a dish covered with foil in a low oven, while the plates are warming; the confit shouldn't be hot – just warm. After that, increase the heat under the frying pan, then pour in the cider for the glaze and let it bubble briskly and reduce to half its original volume, which should take about 5 minutes. Serve the pork chops on the warmed plates, with the cider glaze spooned over them and some confit on the side.

Serves 4
4 thick pork chops
1½ tablespoons seasoned flour
1 tablespoon peanut or other mildly flavored oil
1 tablespoon (10 g) butter

For the confit:
5 oz (150 g) pitted soft prunes (preferably pruneaux d'Agen)
1 good-sized Granny Smith apple
4 shallots, peeled and cut into 6 wedges through the root
1¼ cups (275 ml) hard cider
¼ cup (55 ml) cider vinegar
1 tablespoon dark brown sugar
¼ teaspoon powdered cloves
⅛ teaspoon powdered mace

For the cider glaze:
1 cup (250 ml) hard cider

You will also need a solid frying pan with a diameter of 10 inches (25.5 cm).

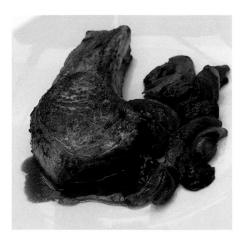

319

Roast Leg of Lamb with Shrewsbury Sauce

This is one of my favorite ways of cooking lamb, particularly in winter – plainly roasted with lots of basting to keep it juicy and succulent, then incorporating all the meat juices and crusty bits into what is truly one of the best sauces ever created. It's sweet and sharp at the same time and complements the lamb perfectly.

Serves 6-8
5 lb (2.25 kg) leg of lamb
1 small onion, peeled and sliced
a few sprigs fresh rosemary, to garnish
salt and freshly ground black pepper

For the Shrewsbury sauce:
2 tablespoons all-purpose flour
1½ teaspoons mustard powder
2½ cups (570 ml) beaujolais or other light red wine
8 tablespoons good-quality red currant jelly, such as Tiptree
3 tablespoons Worcestershire sauce
juice 1 lemon
salt and freshly ground black pepper

You will also need a heavy flameproof roasting pan.

Preheat the oven to 375°F (190°C).

First of all, place the meat in the roasting pan, tucking the slices of onion underneath it. Season the surface with salt and freshly ground black pepper, then place it, uncovered, in the preheated oven on the middle shelf. Roast for 30 minutes per lb (450 g) – for a 5lb (2.25 kg) leg this will be 2½ hours. Make sure that you baste the lamb at least 3 times while it is cooking because this will help keep it juicy and succulent. If you like to serve your lamb quite pink, give it 30 minutes less cooking time. To tell if the lamb is cooked to your liking, insert a skewer into the center, remove it, then press the flat of the skewer against the meat: as the juice runs out, you will see to what degree the meat is cooked – the pinker the juice, the rarer the meat. When it is cooked as you like it, remove it to a carving board and keep it in a warm place to rest for 30 minutes.

Now, to make the sauce, spoon off any surplus fat from the roasting pan, tipping it to one side and allowing the fat to separate from the juices; you need to leave about 2 tablespoons of fat behind. Now, place the roasting pan over a direct heat turned to low and stir in the flour and mustard powder until you have a smooth paste that has soaked up all the fat and juices. Next, add the wine, a little at a time, mixing with a wooden spoon after each addition. Halfway through, switch from the spoon to a whisk and continue to whisk until all the wine has been incorporated. Now, simply add the red currant jelly, Worcestershire sauce, lemon juice, and seasoning, then whisk again until the jelly has dissolved.

Now, turn the heat to its lowest setting and let the sauce gently bubble and reduce for about 15 minutes, then pour it into a warm serving pitcher. Carve the lamb, garnish with the rosemary, pour a little of the sauce over and pass the rest round separately.

14
Chicken and other birds

If you sometimes feel depressed or let down, if you're suffering from the pressures of life, or simply having a plain old gray day, my advice is to roast a chicken. I'm not precisely sure why, but there is, and always has been, some magical "cure-all" involved in the whole process. Sometimes you need to turn your back on the complications of life, give yourself some space, and become homespun and happy for just a couple of hours. It really does act as a kind of therapy.

For a start, just imagine the smell of it: that evocative come-hither aroma that hits you even when you wander past some fast-food chicken rotisserie – and multiply that 10 times over when you have one roasting in your own kitchen. And what about the sound of it? All those juices sizzling and spluttering. Finally, the vision of it – plump, bronzed, and shining as it emerges from the oven! It doesn't have to be complicated, either. A simple roast chicken can be served just as it is, with chunky potato wedges or crusty bread and a salad. And really good roast chicken is just as much of a treat when it's cold. But then it *can* be all kinds of other things, too: very sophisticated and special, stuffed with herbs, served with sauces... Can there be anyone on earth who doesn't long to eat roast chicken? (Except vegetarians, of course!) There's one requirement, of course, and that is that the chicken has to be a really good one to start with - one raised for the table traditionally and naturally to provide the best eating quality.

First catch your chicken

Seventy-five years ago chickens were raised slowly and then fattened for the table. They were fine birds: strong and plump with lots of succulent, juicy flesh and luscious, concentrated chicken flavor. A whole family could dine on a roast chicken and still have some left over. Roast chicken was very special – not an everyday thing, but something to be anticipated and savored. The sad thing is there are young (and not-so-young) people who have never actually tasted the real thing. The reason? Progress. Now, I'm not against progress – far from it – but it can sometimes run away with us, forcing us to rein in a bit and to try to get back on track.

What's gone wrong?

Mass production means masses of cheap chickens. We have created new breeds of fast-growing chickens that can be raised very intensively, almost like a production line, which means limited living space in a computer-controlled environment with feed containing antibiotics and hormones The average life span of one of these hens is less than 50 days. At the end of this short, uncomfortable life the chicken is often then plunged into scalding-hot water, after which a mechanical process removes its feathers. During this process it is absorbing water and then it's likely to be frozen, water and all. The result is coarse-grained, watery, limp chicken that has no flavor at all.

How can we put this right?

For the most part we can't, because a large section of the community wants cheap chicken and doesn't care about flavor. OK, everyone is free to choose, but ironically, up until now, that has not been the case. People who really do care about flavor have been very limited in their choice, and tracking down a real, naturally raised old-fashioned chicken has not been easy. This has to change. I am reminded of how often I've been told, when attempting to improve the quality of ingredients, that there's no demand for it. But here I am campaigning again and, hopefully, I can help to create a demand that will ultimately provide us all with a real choice.

What is a proper old-fashioned chicken?

1) The first thing we need to be concerned with is breeding. The bird has to be slow-growing, or rather it has to grow naturally as nature intended. It must have a reasonable life span – not less than 81 days.

2) It needs to have its own space and not live in overcrowded conditions.

3) It has to be truly free range. There is a bit of a free-range fantasy that has made the rounds. If you buy a chicken that is labeled "free range." what that can mean is "sort-of free range." The best type of chicken is truly free to *range*, to have 24-hour access to the outdoors, to breath fresh air, to have access to a large field, meadow, or orchard to peck and scratch about, and to have a truly natural existence; to be protected from predators like dogs or foxes by an electric security fence, to have shelter from the weather when needed, and to have a place to roost, a plentiful supply of grain, and fresh water.

4) The next question to ask is has it been dry-plucked? Real chicken does not get dunked into hot water. For the flavor to be at its best, dry-plucking is the optimum process.

5) A little age adds a lot of flavor! This old adage was never more true. If you hang an intact, ungutted chicken in a controlled temperature, it will mature naturally (like cheese) and its flavor will become concentrated.

   I repeat, I'm all for progress, but I've never wanted good food to be only for the privileged few who are in the know. What I've observed is that the very best food producers in the world today are those who use traditional skills and methods alongside the latest technology.

Where can you buy real chicken?
Free-range and organic poultry is available from a number of suppliers. One of the best-flavored chickens, I've found out, is produced by D'Artagnan (see Suppliers, pages 481-2). This type of chicken is also great for casseroles and other cooking processes for chicken. Kosher chickens are also flavorful and are widely available. A chicken weighing about 3 lb (1.35 kg) is suitable for fast roasting (see page 332), and for a traditional slow-roast chicken, the best size is about 5-6 lb (2.25-2.7 kg).

How to roast a chicken

I want to give two options here: one is for a traditional home-roast Sunday chicken and the other a fast-roast chicken that can be adapted in various ways with different sauces and flavors. But first a few points to remember.

Does it need to be trussed?

No. The original idea of trussing was merely to make the bird look neater, but I find it's easier to cook if it isn't tightly tied. So cut away and discard any trussing strings if they are present.

Which way up should I roast it?

On its back is my favored way, placing it directly in the roasting pan. Why? Because I have found that the more robust meat of the chicken is sitting next to the direct heat this way, and this, in the end, provides delicious crispy bits a) to serve and eat, and b) to be scraped up into the sauce or gravy, giving it an extra dimension. Some cooks say you should begin by roasting a chicken upside down, then on its side, then on its back, but I don't think the breast part, which is the most delicate, should be in direct contact with the heat of the roasting pan. Also, turning very hot, slithery chicken over onto its side, or breast, and so on, during cooking is not a good idea. I tend not to use a rack for chicken for the reason outlined above, but I do use one for duck (see page 331).

Will it be dry?

No, I promise it won't, as long as you are careful, follow the guidelines given and don't overcook it. With the slower, traditional roasting, bacon placed on the breast provides protection as well as a gradual slow-basting of the breast, and the pork in the stuffing provides the same protection internally, so all this – and the chicken's natural juices – keeps it moist. Don't forget that the better the quality of chicken, the moister and easier it will be to cook. In the case of fast-roast chicken, because the bird is in the oven for a much shorter time, less evaporation occurs and the chicken stays beautifully moist.

When is it cooked?

Obviously if you stick to the timings for slow-roasting given on page 338 you can't go far wrong, but there are two tests: one is to insert a thin skewer into the thickest part of the leg, remove it, and press it flat against the flesh to see if the juices run clear; the second one is to give the leg a tug – if it has some give in it and is not too resistant, that indicates the chicken is cooked. If you are in real doubt, cut a bit of the leg away and look at the area of meat where the thigh joins the body – there should be no visible pink juices.

Fast- or slow-roasting?

After a number of experiments, I have come up with a method of roasting a smaller chicken at the highest temperature in the oven, and I have to say the method produces a wonderful result. With a bigger bird, slow-roasting is recommended: here you have a more melting, tender, finished texture, whereas with fast-roasting, the flesh is firmer but still tender since the chicken is younger. What's good is to have a choice – the slower method for leisurely family meals at weekends and the fast method for weekday evening suppers.

Why does it need to rest before carving?

When a chicken is cooked, the heat in the oven causes all the internal juices to bubble up to the surface just under the skin – sometimes you can see the skin almost flapping with the amount of juice inside it. Because of this you should always allow the bird to rest for at least 15 minutes before carving it, so that all these wonderful juices are absorbed back into the chicken keeping everything tender and moist. The fibers of the chicken will also relax, and this will make carving easier.

How do I carve a chicken?

Very easily, provided you have a sharp knife (see page 299) and follow the instructions given below.

To carve a chicken, insert the knife between the leg and body and remove the thigh and drumstick in one piece

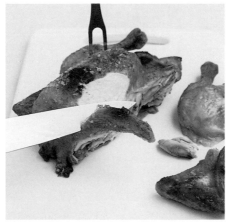

Remove the wing on the same side, then slice the breast. Repeat this on the other side of the bird

Finally, divide the drumstick and thigh, cutting through the joint so you have two leg portions

Cutting up a chicken

1) Using a very sharp knife, begin by cutting through the tail, then stand the chicken in a vertical position

2) Now, insert the knife into the cut you've just made and cut straight down the back of the chicken

3) Place the chicken skin-side down, open it out flat like a book, and cut right through the breastbone

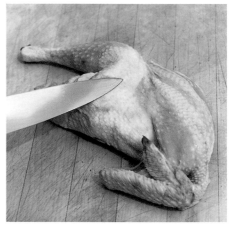

4) Turn the chicken halves over, stretch out the leg, and cut along the line dividing the leg from the breast

5) For six portions, turn the legs over, find the thin white line at the center of the joint and cut through it

6) If you need eight portions, simply cut the breast portion in half

Chicken Cacciatora

This is my version of the famous Italian classic – best made in late summer when there's an abundance of red, ripe, full-flavored tomatoes, but it's still good in other seasons since there are now some well-flavored varieties available in supermarkets. Either way, the tomatoes need to be very red and ripe.

First of all, heat the oil in the casserole over a high heat and season the chicken pieces with salt and pepper. Then, when the oil gets really hot and begins to shimmer, fry the chicken – in 2 batches – to brown it well on all sides: remove the first batch to a plate while you tackle the second; each piece needs to become a golden-brown color all over. When the second batch is ready, remove it to join the rest. Now, add the onions to the casserole, turn the heat down to medium, and cook for 8-10 minutes, or until they are softened and nicely browned at the edges.

Meanwhile, peel the tomatoes. To do this, pour boiling water over them and leave them for exactly 1 minute before draining and slipping off their skins (protect your hands with a cloth if they are too hot), then chop them into small pieces.

When the onions are browned, add the garlic to the casserole, let this cook for about 1 minute, then add the tomatoes, tomato paste, rosemary, bay leaf, white wine, and white wine vinegar. Now, add some seasoning and bring it up to a boil, then let it bubble and reduce (without covering) to about half its original volume, which will take about 20 minutes. Now, add the chicken pieces, stir them around, then put on the lid, and simmer gently for 40 minutes, until the chicken pieces are cooked through. This is good served with green tagliatelle, noodles, rice, or a simple vegetable.

Serves 4

1 x 3 lb (1.35 kg) free range chicken, cut into 8 pieces (see opposite page)
1 tablespoon olive oil
2 large onions, peeled and thickly sliced
1 lb 8 oz (700 g) ripe red tomatoes
2 large cloves garlic, peeled and crushed
1 tablespoon tomato paste
1 tablespoon fresh rosemary leaves, bruised and finely chopped
1 bay leaf
1¼ cups (275 ml) dry white wine
1 tablespoon white wine vinegar
salt and freshly ground black pepper

You will also need a lidded flameproof casserole with a capacity of 4 quarts (3.5 liters).

Other birds

These are simply those birds, besides chicken, that are specifically bred for the table – what used to be sometimes raised as domestic poultry. In this chapter I have included guinea fowl, quail, Rock Cornish game hens, and farmed duck.

Guinea fowl

Guinea fowl are unusual in that they are neither totally wild nor truly domesticated. The fowl are raised for the table and can be bought from specialist game suppliers (see Suppliers, pages 481-2). The flavor is somewhere between pheasant and chicken, and though it isn't as plump as chicken (one will really only serve two people), it does have an extra-gamey flavor. You can use it for any chicken recipe, but if you want to make something like coq au vin, where the bird needs to be cut up, ask the butcher to do it because it's quite a difficult job.

Quail

These are completely domesticated game birds, bred for the table. Don't be taken in by their tiny appearance, which is, in fact, quite deceptive – they are surprisingly plump and the flesh is delicious. Serve two quail per person, and apart from the very special recipe for Roast Quail Wrapped in Pancetta and Grape Leaves with Grape Confit on page 340, another good way to serve them is to place a sage leaf on the breast of each bird, wrap each one in bacon, them place them on a bed of previously softened onions and mushrooms, along with ⅔ cup (150 ml) of dry white wine, cider, or Madeira. Then braise them in a medium oven at 350°F (180°C) – and give them 40-45 minutes.

Rock Cornish game hens

The Cornish game hen is a very small chicken weighing around 2½ lb (1.15 kg), delicious stuffed and roasted or split and barbecued. They are attractive and convenient for serving since one hen will serve one person.

Duck

Ducks, or ducklings as they are sometimes known, come in a variety of sizes, usually from 3 lb (1.35 kg) to 6 lb (2.7 kg). The Long Island or Chinese Peking duck is one of the most common kinds of duck available in the US. It is a delicious but fairly fatty bird; if the ones available to you are small, buy two to serve four people. Muscovy ducks, similar in taste to French Barbary ducks, are less fatty than other varieties, and they are meaty with an excellent flavor. Easier to overcook than the Long Island duck, check them regularly toward the end of the cooking time to guarantee the flesh is still moist when you serve it. Wild mallard is available during the fall and is much less fatty than farmed duck.

Roast duck at last!

In over 30 years of cooking and writing recipes, duck has posed some problems. It is a magnificent bird – rich and succulent, with an abundance of flavor; it also has masses of fat, but that is not a problem because the fat all comes out in the cooking; but what the cook has to aim for is that elusive, really crunchy, almost crackling-like skin, with moist, tender flesh beneath. I used to belong to what I call the semi-Chinese school, which meant vastly overcooking a duck to get it really crisp but losing much of the succulent flesh in the process. I've also tried the complicated Chinese method of boiling it first, then drying and roasting it. Both methods were never quite right. Now, after all these years, I've figured it out – fast-roasting is the answer (see the recipe on page 334): perfect roast duck every time without a worry.

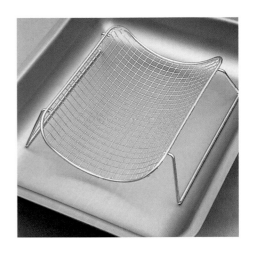

Because so much fat comes out of the duck while it is cooking, it needs to be placed either on a roasting rack, *right*, or on some crumpled aluminum foil to allow the fat to drain away from the bird, making the skin really crisp.

Carving

It has to be said that this is another "at last," after years of cutting a roast duck into rather inelegant quarters. I have now discovered the correct way to carve the whole thing into eight perfect portions to serve four people. This is thanks to my friend and poultry specialist Bill Curran, and below we have photographed his ingenious method.

Turn the bird onto its breast and cut down through the meat along the full length of the back bone on either side, then turn the duck onto its back

Next, cut the meat away from the carcass, keeping the knife close to the bone. When you reach the base of the bird, carefully cut through the leg joint

Cut each half of the duck between the leg and the breast, then cut the leg into two pieces at the joint. Finally, divide the breast into two

Fast-Roast Chicken with Lemon and Tarragon

Here is a revolution in the best way to roast a small chicken. The flavorings can vary in any way you like — crushed chopped rosemary leaves, sage leaves, or thyme can be used, or a mixture of herbs, and you could replace the garlic with a couple of finely chopped shallots. It's a great recipe for adapting to whatever you have handy.

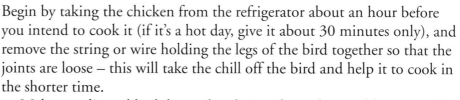

Serves 4

1 x 3 lb (1.35 kg) free range chicken
½ small lemon, thinly sliced and the slices halved, plus the juice of the remaining lemon
2½ tablespoons chopped fresh tarragon leaves
2 cloves garlic, peeled and crushed
1 tablespoon (10 g) softened butter
2 teaspoons olive oil
1¼ cups (275 ml) dry white wine
salt and freshly ground black pepper

You will also need a heavy roasting pan measuring approximately 9 x 11 inches (23 x 28 cm), 2 inches (5 cm) deep.

Preheat the oven to 450°F (230°C).

Begin by taking the chicken from the refrigerator about an hour before you intend to cook it (if it's a hot day, give it about 30 minutes only), and remove the string or wire holding the legs of the bird together so that the joints are loose – this will take the chill off the bird and help it to cook in the shorter time.

Make a garlic and herb butter by placing the garlic, 2 tablespoons of the chopped tarragon leaves, and the butter in a bowl and combine them with a fork, adding some salt and pepper. Then place the herb butter inside the body cavity of the bird, along with the halved lemon slices. Spread a little of the olive oil over the bottom of the roasting pan, place the chicken in it, then spread the rest of the olive oil all over the skin of the bird. Lastly, season well with salt and black pepper, and then place the roasting pan into the lower third of the oven. Now, let it roast for 45 minutes without opening the oven door. When this time is up, remove the bird from the oven. Next, put a wooden spoon into the body cavity, and using a spatula to hold the breast end, tip the chicken to pour out the buttery juices and slices of lemon into the roasting pan. Transfer the bird on to a carving board, cover with foil, and let it rest for 20 minutes.

Meanwhile, using a tablespoon, skim off the excess fat from the juices in the roasting pan, then place the pan over direct heat, add the wine and lemon juice, and let the liquid bubble and reduce to about half its original volume. Now, add the remaining tarragon, then taste and check the seasoning. Carve the chicken onto warm plates and add any juices to the sauce. Spoon the sauce over the chicken and serve.

Crisp Roast Duck with Confit of Sour Cherries

This is it – the best method of roasting duck I've found to date, and of all the lovely sauces, this one – made with dried sour cherries – is the best. It's important to remember, however, that the duck should be as dry as possible, so buy it 24 hours in advance, remove and discard the wrapping and giblets, dry it with a clean dish towel, and leave it uncovered on a plate in the refrigerator until needed.

Serves 4
1 x 4 lb (1.8 kg) meaty duck (weight with giblets)
fresh watercress, to garnish
sea salt and freshly ground black pepper

For the confit of sour cherries:
3 oz (75 g) dried sour cherries or dried cranberries
¾ cup plus 2 tablespoons (200 ml) dry red wine (cabernet sauvignon, for example)
2½ tablespoons (25 g) granulated sugar
1 tablespoon red wine vinegar

You will also need a roasting rack or some aluminum foil, and a heavy roasting pan measuring 9 x 11 inches (23 x 28 cm), 2 inches (5 cm) deep.

Preheat the oven to 450°F (230°C).

You need to start this recipe the day before you want to serve it by first soaking the cherries for the confit in the red wine overnight.

The next day, prepare the duck by wiping it again with a dish towel. Now, using a small skewer, prick the fatty parts of the duck's skin, particularly between the legs and the breast. Now, either place the duck on the roasting rack in the pan or make a rack yourself by crumpling the aluminum foil and placing it in the bottom of the roasting pan. Season with coarse sea salt and freshly ground black pepper, using quite a lot of salt since this encourages crunchiness. Now, place the pan on the center shelf of the preheated oven and roast the duck for 1 hour and 50 minutes. During the cooking time, using an oven mitt to protect your hands, remove the pan from the oven and drain the fat from the corner of the pan – do this about 3 times (the fat is perfect for roasting potatoes, so don't throw it away).

Meanwhile, to make the confit, place the soaked cherries and wine in a saucepan, along with the sugar and wine vinegar. Bring the mixture up to a gentle simmer, give it all a good stir, and let it barely simmer, without a lid, for 50 minutes to 1 hour, stirring from time to time. What will happen is that the wine will slowly reduce so there's only about 3 tablespoons of liquid left.

When the cooking time is up, allow the duck to rest for 20 minutes or so, then carve (see the photographs on page 331) and serve garnished with the fresh watercress. Pour some of the sour-cherry confit over each portion and pass the rest in a pitcher at the table.

Paella

I've had lots of hits and misses with this Spanish classic, adding ridiculous, overwhelming amounts of saffron to get it as yellow as it is in Spain. Then I found out the Spanish sometimes use coloring! So here at last is the Delia paella – easy, no fuss, and the good thing is it serves six people as a complete meal needing no accompaniment.

Serves 6

1¾ cups (350 g) Calasparra paella rice
2 tablespoons olive oil
1 x 3 lb (1.35 kg) free range chicken, cut into 8 pieces (see page 328)
1 large onion, peeled and roughly chopped
1 red bell pepper, seeded and roughly chopped into chunks
4 oz (110 g) Spanish chorizo sausage in a piece, skin removed and cut into ½ inch (1 cm) dice
2 cloves garlic, peeled and crushed
1½ teaspoons paprika
¼ teaspoon cayenne pepper
½ teaspoon saffron strands
8 oz (225 g) ripe red tomatoes, peeled and roughly diced
5 cups (1.2 liters) boiling water
12 medium-sized shrimp, shell-on, defrosted if frozen, 4 with heads, 8 without
⅓ cup (50 g) fresh or frozen shelled peas
1 lemon, cut into wedges, to garnish
salt and freshly ground black pepper

You will also need a shallow paella pan with a bottom diameter of 10 inches (25.5 cm), a top diameter of 13 inches (32.5 cm) and a capacity of 4½ quarts (4 liters).

Once you have peeled, chopped, prepared, and assembled everything, heat the oil in the pan over a fairly high heat. Now, season the chicken pieces, adding 4 of them to the hot oil to sauté on all sides until golden brown, then remove them to a plate and do the same with the other 4 pieces. Next, add the onion, bell pepper, and chorizo and fry these over a medium heat for 6-8 minutes, or until they're nicely tinged brown at the edges. Now, add the garlic, paprika, cayenne, and saffron and cook for another minute, then return the chicken to the pan, followed by the tomatoes, plenty of seasoning, and the boiling water. Next, bring everything to a gentle simmer, turn the heat down, and cook, uncovered, for 10 minutes.

After that, remove the chicken pieces and set them aside, then pour the rice into the center of the pan. Bring everything back up to a boil, give a final stir, and simmer, still uncovered, for about 10 minutes. During that time, shake the pan occasionally and move it around on the heat a little if the burner is not as big as the bottom of the pan. Next, return the chicken, along with the shrimp and peas, to the pan and continue to simmer for 15-20 minutes, or until the rice is cooked, adding a little more hot liquid if you think it's necessary. Now, shake the pan again, making sure the rice is completely immersed. Turn the shrimp over halfway through the cooking time – they will turn pink when cooked. The rice at the edges of the pan will take longest to cook, so to test that the paella is ready, take a little of the rice from the edges to check whether it has cooked through, then remove the pan from the heat and cover with a clean dish towel for 5 minutes to absorb some of the steam. The paella is now ready – just garnish with the lemon wedges and don't forget to have hot plates ready for serving it.

Stir-Fried Chicken with Lime and Coconut

It's hard to credit that a recipe as simple and as quick as this could taste so good, but I can assure you it's an absolute winner.

First of all, chop the chicken into bite-sized pieces and place them in a bowl with the lime juice and zest. Stir well and let them marinate for an hour.

When you're ready to cook the chicken, heat the oil in the pan or wok over a high heat, add the chicken pieces, and stir-fry for 3-4 minutes until they're golden. Then add the chili, stir-fry for 1 more minute, and add the coconut milk, fish sauce, and half the cilantro and scallions. Cook for another 1-2 minutes, then serve with Thai fragrant rice and the remaining cilantro and scallions sprinkled on top.

Serves 2

2 free range boneless, skinless chicken breast halves
grated zest and juice 1 large lime
⅔ cup (150 ml) canned coconut milk
2 teaspoons olive oil
1 green chili, seeded and finely chopped
2 teaspoons Thai fish sauce
6 tablespoons fresh cilantro
4 scallions, cut into 1 inch (2.5 cm) shreds, including the green parts

You will also need a frying pan with a diameter of 10 inches (25.5 cm), or a wok.

Traditional Roast Chicken with Apple, Sage, and Onion Stuffing, Cranberry with Sage Sauce, and Chicken-Giblet Gravy

This is what I described at the beginning of this chapter – a family roast chicken, moist and succulent for Sunday dinner, with lots of crispy bacon, real chicken gravy, some very savory stuffing, and a sauce. All it needs is some vegetables with a bowl of crunchy roast potatoes, and some family and friends to share the feast.

Apple, sage, and onion stuffing

If you have a food processor, making stuffing is a breeze: all you do is turn the motor on, add the pieces of bread, and process into crumbs, then add the parsley, sage, apple, and onion quarters and process until everything is finely chopped. Next, trim any sinewy bits from the chicken livers, rinse under cold water, pat them dry, then add them, along with the sausage meat, mace, and seasonings. Give a few pulses in the food processor until it is thoroughly blended, remove the stuffing from the processor with a spatula, then place in a plastic storage bag and store in the refrigerator until you are ready to stuff the chicken (within a couple of hours). If you're doing this by hand, just finely chop all the ingredients, combine in a bowl, and refrigerate as above.

Traditional roast chicken

Preheat the oven to 375°F (190°C).

First of all, the chicken needs to be stuffed. To do this, you begin at the neck end, where you'll find a flap of loose skin: gently loosen this away from the breast and you'll be able to make a triangular pocket. Pack about two-thirds of the stuffing inside, as far as you can go, and make a neat round shape on the outside, then tuck the neck flap under the bird's back and secure it with a small skewer or toothpick. Take the remaining stuffing and place it in the body cavity (the fat in the pork will melt and help to keep the bird moist inside). Now, place the chicken in the roasting pan and spread the butter over the chicken using your hands and making sure you don't leave any part of the surface unbuttered.

Season the chicken all over with salt and black pepper, then arrange 7 slices of the bacon, slightly overlapping, in a row along the breast. Cut the last strip in half and place one piece on each leg.

Place the chicken in the oven on the centre shelf and cook for 20 minutes per lb (450 g), plus 10-20 minutes extra – this will be 1 hour and 50 minutes to 2 hours for a 5 lb (2.25 kg) bird, or 2 hours 10 minutes to 2 hours 20 minutes for a 6 lb (2.7 kg) bird. The chicken is cooked if the juices run clear when the thickest part of the leg is pierced with a skewer. It is important to baste the chicken at least 3 times during the cooking – spooning over the juices mingling with the bacon fat and butter helps to keep the flesh succulent.

During the last basting (about half an hour before the chicken is cooked), remove the now-crisp bacon strips and keep them warm. If they

Serves 6-8

For the roast chicken:
1 x 5-6 lb (2.25-2.7 kg) free range chicken
4 tablespoons (50 g) butter, at room temperature
8 strips bacon
salt and freshly ground black pepper

For the apple, sage, and onion stuffing:
1 sweet apple, eg McIntosh, cored and quartered
1½ tablespoons fresh sage leaves
1 small onion, peeled and quartered
4 oz (110 g) fresh white bread, crusts removed
1 tablespoon fresh parsley leaves
reserved chicken livers from the giblets
8 oz (225 g) ground pork or pork sausage meat
¼ teaspoon powdered mace
salt and freshly ground black pepper

You will also need a flameproof roasting pan measuring 10 x 14 inches (25.5 x 35 cm), 2 inches (5 cm) deep.

are not crisp, leave them around the chicken to finish off. For the final 15 minutes of cooking, raise the heat up to 425°F (220°C), which will give the skin that final golden crispiness.

When the chicken is cooked, it is important to leave it in the warm kitchen (near the oven), covered in foil, for 30 minutes, which will allow it to relax. This is important because while the chicken is cooking all the juices bubble up to the surface (if you look inside the oven you will actually see this happening just under the skin), and allowing the chicken to relax allows all these precious juices to seep back into the flesh. It also makes the chicken much easier to carve. When you serve the chicken, make sure everyone gets some crispy bacon and stuffing. Serve with the Chicken-Giblet Gravy and Cranberry and Sage Sauce.

For the chicken-giblet gravy

Simply place the giblets, water, carrot, onion, herbs, peppercorns, and salt in a medium-sized saucepan and simmer very gently with the lid almost on for 2 hours. Strain the stock into a large measuring cup, cool it, and chill in the refrigerator. Any fat on the surface is easily removed after it becomes cold. To make the gravy, after removing the chicken from the roasting pan, tilt the pan and remove most of the fat which, you will see, separates clearly from the juices; you need to leave about 2 tablespoons of fat behind. Now, place the roasting pan over direct heat turned to fairly low, and when the juices begin to sizzle, sprinkle in the flour, stirring vigorously until you get a smooth paste; then add the giblet stock, little by little, exchanging the wooden spoon for a whisk. Whisk thoroughly until all the stock is incorporated, bring the mixture up to simmering, then taste and season with salt and freshly ground black pepper.

For the cranberry and sage sauce

Combine all the ingredients in a small saucepan and whisk over a gentle heat until the cranberry jelly has melted. Then pour the sauce into a serving pitcher and leave until needed (it doesn't need re-heating – it's served at room temperature). Although I love to serve this sauce in the summer, in winter my favorite accompaniment is Traditional Bread Sauce from my Christmas book.

For the chicken-giblet gravy:
8 oz (225 g) frozen chicken giblets (reserving the livers for the stuffing),
3¾ cups (850 ml) water
1 medium carrot, roughly chopped
½ onion
a few fresh parsley stalks
sprig fresh thyme
1 bay leaf
½ teaspoon black peppercorns
3 tablespoons all-purpose flour
salt and freshly ground black pepper

For the cranberry and sage sauce:
6 tablespoons cranberry jelly
4 teaspoons chopped fresh sage
3 tablespoons balsamic vinegar
salt and freshly ground black pepper

Roast Quail Wrapped in Pancetta and Grape Leaves with Grape Confit

I am a self-confessed quail convert, having shunned them for years as being undersized and troublesome. I was wrong. They are plump and meaty and, because they are self-contained, they are one of the easiest birds to cook and serve. Grape leaves, which impart a delicious flavor, are available in some stores and specialized food shops, but if you can't find them, you can use foil loosely crumpled around each quail instead.

Serves 4

8 quail
3 oz (75 g) sliced pancetta, preferably smoked
16 fresh grape leaves or preserved grape leaves in brine
a little olive oil
salt and freshly ground black pepper

For the grape confit:

6 oz (175 g) red or black seedless grapes, halved
1 teaspoon granulated sugar
3 tablespoons red wine
1 tablespoon red wine vinegar

You will also need a shallow baking pan measuring 10 x 14 inches (25.5 x 35 cm), and some string.

Preheat the oven to 425°F (220°C).

First of all, make the grape confit by dissolving the sugar in the wine and wine vinegar, then add the grapes and let them simmer very gently, without a lid, for 40 minutes until the liquid has reduced to a syrup.

If you are using fresh grape leaves, blanch them by dipping them in boiling water for a few seconds until they become limp, then pat them dry and remove the stems. If you have preserved grape leaves, rinse them under running water, and pat them dry. Now, wipe the quail with paper towels and remove any trussing string, then rub them with olive oil and season.

Next, cover the breasts with the pancetta, dividing it equally among the quail. Now, place each bird on a grape leaf with the legs pointing toward the stem end, and wrap the leaf up each side; put another leaf over the breast, and tuck it in underneath the quail. Tie each quail with a piece of string to keep the leaves in place, then lay them in the baking pan and cook on a high shelf of the oven for 15 minutes. After that, take them out, untie the string, and holding the quail in a cloth, unpeel the top leaf (leaving the second leaf and pancetta intact). Return the quail to the oven to brown and crisp, which takes another 15 minutes. When you've removed them from the oven, let them rest for about 10 minutes before serving with the grape confit.

Guinea Fowl Baked with Thirty Cloves of Garlic

Before you balk at this recipe, you might like to know that garlic, simmered gently for 1¼ hours, mellows deliciously, losing much of its pungency. I have to admit, it's probably not the thing to eat before a first date, but otherwise it's utterly sublime. In this recipe, an inedible huff paste, prepared in moments, is used to make a perfect seal for the lid of the casserole, guaranteeing that all the juices and fragrances remain intact. If you want, you could use foil instead, bearing in mind it will not be quite as effective.

First of all, dry the guinea fowl as much as possible with paper towels and season it well. Next, melt the butter and oil in the casserole, then keeping the heat fairly high, brown the guinea fowl carefully on all sides. This will seem a bit awkward, but all you do is protect your hands with a cloth and hold the guinea fowl by its legs, turning it into different positions until it is a rich golden color all over; this will take 10-15 minutes in all. After that, remove the guinea fowl from the casserole, add the cloves of garlic and rosemary sprigs, toss these around, then replace the guinea fowl and sprinkle with the chopped rosemary. Next, pour the wine all around it and let it gently come to simmering point.

Meanwhile, to make the huff paste, place the flour in a bowl and add the water – it should be enough to make a soft but not a sticky dough – then divide the dough into 4 pieces and roll each one into a cylinder about 9 inches (23 cm) long on a lightly floured surface. Now, position these all around the rim of the casserole – it doesn't matter what they look like. Place the casserole lid carefully on top, pressing down gently and making sure there are no gaps. Alternatively, simply place a double sheet of foil over the casserole before putting the lid on. Now, place the casserole in the oven and cook for 1 hour exactly, then remove the lid and let the guinea fowl continue to cook for another 10 minutes, to re-crisp the skin. Next, remove the guinea fowl from the casserole and allow it to rest for 10 minutes before carving.

Serve the carved guinea fowl with the garlic cloves alongside and the cooking juices poured around it. The idea is to mash the garlic cloves with a knife to release all the creamy pulp, and as you eat, dip the pieces of guinea fowl into it. Creamy mashed potatoes would be a wonderful accompaniment here.

Serves 4
1 x 4 lb (1.8 kg) guinea fowl
30 cloves garlic, unpeeled (3-4 heads)
1 tablespoon (10 g) butter
2 teaspoons olive oil
6 small sprigs fresh rosemary
1½ tablespoons rosemary leaves, bruised and chopped
1¼ cups (275 ml) white wine
salt and freshly ground black pepper

For the huff (sealing) paste:
1¾ cups (225 g) all-purpose flour, plus a little extra for dusting
⅔ cup (150 ml) cold water

You will also need a lidded flameproof casserole large enough to hold the guinea fowl comfortably – about 5 quarts (4.5 liters).

Preheat the oven to 400°F (200°C).

Broiled Lemon Chicken Kebabs with Gremolata

This is what we all need – something easy to prepare, really fast to cook, and that also tastes exceptionally good. Serve with rice or salad or both, or, instead of the rice, warm crusty bread to dip into the juices.

Serves 2
2 free range boneless chicken breast halves, skin-on
juice 1 lemon, plus 1 teaspoon grated lemon zest
3 thick slices lemon, cut into quarters
¼ cup (55 ml) olive oil
1 clove garlic, peeled and crushed
2 teaspoons chopped fresh oregano
1 teaspoon white wine vinegar
2 bay leaves, torn in half
salt and freshly ground black pepper

For the gremolata:
1 clove garlic, peeled and finely chopped
1½ teaspoons grated lemon zest
1 tablespoon chopped fresh parsley

You will also need 2 wooden skewers, 10 inches (25.5 cm) long, soaked in water for at least 30 minutes before you start cooking.

Begin by chopping each piece of chicken into 5 chunky pieces, leaving the skin on, and place them in a bowl along with the lemon juice and zest, oil, garlic, oregano, white wine vinegar, and plenty of seasoning. Cover and let the pieces marinate in the refrigerator overnight or for a few hours – or for as much time as you have.

To cook the chicken, preheat the broiler to its highest setting at least 10 minutes ahead, then first thread half a bay leaf on to the first skewer, followed by a quarter-slice of lemon, then a piece of chicken. Continue alternating the lemon and chicken until you have used 5 pieces of chicken, finishing with a lemon quarter and another bay-leaf half at the end and making sure you pack everything together as tightly as possible. Repeat with the second skewer, then place them both on a broiler rack, and underneath the rack place a heatproof dish to catch the juices. The kebabs should be 4 inches (10 cm) from the broiler, and as they cook you need to baste them with the marinade juices. They will need 10 minutes on each side to cook through and to become nice and dark and toasted at the edges.

While they're under the broiler, mix the gremolata ingredients together and have them ready. When the chicken is done, transfer it to a serving plate and keep warm. Now, put the rest of the marinade, plus the basting juices, into a saucepan and boil to reduce to a syrupy consistency, which will take about 2 minutes. Pour this over the chicken and sprinkle with the gremolata when you serve it at the table.

15

A vegetable calendar

I will always remember the comedienne Victoria Wood at the Albert Hall in 1996 doing one of her splendid monologues in which she described how an aunt of hers always put the sprouts on for the Christmas lunch in November! It was the older people in the audience who laughed the loudest because, of course, we all remembered the waterlogged, rather gray, overcooked vegetables of our schooldays.

Though the citizens of most of the world's affluent nations are still very much meat-loving people, they have of late developed a much more healthy reverence and respect for vegetables. Instead of being some "also-ran" to help the meat go down, vegetables have now become absolute stars in their own right.

How to cook perfect vegetables

The answer to this lies in just one word - carefully. Vegetables need care and attention if we're going to get the best out of them. "Catch the moment" is a good phrase, because there is a moment when they are cooked to perfection and then, beyond that, they begin to deteriorate.

The problem of overcooking, I suspect, was related to a fear of the vegetables not being quite done enough, but now, we seem to be facing the absolutely opposite problem - a fear of overcooking that results in almost raw, inedible vegetables that you can't get your fork into. So while it can be argued that overcooked vegetables should be banned for ever, I would like to see the opposite extreme banned, too. I have nothing against good, honest, raw vegetables, but if they're meant to be cooked to bring out their best flavor, then they must be.

Catching the moment?

I am always being asked what my favorite piece of cooking equipment is, and the answer is unequivocal - a small, flat skewer! I keep a whole bunch of them hanging near where I cook. Using them is the only way I can tell if, say, a cauliflower floret, a potato, or a Brussels sprout is cooked. As the skewer slides into the thickest part of the vegetable, you can feel if it's tender by the amount of give. A very small, sharp paring knife will do the same job, but a skewer is better. If you practice the skewer test every time you cook vegetables you'll soon get the feel of "catching the moment."

Is water the enemy?

I would say yes to this question - most of the time, but not always. On the whole, the more water you have, the more it dilutes the flavor of the vegetables. If you're boiling, the water should barely cover the vegetables, because a brief encounter is what we're really looking for. Always use water you have boiling in a kettle so that you can control how much you are adding; you'll be able to see instantly when the water barely covers the vegetables and doesn't need more. So, always be very sparing with water, except when you are boiling cabbage, where, I have concluded after many years of experimenting, that cabbage needs plenty of boiling water to cover so that its brief encounter with the fast-boiling water cooks and tenderizes it as quickly as possible. All vegetable cooking water contains nutrients, so use it as stock whenever possible. In the vegetable cooking methods that follow, I will indicate the amounts of water needed.

Is steaming better?

Sometimes steaming is very definitely better, other times not. As we have prepared *How To Cook*, my team and I have conducted comparison tests so that when steaming is better, it will be indicated. In some cases, steam rather than water helps to preserve more flavor, but in other cases, steaming does not tenderise sufficiently, and, because it takes longer, it can affect flavor. I would urge you to invest in a collapsible basket steamer – a wonderful piece of equipment that can be slipped into any-sized saucepan, allowing you to always have the choice of being able to steam.

Oven-roasting

When broiled vegetables became fashionable in many parts of the world, the vagaries of the domestic oven broiler were never going to be able to cope without a great deal of hassle. Since my first experience with high-temperature oven-roasting of vegetables in my book, *Summer Collection*, I am now thrilled and delighted to have discovered this method of oven-roasting vegetables. I now almost never broil or sauté, which demands time, standing around watching, waiting, and turning, whereas oven-roasting, besides leaving you in peace, has the huge advantage of requiring less fat. I do, however, sometimes use a ridged grill pan, which gives plenty of vision and no bending backaches from peering under a conventional oven broiler.

Which is the best method?

There isn't one best method for all vegetables. All of them respond differently to different ways of cooking, so what I will do is indicate which method I think is best for each specific vegetable.

Serving vegetables in season

Nature used to provide us with a perfectly varied diet, leaving us blissfully free of a large amount of decision-making. This in turn gave an added dimension to everyday eating in that we could enjoy anticipating what each month in each year would bring and really look forward to it.

Now modern technology and progress have provided airline shipping. At any given time in the calendar, produce from around the world can be dispatched within hours and absolutely everything is always available all year round. What this means is that, along with the good fortune of being able to eat almost anything we feel like when we like, we have also lost something, and that is an appreciation of what individual items taste like when they are harvested in their natural environment, in their best season. Thus we have pallid sprouts in July and woolly strawberries at Christmas. There's also the added problem of travel time and distribution, which often means fruits and vegetables are picked when immature and unripened, with a resulting loss of flavor and quality.

I am not against progress and I do appreciate imported fresh shelled peas – they don't have the tender melt-in-the-mouth flavor of home-grown peas in June, but they're better than frozen. I also love having fresh basil in the winter months when mine has died off. However, if we want to know how to cook we first need to know the season that vegetables have the finest quality and flavor - tight little Brussels sprouts after the first frost has sharpened their flavor; the finest young green stalks of asparagus in early May; the very red, sweet, sun-ripened tomatoes of late summer; and the unmatched flavor and melting texture of runner beans from your garden. For this reason I will indicate the best season for each vegetable and hopefully encourage you to reintroduce this natural rhythm of nature into your day-to-day eating.

Asparagus

April to the end of May, depending on the weather

I have now almost completely given up making things with asparagus, because apart from the very tender tips, which I like to chop and put in Eggs en Cocotte (page 39), I think asparagus is best eaten as it is, hot with foaming melted butter or hollandaise sauce poured over it, or served warm or cold with a good vinaigrette (see page 383).

To cook asparagus, take each stalk, one by one, in both hands and bend and snap off the woody end, then trim the ends with a knife to make them neater. Lay the asparagus stalks in a collapsible basket steamer (or an ordinary steamer will do) – they can be piled one on top of the other – then place them in a saucepan, pour in about 1 inch (2.5 cm) of boiling water from the kettle, then season with salt, put on a lid, and steam for 5-6 minutes, or until they feel tender when tested with a skewer.

Serve the asparagus on hot plates with some sauce poured over the tips. Pick them up with your hands and eat down to the ends, dipping in the sauce after each bite. Also, don't forget to have finger bowls and napkins for each person. 1 lb 4 oz (570 g) of asparagus will serve 4 as an appetizer.

Eggplant

Available all year, best late July to September

Chefs and cooks seems to have an endless debate about eggplant – to salt and drain or not to salt and drain. I'm for the former. I do take the point that the modern eggplant has evolved to a state where it does not contain bitter juices, but the juices are there nonetheless and I find salting and draining gets rid of excess moisture and concentrates the flavor – there's nothing worse than a watery eggplant.

Eggplant also have a capacity to absorb other flavors, so are great mixed with tomatoes and spices, cheese or legumes. They also absorb oil at an incredible rate, so frying is not recommended. I find the best way to cook them is either by oven-roasting (page 366) or char-broiling (page 388).

Beets

Available all year round, best June through September

A truly magnificent vegetable, but sadly poor old beets are often despised as a consequence of formerly being confined to the pickle jar. This is particularly true if the beets are preserved in poor quality vinegar, which can be a lethal culinary weapon that kills the beets' flavor. Yet cooked as a vegetable or in a salad beets have a superb earthy flavor and a wonderful rich, vibrant color.

To cook beets: there are two methods here; one is a long, slow method in the oven, suitable for larger, older beets; and the other method is right for the first small bunches of fresh beets that appear in June.

To cook 1 lb (450 g) of winter-storage beets in the oven (try to use even-sized beets if you can) begin by preheating the oven to 325°F (170°C). Prepare the beets by leaving the trailing root intact but trimming the green stalk so only 1 inch (2.5 cm) is left. Wash well under cold running water, but don't peel them. Now, place the beets in a package of double aluminum foil, sealing well. Place the package on a baking sheet and bake on the middle shelf of the preheated oven for 3 hours. To test if they are done, you should be able to ease the skin away with your thumbs.

For boiling young summer beets, take one bunch of beets, prepare as above, and place it in a medium saucepan; then add salt and enough boiling water to barely cover them. Simmer, covered, for 20-30 minutes, until the skin eases away when pushed away with your thumbs.

Peel and serve hot as a vegetable or cold with vinaigrette in a salad.

Fava beans

Best late-June and July

In one of my earlier cookbooks, I gave a recipe for very young fava beans in their pods; in fact, the beans are hardly formed and the finger-thick pods are delicious. If you grow fava beans in your own garden or know someone who does, cooking the young pods is worth a try. The beans themselves, however, when they've developed in the pod, have much to offer. When they're young and tender just steam them for about 3 minutes; if they're a bit older, boiling is best because it softens and tenderises the skin – add salt, barely cover with boiling water, and give them 3-4 minutes.

Older fava beans, when quite large, can be blanched in boiling water for 1 minute, then drained, cooled enough to handle, and the skins slipped off. As you do this they will split in two. Finish cooking them in steam until tender – 2-3 minutes. Fava beans have a wonderful affinity for boiled ham and ham steaks, and they taste great partnered with pancetta (Italian cured bacon). They make a delicious salad (see page 385). 1 lb (450 g) of fava beans in the pod will serve 2.

Broccoli

Available all year, best August through April

Broccoli is a vegetable that, because it's imported all year round, turns up far too often on menus. It's good to enjoy it in season, however. Prepare it by cutting it into even-sized florets measuring about 2 inches (5 cm) each, then steam them until tender – 4-5 minutes. Serve with a squeeze of lemon juice, a little butter, or a sprinkle of grated cheese to melt into the flower heads. You can also roast broccoli tossed in a little oil and seasoning – just place in a preheated oven at 400°F (200°C) for 25 minutes.

Alternatively, you can stir-fry it for 2 people by separating 8 oz (225 g) of florets into 1 inch (2.5 cm) pieces and slicing the stalks into tiny diagonal slices. Stir-fry in 2 teaspoons of very hot oil for 1 minute, then add 1 teaspoon of grated ginger and a crushed clove of garlic; stir-fry for another minute, then add 1 tablespoon of soy sauce and 1 tablespoon of dry sherry. Cover with a lid and continue to cook until tender – about 2 more minutes.

Broccoli raab

Best from late September through March

After the lean winter months, the first fresh green vegetable to herald spring is broccoli raab, with its purple or white flowery heads. It has a lovely, sweet, very green kind of flavor and tender stalks. I like to eat the leaves, stalks, and heads when it's very young. Steam them, sprinkled with salt, for 3-4 minutes. You will need 4 oz (110 g) per person.

Brussels sprouts

Best from September through December

Mini cabbages that grow on thick stalks is how I would describe Brussels sprouts. I am able to buy them in season near my home still attached to their two-foot-high stalks, which means I can "pick" them fresh as I need them throughout the week.

People either love or hate Brussels sprouts, and I am devoted to them – with certain requirements. I never buy them until the first frost, because I think that frost sharpens their flavor - sprouts at the end of summer are never as good. Also, if too large, they're difficult to cook, so small, tight buttons about 1 inch (2.5 cm) in size are best. The larger, more opened, walnut-sized sprouts are more difficult to cook but can be used in purées or soups.

To cook Brussels sprouts, there's no need to make incisions in the stalks. All you need to do for 1 lb (450 g) of sprouts is take off the outer leaves if they look a bit weary (if not leave them on), sprinkle with salt and steam them for 5-8 minutes, depending on their size, but watch carefully and remember undercooking is just as bad as overcooking, so use a skewer to test when they're tender. Another way to serve them is to have a frying pan with ½ a teaspoon of butter and ½ a teaspoon of oil very hot, then, after giving them about one minute's less steaming, toss them around in the hot pan to finish cooking and to turn them fairly brown at the edges. This last method can be varied by adding a couple of strips of bacon, cooked first until crisp. At Christmas it's nice to add 4 oz (110 g) of chopped, peeled, cooked chestnuts and brown these, too. 1 lb (450 g) of Brussels sprouts will serve 2-3 people.

Cabbage

Available all year

A cabbage is honest, down to earth goodness with no pretensions. It is a supremely beautiful vegetable, an absolute work of art visually. With its tight, audibly squeaky leaves bursting with vitality and flavor, especially sweet after the first frosts in the fall, why is it not acknowledged and revered? The overcooking of former years has made it a much-maligned vegetable in the western world. Chefs and restaurants continue to largely ignore its seasons, preferring to offer endless dull green string beans and the ever in-season broccoli.

When were you last offered a bowl of fragrant, buttered green cabbage in a restaurant? Isn't it time for a rethink? Fresh cabbage lightly cooked is full of goodness, packed with vitamins, minerals, and flavor, and it's not expensive. So I hope I can encourage you to start eating more of it.

Types of cabbage

Round white and red

Available in winter round white cabbage has green outer leaves but gets whiter toward the center and is good for coleslaw. Red cabbage is particularly good for pickling and baking with spices and apples. Both these cabbages are firm.

Savoy cabbage

Available in winter

The savoy, *right*, a round variety with crinkly leaves has a superb flavor.

Pointed cabbage

Available in winter

This is a lovely variety – tight, green, and leafy. Best after the first frost.

Kale

Available in late September through December

Kale has frilly leaves and a pleasant, strong flavor. It can be used raw or cooked. Its flavor is best in the winter months but you can usually buy it throughout the fall and winter.

Collards

Available in fall

These greens have a strong but sweet broccoli-like flavor. The greens are cooked in the same way as round white cabbage

Available in fall

These spicy, peppery greens are the leaves of the mustard plant and are delicious simmered with a very small amount of water flavored with a cut clove of garlic or sauteed in a little olive oil and butter.

Buying cabbage

Cabbage should always be eaten as fresh as possible – it loses nutrients if stored for too long. A fresh cabbage will look bright and crisp, with its outer leaves intact (often if it's had its outer leaves removed, it was because they were limp, which is not a good sign). The heart should feel firm and the leaves should squeak as you pull them apart.

To prepare cabbage: With a leafy variety it's best to discard any tired, floppy outside leaves, then separate the other leaves down to the central bud and place them one by one on a flat board. Then, using a sharp paring knife, cut out the stalks, running the point of the knife down each side. When the stalks have been removed, pile the leaves on top of each other and, using a larger knife, shred the cabbage into strips, then do the same with the center bud to shred that, too. For a more compact variety, such as Savoy, once the outer leaves have been discarded, halve and then quarter the cabbage lengthwise, then cut out the hard core from each quarter and discard. Finally, slice thinly across each quarter to shred it.

To cook cabbage: I have tried every method under the sun and I am now convinced that boiled cabbage needs plenty of water. The secret is to shred it quite finely and cook it briefly in rapidly boiling water. What I do is pack it down quite tightly into a saucepan, sprinkle with salt, then place the pan over a high heat, pour boiling water from the kettle over it so that it re-boils instantly, and time it for 3-5 minutes.

The one way to tell if it's cooked is to bite a piece, as you would pasta. Then tip it into a colander and squeeze as much excess water out as you can, using a saucer to press the cabbage down. Then turn the saucer on its side and use chopping movements, which pushes any excess water out. Serve it immediately in a hot bowl, tossing it with a minute amount of butter, and season it with salt and pepper. One medium-sized cabbage will serve 4 people.

Carrots

Available all year

Home-grown bunches of summer carrots are my favorites – sweet and delicate, great for simply munching raw or grated into salads. The first of these to appear in spring have a particularly good flavor.

To cook summer carrots, there's no need to peel them – just rinse them under cold running water and cut off the tops only, a fraction above the end. This leaves the inside of the carrot intact and preserves the flavor.

Place them in a steamer, sprinkle with a little salt, and steam for about 7 minutes, or until tender when pierced with a skewer but still retaining some firmness and bite. Serve plain, or tossed in butter and mixed with some chopped fresh tarragon leaves.

To cook winter carrots: these are available from storage all year round. Cook them plainly by scraping off the skins and cutting them into 2 inch (5 cm) chunks, then placing them in a saucepan with salt and enough boiling water to barely cover them. Cook for 20 minutes, or until tender but with a little firm bite in the center, then drain and drop them into a food processor, and, using the pulse button, "chop" the carrots quite small - don't overdo it or you'll have a purée. Quickly return the carrots to the pan using a spatula, add a pat of butter and some freshly ground black pepper, then place them over a gentle heat and stir them around for a couple of minutes to get them hot again. 1 lb (450 g) of carrots will serve 4.

Cauliflower

Late October through March

Imported cauliflower is available all year, but you can buy freshly-grown cauliflower in the winter months. There is also on the market a variety with dark-purple curds instead of the creamy-white. This has a more distinctive flavor and is good, I think, for a change. Both varieties are cooked in the same way. Prepare them by discarding the tough outer green leaves and saving the younger tender ones, which not only can be cooked and eaten, but their presence in the cooking imparts extra flavor.

To cook a cauliflower, first of all separate it into florets by turning the cauliflower upside down, inserting a small sharp knife, and cutting through to separate the heads into about 3 inch (7.5 cm) florets. Then place them, along with the leaves, in a steamer, standing them up vertically (ie stalk-side down, flower heads up). Now, drop in a bay leaf, which has a fragrant affinity for cauliflower. Add some salt and some nutmeg, which I like to grate lightly over the surface of the florets. Now, pour in boiling water from the kettle and steam for 6-7 minutes, or until tender when tested with a skewer. Serve with a little butter, or grated cheese, or the recipe for cauliflower with cheese on page 365. One medium cauliflower will serve 4 people.

Celery root (celeriac)

Best through the winter months

Celery root, at first sight, is probably the ugliest, oddest-looking vegetable there is, but there is a hidden agenda here, for underneath the spiney roots and ugly skin is a soft, velvety flesh that, when mashed, has the creaminess of potato with the added subtle flavor of celery. But that's not all: celery root is excellent roasted in the oven and also raw in a salad, cut into tiny julienne matchstick strips and served with a creamy dressing.

To prepare celery root, first of all have no fear in paring off the skin really thickly. What you need to do is peel off enough to leave behind only the creamy-white flesh, with no brown bits left behind. Because the root channels are interwoven into the base of the bulb you will need to cut all this away, so it's always useful to remember only three-quarters of what you buy can be used. Cut the rest into chunks and, as you do so, drop this them into some cold salted water to prevent discoloring. Now, you can either dry them well and roast (see page 364) or boil them and combine and mash them with equal quantities of boiled potatoes.

Celery

Available almost all year round

Celery is delicious partnered with Stilton cheese it's often perhaps enjoyed best of all served fresh, crunchy, and crisp in the autumn with a good cheese board, some fresh-shelled walnuts, and a glass of vintage port.

In the United States, we find two main varieties. The first, Pascal, is pale green. The second variety is white and known as garden celery.

To prepare celery, first of all remove the tough, large outer stalks, and, because these are usually distinctively stringy, take a sharp paring knife and pare off the strings, *above left*. Now trim off the outer skin around the root and cut the head vertically so that some of the sweet, edible root is still intact; then cut into 6-8 layered vertical strips, *left*.

Zucchini

Best home-grown from early to late summer

Zucchini are a variety of summer squash. I used to grow them; now I would rather buy them small and tender. The reason is - if I wasn't vigilant about going to my garden every day to pick them, they seemed to turn into giants overnight. And serving overgrown zucchini for supper night after night is *not* a good idea! Young small zucchini are delicate and don't have a great deal of their own flavor. Like eggplant they have a high water content that can render them watery and dull. I like them cut in chunks and roasted in the oven, as in Oven-Roasted Ratatouille in my book, *Summer Collection*, or marinated in a vinaigrette with herbs (see page 369), which allows them to absorb some real flavor.

Fennel

Available in markets and home-grown, September to June

Sometimes called Florence fennel and also known by its charming Italian name *finocchio*, fennel looks like a fat, bulbous celery and has the same crunchy texture but with a marked aniseed flavor. Fennel can be thinly sliced and eaten raw in salads or shaved very finely with a mandolin and dressed with vinaigrette. It's also very good cooked and served as a vegetable dish.

To prepare fennel, first trim off the green shoot at the top; if the fronds aren't too droopy you can use them as a garnish. Then cut it diagonally into a pointed shape. Next slice off the root part at the other end and remove any outer toughened or brown layers. Slice the bulb in half and then again into quarters. Now you can take a little of the stalky core out, but not all, because you want the layers, including the inner green part, to stay intact.

To cook fennel, cut it into quarters, steam it for 10 minutes, or until tender, then have a frying pan with 1 teaspoon each of oil and butter really hot and sauté the fennel until it's golden brown at the edges. Finally, sprinkle with a tablespoon of freshly grated Parmesan while it's still in the pan and let it rest for a few seconds, then serve sprinkled with a little more grated Parmesan and some of the chopped feathery fronds. Serves 2.

Leeks

Best home-grown from early October through December

Leeks are a very fine vegetable indeed. Though they are related to onions, they have a far more subtle and somehow nobler taste, I think. Leeks lend themselves to other flavors superbly, too: great with potatoes, in a soup or with cheese (see Leek and Goat Cheese Tart, pages 110-11), in salads with vinaigrette, and they also respond beautifully to quick stir-frying. Watch the season, though, since home-grown leeks taste much more flavorful and sweet in the early fall and winter, and the imported ones never seem quite as good. Remember, too, that the smaller and thinner the leeks are the sweeter their flavor is, so avoid the very thick, heavy ones.

To prepare leeks, buy a little more than you need, because there's going to be quite a bit of waste in trimming. First take off the tough outer leaves and trim off most of the very green part. Now, using a sharp knife, place the leek on a flat surface and make an incision vertically about halfway down (because of the intricate layers, there can be garden dirt and grit trapped inside the layers, usually in the upper part). Now, under cold running water, fan out the layers of leek and rinse them thoroughly to rid them of any hidden dirt, *right*.

This is my favorite way of cooking leeks – very gently, in their own juices and served as a vegetable, particularly at the end of winter when there's not a lot of other fresh vegetables available.

When the leeks are trimmed and washed, cut them all the way through vertically, then chop them into 1 inch (2.5 cm) pieces. Place a small frying pan over a medium heat, add the butter, and let it melt so that it lightly coats the surface of the pan. Now, add the leeks and seasoning, stir them around, turn the heat down to low, and let them cook gently for about 5 minutes without a lid, stirring them 2 or 3 times. There will be a lot of juice collecting in the pan, so use a perforated spoon when serving them.

Buttered Leeks

Serves 2
1 lb (450 g) leeks, trimmed – you need
12 oz (350 g) trimmed weight
½ teaspoon butter
salt and freshly ground black pepper

Mushrooms

"Mushrooming" is a word used to describe something that explodes in growth, and I have to say that's precisely the word I would use to describe the mushroom market. While once we could buy only commercial button mushrooms, we are now presented with an amazing variety of sizes, shapes, and colors. Don't be too dazzled by appearances, though, because some of them look more interesting than they actually taste.

Because the seasons and availability of mushrooms fluctuate, here we need to concern ourselves mostly with how to get the best out of whatever is available. My own firm favorite cultivated mushrooms are the flat, open, dark-gilled variety and the smaller pink-gilled open caps. (I have never thought the pale, insipid button mushrooms you can find at most supermarkets were even worth bothering with.) There are now commonly available cremini mushrooms, or chestnut, and the large version of them called portabella. I also like shiitake (particularly in an omelette), a saffron-yellow variety called pied de mouton, and now we can buy porcini (known as ceps in France), the best-flavored wild mushrooms of all. Another delicious variety called morel grows wild in some parts of the United States. I now find getting the finest mushroom flavor in cooking is never a problem.

To prepare mushrooms, don't wash them is the first rule – they already have a lot of moisture and washing them means they absorb even more, which can make them soggy. Take a damp piece of paper towel and wipe each mushroom clean, or use a special mushroom brush, which brushes away any dirt. Don't peel them because the peel itself has lots of flavor. I always use the mushroom stems, except with shiitake because their stems are a bit too chewy and have to be trimmed down almost to the cup. If the mushrooms are small, leave them whole; if large, cut through the stem, then into halves or quarters.

First imagine a plump, round, fat, juicy mushroom, then think of a shrivelled dried mushroom – the difference is moisture, and because the dried one has masses more flavor, having lost the moisture, I feel that the thing to aim for when cooking mushrooms is to get as much of the moisture out as possible so as to concentrate the flavor. Don't use very much oil or butter since mushrooms tend to soak this up at an alarming rate. Always remember, too, that as the moisture evaporates the mushrooms will lose half their original volume.

Heat the olive oil or butter in a frying pan, and, when it's hot, throw in the mushrooms and toss them around by shaking the pan. Season with salt and pepper, then turn the heat down to very low and let the mushrooms cook gently, uncovered, so that all the juice evaporates and the flavor of the mushrooms becomes more concentrated. Leave them like that for 30 minutes, stirring them around once or twice.

Sautéed Mushrooms

Serves 2
8 oz (225 g) mushrooms, prepared as described
1 teaspoon olive oil or butter
salt and freshly ground black pepper

Once the mushrooms have lost much of their moisture content they can then be used in an omelette or simply as they are. You could also add a peeled and chopped clove of garlic 5 minutes before the end and finish off with a sprinkling of chopped fresh flat-leaf parsley.

Onions and shallots

Available all year

Where would cooks be without onions? One of the principal flavor-makers in the kitchen, stews, soups, casseroles, salads, and sauces are all enhanced by this most humble but wonderful of vegetables, along with the shallot, its tiny, milder cousin, which also plays an important role.

Over the years I've been given countless methods of how not to cry when preparing them. One enterprising person even sent me a battery-operated fan to fan away the fumes, but I can honestly say that nothing really works. For chopping, however, food processors have made things a lot easier, and now there aren't as many tears as there used to be.

How to prepare onions

Slicing: if you want to slice them, cut off the root end, then peel away the skin. Slice in whole round slices and separate into rings, or else cut the onion in half first and then slice into half-moon shapes.

Chopping: rough chopping is as above, making about 3 cuts vertically across each onion and then 3 horizontally.

Chopping small (without a processor): this time leave the root intact, then peel away the skin from the top end. Now, cut the onion in half and place each half on a flat surface, round-side up. Next, make cuts vertically from the root end but leaving the root intact to hold it together, *top right*. Then make horizontal cuts across the vertical cuts while you hold onto the root end firmly, *right*. The last cut will be the little root bit, and this can be discarded.

Here, the onions are actually roasted, but you get the same effect without having to stand over them. They are particularly lovely served with sausages and mashed potatoes or for steak and onions.

First of all, you need to cut the onions into ¼ inch (5 mm) slices, then place them in a bowl, add the oil and sugar, and toss them around to get the lightest coating. Then spread them out on a baking pan and place on a high shelf of the oven for 14-15 minutes – they need to be nicely blackened round the edges.

Oven-Fried Onions

Serves 2

8 oz (225 g) onions, peeled
1 teaspoon peanut or other mildly flavored oil
1 teaspoon superfine sugar

Preheat the oven to 425°F (220°C).

Shallots

These are similar to baby onions, sometimes bright purple-pink and sometimes creamy-white. Cooked slowly as a confit they make a lovely accompaniment to beef. In a medium pan, simmer 12 oz (350 g) of peeled whole shallots with ¾ cup (200 ml) of red wine, 1½ tablespoons (25 ml) of red wine vinegar, and seasoning. Keep the heat very low and cook, without a lid, for about 1 hour and 10 minutes, turning the shallots over halfway through. After this time, add half a teaspoon of sugar to give a lovely sticky glaze, and cook for another 5 minutes. Serves 4.

They are lovely pickled, served as a condiment, or simmered whole in casseroles and braised dishes, and I love them chopped very finely in salads (see pages 385 and 391).

Parsnips

Best late October through February
What an absolute star a parsnip is – full of soft, juicy flesh and fragrant, sweet flavor. They are lovely plain, steamed, mashed, or roasted, and one of my favorite ways to serve parsnips is to sprinkle them with Parmesan and bake them in the oven.

Parsnips seem to taste best after the frosts have arrived, which really does intensify their flavor. Because parsnips are stored, they tend to become somewhat woody toward the end of the winter, so enjoy them at their best between late October and February. If you can, buy small, young parsnips that don't need peeling and coring; the older, larger, late-winter parsnips need to be peeled and cored. Cut them into even-sized pieces, steam them for 10-15 minutes, and serve with plenty of salt and freshly ground black pepper along with a little butter. For roasting, prepare them in the same way, tossed with a little oil and seasonings. Place in a preheated shallow baking pan and roast in the oven preheated to 425°F (220°C) for 30-40 minutes, depending on the size of the parsnips. 1 lb (450 g) of parsnips will serve 4 people.

Peas

Home-grown, best from early June to early July
One sad but thought-provoking incident happened to me a few years ago. I was buying fresh peas in the pod in a supermarket, and the high school student with her Saturday job working the checkout register asked me if I could tell her what they were! Perhaps the positive side of that comment was a kind of affirmation that I really needed to write *How To Cook*.

Fresh-shelled peas are one of the most delightful vegetables of all – young and tender, they melt in the mouth when they are cooked and taste wonderful when eaten raw. Sure, it takes a bit of time to shell them, but sitting by an open window or in the garden on a bright summer's day shelling peas can be wonderful therapy. When they first arrive they're incredibly sweet and tender, but later on they get bigger and have almost a completely different character and flavor. I like both equally. Some markets carry imported peas all year round, both shelled and in the pods.

To cook young, fresh shelled peas, first remember to buy 8 oz (225 g) in the pod per person. After shelling, place them in a steamer with some salt and give them 1 minute before you bite one; they shouldn't take any longer than 2 minutes in all. Peas that are a bit older may need 3-4 minutes.

Braised Peas, Arugula, and Scallions

This is a good recipe for older peas, which sometimes, in my opinion, have more texture and flavor than the younger ones. If the peas you are using are very young, however, give them far less cooking time – 8 minutes at the most.

First trim the scallions: you need only the white bulbs (the rest can be chopped and saved for something such as a stir-fry). Pull off any thick stems from the arugula and tear the larger leaves in half. Now, all you do is put all the ingredients in a large saucepan, cover with a lid, bring them up to simmering point, and simmer gently for 8-15 minutes, depending on the age of the peas.

Serves 6
3 lb (1.35 kg) peas (unshelled weight), freshly shelled
2½ oz (60 g) fresh arugula
12 bulbous scallions
3 tablespoons (40g) butter
3 tablespoons water
pinch superfine sugar
1¼ teaspoons sea salt

Bell peppers
Available all year, best seasons, summer and autumn
Bell peppers actually come in all kinds of colors, but red, green, and yellow are the most widely ones available. When bell peppers are grown they begin green, and then, if left on the stalks to mature, this mellowing results in red bell peppers, with a sweeter flesh (which is better if they are to be eaten raw or only lightly cooked). But the green ones do have a special character of their own – a sharper, more robust flavor, which stands up to long, slow cooking. For this reason I am very much against any dismissal of green bell peppers as being somehow inferior. In fact certain cuisines, such as Cajun and Creole, seem to only include green bell peppers in their recipes. Yellow bell peppers are more like red in flavor, and their golden-yellow color can look very pretty in certain dishes.

To prepare bell peppers, first, slice the top off the bell peppers, including the stems, then, with the tip of a small knife, scrape out the seeds and the cores. Now, slice the bell peppers into quarters, and again, using the tip of the knife, slice away any white, pithy bits. Then slice or chop according to the recipe. If the recipe calls for finely chopped bell peppers, you can use the round lid parts around the stems and chop those, too.

To cook bell peppers: to peel or not to peel is the question. I say don't bother. After discovering the recipe for Piedmont-Roasted Bell Peppers – which are lovely in the autumn when the bell peppers are in season and the tomatoes are ripe and red – and publishing it in the *Summer Collection*, I decided they were the very best cooked peppers I'd ever tasted, so I stopped going to the bother of peeling them. So all the recipes I have done since then use the bell peppers as they are, skins and all. They can be sautéed, stir-fried in strips until blackened at the edges and tender, or oven-roasted, sprinkled, first, with olive oil and then seasoned before you place them in the oven at 450°F (230°C) for 30-40 minutes.

Chili peppers
Available all year
Forgive the pun, but the whole subject of chilies is a hotbed of confusion! There are so many varieties, and availability fluctuates from one variety to another. The only real guide is individual taste. I would avoid the round, scorching Scotch bonnet pepper unless you are a real hot-chili lover. What I tend to do is buy the larger, fatter kind, which are usually not so fiercely hot, and if I want really fiery hot then the tiny Bird Eye chilies used in Asian cooking are the ones to go for because they are always extremely hot. The other point to remember is that green ones are usually marginally hotter than red. There is a back-up, though - if you find you're using fresh chilies and they haven't given you quite enough heat, all you do is add a few drops of Tabasco (see page 246) to increase the fire.

How to prepare chilies: very carefully. Why? Because the membrane and the seeds inside are the hottest parts and can burn delicate skin. Some cookbooks advise wearing rubber gloves, but if you wash your hands with soap and water after handling, you should be safe enough. What happens is that if your hands touch the delicate skin on your face or, even worse, your eyes, the oils from the chilies can burn. So slice the tops off, cut them in half lengthwise, hold down the chili half with your finger, and, using a sharp knife, scrape away all the membrane and seeds and discard them. After you finely slice or mince the chili, then carefully wash your hands.

Winter squash and pumpkin
Winter squash: available imported all year, home-grown October to November. Pumpkin: home-grown, October and November; imported, September through December.
The bright-orange jack-o-lantern pumpkins available around Halloween do not have a great deal of flavor, so in my opinion are not worth serving as a vegetable. Their smooth, silky texture, however, makes wonderful soups and pies gives the best texture in Pumpkin Pie (see page 114) or in pumpkin and corn soup (page 373).

Butternut squash available home-grown in season (see previous page), as above, or you can buy it all year, imported. Its buttery, nutty texture is one of my own favorites. It is shaped somewhat like a bottle and has both a nutty flavor and a good firm texture making it excellent for roasting and braising (see the recipes on pages 364 and 312 respectively).

To prepare pumpkin or squash, you need a good, sharp, heavy knife. First you cut the vegetable in half and then into quarters. After that scoop out the fibrous parts and all the seeds with a spoon or knife, then, this time using a small but very sharp knife, peel away the tough skin. Finally, cut the pumpkin flesh into cubes or slices.

Runner beans

Best home-grown during the summer months

Runner beans are are so delicious that I could happily eat a whole plateful and nothing else. They are difficult to find at the markets but can be easily grown at home, and I encourage you to try them. A planting will provide delicious feasts over the course of a month or two. The beans must be harvested young because the whole pod is eaten. The problem is that people rarely know how to prepare and cook them. If they're simply chopped into small sections, the skins take longer to cook than the insides, and they end up being either gray and overcooked or undercooked and tough. To solve this problem, I use something called a bean slicer, *right*. The runner beans are simply fed through a channel, and a wheel with blades is turned by hand so that the runner beans are sliced very finely. Then, only the briefest cooking time is needed and the beans can be simply cooked with a little of butter and some salt and black pepper.

To prepare and cook runner beans, first, take a sharp paring knife and strip away the stringy part at the seam on either side of each bean. Then feed them through a bean slicer, which should be attached to the edge of a table with a plate underneath to catch the slices. If you don't have a bean slicer, cut the beans in exactly the same way using a paring knife. 1 lb 8 oz (700 g) of runner beans will serve 4 people.

Spinach

Home-grown, best from January through June

Spinach is very green and very good for you. It is packed with vitamin C. What you need to be most aware of is that spinach contains a great deal of water, so what looks like a huge amount won't be when it's cooked.

To prepare spinach: fresh spinach can be rather dirty or muddy. The best way to deal with this is to pick out and discard any damaged or brown leaves, remove the tough stems, plunge the spinach in a sink filled with cold water, and swirl the leaves around. Do this in two or three changes of water, then let it all drain in a colander, shaking it well over the sink. Young spinach leaves can be wiped and used raw in a delicious salad.

To cook spinach: absolutely no water ever. For 1 lb (450 g) of spinach leaves, melt 1 tablespoon (10 g) of butter in a large, heavy saucepan, then, keeping the heat at medium, pack in the spinach leaves. Add some salt, put on a tight-fitting lid, and let it cook for about 30 seconds; then take the lid off and you'll find the spinach has collapsed down into the butter. Give it a stir so that the top leaves get pushed down to the bottom of the pan, replace the lid and give it another 30 seconds or so, shaking the pan a couple of times – I find the whole operation takes less than 2 minutes. Next, drain the spinach in a colander, pressing it well with a saucer to get rid of any excess water. You can now return it to the pan and add seasoning; spinach is enhanced beautifully with a little cream or crème fraîche. Like cauliflower, it also has an affinity for nutmeg, so season with salt and freshly ground black pepper and a few gratings of whole nutmeg. Spinach as a vegetable goes beautifully with finnan haddie (see the recipe on page 404). If you're serving spinach as a vegetable you will need 8 oz (225 g) per person.

Rutabaga

Home-grown, best in winter

I love the unique flavor of rutabagas, which seems to epitomise all the goodness of home cooking. They have long been of service to cooks because their presence in stews and casseroles not only ekes out the meat to make it go further, but also adds a presence that offers something of its own flavor, while at the same time absorbing some of the meat flavors as well. Rutabaga is also good served solo as a vegetable.

To prepare rutabaga, all you need here is a potato peeler to peel it in precisely the same way as a potato, slicing off the root end first with a knife. Then simply cut the rutabaga into suitably sized chunks.

To cook rutabaga, cut it into 1 inch (2.5 cm) dice and steam for about 10 minutes, or until tender, then whiz to a purée in a food processor or mash with a fork, adding a pat of butter, salt and lots of freshly ground black pepper. This method also works very well using half rutabaga and half carrot, but in this case I like it chopped small rather than puréed.

For roast rutabaga cut the chunks larger – 1½ inches (4 cm) – place the cubes in a bowl, adding (for 1 lb/450 g) 2 teaspoons of olive oil and some seasoning. Toss the rutabaga around to get all the pieces coated in the oil, then place them in a shallow baking pan and roast in a preheated oven set at 425°F (220°C) for 30-35 minutes, until the rutabaga is nicely toasted brown at the edges. This amount will serve 4 people.

Corn

Home-grown from July to the end of September

I think of corn as aesthetically one of the most beautiful vegetables – such a visual work of art. The pale-green husks cover firm, silky-white threads, and all this to protect the plump, golden kernels, full of juicy sweetness.

To prepare corn you'll need to remove the kernels, so first of all tear off the green part along with all the silky threads. Then stand the ear of corn upright on a flat board, and using a very sharp paring knife, carefully cut off all the kernels, keeping the knife pressed close to the center cob so that you get the whole kernel.

To cook corn: for corn on the cob, one way is to simply steam the ears for about 15 minutes or until the kernels feel tender when tested with a small skewer. Then serve with a little melted butter and season well with plenty of salt and freshly ground black pepper to be eaten straight from the cob. If you stick a small fork into each end, you can pick the whole thing up, or you can chop the cob into smaller sections that can be lifted with your hands. Don't forget the napkins and finger bowls.

By far the best and most delicious way to cook and eat corn on the cob is to strip the husks and silky threads off as described above, toss the cobs in a little olive oil, season well with salt and black pepper, and roast on an open barbecue grill. Watch them carefully, turning them all the time, until they're toasted golden brown – 5-10 minutes. You will need one medium ear of corn per person.

Warning: never try to cut the ears of corn before cooking because it's virtually impossible. After cooking, a very sharp knife will cut them into chunks you can bite straight into. Finally, corn kernels stripped from the cob and oven-roasted can be served as a vegetable or used to make the Pumpkin Soup with Toasted Corn on page 373.

Turnips

Baby turnips, best in June and July; winter turnips, October to February

In early June I love seeing the first young bunches of carrots, and the same goes for turnips – so pretty, about the size of golf balls, with deep-purple tinges to their creamy-white flesh and topped with frilly leaves. Further into winter they're less tender and can be steamed and mashed to a purée with an equal amount of steamed potatoes, with the addition of a little cream and butter. I love them sliced wafer-thin in Cornish pasties and roasted as a vegetable (they can be used in the recipe on the following page). Turnips are prepared in exactly the same way as rutabagas (see left).

To cook baby turnips, dice 1 lb (450 g) of peeled turnips into ¾ inch (2 cm) cubes. Steam them for 3 minutes, sprinkled with a little salt, then sauté in melted butter, tossing them around for about 10 minutes, until tender. This quantity of turnips will serve 4 people.

Oven-Roasted Winter Vegetables

This recipe is always going to be a good choice if you're entertaining, since the vegetables don't require attention as they cook. Another thing I have found invaluable is being able to prepare them well in advance, giving you that organized feeling. This is a delicious combination of vegetables, but you can vary it with whatever is available.

All you do is cut the vegetables into large, chunky pieces (no smaller than 1½ inches/4 cm) – leaving the celery root until last since it discolors if left for too long – place in a large bowl, then add the herbs, garlic, olive oil, and lots of seasoning. Simply mix the vegetables with your hands. The prepared vegetables can now be kept in a sealed plastic bag in the refrigerator for 2-3 days.

When you're ready to cook the vegetables, spread them out in the baking pan and cook in the preheated oven on a high shelf for 30-40 minutes until they're tender and turning brown at the edges.

Serves 6
Vegetable quantities are prepared weights
12 shallots, peeled
12 oz (350 g) peeled and seeded butternut squash
12 oz (350 g) peeled sweet potato
12 oz (350 g) peeled rutabaga
12 oz (350 g) peeled celery root
1 tablespoon freshly chopped mixed herbs (rosemary and thyme, for example)
2 large cloves garlic, peeled and crushed
3 tablespoons olive oil
salt and freshly ground black pepper

You will also need a shallow baking pan measuring approximately 11 x 16 inches (28 x 40 cm).

Preheat the oven to 425°F (220°C).

Cauliflower with Two Cheeses and Crème Fraîche

There's no need to make a white sauce for this one – the beauty of crème fraîche is that you can simmer it into a creamy sauce in moments. This could be an accompanying vegetable for four or a main course for two served with rice. I like it with penne pasta.

First of all, place the cauliflower florets and a few of the inner leaves in a steamer with the pieces of bay leaf tucked amongst it. Pour in some boiling water from the kettle, add some freshly grated nutmeg and salt, then cover and steam the cauliflower until tender – about 12 minutes. After this, test the thickest parts with a skewer to see if they are tender, then remove it to the baking dish and cover with a cloth to keep warm.

Now, pour ⅓ cup (75 ml) of the steaming water into a saucepan, add the crème fraîche, and simmer, whisking well, until it has thickened very slightly, then add the cheeses. Heat this gently for about 1 minute, whisking, until the cheeses have melted, then season the sauce to taste. Now, pour the sauce over the cauliflower and scatter the scallions and remaining Parmesan on top, then sprinkle with the cayenne. Finally, place the dish under the hot broiler until the cauliflower has browned and the sauce is bubbling hot.

Serves 4 as a vegetable or 2 for supper

1 medium cauliflower, separated into florets
1½ oz (40 g) Parmesan (Parmigiano Reggiano), finely grated, plus 1½ tablespoons extra to finish
1½ oz (40 g) Gruyère, finely grated
3 tablespoons crème fraîche
2 bay leaves, torn in half
a little freshly grated nutmeg
2 scallions, very finely chopped, including the green parts
pinch cayenne pepper
salt and freshly ground black pepper

You will also need an ovenproof baking dish measuring 8 inches (20 cm) square and 2 inches (5 cm) deep.

Preheat the broiler to its highest setting.

365

Tunisian Eggplant Salad with Cilantro and Yogurt

This is my adaptation of an Elizabeth David recipe. I never actually made it from her book, but one of my favorite restaurants, Chez Bruce, in London, regularly serves it as a first course. It's so wonderful I never have anything else if it's on the menu.

Serves 4 as an appetizer
1 lb 8 oz (700 g) eggplant, chopped into ½ inch (1 cm) cubes
3 tablespoons chopped cilantro
1 lb 8 oz (700 g) ripe red tomatoes
about 3 tablespoons olive oil
1½ teaspoons cumin seeds
1 teaspoon allspice berries
1 large onion, weighing about 10 oz (275 g), peeled and finely chopped
1 large red chili, seeded and finely chopped
4 cloves garlic, peeled and finely chopped
3 tablespoons chopped fresh mint
salt and freshly ground black pepper

To serve:
1 tablespoon olive oil
8 pita breads, warmed
4 tablespoons Greek yogurt
1½ tablespoons chopped cilantro
1½ tablespoons chopped fresh mint

You will also need 2 shallow baking pans, one measuring approximately 11 x 16 inches (28 x 40 cm), the other measuring 10 x 14 inches (25.5 x 35 cm).

You'll need to start this recipe the day before you want to serve it. First, salt and drain the chopped eggplant by placing it into a large colander, sprinkling with 1 tablespoon of salt as you add the pieces. Cover with a plate and press the eggplant down using an unopened can as a weight. Now, place the colander over a plate and let the eggplant drain for 1 hour. When it has been draining for 30 minutes, preheat the oven to 450°F (230°C).

Meanwhile, peel the tomatoes. To do this, pour boiling water over them and leave for exactly 1 minute before draining and slipping off their skins, protecting your hands with a cloth if they are too hot. Cut them in half and place them cut-side up on the smaller baking pan, which should be lightly oiled, and brush the tomatoes with a little olive oil as well. Set to one side.

Now, you need to dry-roast the cumin seeds and the allspice berries. To do this, place them in a small frying pan or saucepan over a medium heat and toss them around for 1-2 minutes, or until they begin to look toasted and start to jump in the pan. Now, transfer them to a mortar and pestle and crush them to a powder.

When the eggplant pieces are ready, squeeze them to get rid of any excess juices, dry them in a clean dish towel, then place them in a bowl, add 1 tablespoon of the oil, and toss them around so they get a good coating. After that, spread them out on the larger baking pan and place both pans into the oven with the eggplant on the top shelf and the tomatoes on the next one down. Give them about 25 minutes, by which time the eggplant should be tinged golden brown at the edges and the tomatoes soft. Remove the vegetables from the oven, and when the tomatoes are cool enough to handle, chop them into small pieces.

Meanwhile, heat 2 more tablespoons of the oil in a large frying pan over a medium to high heat and fry the onions until soft and pale gold – about 5 minutes – then add the chili and garlic and fry for 1 more minute. Next, add the chopped tomatoes, eggplant, and crushed spices; stir well, add the herbs and season with salt and freshly ground black pepper. Bring everything up to a gentle simmer, then remove the pan from the heat and pour everything into a serving dish. Leave for 24 hours, or longer if possible, covered in the refrigerator. Serve the salad at room temperature, drizzled with the olive oil. Serve with the warm pita breads, about a tablespoon of Greek yogurt with each serving, and the fresh herbs scattered on top.

Quick-Braised Celery

Serves 4-6
1 bunch celery, trimmed with, strings removed, cut into 3 inch
(7.5 cm) pieces
2 tablespoons (25 g) butter
1 medium onion, peeled and thinly sliced
3 oz (75 g) carrot, peeled and thinly sliced
1 cup (225 ml) hot vegetable stock
1 tablespoon chopped fresh parsley
salt and freshly ground black pepper

You will also need a frying pan with a diameter of 10 inches (25.5 cm).

Celery has such a lot going for it as a raw ingredient in salads, and because of that we forget how good it is cooked to be served as a vegetable on its own. The method below is delightfully quick and easy, and tastes simply wonderful.

First of all, melt the butter in the frying pan and begin to cook the onions for 3-4 minutes over a medium to high heat until lightly golden. Add the carrots and cook for a further 2 minutes. Now, add the celery and continue to fry for 5 minutes more, or until everything is slightly browned at the edges. Season with salt and black pepper, then pour in the hot stock and cover the pan with a lid. Turn the heat down and simmer gently for 20 minutes until the vegetables are almost tender, then take the lid off and increase the heat to medium and continue to simmer until the liquid has reduced to become slightly syrupy – about 5 minutes. Serve the celery with the juices poured on top and sprinkled with the parsley.

Oven-Roasted Carrots with Garlic and Coriander

Serves 4
1 lb (450 g) winter carrots, scraped
2 cloves garlic, peeled and crushed
2 teaspoons coriander seeds
½ teaspoon black peppercorns
½ teaspoon sea salt
2 teaspoons olive oil

You will also need a shallow baking pan measuring approximately 10 x 14 inches (25.5 x 35 cm).

Preheat the oven to 450°F (230°C).

This is a recipe for the large, chunky carrots of winter, which lack the sweet, delicate flavor of new carrots in summer. They are given an added flavor dimension by being roasted in the oven, along with coriander seeds, turning slightly blackened and caramelized at the edges.

Begin by cutting the carrots into 1½ inch (4 cm) chunks, but no smaller. Next, dry-roast the coriander seeds and peppercorns in a small frying pan or saucepan over a medium heat, stirring and tossing them around for 1-2 minutes, or until they begin to look toasted and start to jump in the pan. Now, empty them into a mortar and pestle and crush them coarsely. Then mix the carrot chunks and crushed spices together in a bowl.

Next, put the garlic cloves and salt in the mortar, crush to a purée, and whisk in the oil. Now, toss this mixture around with the carrots and spices, then spread it out in the baking pan. Place the pan into the oven on a high shelf and roast until the carrots are tender when tested with a skewer – 30-40 minutes.

Note: the carrots can be prepared well in advance and kept in a plastic storage bag in the refrigerator.

Marinated Zucchini with a Herb Vinaigrette

If you grow zucchini, then this recipe is superb for serving the ones that – if you happen not to have kept a sharp eye on them – become giants overnight. If you don't grow them, this is still a superb way to serve zucchini as a salad with cold cuts.

To prepare the zucchini, trim off the stem ends, and if they are small, simply slice them in half lengthwise; if they are larger, cut them in 4 lengthwise. Then place them in the steamer, pour in some boiling water, sprinkle the pieces with a little salt, and let them cook, covered, for 10-14 minutes depending on their size. They need to be firm but tender.

Meanwhile, prepare the dressing by pounding the garlic with the salt in a mortar and pestle until it becomes a creamy paste. Now, work in the mustard, then the vinegar and a generous amount of black pepper. Next, add the oil and give everything a good stir; then add the herbs. When the zucchini pieces are ready, remove them to a shallow serving dish and pour the dressing over them. Allow them to become cool, then cover with plastic wrap and leave in the refrigerator for several hours, turning them over in the marinade once or twice. The zucchini will still taste good after 3 days, so you can make this recipe in advance if you prefer.

Serves 4
1 lb (450 g) zucchini
sea salt

For the herb vinaigrette:
1 teaspoon snipped fresh chives
1 teaspoon finely chopped
fresh tarragon
1 teaspoon finely chopped fresh parsley
1 teaspoon fresh rosemary leaves,
bruised and finely chopped
1 clove garlic, peeled
1 teaspoon sea salt
1½ teaspoons wholegrain mustard
2 tablespoons white wine vinegar
4 tablespoons olive oil
freshly ground black pepper

You will also need a steamer.

Below, left to right: Quick-Braised Celery, Oven-Roasted Carrots with Garlic and Coriander, Marinated Zucchini with a Herb Vinaigrette

Cabbage with Bacon, Apples and Cider

The flavors of this recipe combine beautifully, and I think it's an exceptionally good accompaniment to sausages and mashed potatoes.

Serves 4-6

1 lb (450 g) green cabbage, cut into
4 sections and core and stalk removed
4½ oz (125 g) cubetti (cubed)
pancetta or chopped bacon
1 Granny Smith apple, cored and
chopped small
2 tablespoons hard cider
2 tablespoons cider vinegar
2 teaspoons olive oil
1 small onion, peeled and
finely chopped
2 cloves garlic, peeled and crushed
1 bay leaf
1 sprig fresh thyme
salt and freshly ground black pepper

You will also need a frying pan with
a diameter of 10 inches (25.5 cm).

First of all, shred the cabbage into ¼ inch pieces, then place the frying pan over direct heat and dry-fry the pancetta or bacon until crispy and golden, about 5 minutes, and remove the pancetta or bacon to a plate. Now, add the oil to the pan, and when it's hot, fry the onions over a medium heat for 5 minutes - they also need to be turning golden brown at the edges. Now, turn the heat up to its highest setting and add the cabbage, stirring continuously for about 3 minutes, keeping it on the move and tossing it around. Return the pancetta or bacon to the pan and add the apple, garlic, bay leaf, and thyme, seasoning well with salt and black pepper. Toss the mixture around for a few seconds, then add the cider and cider vinegar, and continue to cook with the heat still high for 1-2 minutes. Finally, remove the bay leaf and thyme; taste, season, and serve as soon as possible.

Slow-Cooked Root Vegetable Soup

Something happens to vegetables when they're cooked very slowly for a long time: their flavor becomes mellow but at the same time more intense, and your kitchen is filled with aromas of goodness. This soup is also completely fat-free.

There's not much to do here once everything is peeled and chopped. All you do is place everything in the casserole and bring it up to a gentle simmer, then put on the lid, place the casserole in the lowest part of the oven, and leave it there for 3 hours, by which time the vegetables will be meltingly tender. Next, remove the bay leaves and process or liquidise the soup in several batches to a purée. Then, gently re-heat the soup, and serve it in bowls with a teaspoon of Greek yogurt swirled into each serving and garnished with the fresh chives.

Serves 6

Vegetable quantities are prepared weights
8 oz (225 g) peeled carrots, cut into 2 inch (5 cm) lengths
8 oz (225 g) peeled celery root, cut into 2 inch (5 cm) pieces
8 oz (225 g) trimmed and washed leeks, halved and cut into 2 inch (5 cm) lengths
8 oz (225 g) peeled rutabaga, cut into 2 inch (5 cm) pieces
1 small onion, peeled and roughly chopped
1½ quarts (1.5 liters) hot vegetable stock
3 bay leaves
salt and freshly ground black pepper

To serve:
6 teaspoons fat-free Greek yogurt
a few fresh chives, snipped

You will also need a lidded flameproof casserole with a capacity of 4 quarts (3.5 liters).

Preheat the oven to 275°F (140°C).

371

Bubble and Squeak Rösti

Bubble and squeak is a classic recipe for leftover greens, but making it rösti-style and adding some sharp Cheddar adds a new dimension. These little potato cakes are delicious served with sausages or cold leftover turkey and ham along with a selection of pickles.

Serves 4 (makes 8 rösti)
1 lb (450 g) round red or white potatoes (this should be 3 evenly sized potatoes weighing about 5 oz/150 g each)
3 oz (75 g) green cabbage (trimmed weight)
2 oz (50 g) sharp Cheddar, coarsely grated
1 tablespoon all-purpose flour
2 tablespoons (25 g) butter
2 teaspoons olive oil
salt and freshly ground black pepper

You will also need a shallow baking pan measuring approximately 10 x 14 inches (25.5 x 35 cm).

First, scrub the potatoes and place them in a medium saucepan with a little salt. Pour boiling water over to just cover them, then simmer gently, covered with a lid for 8 minutes. Drain the potatoes, then while they are cooling, finely shred the cabbage into about ¼ inch (5 mm) shreds. This is easy if you form them into a roll and then slice them. Drop the cabbage into boiling water for 2 minutes only, then drain and dry well.

When the potatoes have cooled, peel them, and then, using the coarse side of a grater, grate them into a bowl. Season with salt and freshly ground black pepper; add the grated cheese and cabbage and lightly toss together using 2 forks.

To assemble the rösti, shape the mixture into rounds 3 inches (7.5 cm) wide and ½ inch (1 cm) thick. Press them firmly together to form little cakes and dust lightly with the flour. If you want to make them ahead, place them on a plate and cover with plastic wrap – they will happily rest in the refrigerator for up to 6 hours.

To cook the rösti, preheat the oven to 425°F (220°C) with the baking pan on the top shelf of the oven. Melt the butter and add the oil, then brush the rösti on both sides with the mixture. When the oven has reached the right heat, place the rösti in the baking pan and return it to the top shelf of the oven for 15 minutes; then turn the rösti over and cook them for a further 10 minutes. After they have cooked, it's all right to keep them warm for up to 30 minutes.

Pumpkin Soup with Toasted Corn

This is a very fine combination - the soft, velvety texture of the pumpkin makes the soup deliciously creamy, and the toasted corn provides contrasting flavor and some crunch.

Begin by melting the butter in the saucepan, then add the onion and soften it for about 8 minutes. After that, add the chopped pumpkin (or the butternut squash), along with half the corn kernels; then give everything a good stir and season with salt and pepper. Put on the lid, and, keeping the heat low, allow the vegetables to sweat gently to release their juices – this should take about 10 minutes. Next, pour in the milk and stock and simmer gently for about 20 minutes. Cover the pan with the lid for this but leave a little gap (so it's not quite on) because, with the presence of the milk, it could boil over. Keep a close eye on it anyway.

While the pumpkin is simmering, preheat the broiler to its highest setting for 10 minutes. Mix the rest of the corn with the melted butter, spread them out in a shallow baking pan, season with salt and pepper, and place it under the hot broiler about 3 inches (7.5 cm) from the heat – it will take about 8 minutes to become nicely toasted and golden, but remember to move the corn around on the baking pan halfway through. When the soup is ready, pour it into a food processor or blender and blend it to a purée, leaving a little bit of texture – it doesn't need to be absolutely smooth. You will probably need to do this in 2 batches. Serve the soup in warm bowls with the toasted corn sprinkled on top.

Serves 6

1 lb 8 oz (700 g) pumpkin or butternut squash, peeled, seeded and chopped into 1 inch (2.5 cm) dice
1 lb 4 oz (570 g) corn (off the cob weight, from 5-6 ears of corn)
2 tablespoons (25 g) butter
1 medium onion, peeled and finely chopped
1¼ cups (275 ml) whole milk
3 cups (750 ml) hot vegetable stock
1 teaspoon melted butter, for the corn
salt and freshly ground black pepper

You will also need a lidded saucepan with a capacity of 2 quarts (1.75 liters).

16

Salads and dressings for beginners

The title of this chapter is meant, hopefully, to reassure those who find themselves rather confused about precisely what a well-dressed salad should actually be, something that has somehow eclipsed the simple joy of dressing and eating a salad.

Thirty years ago olive oil was, in England, for medicinal use and came from drugstores, and because England is a beer-brewing country rather than a winemaking one, vinegar was distilled from malt. These ingredients were, as you can imagine, not the desired components of a good salad dressing, and in the lean post-war years salads in ordinary households were served with salad dressing from a jar, a modern commercial version of an 18th-century recipe for English salad sauce made with cream and egg yolks.

Thankfully, we have all now moved on from there, but in my opinion, we have perhaps gone too far. Yes, it's wonderful to have a choice of olive oils and a selection of wine vinegars, but supermarkets now have wall-to-wall oils and sometimes half as many vinegars. It seems that every country in the world produces oils and vinegars, and not merely from the humble olive or the grape but from everything under the sun – witness pumpkin seed oil, grapefruit oil, seaweed vinegar, rose petal vinegar! Even tourist and gift shops sell designer oils and vinegars, which are often made from some unlikely ingredients. They are utterly superfluous to most people's everyday needs and end up lurking unused and abandoned in the back of a pantry. Even worse, I get letters asking me what to do with them!

Because I feel that if I were a beginner today, I wouldn't actually know where to start, I think it might be helpful to concentrate on basic everyday salads and dressings. Oils do not have a very long shelf life, so if you want to enjoy them at their best, having half a dozen varieties on the go is not helpful unless you are doing an awful lot of cooking on a daily basis. So let's start with what, in my opinion, is the best type of olive oil for a salad dressing and tackle the most pertinent question first.

What is extra virgin olive oil?

Before we can understand "extra virgin" we first have to clarify the word "virgin." What it describes, simply, is oil pressed from the fruit of the olive tree under conditions that cause no deterioration of the finished oil – the olives are not damaged, bruised, or subjected to adverse temperatures or too much air, and they must not have undergone any additional treatment such as heat or blending (except with other virgin olive oil). The supreme quality is measured by acidity, or more precisely, the lack of it – too much acidity gives a harsher flavor, which with skill, can be refined out. What is simply termed olive oil is often a blend of lesser-quality refined oils with some virgin added to give the right balance of flavor.

Extra virgin olive oil could, in fact, have another name – perfect virgin olive oil, because this is precisely what it is – virgin olive oil with no flaws whatsoever. By law the acidity of extra virgin olive oil is never more than 1 percent, and what does this mean? Flavor. First, there is an aromatic fragrance, then a sweetness not marred by acidity, and then an abundant taste of fruit, verdant and luscious, not tasting like olives exactly but like some other mysterious, unique fruit. Like very fine wine, extra virgin olive oil is both rich and flavorful.

Which country produces the best olive oil?

It's difficult to answer, this. The olives of each country have their own character and flavor, even varying from region to region; a Tuscan olive oil, for instance, is different from a Ligurian olive oil. If I were a purist I would suggest that Provençal dishes should be made with oils made in Provence, and Italian, Greek, or Spanish dishes made with the oil produced in these countries. But unless you do masses of cooking it's best to find an olive oil you're happy with. My recommendation is to have an extra virgin oil for special occasions, along with a blended oil for everyday.

What about other oils?

What you need to be careful of is having endless bottles of oils that you hardly use, because, as I've said, the shelf life of any oil is never very long. However, I would include the following in my pantry – along with olive oil – as a good selection for both cooking and making dressings:

Peanut oil

Peanut oil is excellent for general use with the advantage of having no marked flavor yet at the same time being rich and smooth. It is perfect for making mayonnaise, with a little olive oil added for flavor, it's an extremely useful oil for cooking, especially in Asian dishes for which the flavor of olive oil would be alien and too strong. Warning: because peanut oil is made from peanuts, people who suffer from nut allergies should avoid it (and warn anyone cooking for people with allergies as well).

Grapeseed and canola oils

These are alternative mildly flavored oils. If you are at all worried about the nut-allergy problem, grapeseed and canola oils will do the same work both in dressings and in cooking.

Sesame oil

An excellent oil, and rich in nutty sesame flavor. It's great in Asian dishes and dressings, but needs to be used very sparingly, because the flavor can be overwhelming.

Walnut oil

This is a great addition to the repertoire of oils. It has all the flavor of crushed walnuts and is therefore particularly good in salads that contain walnuts. It does become rancid quite quickly, however, so monitor its shelf life once it's opened.

Flavored oils

These are definitely not for me. Apart from the fact that they take up valuable storage space, it seems logical that if you want to incorporate other flavors in your oils, they are best added fresh. So add your own garlic, chili, lemon, or herbs, whenever you want to.

How to store oils

Keep oils in the coolest-possible place, though not the refrigerator, since oil solidifies when it gets too cold. Light is not good for oils, either, so a cool, dark corner is be the best place to store them. Most oils have date stamps, so watch these, and although it is more expensive to buy in smaller quantities, it is still cheaper than throwing out stale oil that never got used.

Vinegars for salads

Personally I would want to have about half a dozen vinegars available. They keep better and for longer than oils, so it's good to have a varied selection suitable for different kinds of salads, confits, and sometimes cooked dishes. You will find dozens of designer varieties available, but as always, I say keep it simple and buy the best quality you can afford – some cheaper vinegars are too acidic and lack flavor.

Wine vinegar

Originally the French word *vinaigre*, from which we get our word vinegar, meant sour wine, but now it embraces all similar liquids where alcohol is turned into acetic acid. As you might expect, wine vinegar comes either red or white, and the best quality is that made by the Orléans method, which, because of its long, slow fermentation in oak casks, has depth of flavor without the overpowering acidity.

Balsamic vinegar

After struggling in the past to find good-quality wine vinegar, when *aceto balsamico* (as it's called in Italy) appeared, it was like discovering heaven. It is not a wine vinegar but a grape vinegar, made from fresh-pressed grape juice, aged in barrels of oak, ash, cherry wood, mulberry, and juniper – all contributing to its unique flavor. Each year new grape juice is added and skillfully blended over a period of 8 to 12 years to produce the dark, sweet-sour amber liquid that makes one of the best salad dressings of all.

Sherry vinegar

A very special vinegar made, if I may say, from a very special drink. I love Spanish sherry, both to drink and for cooking, and the vinegar from the sherry grape must has its own delightfully rich, sweet, nutty flavor. Though quite different from *balsamico*, it is equally good sprinkled over salads and cooked vegetables just by itself.

Cider vinegar

As you'd expect, a vinegar distilled from cider, milder and less acidic than wine vinegar. It has a lovely fragrant apple flavor and is good for salad dressings, particularly if the salad contains fruit.

Rice vinegar

It's marvellous how vinegar turns up around the world distilled from whatever grows locally, so it's not surprising that in the Far East vinegar is made from rice. The Japanese have the best quality, and I always have some handy for making Asian salads and dipping sauces.

There are times when vinegar can be dispensed with and the acidic content of a salad dressing can be provided by lemon or lime juice. In fact I would say that if you want to cut the fat in your diet for any reason, lemon and lime juice alone squeezed over salad ingredients give a lovely zest and piquancy of their own. Lime is especially good for Asian dressings, while the combination of lemons and olive oil gives the classic flavors of the Mediterranean to a bowl of very simple salad greens.

Other ingredients

Mustards, both plain and wholegrain, have an emulsifying effect that thickens the dressing. Garlic, if you like it, adds flavor, and sea salt and freshly ground black pepper are two absolute essentials.

What makes the perfect dressing?

For once there are no rules. Food snobs sometimes like to make them, but the truth is it's about personal taste – some like more vinegar, some less, some like to add sugar, others (me) never do. So when you begin to make salad dressings, it's you who should taste and you who should decide just how much of this or that you want.

Equipment

Do invest in a mortar and pestle, a simple time-honored item that will serve you for a lifetime. With a mortar and pestle you can pound and crush the ingredients needed for making most salad dressings. Blenders will do the job and are occasionally preferable for large quantities, but you don't always want to be bothered with them for small amounts. Once you have blended your dressing, a small loop whisk, *right*, will combine it quickly and efficiently; alternatively you can keep a small screw-top jar handy and use it to shake and amalgamate the ingredients together.

Salad ingredients

This could be a subject for a book by itself since most ingredients can be made into salads – meat, fish, vegetables, rice, and so on. Here I will confine myself to specific salad vegetables, starting with a pertinent point.

Lettuce or other salad greens?

For me it would be lettuce all the way; a salad needs bite, crunchiness, and some substance. Yes, there are greens that make good salads, but there are now too many kinds of designer greens grown, bought, and used merely for their looks. That's OK up to a point – we can all appreciate a pretty garnish of colorful greens – but delicate greens that get soggy when they're washed, before being packed in plastic bags, and that disintegrate once they meet with a dressing are to be avoided (except for garnishing).

What kind of lettuce?

Again, it's what you personally like, but my own recommendations would be as follows.

Arugula

Also known as Rocket, Arugula is one of my favorite salad greens. Why? It's traditionally English and has been used in salads since Elizabethan times. It has a lovely concentrated buttery flavor with a peppery after-taste and goes with any dressing. It's not, I think, good as a salad on its own, because it's not crisp, and a lot of it seems somehow to be too concentrated and "in your face." Mixed half & half with crisp lettuces, however, it makes, I think, one of the nicest green salads of all.

Butterhead lettuce

Butterhead, (Bibb, Boston, and Buttercrunch fall into this category, as well) may not look very promising, but usually has a cluster of crisp, sweet greens nestling in a light cream- or butter-colored center that partner most dressings very well.

Crisphead lettuce

This is a lettuce that forms a tight head with crisp leaves and lots of crunch. Great Lakes and Mission are examples of this type.

Escarole lettuce and Quattro Stagioni (Four Seasons)

A colorful pair, the former has pale-green greens and the latter pinkish-red edges. They are not crisp, but their flavor is good as long as you give them lighter dressings.

Frisée

This comes with very crunchy, curly greens, but because it is related to the chicory family, it has a slightly bitter taste, which is fine if matched with highly flavored dressings.

Mâche

This leaf comes in delicate little sprigs with clusters of leaves, and is good both for garnishing and mixing with other lettuce types. Because it does not keep well, it needs to be used fairly quickly.

Romaine lettuce

If fresh, this is reliably crisp and crunchy, with a good flavor, and can take strong, thick, creamy dressings such as Caesar. Romaine has tightly folded leaves that have an upright form of heading.

Watercress

Popular with everyone, watercress is a bit like arugula, with its own distinctive, fresh, peppery flavor. I think it's too strong to be used on its own, but it's wonderful combined with lettuce, used as a garnish, and for giving its own unmatched flavor to soups and sauces.

Not recommended

Even though everything is largely a matter of personal taste, I would like, nevertheless, to explain why I do not recommend certain lettuces and salad greens. Iceberg is crunchy but that's all: it has no flavor. Lollo Rosso,

Lollo Biondo, Oak Leaf, and others are good to look at but pretty dull to eat; I would not bother with them.

How to prepare salad greens

All lettuces and salad greens should be eaten as fresh as possible, but first of all, I've found the best way to store lettuces is to remove the root, and otherwise, leave them whole enclosed in a plastic storage bag in the lowest part of the refrigerator. I believe washing should be avoided if possible, because once the greens are wet it's difficult to dry them again and you simply can't get dressing onto wet salad greens. What I prefer to do is take a damp piece of paper towel and wipe each leaf – this way the lettuce leaves remain dry and can more easily be coated with dressing. Now, I realize many people will not agree with me here and will want to wash the leaves; in that case, plunge the separated greens briefly into cold water and place them in a salad basket. Then cither hang them up after a good shaking or else swing the basket around and around out-of-doors. Finish off by drying the greens carefully with paper towels.

Never use a knife when you prepare lettuce, because cutting tends to brown the edges of the greens. Breaking up the greens too soon can cause them to go limp quickly, so always leave them whole, if possible, until you're ready to serve the salad (and even then use your hands to tear them rather than a knife).

Other salad ingredients

Avocados

A ripe, buttery-textured avocado, served with a good vinaigrette, is simplicity itself. To tell if an avocado is ripe, hold it in the palm of your hand and give it some gentle pressure; if ripe, you'll feel it "give" slightly.

Scallions

Indispensable in the kitchen, and especially in salads. If you go to a farmers' market, you will find tiny, thin, very young scallions that are delicious served whole with just the root trimmed.

Cucumber

A home-grown cucumber is a luxury for its fragrant, cool, pronounced cucumber flavor. In my opinion, home-grown cucumbers do have the best flavor and it's difficult to find a well-flavored imported cucumber in the winter. For the best results, and if you have time, salting, as you would an eggplant, does draw out some of the excess water content and helps concentrate the flavor.

What about the seeds? No problem. These are part and parcel of the cucumber, so I never bother to remove them. Then there's the question of whether to peel or not to peel. I say not, because I like the color, texture, and flavor of the peel, but if the cucumber has a very tough skin, use a potato peeler so only the outer skin is taken off. It's also possible to just peel off strips of skin, making stripes, as a kind of compromise. Small, ridged cucumbers which sometimes have quite knobbly skins are the exception and are usually better peeled.

Chicory heads

Tight little buds of crunchy greens, sometimes with pale-green edges, sometimes pink-edged. They have a slightly bitter taste that calls for a flavorful dressing.

Fennel

This is delicious cooked, but sliced very thinly it's also lovely raw in a salad.

Beets

These can be added to salads cooked (see page 349), or else raw and thinly shredded into julienne strips.

How to make a vinaigrette dressing

It has to be said that this is always going to be a matter of personal taste according to how much acidity you like and what your preferences are as to flavorings and so on. I seem to suffer from some kind of mental handicap with dressings, which roughly means that other people's salad dressings always seem to taste better than my own — my husband's particularly. Here I have set out my favorite version of vinaigrette, but it's adaptable; you can use red or white wine vinegar, a different mustard, or no mustard; if you like it sharper, use a higher ratio of vinegar, and if you want it less sharp use a higher ratio of oil. The following combination is my own personal favorite.

Begin by placing the salt in the mortar and crush it quite coarsely, then add the garlic, and as you begin to crush it and it comes into contact with the salt, it will quickly break down into a purée. Next, add the mustard powder and really work it in, giving it about 20 seconds of circular movements to get it thoroughly blended. After that, add some freshly ground black pepper.

Now, add the vinegars and work these in in the same way, then add the oil, switch to a small whisk (see the photograph on page 379), and give everything a really good, thorough whisking. Whisk again before dressing the salad.

Note: vinaigrette dressing tastes best made and used as fresh as possible, because once the oil is exposed to the air, it loses some of its fragrance. If you want to prepare things ahead, proceed up to the vinegar stage and leave adding the oil until the last minute.

Serves 4-6; halve the ingredients for 2-3
1¼ teaspoons sea salt
1 clove garlic, peeled
1¼ teaspoons mustard powder
2 teaspoons balsamic vinegar
2 teaspoons sherry vinegar
5 tablespoons extra virgin olive oil
freshly ground black pepper

You will also need a mortar and pestle.

Chef's Salad

A chef's salad is so named because it is supposed to be an innovative way of using whatever you happen to have handy to create a main-course salad. Ham, salami, chicken, turkey, or any cold meat could be used for this one; similarly any kind of cheese or salad vegetable. This happens to be one of my favorite combinations, but once you get the gist of it, I'm sure you'll have lots of other ideas.

Serves 6-8 as a main course
6 oz (175 g) lean bacon
8 oz (225 g) French garlic sausage or
Genoa salami, in one piece
4 oz (110 g) small mushrooms
e.g. cremini
3 oz (75 g) Roquefort or other cheese
2 ripe avocados
1 round head lettuce, outer
leaves removed
1 Romaine lettuce, outer
leaves removed
2 oz (50 g) watercress, stems removed
2 oz (50 g) arugula, stems removed
4 scallions, finely chopped

For the dressing:
⅔ cup (150 ml) sour cream
1 small clove garlic, peeled
and crushed
2 tablespoons good-quality mayonnaise
1½ teaspoons wholegrain mustard
2 tablespoons extra virgin olive oil
1 tablespoon white wine vinegar
1 tablespoon lemon juice
salt and freshly ground black pepper

Before you start, preheat the broiler to its highest setting and let it heat up for at least 10 minutes. Meanwhile, combine all the dressing ingredients in a measuring cup or bowl and whisk them together well, tasting to check the seasoning.

Now, place the bacon on some foil on the broiler pan, and broil until it's very crispy – about 7 minutes – then remove the bacon to drain on paper towels and crumble it into small pieces. Next, slice the garlic sausage, first into ¼ inch (5 mm) slices, then cut the slices into ¼ inch (5 mm) strips. After that, wipe the mushrooms and slice them fairly thinly (but not paper-thin). Next, crumble the cheese and peel and slice the avocados.

To serve the salad, tear up the lettuce leaves and place them in a large bowl with the watercress and arugula. Scatter in the bacon, sausage, mushrooms, cheese, and avocado and mix well. Just before serving, add half the dressing and mix together. Add the remaining dressing and toss again so that everything gets a good coating. Finally, sprinkle the scallions over all and serve immediately. This needs to be served with good rustic bread at the table.

Fava Bean Salad with Pancetta and Sherry Vinegar

Because the fresh fava bean season seems to be so short, I always feel the need to feast on them as much as possible when I can, hence this salad. It's good as an appetizer or to serve alongside other salads in a cold buffet. Remember, when buying fava beans in the shell you'll need 1 lb (450 g) in weight to get 4 oz (110 g) once shelled.

Begin this by preheating the broiler to its highest setting for 10 minutes or so, then place the pancetta (or bacon) on a piece of foil and broil it 3 inches (7.5 cm) from the heat for about 4 minutes; it's important to get it really crisp. Then, as soon as it's cool enough to handle, crumble it into tiny pieces. Now, place the shelled beans in a medium saucepan, add a level teaspoon of salt, and pour in enough boiling water to barely cover them. When they come back to a boil, put a lid on, turn the heat down and simmer them gently for about 5 minutes. It's very important not to overcook them, so a timer would be useful here.

While they're cooking, make the dressing by first crushing the garlic and salt with a mortar and pestle until it becomes a creamy paste, then work in the mustard powder, and follow this with the vinegar and a generous amount of coarsely ground black pepper. Next, add the oil and give everything a good whisk. When the beans are cooked, drain them in a colander, place them in a serving bowl, toss them in the dressing, and give everything a good stir. Now, sprinkle in the pancetta, herbs, and chopped shallots; taste to check the seasoning, give everything one more good mix, then cover the bowl with a cloth and set the salad aside for a couple of hours so the beans can absorb all the flavors.

Serves 4 generously
4 lb (1.8 kg) young fava beans, shelled
4 oz (110 g) sliced smoked
pancetta or bacon
1 tablespoon chopped mixed fresh
herbs (parsley, chives, basil, and
thyme, for example)
2 shallots, peeled and finely chopped
salt and freshly ground black pepper

For the dressing:
2 tablespoons sherry vinegar
1 large clove garlic, peeled
2 teaspoons sea salt
2 teaspoons mustard powder
5 tablespoons extra virgin olive oil
freshly ground black pepper

White Bean and Tuna Fish Salad with Lemon Pepper Dressing

This is my version of an old Italian favorite, and I think the addition of a sharp lemon dressing and some buttery arugula leaves gives a lovely edge.

Serves 4 as a main course or
6 as an appetizer
1⅓ cups (250 g) cannellini beans
2 x 6½ oz (2 x 185 g) cans tuna fish
in oil
1 oz (25 g) arugula, stems removed
2 oz (50 g) red onion, peeled and
sliced into thin rounds
salt and freshly ground black pepper

For the dressing:
grated zest 1 lemon
3 tablespoons lemon juice
1¼ teaspoons black peppercorns
2 cloves garlic, peeled
1 tablespoon sea salt
1½ teaspoons mustard powder
3 tablespoons extra virgin olive oil
3 tablespoons tuna oil, reserved from
the cans of tuna

Begin this the night before you are going to make the salad by placing the beans in a bowl and covering them with cold water to soak. Next day, drain the beans, then put them in a large saucepan, cover with fresh water and bring them up to simmering point. Boil for 10 minutes, then cover and simmer gently for 1¼-1½ hours, or until tender.

Meanwhile, empty the tuna fish into a sieve fitted over a bowl and allow it to drain. Then, to make the dressing, first crush the garlic and salt using a mortar and pestle until the garlic is pulverized, then work the mustard powder into this.Now, push the mixture to one side, add the peppercorns and crush these fairly coarsely. Next, add the grated lemon zest, along with the lemon juice, olive oil and tuna oil (the rest of the tuna oil can be discarded). Whisk everything together very thoroughly, then, when the beans are cooked, drain them, rinse out the saucepan and return the beans to it.Now, pour the dressing over while the beans are still warm, give everything a good stir and season generously.

To serve the salad, arrange three-quarters of the arugula leaves over the base of a serving dish, spoon the beans on top and add the tuna fish in chunks. Then add the rest of the arugula leaves, pushing some of the leaves and chunks of tuna right in amongst the beans. Finally, arrange the onion slices on top and serve straight away, allowing people to help themselves. Warm, crusty ciabatta bread would be an excellent accompaniment.

Note: if you forget to soak the beans overnight, you can rinse the beans with cold water and place them in a saucepan, cover with plenty of water, bring to a boil for 10 minutes, then turn off the heat and leave them to soak for 2 hours. Next, bring them up to a boil again and boil gently for 1½-2 hours, or until the beans are tender.

Char-Broiled Eggplant and Roasted-Tomato Salad with Feta Cheese

I am indebted to Chris Payne, who very generously gave me this splendid recipe. If you don't possess a ridged grill pan, you could broil the eggplant slices until nicely browned and tender. Either way, this is a truly delicious combination of textures and flavors.

Serves 4

2 medium eggplants
8 small, ripe plum tomatoes
7 oz (200 g) Feta cheese, cut into thin slices
8 tablespoons extra virgin olive oil
1½ tablespoons torn fresh basil leaves
2 tablespoons balsamic vinegar
4 oz (110 g) assorted salad greens
¾ cup (200 ml) crème fraîche
a little paprika
salt and freshly ground black pepper

You will also need a shallow baking pan measuring approximately 10 x 14 inches (25.5 x 35 cm), and a ridged grill pan.

Preheat the oven to 400°F (200°C).

First of all, skin the tomatoes by covering them with boiling water for 1 minute, then drain them and slip off their skins. Cut them in half and place them in the baking pan, cut-side up, then season well, drizzle 1 tablespoon of the olive oil over and place them on the top shelf of the oven to roast for 50-60 minutes. After this time, leave them aside to cool.

While they're cooling, cut the eggplants across into ½ inch (1 cm) slices, lay the slices on a board and lightly sprinkle them with salt on both sides. Leave them for 20 minutes to draw out some of the excess moisture, then blot them dry with paper towels. Next, brush them on both sides using 1 tablespoon of the olive oil and season with freshly ground black pepper. Brush the grill pan lightly with olive oil and place it over a high heat, then, when it is very hot, cook the eggplants in batches for about 2½ minutes on each side (this should take about 20 minutes in all).

Now, pour the remaining 6 tablespoons of olive oil into a large bowl, add the basil and balsamic vinegar, then toss the cooked eggplant in this marinade and leave them in a cool place until you are ready to serve.

Divide the salad greens between 4 plates and arrange the tomatoes and eggplants alternately all around. Then place equal quantities of the Feta slices in the middle of each salad and drizzle with the remaining marinade. Finally, put 1 tablespoon of crème fraîche on top of each salad and sprinkle a little paprika on top.

Spiced Carnaroli Rice Salad

This is a lovely spicy salad with Moroccan overtones – perfect for a buffet lunch, a party or for serving with cold cuts and spicy chutneys.

Serves 4

1½ cups (275 ml) carnaroli rice
¾ teaspoon cumin seeds
½ teaspoon coriander seeds
2 cardamom pods
3 teaspoons peanut or other mildly flavored oil
¼ cup (25 g) pine nuts
⅓ cup (40 g) currants
¼ cup (40 g) soft dried apricots, chopped into ¼ inch (5 mm) pieces
1 inch (2.5 cm) piece cinnamon stick
1 bay leaf
2½ cups (570 ml) boiling water
1 large red onion
3 scallions, trimmed and finely chopped
sea salt

For the dressing:

2 tablespoons peanut or other mildly flavored oil
4 tablespoons lemon juice

You will also need a lidded frying pan with a diameter of 8 inches (20 cm).

First, roast and crush the spices. To do this you need to place the cumin and coriander seeds and cardamom pods in the frying pan over a medium heat and stir and toss them around for 1-2 minutes, or until they begin to look toasted and start to jump in the pan. Now, transfer them to a mortar and pestle and crush them to a powder.

After that, add two teaspoons of the oil to the frying pan placed over a medium heat. When the oil is hot, sauté the nuts, currants and apricots until the nuts are golden brown. Next, stir in the rice and roasted spices, cinnamon stick, and bay leaf and turn the grains over in the pan until they're nicely coated and glistening with oil. Now, pour in the boiling water and add some salt, stirring only once; then put the lid on, turn the heat down to its lowest setting, and let the rice cook for exactly 15 minutes. Don't remove the lid, and remember what was said in Part One – absolutely no stirring.

While the rice is cooking, preheat the broiler to its highest setting. Peel and slice the red onion into ¼ inch (5 mm) rounds, then brush one side with half of the remaining teaspoon of oil, place them on a broiling rack directly under the broiler, and cook until the edges have blackened – 4-5 minutes – then turn them over. Brush the other side with the rest of the oil and broil them as before. After that, remove them and let them cool.

When the rice is cooked, take the pan off the heat, remove the lid, and cover with a clean dish cloth for 5 minutes to absorb the steam. Now, empty the rice into a warm serving dish and add about two-thirds of the scallions. Whisk the oil and lemon juice together and pour this over the rice before fluffing it up with a fork, then garnish the salad with the broiled onions and remaining scallions before serving.

Salade Niçoise

Nothing has changed much here over the long years I've been cooking and writing recipes – this is still one of the best combinations of salad ingredients ever invented. Fancy restaurants often attempt to do trendy versions with salmon, char-broiled tuna, and the like, but the original reigns supreme. In Provence, lettuce was sometimes used, sometimes not, but I now like to abandon the lettuce in favor of a few arugula leaves.

To make the vinaigrette dressing, start off with a mortar and pestle. First of all, crush the flakes of sea salt to a powder, then add the peeled clove of garlic and pound them together, which will immediately bring out the garlic's juices and turn it into a smooth paste. Next, add the dry mustard powder, work that in, then add the vinegar and some freshly ground black pepper and mix thoroughly until the salt dissolves. Finally, add the olive oil. Now, stir the herbs into the vinaigrette – it will look rather thick but will spread itself out beautifully once you toss it into the salad. Just before you dress the salad, pour everything into a screw-top jar and shake vigorously so it's thoroughly blended.

For the salad, begin by preparing the tomatoes. Place them in a bowl, pour boiling water over them, then, after 1 minute, drain and slip off their skins, protecting your hands with a cloth if you need to. Now, cut each tomato in half and hold each half in the palm of your hand (cut-side up), then turn your hand over and squeeze gently until the seeds come out; it's best to do this over a plate or bowl to catch the seeds. Now, cut each tomato into quarters. Then, in a large salad bowl, arrange the tomatoes, arugula leaves, cucumber, potatoes, beans, and chopped shallots in layers, sprinkling a little of the dressing over the ingredients as you go. Next, arrange chunks of tuna and egg quarters on top; then arrange the anchovies in a criss-cross pattern, followed by a scattering of olives, the chopped parsley, and a final sprinkling of dressing. Try to serve the salad fairly promptly, and needless to say it needs lots of warm, crusty baguette with fresh butter to go with it.

Serves 4-6 as a light lunch
12 oz (350 g) red ripe tomatoes
4 oz (110 g) arugula, stems removed
½ small young cucumber, cut into smallish chunks
1 lb (450 g) new or baby potatoes, cooked and sliced
4 oz (110 g) string beans, cooked
4 shallots, peeled and finely chopped
2 x 6½ oz (2 x 185 g) cans tuna fish in oil, well drained
2 large hard-boiled eggs, peeled and quartered
2 oz (50 g) anchovy fillets
2 oz (50 g) black olives
1 tablespoon chopped fresh parsley

For the vinaigrette dressing:
1 teaspoon sea salt
1 clove garlic, peeled
1½ teaspoons mustard powder
1 tablespoon wine or balsamic vinegar
6 tablespoons extra virgin olive oil
2 tablespoons finely chopped fresh herbs (chives, tarragon, parsley, basil, chervil, or mint, for example); if using fresh oregano and thyme, use just ½ teaspoon each in the mix
freshly ground black pepper

Thai Broiled-Beef Salad With Grapes

This recipe was given to me by chef Norbert Kostner at the Mandarin Asian Hotel in Bangkok when I visited the cooking school there. It's very good served as an appetizer or included in a cold-buffet menu.

Serves 4

1 lb (450 g) rump or sirloin steak
in 1 piece, 1 inch (2.5 cm) thick
6 oz (175 g) red or black seedless
grapes, halved
2-3 medium red chilies, halved
and seeded, or 3-4 Bird Eye
chilies, whole
2 cloves garlic, peeled
1 inch (2.5 cm) piece fresh
ginger, peeled
6 sprigs cilantro, plus 3 tablespoons
chopped cilantro
1 sprig fresh mint, plus 3 tablespoons
chopped fresh mint
3 tablespoons Thai fish sauce
grated zest 1 lime, plus 3 tablespoons
lime juice (juice of about 2 limes)
2 teaspoons palm sugar or light
brown soft sugar
3-4 stems lemon grass, very finely sliced
6 kaffir lime leaves, rolled into a
cigar shape and very finely
shredded (optional)
4 oz (110 g) arugula, stems removed

To garnish:

1 teaspoon toasted sesame seeds
1 teaspoon chopped fresh chives

Preheat the broiler to its highest
setting.

First, you need to broil the beef in advance, and for medium-rare give it 2-3 minutes on each side. Be careful not to overcook the steak: it needs to be quite pink since the lime juice in the dressing "cooks" the beef a bit further. If you'd prefer to use a ridged grill pan, preheat it for 10 minutes, then cook the steak for 1½-2 minutes on each side. Once the beef is broiled, allow it to rest for 10 minutes before slicing it into thin strips.

Meanwhile, to make the dressing, blend the chilies, garlic, ginger, and sprigs of cilantro, and mint in a food processor until finely chopped; then add the fish sauce, lime juice, and sugar and whiz again to blend everything. Pour the dressing over the beef strips, then sprinkle with the lemon grass, lime leaves (if using), lime zest, and remaining herbs. Add the arugula and grapes and toss everything together, then scatter the garnish on top.

Blue Cheese Dressing

I especially love this dressing. The blue cheese can be Roquefort, or Gorgonzola, which crumbles particularly well. The only stipulation is that the cheese has to be gutsy; a subtle, faint-hearted one will get lost among all the other strong flavors.

Start off by crushing the garlic clove (or cloves), together with the salt, to a creamy mass in a mortar and pestle, then add the mustard and work that in. Next, add the lemon juice, vinegar, and then the oil. Mix everything together thoroughly; then, in a bowl, combine the sour cream and mayonnaise and gradually whisk this combination into the dressing ingredients. When everything is thoroughly blended, add the chopped scallions and the crumbled blue cheese and season with freshly ground pepper. The dressing is now ready to use. I think a few crunchy croutons are a nice addition here.

To make these, toss ¼ inch (5 mm) cubes of bread – approximately 4 oz (110 g) in all – in a bowl with two teaspoons of olive oil, spread them out on a baking sheet, and bake in an oven preheated to 375°F (190°C) for 10 minutes.

Serves 4-6

1½ oz (40 g) blue cheese, crumbled
1 large or 2 small cloves garlic, peeled
1 teaspoon sea salt
1½ teaspoons mustard powder
1 tablespoon lemon juice
1 tablespoon balsamic vinegar
2 tablespoons light olive oil
⅔ cup (150 ml) sour cream
2 tablespoons mayonnaise
2 scallions, finely chopped
freshly ground black pepper

Marinated Trout Fillets and Potato Salad with Coriander Seeds and Cracked Pepper

This is a salad that can mostly be made way, way ahead – up to a week, believe it or not. Then all you do is steam some potatoes to go with it, or alternatively you can serve the trout fillets as they are, and instead of the potatoes, have a basket of buttered whole wheat bread at the table.

To get the best fragrance from the coriander seeds and peppercorns, drop them into a small frying pan and place them over a medium heat to dry-roast for 2-3 minutes. Move them around the pan until they start to jump, then put them in a mortar and pestle and crush them fairly coarsely.

Next, prepare the trout fillets by turning them skin-side up on a flat surface, then, with a sharp knife, lift the skin away at the tail end. Now, discard the knife and simply pull the skin from the flesh. If it clings at any point, just use the knife again and ease it away. Now, snip each one in 4 lengthwise, then cut them into 1½ inch (4 cm) pieces and lay the strips in the dish – this will probably have to be in 2 layers to fit them in – sprinkling the pepper and coriander mixture all over each layer. Next, scatter the shallot rings, bay leaves, and lemon slices all over, tucking them in-between the trout fillets here and there.

Now, in a bowl, whisk together the lemon juice, sugar, mustard, and oil. When they're very thoroughly mixed, pour the mixture over the trout. Cover with plastic wrap and put a plate on top with some kind of weight on it to keep the trout submerged; then place the trout in the refrigerator and let it marinate for a minimum of 24 hours or up to a week.

When you want to serve the salad, it's important to remove the trout from the refrigerator at least an hour beforehand. Now, steam the potatoes, generously sprinkled with salt, for 20-30 minutes (depending on their size), and, when they're cooked, place a cloth over them to absorb the steam for 5 minutes. Chop them roughly, divide them between the plates, spoon some of the trout marinade over, then arrange the trout and everything else on top. Finish off with a few sprigs of flat-leaf parsley.

Serves 4 as a main course or 8 as an appetizer
4 smoked trout fillets, weighing approximately 1 lb (450 g)
2 teaspoons coriander seeds
2 teaspoons black peppercorns
6 shallots, peeled and cut into thin rings
2 bay leaves, each snipped into 3-4 pieces
1 lemon, thinly sliced and cut in half
juice 2 lemons
2 teaspoons dark brown sugar
3 teaspoons wholegrain mustard
1 cup (250 ml) extra virgin olive oil

To serve:
1 lb 8 oz (700 g) new or baby potatoes, scrubbed but skins left on
a few sprigs fresh flat-leaf parsley
Sea salt

You will also need a shallow dish with a capacity of approximately 1 quart (1 liter).

17
What's new in the dairy

"You may drive out Nature with a pitchfork, but she will ever hurry back to triumph in stealth over your foolish contempt."
Never were these words, from Horace, *Epistles*, more true than in the dairy. In my long career of food writing, I have seen fashions, fads, and so-called health scares arrive with the force of a destructive tidal wave one moment, then recede and disappear without trace the next, leaving everyone reeling in confusion.

My conclusion is that nutritionists a) often disagree with each other, and b) change their minds anyway as more and more facts come to light.

Meanwhile nature, thankfully, remains steadfast and still has the last word – if you wait long enough. Perhaps dairy foods more than any other have suffered being in the nutritional firing line in the past, but thankfully they have now been reinstated, as everyone's now discovered that the so-called-healthy hydrogenated-fat alternatives were not so healthy after all. Added to that, nature's very own dairy products have a unique and magical property called flavor that no man-made alternative has ever been able to match.

The fat problem

Yes, it's true that since we have evolved a more sedentary way of living we have had to cut the fat content in our diets. We now no longer serve our vegetables swimming with butter; perhaps we spread a little less of it on our bread. And, of course, we now all love and applaud olive oil. But believe me, the home kitchen is not where our excess of eating fat has come from – we cannot blame dairy foods or the fat content of a good square meal. If we want to know why we consume more fat, we have to look, I'm afraid, at how our consumption of processed and snack foods and chocolate bars has grown. These have hidden amounts of fat that we don't take into account. What we eat per head in England in chocolate bars alone adds up to 1¼ cups (275 ml) of heavy cream per person per week. Not that chocolate bars and other snacks foods are bad in themselves, but we desperately need to find the balance that so often gets overlooked in the heat of the health debate.

There is a crazy kind of imbalance, largely due to ignorance, that people seem hardly aware of – we eat fattening snacks and then have only fat-free milk because we are "cutting down," or a Danish pastry with a high fat content accompanied by an artificial sweetener in our coffee. Someone who never eats snack foods but pours heavy cream on their apple pie at the weekend is, I'm quite positive, consuming far less fat. So, let's get dairy foods out of the firing line and enjoy them not in excess but in the perfect balance of a normal healthy diet.

A dairy explosion

When I first started writing about cooking, the dairy foods that were sold widely in stores were simply whole milk and two types of cream. Sour cream was not that widely available – perhaps just sometimes in specialized food shops; yogurt was only available in health food stores; and you only ate clotted cream if you went to the West Country of England where it was made. Now if you approach the dairy section in any large supermarket you can see a veritable explosion has taken place: miles of yogurts of every type and flavor, and an enormous range of different kinds of dairy products that, for me personally and for cooks everywhere, have been such a delight to discover and introduce into a whole range of cooking and recipes. But, with all this enormous choice available, it can be confusing, so here, before we move into the recipes, I want to give each dairy product an explanation.

Whole milk

The reason whole milk is so good for growing children is that it has many of the nutrients needed for good health. It has a natural fat content of 3.5 percent, contains protein and carbohydrates, and is a good source of calcium, an essential and important mineral for growing children's bones and teeth. In addition to all that, milk is packed with vitamins and minerals. Because of these reasons, anyone living on a strict budget should choose milk first and foremost – in fact in the long run, milk is the cheapest nourishment on offer.

In cooking, whole milk should be used to make white sauces and puddings, and substituting milk for half the amount of stock needed when making vegetable soups gives a lovely creamy texture and flavor.

Low fat milk

This has all the virtues of whole milk, except that some of the fat has been removed, leaving between 1 and 2 percent. Because of this, it is actually better in tea and coffee, and, I think, works better in batters for pancakes or Yorkshire puddings. For anyone wishing to cut some of the fat content in their diet, low fat milk is an excellent choice because it still retains some creaminess.

Skim milk

This is the one for people who are following a low fat diet, as only a trace (less than 0.5 percent) remains. Even so, skim milk is still highly nutritious and is an excellent source of calcium; it contains everything whole and low fat milk have without the fat. It can be used in all recipes requiring milk, but it obviously won't give the same degree of creaminess.

Soy milk

This is a dairy-free milk that is increasing in popularity. It has a high protein content and is perfect for those with a milk (lactose) intolerance and for vegans.

Pasteurized milk

This is simply milk that has undergone heat treatment: a mere 5 seconds at 72°C purifies it but, at the same time, leaves all the important vitamins, minerals and proteins virtually unchanged.

Homogenized milk

When you leave pasteurized or other milk to stand, the small amount of cream present rises to the top. What homogenization does, through a special treatment, is distribute the cream (milk-fat globules) evenly throughout the milk so this separation does not occur.

Buttermilk

This used to be a by-product of butter-making, hence its name, but now we have specially cultured buttermilk, which is made by adding a culture to skim or low fat milk. It has the same acidic flavor as the original and is perfect for making extra-light scones, soda bread, and pancakes.

Heavy cream

When cows' milk reaches the dairy, it contains a liquid substance called butterfat, and this, when it's skimmed off the surface of the milk, is cream, or what we know as heavy cream. It is extremely rich, with a fat content between 36-40 percent. Because of this it can stand being boiled in cooking without separating, and it can be whipped to a fluffy, spreadable consistency.

When whipping heavy cream, though, you have to be extra careful, as overwhipping can give a grainy, slightly separated appearance (and if you really overwhip it, you'll end up with butter). One of the ways to prevent this from happening is to add a couple of tablespoons of milk per 2 ½ cups (570 ml) of cream, and if you are using an electric hand mixer, make sure that you turn the speed down when it looks thick enough. Heavy cream is also rich and luscious served just as it is, chilled, as a thick heavy cream. If you're not Scottish (Scots don't approve), try pouring heavy cream over hot cooked oatmeal, along with some all-natural brown sugar to melt and marble into little pools.

Light cream

This is a much thinner cream, good for pouring and for cooking with when you need more creaminess than milk. Light cream contains between 18 and 30 percent fat. It is not suitable for whipping but is useful as a lighter alternative to heavy cream.

Half and half

This is a mixture of half milk and half cream. The fat content of half and half ranges from 10 to 12 percent.

Sour cream

This is a wonderful product; it's flavor is unique, and in my opinion, it is the very best topping for baked potatoes (mixed with snipped fresh chives). There is a low fat sour cream available that you might like to try. If you are lucky enough to get some caviar, sour cream and chives make wonderful accompaniments.

Crème fraîche

For me, crème fraîche is the number one top cooking ingredient in the cream family. Because by law, milk and cream have to be pasteurized, the flavor has undoubtedly been affected, making them blander than in former times. The French (more particularly the Normans, since Normandy is the world's richest dairy area), not content with this diminished flavor, created a special way of adding a culture to their cream allowing it to mature and develop the faintly acidic flavor that was lost in pasteurization.

The best crème fraîche comes from a strictly controlled area of Normandy and has all the rich, luscious flavor that the area is famous for. If you open a container and closely look at it, you can see the wonderful creamy-yellow color of the real thing, *right*. Crème fraîche is now being produced in the US, particularly in Vermont where an excellent product is made; it is available at some gourmet food markets. The reason crème fraîche is especially loved by cooks is it has a longer shelf life than heavy cream, so you can take a spoonful here and there, replace the lid and use it again. Finally, the other supreme virtue of crème fraîche is that when you use it in cooking, it never curdles and separates – you can bubble and boil it and never be afraid.

Clotted cream

Wait for it – this is the big one! Perhaps you'd rather not know, but it has at least 55 percent butterfat. Clotted cream has a unique and special dairy color, like pale buttercups, and is thick, rich and utterly irresistible. It is a speciality of the rich pastureland of the West Country of England, and is made by heating the cream to evaporate some of the liquids, so, in a sense, you could call it concentrated cream. It is heaven spread on scones with home-made preserves, and extra special on tart fruit pies. It's not for every day, but everyone should treat themselves to some just once in a while. It is available at some gourmet food markets.

Yogurt

The staple snack of the 1980s and 1990s has proved to be yogurt, and producers never seem to tire of yet more variations and flavors. In the kitchen, yogurt is a useful dairy ingredient and can be used in many ways. But what exactly is yogurt? Very briefly, it's milk – whole, low fat, skim, or dried – first pasteurized by heat treatment, then cooled and inoculated with a specially prepared culture. Then the whole thing is incubated at a warm temperature until the acidity reaches a certain level and setting takes place. The yogurt is then cooled and chilled, ready to be eaten or stored. Apart from preserving the milk, the process adds acidity to the flavor, which is pleasant to eat as it is but is also incredibly good for adding character and flavor to all kinds of dishes. The fat content of yogurt depends on the milk it is made from - wholemilk, low fat, or fat-free.

Organic wholemilk yogurt

This is a yogurt made with organic whole milk produced at dairies that meet requirements relating to animal feeds and pastureland. It is a completely natural product, suitable for vegetarians and available in low fat versions.

Genuine Greek yogurt

This is another of my absolute favorite dairy ingredients. It's a special yogurt made from cows' or sheep's milk, which is boiled in open vats so that its liquid content is reduced. The result is a much thicker consistency, giving a more concentrated yogurt with a fat content of 8-10 percent. I have a special fondness for it, and I love serving it well chilled with lots of lovely Greek mountain honey poured over it and pistachios sprinkled on top – in fact I think this is one of the simplest and nicest desserts. Greek yogurt is also a very useful ingredient in cooking, since it can replace some of the cream when you wish to lighten dairy desserts. Now you can buy low fat Greek yogurt, with 9 percent fat, and an amazing 0 percent, too. You may have to hunt for Greek yogurt in gourmet food markets but it is really worth seeking it out.

Cottage cheese

This is a very popular cheese because of its low fat content; it is a firm friend of the waistwatcher. It is made from low fat or skim milk that is first heat-treated, then a starter culture is added that forms the curds and whey. These are then washed several times in chilled water to remove the whey, and the curds are then drained and, finally, they are given a very light dressing of cultured cream. The result is a mild, faintly acidic cheese with just a hint of creaminess but not a great deal of character and flavor. Cottage cheese should always be eaten as fresh as possible, and it is good served with a sprinkling of snipped fresh chives and seasoned with coarse salt and black pepper.

Cream cheese

This has a soft, smooth, buttery texture and varies enormously according to its fat content. Standard cream cheese has a minimum of 33 percent fat content, but there are many variations, such as the Neuchatel and non-fat versions, which can be used in recipes to replace full-fat cream if a lower fat content and fewer calories are required.

Farmers cheese

This is a type of cottage cheese which is fairly solid because most of the moisture has been removed. It may be used in recipes or enjoyed as a regular eating cheese.

Quark

This is a soft white cheese made from low fat milk; it is mildly flavored and ideal for dieters. Use it instead of butter in scrambled eggs or mashed potatoes (see pages 36 and 178).

Ricotta

This, strictly speaking, is not really a cheese but a sort of by-product of cheesemaking. It is made from the drained whey and then cooked; in Italian, the word ricotta means re-cooked. It has a mild, fresh lactic flavor and contains only 14 percent fat. It is actually delicious just by itself served with summer fruit, and I have eaten it freshly made in Apulia, Italy, sprinkled with coarse salt, pepper, and olive oil, along with a really good quality bread.

Mascarpone

In my opinion, Mascarpone is the richest and most aristocratic of the new wave of dairy products. Thick, yellow, and creamy, with a very high fat content (40 percent) but a distinctive, rich dairy flavor, it forms the main part of the famous tiramisu. There again, it is lovely served alone with berries or in a cheesecake. Because of its high fat content, it can be lightened by mixing it with an equal quantity of fromage blanc and used as a filling for sponge cakes or as a topping for desserts. Add a small amount of sugar to sweeten the mixture and what you get is the flavor of Mascarpone as well as a lighter texture, and, if you are watching your waistline, far less guilt! I can also recommend Mascarpone spread on sweet oat crackers (or Digestives Biscuits from England) with fresh strawberry jam. Mascarpone is also excellent for adding to sauces.

Fromage frais and fromage blanc

Fromage frais is a fresh curd cheese originating in France and made from pasteurized cows' milk. Basically, it has very little fat, but cream is added to make 4 percent (or 8 percent) fromage frais. In the US, something very similar called fromage blanc is being produced. It has a 0 percent fat content so is ideal for anyone on a low fat diet. It is also ideal for use in dips. For a cool, light, low fat dessert, see the recipe for Fromage Blanc Creams on page 416.

Finnan Haddie with Crème Fraîche, Chive, and Butter Sauce

This is a great recipe, a) because it's the most wonderful combination of flavors, and b) because it takes only 12 minutes from start to finish. Serve it with spinach cooked in its own juices with a little butter, then drain well and you'll have a sublime meal in no time at all.

Serves 2

12-14 oz (350-400 g) finnan haddie or smoked cod, skinned
3 tablespoons crème fraîche
1½ tablespoons snipped
fresh chives
1 tablespoon (10 g) butter, diced
⅔ cup (150 ml) whole milk
freshly ground black pepper

You will also need a frying pan with a diameter of 10 inches (25.5 cm).

First, place the fish in the frying pan and add a little freshly ground black pepper but no salt. Then pour in the milk (it won't cover the fish, but that doesn't matter), bring it up to simmering, and cook gently, uncovered, for 8-12 minutes. You will be able to see clearly when the fish is cooked beacuse the fish will become pale and opaque.

Now, carefully remove the fish to a plate using a spatula, increase the heat and add the crème fraîche to the pan. Continue to simmer, uncovered, for 2-3 minutes, until the sauce reduces and thickens slightly, then whisk in the butter and return the fish to the sauce briefly. Scatter in the chives, let it bubble for about 30 seconds, and it's ready to serve.

Sirloin Steak with Crème Fraîche and Cracked Pepper Sauce

This is a special supper dish for two people celebrating a birthday or anniversary or for those who simply want a treat. It needs a good bottle of red wine, and baked potatoes with a leafy salad would be good accompaniments.

First of all you need to reduce the stock to half its original volume, so put it in a small saucepan and boil rapidly for about 10 minutes, then taste and add some salt if it needs it. Now, measure the Cognac into a jug.

When the steaks are at room temperature, season them well with salt, then place the frying pan over a high heat, and when it's really hot, add the butter and oil, which should start to foam immediately. Now, drop the steaks into the hot pan, and keeping the heat high, give them 3 minutes on one side for medium or 2 minutes for rare. Use a timer and try to leave them alone – no prodding! Now, turn them over and give them another 2 minutes on the other side for medium or 1 minute for rare. After that pour in the Cognac, let it splutter and reduce; then add, first, the reduced stock and finally the crème fraîche and crushed pepper. Give it all a good stir, then let everything bubble, reduce, and amalgamate for about 1 more minute, then serve the steaks on warmed plates with the sauce spooned over them.

Serves 2

2 x 8 oz (225 g) sirloin steaks, at least 1 inch (2.5 cm) thick, removed from the refrigerator about 1 hour before you need them
3 tablespoons crème fraîche
2 teaspoons black peppercorns, coarsely crushed
1¼ cups (275 ml) fresh beef stock
2 tablespoons Cognac
1 teaspoon butter
1 teaspoon oil
Sea salt

You will also need a solid frying pan with a diameter of 10 inches (25.5 cm).

Rhubarb Yogurt Fool

I now find that lusciously thick genuine Greek yogurt makes the best fruit fool of all because it allows the full flavor of the fruit to dominate. If you're serving this to someone who doesn't like yogurt, don't worry — they won't know.

Serves 4

1 lb 4 oz (570 g) rhubarb, cut into 1 inch (2.5 cm) chunks
⅓ cup (75 g) superfine sugar
1 teaspoon fresh ginger, chopped
¾ cup (200 ml) Greek yogurt
2 pieces stem ginger

You will also need a shallow square or round ovenproof baking dish and 4 serving dishes, each with a capacity of 6 fl oz (175 ml).

Preheat the oven to 350°F (180°C).

After you've trimmed, washed, and cut the rhubarb, place it in a baking dish, sprinkle with the sugar and fresh ginger, and bake in the oven for 30-40 minutes, until tender. Now, drain the rhubarb, reserving the juice, and purée the rhubarb in a food processor, along with 2 tablespoons of the reserved juice. When it's cool, fold half of the purée into the Greek yogurt in a bowl, then divide it among the serving dishes and spoon the remaining purée on top. Finally, cut the 2 pieces of stem ginger into matchstick lengths and use them to garnish the fool. Cover and refrigerate until needed.

Gooseberry Yogurt Fool

If you can find gooseberries, try this delicious variation on the recipe above. You will need 2 lb (900 g), stems removed. I think gooseberries are best cooked in the oven, so place them in a 9 inch (23 cm) square or round ovenproof baking dish, sprinkle them with ½ cup plus 2 tablespoons (150 g) superfine sugar, and bake them on the center shelf of the oven, uncovered, for 20-30 minutes, or until tender when tested with a skewer. After that, tip them into a sieve set over a bowl to drain off the excess juice. Now, reserve about a quarter of the cooked gooseberries for later, then place the rest in the bowl of a food processor, add 4 tablespoons of the reserved juice and whiz to a thick purée.

After the purée has become cold, empty 1¼ cups (275 g) Greek yogurt into a bowl, give it a stir, and fold in half the gooseberry purée. Now, spoon this mixture into six serving dishes, spoon the rest of the purée on top, and, finally, add the reserved gooseberries. Cover the dishes with plastic wrap and chill until you're ready to serve, then serve with some Pecan Shortbreads (see page 414) cut into small rounds. This amount will serve 6 people.

Toffee Bananas with Toasted Nuts

The world record for making this recipe is not five minutes, but just three — it's quite simply the fastest dessert recipe I've ever come across. It's also amazingly good, and if it is conceivable that anybody on this earth does not love delectably thick Greek yogurt, then you can make it just as well with whipped cream.

Right, on your marks, get ready… Place the brazil nuts, spread out on some foil, under the broiler about 4 inches (10 cm) from the heat and put a timer on for 3 minutes (if you don't have a timer keep an eye on them, because they will easily burn), then place them to one side for later.

Now, peel and slice the bananas into thin rounds and place them in a large bowl, then add the yogurt and mix well. Next, divide the mixture among the serving dishes and simply sprinkle the sugar equally over the 4 portions of banana. Now, cover with plastic wrap and leave in the refrigerator for about 3 hours — after this time the sugar will have transformed itself into lovely pools of toffee sauce. Now, all you need to do is chop the toasted nuts, sprinkle them on top, serve the desserts, and wait for the compliments.

Serves 4
2 large, ripe bananas
2 oz (50 g) brazil nuts
2 cups (500 g) Greek yogurt
¾ cup (150 g) dark muscovado or dark brown sugar

You will also need 4 individual serving dishes, each with a capacity of 1 cup (250 ml).

Preheat the broiler to its highest setting.

Classic Crème Caramel

Over the years I've experimented with what should be the best crème caramel, using heavy cream, crème fraîche, and half and half of these in the mixture. Now, I prefer to use light cream, which gives the whole thing a sort of wobbly lightness. So this, I now think, is the ultimate.

Serves 4-6

For the caramel:
¾ cup (175 g) superfine sugar
2 tablespoons hot tap water

For the custard:
⅔ cup (150 ml) whole milk
1¼ cups (275 ml) light cream
4 large eggs
1 teaspoon pure vanilla extract

To serve:
about 1¼ cups (275 ml) heavy cream

You will also need a soufflé dish with a capacity of 1 quart (850 ml), 5 inches (13 cm) in diameter, 3 inches (7.5 cm) deep, and a deep roasting pan.

Preheat the oven to 300°F (150°C).

Begin by making the caramel (see the pictures on page 477). To do this put the sugar in a saucepan and place it over a medium heat. Leave it like that, keeping an eye on it, until the sugar begins to melt and begins to turn liquid around the edges, which will take 4-6 minutes. Now, give the pan a good shake and leave it again to melt until about a quarter of the sugar has melted. Now, using a wooden spoon, give it a gentle stir and continue to cook and stir until the sugar has transformed from crystals to liquid and is the color of dark honey – the whole thing should take 10-15 minutes. Then take the pan off the heat and add the water, being cautious here because it sometimes splutters at this stage. You may now need to return the pan to a low heat to re-melt the caramel, stirring until any lumps have dissolved again. Then quickly pour two-thirds of the caramel into the soufflé dish, turning it round the bottom and sides to coat.

Now, for the custard: Pour the milk and cream into the saucepan containing the rest of the caramel, then place this over a gentle heat and use a whisk to thoroughly combine everything. Don't panic if you get a great glob of caramel clinging to your whisk or if there's some stuck around the edges of the pan – remember that the saucepan is heating up and the heat *will* melt it. "Eventually" is the word, so be patient. When it's all melted, remove the pan from the heat. Next, break the eggs into a large bowl or measuring cup and whisk them; then pour the hot milk that's now blended with the remaining caramel into this mixture, whisking it in as you pour. Next, add the vanilla extract, and after that, pour the mixture through a sieve into the caramel-lined dish. If you have any unmelted caramel left on the bottom of the pan, fill the pan with hot water, add a drop of dish-washing liquid, and heat again to clean it off.

Now, place the soufflé dish in the roasting pan and pour in enough tap-hot water to come two-thirds of the way up the dish. Place the whole thing on the center shelf of the preheated oven and leave it there for 1¼ hours, until the custard is set in the center, which means it should feel firm and springy to the touch. Then remove it from the roasting pan, and when it's completely cold, cover with plastic wrap and chill thoroughly for several hours in the refrigerator before turning out.

When you're ready to serve, loosen it around the sides with a spreading knife, put quite a deep serving plate on top and then turn it upside down and give it a hefty shake. What you will then have is a delicious, light, set caramel custard surrounded by a pool of golden caramel sauce. Serve it cut in slices with some heavy cream to mingle with the caramel.

Buttermilk Scones with Clotted Cream and Raspberry Butter

These are the lightest little scones you'll ever come across, but what is raspberry butter, you're wondering. The answer is that, traditionally, country people used to use up surplus summer fruits by making fruit cheeses. The fruit was cooked long and slow until it was concentrated into a thick, paste-like consistency. Fruit butters are similar, but not quite so thick. This version, made with raspberries, has all the concentrated flavor and aroma of the fruit, perfect for spooning onto scones with generous amounts of clotted or whipped cream.

To make the raspberry butter, purée the raspberries in a food processor, then pass them through a fine sieve, pressing with a wooden spoon so that as much juice as possible gets through – you should get about 1¾ cups (425 ml). Now, place the purée in a medium saucepan with the sugar and heat very gently until the sugar has dissolved. Then turn up the heat so the mixture boils rapidly for 8-10 minutes, but keep stirring from time to time so it doesn't catch on the bottom. When it's ready, the mixture should have reduced by one third and a wooden spoon drawn across the bottom of the pan should leave a trail for 1-2 seconds only, but be careful not to overcook it, or you will get glue. Then pour it into a serving dish and leave to one side to cool and set for at least an hour.

For the scones, begin by sifting the flour and salt into a bowl, rub the butter lightly into the mixture until it looks like breadcrumbs, then add the sugar. Now, in a measuring cup, beat the egg and 2 tablespoons of the buttermilk together and begin adding this to the rest, mixing the dough with a spreading knife. When it begins to come together, finish mixing it with your hands – it should be soft but not sticky (if the dough seems too dry, add a little more buttermilk, a teaspoon at a time).

When you have formed the dough into a ball, turn it onto a lightly floured surface and roll it into a circle at least 1 inch (2.5 cm) thick – be very careful not to roll it any thinner; the secret of well-risen scones is to start off with a thickness of no less than an inch. Cut out the scones by placing the cutter on the dough and giving it a sharp tap – don't twist it, just lift it up and push the dough out. Carry on until you are left with the trimmings, then bring these back together to roll out again until you can cut out the last scone.

Place the scones on the baking sheet, brush them lightly with the buttermilk and dust with a little flour. Now bake on the top shelf of the oven for 10-12 minutes, or until they are well risen and golden brown, then remove them to a wire rack to cool. Serve the scones spread thickly with raspberry butter and lots of cream.

Note: don't forget that scones don't keep well, so in the unlikely event of there being any left, place them in the freezer. The raspberry butter, however, can be kept in the refrigerator for a couple of weeks.

Makes about 10 scones
2-3 tablespoons buttermilk, plus a little extra for brushing
1½ cups (225 g) self-rising flour, plus a little extra for dusting
6 tablespoons (75 g) butter, at room temperature
¼ cup (40 g) superfine sugar
1 large egg, beaten

For the raspberry butter:
1 lb (450 g) raspberries
¾ cup (175 g) granulated sugar

To serve:
clotted or whipped cream

You will also need a lightly greased baking sheet dusted with flour, and a 2 inch (5 cm) cookie cutter.

Preheat the oven to 425°F (220°C).

Meringues with Cream and Strawberries

This recipe, inspired by the strawberry and cream dessert traditionally served at Eton College on the 4th of June, is great for anxious meringue makers – because the meringues are broken up it simply doesn't matter if they weep, crack, or collapse. So you can practice making them over and over with this dish until you get them perfect and, at the same time, enjoy this amazingly good summer dessert. Don't forget, though, to make the meringues the day before you want to serve it.

Serves 6

¾ cup (175 g) superfine sugar

3 large egg whites

1 lb (450 g) fresh strawberries, hulled

1 ½ tablespoons confectioners sugar

2½ cups (570 ml) heavy cream

You will also need a baking sheet measuring approximately 11 x 16 inches (28 x 40 cm), lined with non-stick parchment paper.

Preheat the oven to 300°F (150°C).

First, have the superfine sugar measured out ready, then place the egg whites in a scrupulously clean bowl and whisk until they form soft peaks that slightly tip over when you lift the whisk. Next, add the sugar, about a tablespoon at a time, and continue to whisk until each tablespoon of sugar has been thoroughly absorbed. Now simply take tablespoonfuls of the mixture and place them in rows on the lined baking sheet. Place the baking sheet in the oven on the center shelf, turn the heat down to 275°F (140°C) and leave the meringues there for 1 hour. After that, turn the oven off and leave the meringues in the oven to dry out overnight, or until the oven is completely cold.

When you're ready to make the dessert, chop half the strawberries and place them in a blender together with the confectioners sugar. Whiz the mixture to a purée, then pass it through a sieve to remove the seeds. Now, chop the rest of the strawberries and whip the heavy cream to the softly whipped stage.

All the above can be done in advance, but when you are ready to serve, break up the meringues into roughly 1 inch (2.5 cm) pieces, place them in a large mixing bowl, add the chopped strawberries, then fold the cream in and around them. After that, gently fold in all but about 2 tablespoons of the purée to give a marbled effect. Finally, pile the whole lot into a serving dish, spoon the rest of the purée over the surface, and serve as soon as possible.

Pecan Shortbreads with Raspberries and Raspberry Purée

If you like classic crème pâtissière (French pastry cream) but have no time to make it, a combination of store-bought custard and crème fraîche makes a good alternative. If you use it to sandwich together crisp, wafer-thin pecan shortbreads, raspberries, and raspberry purée, you have a real winner for summer entertaining.

To begin, toast the pecans by spreading them out on a baking sheet and placing them in the oven for 8 minutes. Then, once cool, place them in a processor and grind them down until they look rather like ground almonds.

Now, in a mixing bowl, cream the butter and confectioners sugar together until light and fluffy, then gradually work in the sifted flours, followed by the ground pecans, bringing the mixture together into a stiff ball. Place the dough in a plastic storage bag and leave in the refrigerator to rest for 30 minutes. After that, roll it out to a thickness of ¼ inch (5 mm), then cut out 16 rounds by placing the cutter on the pastry and giving it a sharp tap, then simply lift the cutter and the piece will drop out. Now arrange the biscuits on the baking sheets and lightly prick each one with a fork. Bake for 10-12 minutes, leave on the baking sheets for about 10 minutes, then remove to a wire rack to cool completely.

While the shortbreads are cooling, place the raspberries for the purée in a bowl, sprinkle them with the sugar and leave for 30 minutes. After that, purée them in a processor and pass through a nylon sieve to remove the seeds, then place in a serving bowl, cover and chill until needed.

For the raspberry filling, beat the crème fraîche in a mixing bowl with an electric hand mixer until it becomes really stiff, then add the custard and vanilla extract and beat again, also until thick. Cover and chill until needed. Just before serving, spread equal quantities of the cream mixture over 8 of the cookies, then arrange the raspberries on top, reserving 24 for decoration. Spoon some purée over the cream, then sandwich with the remaining shortbreads. Place 3 raspberries on top of each one, and lightly dust with the confectioners sugar.

Note: don't be tempted to prepare these too far in advance, because once the filling goes in the shortbreads begin to lose their crunchiness.

Serves 8
For the pecan shortbreads:
1 cup (110 g) pecans
10 tablespoons (150 g) softened butter
½ cup (60 g) confectioners sugar
1 cup (150 g) all-purpose flour, sifted
⅓ cup plus 1 tablespoon (60 g) rice flour or ground rice, sifted

For the raspberry purée:
8 oz (225 g) fresh raspberries
2 tablespoons superfine sugar

For the raspberry filling:
1 lb (450 g) fresh raspberries, reserving 24 for the garnish
¾ cup (200 ml) crème fraîche
⅔ cup (150 ml) fresh custard
¼ teaspoon vanilla extract

To garnish:
24 whole fresh raspberries, reserved from the filling
confectioners sugar, to dust

You will also need 2 baking sheets measuring approximately 11 x 16 inches (28 x 40 cm), lightly greased, and a 3½ inch (9 cm) round cookie cutter.

Preheat the oven to 350°F (180°C).

Fromage Blanc Creams with Red Fruit Compote

In my book Winter Collection, *I made these with Mascarpone, but this low fat alternative is, I feel, every bit as good as the rich version and the perfect accompaniment to any fruit compote. I like this best made with leaf gelatin, but I've also included instructions for powdered gelatin.*

Serves 6
3½ cups (800 g) fromage blanc
6 sheets (0.33 oz) leaf gelatin
⅔ cup (150 ml) low fat milk
½ cup (75 g) superfine sugar
1 vanilla bean, split lengthwise

For the compote:
8 oz (225 g) fresh plums
8 oz (225 g) fresh cherries
8 oz (225 g) fresh blueberries
8 oz (225 g) fresh strawberries
8 oz (225 g) fresh raspberries
¼ cup (50 g) superfine sugar

You will also need 6 x ¾ cup (175 ml) mini pudding molds, lightly oiled with a flavorless oil, and an ovenproof baking dish measuring 9 inches (23 cm) square and 2 inches (5 cm) deep.

Preheat the oven to 350°F (180°C).

If you are using leaf gelatin, simply place the sheets in a bowl and cover with cold water, *below left*, then leave them to soak for about 5 minutes, till softened, *below center*. Meanwhile, place the milk in a saucepan with the sugar and vanilla bean and heat gently for 5 minutes, or until the sugar has dissolved. Then take the pan off the heat. All you do now is squeeze the leaf gelatin in your hands to remove any excess water, then add it to the hot milk, *below right*. Give it all a thorough whisking and let it cool.

Next, in a large mixing bowl, whisk the fromage blanc until smooth, then add the cooled gelatin and milk mixture, removing the vanilla bean, and whisk again really well. Now, divide the mixture between the pudding basins, filling them to within ½ inch (1 cm) of the rims. Finally, cover with plastic wrap and chill in the refrigerator for at least 3 hours.

To make the compote, begin by preparing the plums: cut them around their natural line into halves, remove the pits, then cut each half into 4 and place in the ovenproof dish, along with the whole cherries and blueberries. Now, sprinkle in the sugar, then place the dish on the center shelf of the oven without covering and leave it there for 15 minutes. Next stir in the strawberries, halved if large, and return the dish to the oven for 10-15 minutes, or until the fruits are tender and the juices have run out of them. Finally, remove them from the oven and stir the raspberries into the hot juices, then allow it to cool, cover with plastic wrap and chill.

To serve the creams, gently ease each one away from the edge of the mold using your little finger, then invert them onto serving dishes and serve with the compote spooned all around.

If you'd prefer to use powdered gelatin instead of leaf, place 4 tablespoons of the milk in a small bowl, then sprinkle the contents of one envelope unflavored gelatin over the milk and let it stand for 5 minutes. Meanwhile, heat the rest of the milk in a small saucepan, along with the vanilla bean and sugar until the sugar has dissolved, then remove it from the heat and whisk in the soaked-gelatin mixture. Allow to cool, then just whisk into the fromage blanc and continue as for the main recipe.

Coffee Cappuccino Creams with Cream and Sweet Coffee Sauce

If you are a coffee fan, this is the coffee dessert – the best ever! It is based on an old-fashioned recipe for honeycomb mold, which sometimes separates into layers, but sadly it often doesn't. Therefore, I have now given up on layers because it tastes absolutely divine anyway. You can make this and serve it in Irish coffee glasses or plain glasses. The contrast of the unsweetened coffee cream mingling with the sweetened sauce and a generous amount of heavy cream poured over it is simply gorgeous.

Serves 6
9 teaspoons instant espresso coffee powder
⅔ cup (150 ml) water
1 envelope unflavored gelatin
1¼ cups (275 ml) whole milk
3 large eggs, separated
1½ teaspoons cornstarch
¾ cup (200 ml) crème fraîche

For the sauce:
5 teaspoons instant espresso coffee powder
¾ cup (175 g) granulated sugar
1 cup (250 ml) water

To serve:
⅔ cup (150 ml) heavy cream

You will also need 6 x 1 cup (200 ml) serving dishes.

Begin by soaking the gelatin: pour the water into a small bowl, sprinkle in the gelatin and let it soak for 5 minutes. Meanwhile, pour the milk into a medium saucepan and place it over a gentle heat. Then, in a bowl, whisk the egg yolks and cornstarch together, and when the milk is very hot and just about to simmer, pour it over the egg-yolk mixture, whisking as you do. Now, return the mixture to the same saucepan, adding the soaked gelatin and coffee powder, then return the pan to the heat and continue to whisk until the custard is thickened and the gelatin and coffee are completely dissolved. Remove the pan from the heat and pour the custard into a large mixing bowl, let it cool, then whisk in the crème fraîche.

In another bowl, and using a clean whisk, whisk the egg whites to the soft-peak stage. Now, fold 2 tablespoons of the egg whites into the coffee custard to loosen the mixture, then gently fold in the rest. Pour the mixture into the dishes and cover them with plastic wrap, leaving them in a cool place for about 2 hours before chilling them in the refrigerator until needed.

To make the coffee sauce, gently heat the sugar and water together and whisk until all the sugar granules have completely dissolved, then simmer gently for 15 minutes without a lid until it becomes syrupy. Next, dissolve the coffee in 2 teaspoons of warm water, stir this into the syrup and transfer it to a serving pitcher to cool. Meanwhile, whip up the cream to the soft peak stage, and when you're ready, serve the coffee creams topped with whipped cream with the coffee syrup poured on top.

Note: this recipe contains raw eggs.

18
Fruit for cooking

I think a good sub-title for this chapter might be "How to preserve our heritage." There is, unfortunately, a price to pay for progress, and while fruit from around the world arrives at our supermarkets daily bringing a permanent abundance of choice, it's sad that some local and regional fruit growers are being forced into decline.

I am not against progress; I enjoy having such a wide choice. I feel privileged that I can shop around the world just a few miles from where I live and I love being able to bite into a crunchy fresh apple in June that hasn't gone mealy with storage. But at the same time I hope that local fruit growers won't ever give up, and we need to encourage them by buying their produce wherever possible. It's important that with all the dazzling choice before us we look at labels to find out the regions or countries of origin and give our local fruit growers all the support we can.

On the pages that follow, I have tried to give a kind of first-time overall view of various fruit and how to prepare and cook them. This is not, by any means, a comprehensive list, but a look at kinds of fruit that are most likely to be used in any day-to-day cooking repertoire.

Apples

It's on the subject of the apple, more than any other fruit, that chefs and cooks often part company. As one of the latter, and having been born and bred in England, I am quite definitely a Bramley lover. A few apple growers in the US are now beginning to trial grow the Bramley, and it may be available in years to come. Suitable alternatives to the Barmley apple include Rome, Stayman Winesap, Granny Smith, Northern Spy, Macoun, McIntosh, and Cortland. Some recipes require firmer apples to keep their shape, and Granny Smiths, McIntosh, and Stayman Winesap are excellent for this purpose.

There are always several of the varieties listed above widely available, but their best season is from the end of August through November. As the seasons go I tend to cook with apples more frequently in the winter months and use other fruit as it becomes more plentiful during the summer. When I first started cooking, seasons were so important and truly dictated the rhythm of cooking through the year, and as I've said elsewhere, I still find this variation makes cooking more interesting.

When it comes to preparing apples for cooking, unless you're going at the speed of lightning, you will need a bowl of lightly salted water, since this will prevent them from browning. First of all, you need a small, sharp knife and a potato peeler. Cut each apple in half, then cut one half into quarters using the knife, taking out the core and seeds. Now, using the peeler, peel off the skin (if the recipe requires it), then, depending on the recipe, slice or chop the apples and add them to the bowl of water as they are prepared. Use them as quickly as possible, draining in a colander and drying them with a dish towel first.

Apricots

Here's a fruit that cannot be grown without warm sunshine. The majority of apricots available in the US come from California. The ones on the market in June and July are the seasonal California apricots; otherwise, the ones you will find are imported. Picked straight from the tree, an apricot can be delightful to eat raw, warm from the sun. But usually, by the time they arrive at most markets, I feel they need light cooking to bring out the best apricot flavor. The season for buying fresh ones is short, but dried apricots are now available all year round and can nearly always be used in apricot recipes.

When it comes to preparing apricots, there's no need to peel them – all you do is cut the apricot around the natural line into two halves, then, holding the half containing the pit in one hand, give a little twist and squeeze as you remove the pit with the other hand. To cook apricots, you can use them in place of plums in the recipe on page 435.

Bananas

A little bit of heaven is a ripe, fragrant, soft-fleshed banana mashed with a fork with just a little brown sugar and piled on to thick slices of buttered crusty whole wheat bread (homemade, see page 84). That and a cup of freshly brewed tea can give anyone renewed strength in the middle of a working day.

When choosing bananas, remember that to be ripe enough to eat the peeling must be all yellow with no green areas near the stalk. Also, the riper they are the better they taste – sweeter and more fragrant. A really ripe and ready-to-eat banana will have little brown freckles on its yellow skin, but be warned: ripe and ready means just that, so eat it soon or it might be a little too ripe tomorrow! Remember, too, that bananas come from hot countries and hate the cold, so never, ever put them in the refrigerator, because the shock of it turns them black. Bananas also tend to discolor if they are exposed to the air, so if you are preparing them for a recipe they should be tossed in lemon juice if they have to wait around. When they're submerged and cut off from the air, however, they stay creamy white with no problem. The recipe for Toffee Bananas with Toasted Nuts on page 407 is one of the simplest and easiest desserts I know.

Cherries

In the US, both sweet and sour cherries grow. I am grateful for this because a percentage of the sweet cherries are exported to Britain to provide us with a plentiful supply throughout the summer. Cherries are expensive because they must be laboriously hand-picked. Since the season is relatively short, I always make the most of it and seem to eat them practically every day.

The sweet cherries grown in the US are usually the Bing variety, and the common sour cherry variety is called Morello. Morellos are exceptionally good for cooking, with a wonderful, quite unique, concentrated cherry flavor. Sour cherries can be bought dried. Cherries sold in jars can be good, and Morello cherry preserves are superb both spread on bread and scones and used in a sauce to serve with duck. I have lately discovered that sweet cherries cooked with wine and wine vinegar also make a superb sauce for duck or ham, so I would use fresh ones in the summer, and in the winter make the sauce with dried sour cherries.

Figs

Like apricots, fresh figs ideally need to be eaten picked from the tree, warm from the sunshine, fully ripened and bursting with soft, luscious flesh. If their sweetness is then combined with some thinly sliced Prosciutto or Serrano ham, you would have a feast indeed. The best of the crop are at their most luscious from June to October. They should be dark purple, feel soft to the touch when you buy them and their skins should have a soft bloom, which needs to be wiped off with damp paper towels. Eat them just as they are, as a topping for sweet galettes (page 124), or arranged in overlapping slices, brushed with honey, and baked for 10-12 minutes at 425°F (220°C). Another very unusual way to serve them is as an appetizer; see the recipe for Roasted Figs with Gorgonzola and Honey-Vinegar Sauce on page 438.

Lemons

Imagine a world without lemons or a kitchen that didn't always have a lemon tucked away. Can there be a more widely used fruit or absolutely essential ingredient in cooking in the Western world?

Lemons, which are available all year round, contain lots of sharp, acidic juice, but also a fragrant oil that's found in the zest (the colored outer layer of the peel). In a drink such as a dry Martini or gin and tonic, this pared-off outer peel releases its fragrant oil to give a subtle lemon hint. In cooking, lemon zest is every bit as treasured as the juice, and Christmas fruit cakes, puddings, and mincemeat all contain not only lemon juice and zest but candied lemon peel, giving extra fragrance and flavor. It's always best to use lemons as fresh as possible, but I find extra lemons keep better if they're stored in a plastic storage bag in the salad drawer of the refrigerator.

Squeezing

It is said that rolling the lemon with the palm of your hand on a flat surface using a bit of pressure will allow you to get more juice. When my mother made pancakes, she would put plates to warm in the oven and put the lemon in along with them, because this, she said, produced more juice. Either way, I think a lemon reamer inserted into a half lemon and squeezed and twisted is a wonderfully easy way to extract the juice.

Zesting

If you want finely zested lemon, a grater will do the job, but you need to take care not to include the bitter pith just beneath the zest. Best of all is a lemon zester, which removes only the outer zest and the fragrant oils. A great lemon recipe is the grilled lemon chicken kebabs on page 342.

Limes

Lime trees grow and thrive in California, the Caribbean, and in Mexico. Florida key limes, if you can find a source for them, are wonderful for cooking. Limes are yet another supreme gift of nature. Like lemons, they are filled with fragrant acidic juice and the zest contains the same high flavored oils. Though limes are small green lookalike lemons, their flavor is distinctly different. I love limes and always have them in my kitchen. If you want a low fat salad dressing, look no further – just squeeze lime juice all over a salad. It's remarkable how it offers both its own flavor and at the same time manages to enhance other flavors in the salad. The same applies to the juice, which really enhances the flavor of mango, papaya, and pineapple.

Mangoes

When you're standing before a ripe, plump mango and you can feel its soft ripeness and smell its quite overwhelming fragrance, that is a time to rejoice. Now, because of fast transportation, everybody can enjoy this most luscious and succulent of fruit, with its dazzling orange-yellow flesh. The fruit itself is fragrant, with a custard flavor. That said, a mango is always rather awkward to prepare, but first you need to check that it's ripe. Color is not an indication: the skins are variously green, red, yellow-orange, or even vaguely purple. As with an avocado you need to hold the fruit in your hand and feel a "give" of softness when you exert a little pressure. Smell, too, can help you – the riper it is the heavier the perfume.

I love a mango on its own with just a squeeze of lime to bring out the flavor of the fruit. Mango salsa, page 188, goes beautifully with chicken, and you'll find Thai Fish Curry with Mango, page 433, is quite exquisite.

How to prepare a mango

The best way to begin is to place the mango on a flat surface (I often use a dinner plate to catch the juice). Remember there is a large flat pit in the center, so take a sharp knife, hold the mango in a vertical position, then slice it lengthwise either side of the pit, *top right*. Now, hold each slice, flesh-side up, and this time, using a small knife, cut a criss-cross pattern into the flesh right down to the skin but being careful not to cut through the skin, *right*. Now, you can turn the whole thing inside out and simply cut away the cubes of mango into a bowl, then pour in any juices that are left on the plate.

Slicing the mango

Mangoes can be sliced, but only if they're the exact ripeness and not too soft. This time you need a potato peeler to finely peel off the skin, then hold the mango in one hand, and with a small knife, cut out a slice, *left*, taking the knife down to the pit either side of it, then remove the slice and carry on cutting slices all the way around.

Too ripe

If the mango is too soft and fibrous to chop or slice, cut the cheeks off the mango (as shown on the previous page), then scoop out the flesh and make a purée in the processor with a little lime juice. Lovely as a sauce for something sweet or savory, or add half its quantity of Greek yogurt to make a fragrant mango fool.

Oranges

Oranges feature as regularly as lemons in recipes: the famous French classic bigarade (orange and port) sauce served with duck, for instance, and my own favorite classic sauce, Cumberland, which features orange and lemon, where the juices and finely shredded zest are combined with port and red currant jelly. Then there is also, of course, that great British invention - wonderful marmalade - which is hard to beat. Made with the bitter oranges of Seville that arrive at Christmas, no marmalade made with other citrus fruit has that tangy intensity of flavor, where the sharpness of the oranges wins hands down over the sugar, totally eliminating that over-sweetness that so often masks the true flavor of the fruit in preserves.

Buying oranges is such a hit and miss affair, and a dry, sour or extra-pithy orange is really not pleasant. So, for eating straight there's only one type of orange that never fails to please, and that's navel oranges. They are distinctive in that they have a so-called "navel," and inside there's a sort of baby fruit attached. I'm not saying other varieties of orange are not good, but with navels you're never disappointed. In the US they are grown mainly in Florida and California, and the ones supplied to markets from November through February taste the best.

Peaches and nectarines

Oh to be walking through a fragrant orchard when the peaches are ripe and just about to fall from the trees. The peach, beloved of artists, is a beauteous thing, with its deep-crimson rosy bloom and voluptuous bright-yellow flesh oozing with juice. When we're lucky enough to eat them just like that – ready, ripe, and warm from the sun – we need have no thought of recipes. Home-grown peaches and nectarines are available during the summer months. Imported ones can be found in the winter, but they have often been picked too early so that by the time the hard flesh finally becomes soft enough to eat, it has often turned mealy, dry, and tasteless. There are white fleshed varieties of both nectarines and peaches, but the yellow, in my opinion, has more flavor.

Unripened peaches and their first cousin, nectarines, can be somewhat rescued in cooking, however, so poaching them in Marsala (*Summer Collection*) is a good idea.

Pineapple

When I first started cooking I was slightly afraid of pineapples, not knowing quite how to come at them or where to start with my knife. When I was a child, pineapple came canned in neat rings packed in syrup. My favorite cooking teacher, Elizabeth David (though only through books), came to my aid and, as always, explained it perfectly, which gave me immense satisfaction as I proudly took the pineapple to the table sprinkled with a little sugar and Kirsch.

First, you need to buy a ripe pineapple: look for proud, lively green tufts that don't look too aged or tired. Give one a tug if you can: if it's ripe it should pull off easily. The other thing to look for are the little thorny bits that stick out – they should be brown. The color of the pineapple itself is not always a guide: some from Central America are very green and others from the Ivory Coast are golden amber. Feel the pineapple at the bottom: it should give and feel soft if it's ripe, and don't forget to smell its strong pineapple perfume, probably telling you more than anything whether it's ready to eat.

I have now created my own way of dealing with a pineapple. Needless to say, the tough, elusive-looking object needs a really sharp knife. First slice off the leafy top and about ½ inch (1 cm) of the fruit with it – you need to get this as straight as possible. Put it to one side, then cut off the opposite end, which can be discarded. Now, stand it upright and slice off the skin vertically in slices, *top right*, going all the way round. What you will now have is a whole peeled pineapple; what you need to do next is use the tip of a potato peeler to dig out the "eyes," *center right*, which are similar to those of a potato. Now, slice the pineapple vertically in half, then into quarters. The central core can be somewhat tough, so slice this off along the center of each quarter, *bottom right*, then cut the quarters into slices about ⅓ inch (7 mm) thick. Arrange these in overlapping circles, then sprinkle with a light dusting of sugar and a little Kirsch (rum is also very good) and place the leafy top in the center.

Plums, Greengage plums, and Damsons

In areas of the country without the climate for growing peaches and nectarines, fresh, tangy plums may be available, instead, and these more than make up the difference. Varieties are distinguished by skin color (red, purple, black, or green), aroma (subtle or robust), and, of course, taste (sweet, tart, or mild). I have a small Victoria plum tree in my garden in England, and I love eating them straight from the tree in late summer. I give them a faint squeeze to see which ones are fully ripe, then eat just a few each day for breakfast and lunch until they're all gone. There are several varieties of home-grown plums, all suitable for cooking or eating raw when fully ripe. The best plums for buying fresh are found in the markets during May through early October.

If at all possible, try to find Greengage plums, which rarely appear at markets but are sometimes imported. Because of their green color, they are deceptive – they can look unripe and forbidding but taste very sweet. I like to cook both greengages or other plums in a compote of Marsala wine (see page 215).

Damsons - my favorite member of the plum family - are sometimes home-grown or found at farmers' markets. The true damson is small and oval, almost almond-shaped, with dark indigo-purple skin covered in a soft bloom and bright-green sharp-sour flesh that, when cooked with sugar, produces darker, reddish-purple juice. The secret of the damson's utter charm is that because it's a sharp fruit its flavor is not killed by sugar, so damson jam remains perfectly tart and not over-sweet. One of my all-time favorite recipes is for damson chutney: in 20 years I've never been without a little hoard of it stashed away in my cupboard under the stairs. It does wonders for sausages or makes a very sophisticated accompaniment to cold cuts, and I particularly love serving sausages with baked potatoes and dipping the potato skins into a dish of luscious damson chutney.

Rhubarb

Rhubarb arrives at a very important time in the calendar - early spring when there's absolutely no other interesting fruit in season. Rhubarb really is a curious, wonderfully different fruit – no other comes to us as an elongated stalk. Watching it grow almost secretly under its umbrella of wide green leaves in the garden is fascinating.

We can buy the tender, pink stalks of hothouse rhubarb, which have a delicate, youthful flavor. Then, between early April and June, we begin to see the field-grown rhubarb which is a deeper, rosier red. Later on toward the end of the season, it will be dark crimson, more acid, and less sweet, so a little more sugar is needed at this time. Use it in the crumble recipe on page 440, in one-crust pies, or in the Old-Fashioned Rhubarb Trifle on page 436.

When it comes to preparing and cooking rhubarb, first trim off the leaves and cut the stalks into 1 inch (2.5 cm) chunks. I never, ever simmer or boil rhubarb because it tends to mash up too much, so to keep the pieces intact, it's better to bake it in the oven using ⅓ cup(75 g) of sugar to each 1 lb 8 oz (700 g) of fruit, preheating the oven to 350°F (180°C). Place it in a shallow dish and give it 30-40 minutes, uncovered. This amount will serve 4 people.

Berries

Wild berries

If a crop of wild berries becomes ripe in your area, go out berry picking to discover the different varieties and flavors. The intense flavor of the wild berry is wonderful and something that the cultivated varieties can only try to replicate. Wild berries may contain more seeds, but their taste and the pleasure of picking them is most rewarding.

Blackberries

There is still something very satisfying about blackberry picking, although I usually find someone has been there first, picking all the best ones at the lowest levels! Don't be thwarted – use a long stick to pull down the upper branches. Take some gloves, too, or your hands will be very scratched, and a basket if you're really determined to pick enough to cook with when you return home.

Either way, wild blackberries have a character and flavor that the cultivated ones have never captured. It's tricky, though, because if the summer is a rainy one, they will be plump, fleshy, and juicy; if the summer is dry, they will be very small and more concentrated. So, given the vagaries of wild blackberries, the cultivated kind are better than none. Blackberries are absolutely delicious mixed with apples in a one-crust pie, or why not try them instead of apple in the crumble recipe on page 440?

Blueberries

When I was small my Welsh grandmother used to make tarts with a fruit called bilberry – little berries that grew wild, with purple flesh that yielded dark, deep-red juice. The blueberry is apparently its cousin, and grows wild in North America, but these are dark indigo-blue outside and inside the flesh is green. The cultivated blueberries we buy are larger, plumper, and very handsome to look at, and they are best and cheapest in the summer.

Blueberries are delicious served with buttermilk pancakes for breakfast, in pies, and in blueberry muffins (*Summer Collection*). I have used them in the recipe for Fromage Blanc Creams with Red Fruit Compote on page 416 – a lovely summery combination.

Raspberries

A truly exquisite soft fruit which has an intense flavor and needs hardly any adornment. I like them served on a plate spread out in a single layer with a minute sprinkling of sugar, and I eat them just like that as often as I can during the season, July through October, which is the season for the everbearing varieties. Treat raspberries more or less like strawberries – no water if possible, and covered if you have to keep them in the refrigerator. Raspberries, like strawberries, also lend themselves to countless recipe ideas. Damaged, over-soft fruits make marvellous tarts. Furthermore, if you sieve them and add confectioners sugar to taste you have a wonderful sauce for pouring over ice cream or strawberries. If you get the chance, try golden raspberries which are more delicately flavored than the red but just as delicious. They are pretty to use as a garnish or as part of a dessert.

Red currants

Red currant jelly is an absolute must-have as a pantry ingredient (see page 246). It is almost always available at supermarkets, and there are several brands you can buy to decide which is your favorite. Fresh red currants are rarely to be found, but occasionally, you can find them at a farmers' market. I like the combination of red currants mixed with strawberries and raspberries in equal quantities for one of the simplest of desserts. Pass around sugar and cream and summer is in every spoonful. Still more rarely found are white currants, which would be beautiful used for contrast of color in combination with red currants in the filling for the meringue recipe, page 62.

To prepare currants, all you do to easily separate them from stalks is to take a bunch in one hand, hold the stalk firmly, then slide the stalk in-between the prongs of a fork held in the other hand. Now, pull from top to bottom, sliding them all off in one swift movement.

Strawberries

I think it's true to say that strawberries are one of the best fruits in the world, particularly during the height of the season which runs from late April to June when they are at their most delicious. If you want to really enjoy a feast of strawberries during the late spring and early summer, my advice is to drive to a place in the country where you can pick your own or buy direct from the grower. Always let your nose be your guide: the little plastic baskets that the strawberries are sold in have air holes, so make sure the strawberries have a strong, ripe scent, which indicates a good flavor.

Strawberry know-how

To get the most pleasure out of strawberries it's best to know how to treat them before you eat them. This means a bit of TLC, because their sheer beauty can be lost by bad handling.

1) Try to pick your own.

2) Eat them the same day or store in a cool place with the hulls intact.

3) Refrigerators and strawberries don't like each other. Low temperatures rob them of fragrance and flavor and somehow transfer the flavor to other ingredients in the refrigerator (uncovered milk or cream can quickly absorb strawberry flavors).

4) Please don't wash them. They tend to absorb water, which makes them mushy, so this also means it's not a good idea to buy them after heavy rain. Just wipe them with damp paper towels.

5) Leave the hulls on as long as possible and only remove them an hour or so before eating.

6) If you're forced to put them in the refrigerator, try sugared strawberries, which involves slicing them in half, sprinkling with sugar and storing them in a tightly lidded polythene box. During the storage the juices will mingle with the sugar and form a lovely strawberry-flavored syrup. Remove from the refrigerator about an hour before serving.

Exotics

These are not often used in cooking as such but they do make a very splendid fruit salad (see the following page), so I will briefly explain how to deal with them.

Kiwi fruit

You can use a potato peeler here to peel off the skin and then slice the fruit, or if you want to eat one whole, slice the top off and scoop the flesh out with a teaspoon, as if you were eating a boiled egg.

Lychees

To prepare this fragrant, juicy little fruit, peel off the papery skin, slice the fruit round the middle, separate it into halves, and discard the seed.

Passion fruit

When you buy passion fruit, look for a crinkled skin, which is a sign of ripeness, then just slice the fruit in half and scoop out the edible seeds and all the lovely juicy flesh that surrounds them.

Papaya (or pawpaw)

When ripe a pawpaw should, like an avocado, have some "give" when you hold it in your hand and exert a little pressure. To prepare it, slice it in half vertically, scoop out the seeds, peel off the skin, and slice or chop.

Clockwise from top left: passion fruit, papaya, kiwi fruit, and lychees

Tropical Fruit Salad in Planter's Punch

Planter's punch, a popular drink throughout the Caribbean, is a delicious combination of rum, orange, lime, and pineapple juice, with just a trace of cinnamon and nutmeg. The syrup for this fruit salad is based on exactly the same combination, which makes it very special.

Serves 8

2 bananas, peeled and chopped into 1 inch (2.5 cm) chunks
8 oz (225 g) seedless black grapes, halved
1 papaya, peeled and chopped into 1 inch (2.5 cm) chunks (see page 431)
1 large mango, peeled and chopped into 1 inch (2.5 cm) chunks (see page 425)
1 small pineapple, peeled and chopped into 1 inch (2.5 cm) chunks (see page 427)
2 oranges, peeled and cut into segments
8 oz (225 g) lychees, peeled, pitted and halved (see page 431)
2 kiwi fruit, peeled, halved and cut into ½ inch (1 cm) slices (see page 431)
4 passion fruit, halved
1 whole nutmeg

For the syrup:

½ cup (110 g) granulated sugar
2 small cinnamon sticks
1⅛ cups (275 ml) water
pared zest and juice 2 limes
½ cup (120 ml) freshly squeezed orange juice
½ cup (120 ml) pineapple juice
⅔ cup (150 ml) dark rum

Begin by making up the syrup: put the sugar, cinnamon, and water in a small saucepan, then add the lime zest. Now, over a gentle flame, mix slowly until all the sugar has dissolved – it will take about 10 minutes. Stir it with a wooden spoon: you should have no sugar crystals left clinging to the spoon when you turn it over. After that, remove it from the heat and allow it to cool.

Add the prepared fruit to a large serving bowl, scooping the seeds from the halved passion fruit using a teaspoon, then strain in the cold syrup along with the fruit juices, lime juice, and rum. Stir well before covering with plastic wrap and chilling in the refrigerator. As you serve the fruit salad, sprinkle a little freshly grated nutmeg over each serving.

Thai Fish Curry with Mango

You won't believe how utterly simple and easy this is, and yet it tastes exotic and wonderful, and what's more, it can all be prepared well in advance and the fish added about 10 minutes before you plan to serve it. You can also make this using 1 lb 8 oz (700 g) of raw, peeled shrimp added in place of the fish.

Begin by emptying the coconut milk into the pan or wok and stir while you bring it to a boil, then reduce the heat to medium and cook until the fat separates from the solids, about 20 minutes or so. You will then have about 2½ cups (570 ml) left. Now, to make the curry paste, all you do is put everything in a food processor or blender and whiz until you have a rather coarse, rough-looking paste with everything perfectly blended.

Now, over medium heat, add the curry paste and fish to the pan, and once it reaches the simmering point, cook for 4 minutes. Add the mango and cook for a further 2 minutes. Serve the curry with the cilantro sprinkled on top and Thai fragrant rice as an accompaniment. To prepare the curry in advance, prepare everything, keeping the paste covered in the refrigerator, then, 10 minutes before you want to serve, bring the coconut milk back up to a boil, then add the paste, fish, and mango as above.

Serves 4 generously

2 lb (900 g) firm fish fillet (halibut, cod, or haddock, for example), skinned and chopped into 1½ inch (4 cm) chunks
1 large mango, peeled and cut into ¾ inch (2 cm) pieces (see page 425)
3¼ cups (800 ml) coconut milk

For the curry paste:
2 medium red chilies, halved and seeded
grated zest and juice 1 lime
2 stems lemon grass, roughly chopped
1 inch (2.5 cm) piece fresh root ginger, peeled and sliced
4 cloves garlic, peeled
1 small onion, peeled and quartered
1 teaspoon shrimp paste
3 tablespoons Thai fish sauce

To garnish:
3 tablespoons chopped cilantro

You will also need a deep frying pan with a diameter of 10 inches (25.5 cm), or a wok.

433

Plum and Cinnamon Oat Slices

This is really an all-fruit recipe – it's exceptionally good with plums, but I love it with fresh or soft, dried apricots, apples, raspberries, and blueberries; in fact, you can add whatever fruit is in season. It's wonderful served either warm as a dessert with cream, or cold with ice cream. It's also a great recipe for children to make because it's so easy.

Start by cutting all the plums in half, around and through their natural line, giving a little twist to separate the halves and removing the pits. Then cut them into thin slices. Now, place them in a bowl and toss them around with the cinnamon. Next, mix the flour and rolled oats together with the salt in a mixing bowl. Melt the butter and sugar in a small saucepan over a fairly gentle heat, stirring occasionally until the butter has melted. Now, starting with a wooden spoon but finishing off with your hands, mix the melted butter and sugar with the oat mixture so you end up with a lump of dough. Divide the dough in half and press one of the halves into the baking pan, firmly pressing it all over the bottom to form a wall-to-wall carpet. Next, scatter the plums evenly over the surface, then top with the remaining oat mixture, again pressing down firmly. Now, place the pan on the center shelf of the oven and bake for 25-30 minutes, or a bit longer if you like the top really crispy. Then remove the pan from the oven and allow to cool for about 10 minutes before marking into 15 squares – to do this make 2 cuts lengthwise, then 4 cuts crosswize; don't worry if they're not all even. Unless you want to serve these warm, let them cool completely in the pan.

Note: if you want to serve these as a dessert, it can be made in a round 9 inch (23 cm) springform pan, in which case it can be cut into 8-10 wedges and served warm from the oven.

Makes 15
1 lb (450 g) fresh plums
1½ teaspoons ground cinnamon
2 cups (275 g) whole wheat flour, preferably organic
1½ cups plus 2 tablespoons (150 g) rolled oats, preferably organic
1 teaspoon salt
16 tablespoons (225 g) butter
¾ cup (110 g) light brown sugar

You will also need a non-stick baking pan measuring approximately 10 x 6 inches (25.5 x 15 cm) and 1 inch (2.5 cm) deep, lightly greased.

Preheat the oven to 400°F (200°C).

Opposite, top: Apricot and Cinnamon Oat Slice; bottom: Plum and Cinnamon Oat Slice

435

Old-Fashioned Rhubarb Trifle

I call this old-fashioned because when I was a child – a very long time ago – I used to love jelly trifles, and my mother would always make one for my birthday. This recipe is for a much more adult version, and the sharp, fragrant acidity of the rhubarb makes it a very light and refreshing dessert for spring and early summer.

Serves 6

1 lb 8 oz (700 g) fresh rhubarb
½ cup (110 g) superfine sugar
grated zest and juice 1 orange
½ cup (50 g) pecans
9 ladyfingers, e.g. Boudoir Biscuits
3 tablespoons marmalade
½ cup (120 ml) sercial Madeira
about 1⅓ cups (275 ml) freshly squeezed orange juice
1 envelope unflavored gelatin
12 oz (350 g) fresh custard
¾ cup (200 g) Greek yogurt

To serve:
a little heavy cream (optional)

You will also need an ovenproof baking dish measuring 8 inches (20 cm) square and 2 inches (5 cm) deep, and 6 individual serving bowls or 1 large trifle bowl with a capacity of 2 quarts (2 liters).

Preheat the oven to 350°F (180°C).

To prepare the rhubarb, cut it into 1 inch (2.5 cm) chunks and add these to the baking dish. Then sprinkle in the superfine sugar, together with the zest and juice of the orange. Now, place the whole lot in the oven without covering and let it cook for 30-40 minutes, until the rhubarb is tender but still retains its shape. At the same time, place the pecans in the oven and put a timer on for 7 minutes to toast them lightly, then you can either leave them whole or chop them roughly.

While the rhubarb is cooking, spread the marmalade on the ladyfingers and arrange them either in the individual serving bowls or the large trifle bowl. Then sprinkle the Madeira carefully over them, then leave it all aside so it can soak in.

When the rhubarb is cooked and has become completely cold, taste it – if it is a bit sharp, add a little more sugar. Take a perforated spoon and carefully remove the chunks of rhubarb, placing them in and among the ladyfingers. Now, pour all the juices from the dish into a large measuring cup and make this up to 2¼ cups (510 ml) with the orange juice.

Next, pour 1 cup (250 ml) of this into a small saucepan, sprinkle with the gelatin, whisk it, and let it soak for 5 minutes. Then place the pan over a gentle heat and whisk everything until all the gelatin has completely dissolved – about 2 minutes – then return this to the remaining juice in the measuring cup and give it all another good stir. Now, pour it over the ladyfingers and rhubarb. When it is completely cold, cover it with plastic wrap and leave it in the refrigerator until completely set. The last thing you need to do is whisk the custard and Greek yogurt together in a mixing bowl, then spoon this over the set mixture.

Now, cover with plastic wrap again and chill until you're ready to serve. Don't forget to sprinkle the toasted pecans on top just before serving, and although it doesn't strictly need it, a little chilled heavy cream is a nice addition.

Roasted Figs with Gorgonzola and Honey-Vinegar Sauce

This may sound like an unlikely combination but it's simply delicious – an appetizer that's fast, unusual, and absolutely no trouble to prepare.

Serves 4 as an appetizer
12 ripe figs
6 oz (175 g) Gorgonzola Piccante, chopped into ¼ inch (5 mm) dice
salt and freshly ground black pepper

For the sauce:
2 tablespoons honey, preferably Greek honey
2 tablespoons red wine vinegar

You will also need a shallow baking pan measuring approximately 10 x 14 inches (25.5 x 35 cm), oiled.

Preheat the broiler to its highest setting.

All you do is wipe and halve the figs, then place them, cut-side up, in the baking pan. Season with salt and freshly ground black pepper, then place them under the broiler for 5-6 minutes, until they're soft and just bubbling slightly. When the figs are ready, remove the baking pan from under the broiler and divide the cheese equally among them, gently pressing it down to squash it in a bit. Then place them back under the broiler for about 2 minutes until the cheese is bubbling and faintly golden brown.

Meanwhile, make the sauce by combining the honey and vinegar, then serve the figs with the sauce poured over them.

Spiced Oranges in Port

This is a great recipe for Christmas because you can make it ahead, it keeps well, and it can be used to accompany cold sliced poultry, game, or pork. It is especially good served with cooked ham, hot or cold.

First, you need to dry-roast the coriander seeds and cardamom pods, and to do this place them in a small frying pan or saucepan over a medium heat and stir and toss them around for 1-2 minutes, or until they begin to look toasted and start to jump in the pan, then lightly crush them in a mortar and pestle. Now, arrange the orange wedges in the bottom of the casserole, skin-side down, then sprinkle the spices on top (the pods of the cardamom seeds can go in as well). Next, add the rest of the ingredients. Then, over a gentle heat, slowly bring everything to simmering. Put the lid on and place the casserole in the oven on a low shelf and leave it there for 3 hours, by which time the orange skins will be meltingly tender. When the oranges have cooled, store them in a jar or a lidded plastic container in the refrigerator for a couple of days to allow the flavors to develop.

Serves 6-8
2 navel oranges, each cut into 16 wedges, skin left on
¾ cup (175 ml) tawny port
1 teaspoon coriander seeds
6 cardamom pods
4 whole cloves
1 inch (2.5 cm) piece fresh ginger, peeled and cut into thin slices
½ cinnamon stick
¾ cup (110 g) light brown sugar
½ cup (120 ml) water

You will also need a lidded flameproof casserole with a diameter of 8 inches (20 cm) and a capacity of 2½ quarts (2.25 liters).

Preheat the oven to 275°F (140°C).

Apple and Almond Crumble

This is another moveable feast because absolutely any fruit can be used. I love it with peaches or apricots in summer, in spring it's good with rhubarb, and in autumn I use half blackberries and half apples. Whatever fruit you use, though, the great thing about the topping is that it bakes to a lovely short, crumbly crispness that is almost crunchy.

Serves 6-8
1 lb 8 oz (700 g) Granny Smith apples
8 oz (225 g) McIntosh apples or other sweet apples
3½ tablespoons (25 g) light brown sugar
1 teaspoon ground cinnamon
¼ teaspoon ground cloves

For the crumble:
4 oz (110 g) whole almonds, skin on
6 tablespoons (75 g) chilled butter, cut into small dice
1¼ cups (175 g) self-rising flour, sifted
2 teaspoons ground cinnamon
½ cup (110 g) demerara or raw sugar

To serve:
custard or heavy cream

You will also need either an oval ovenproof baking dish measuring 7½ x 11 inches (19 x 28 cm) and 1¾ inches (4.5 cm) deep, or a round ovenproof baking dish with a diameter of 9½ inches (24 cm) and 1¾ inches (4.5 cm) deep.

Preheat the oven to 400°F (200°C).

Begin by preparing the apples. I always find the best way to do this is to cut them first in quarters, then peel them with a potato peeler and slice out the cores. Now, cut them into thickish slices and toss them in a bowl with the sugar, cinnamon, and ground cloves, then place them in the baking dish and put to one side.

Next, make the crumble, which couldn't be simpler since it is all made in a food processor. All you do is place the butter, sifted flour, cinnamon, and sugar into the food processor and give it a whiz till it resembles crumbs. Next, add the almonds and process again, not too fast, until they are fairly finely chopped making sure there are still a few chunky bits. If you don't have a food processor, use a large bowl, rubbing the butter into the sifted flour until it resembles crumbs, then stir in the cinnamon, sugar, and almonds, which should be fairly finely chopped by hand. Now, simply sprinkle the crumble mixture all over the apples, spreading it up to the edges of the dish, and, using the flat of your hands, press it down firmly all over; the more tightly it is packed the crisper it will be. Then finish off by lightly running a fork all over the surface.

Now, bake the crumble on the center shelf of the oven for 35-40 minutes, by which time the apples will be soft and the topping golden brown and crisp. Let it rest for 10-15 minutes before serving, then serve it warm with custard or heavy cream.

Key Lime Pie

This very famous recipe from Florida is traditionally made with key limes. Their season is short and availability limited; the pie tastes just as good, however, made with other varieties of limes.

Serves 8-10
For the bottom:
7 tablespoons (95 g) butter
6 oz (175 g) sweet oat cookies
½ cup (50 g) Grape-Nuts

For the filling:
1 tablespoon grated lime zest
(zest 3 limes)
⅔ cup (150 ml) lime juice
(juice 4-5 large limes)
3 large egg yolks
1¾ cup (400 g) sweetened
condensed milk

To finish:
a little crème fraîche
lime slices

You will also need a loose-bottomed flan pan with a diameter of 9 inches (23 cm), 1 inch (2.5 cm) deep, and a solid baking sheet.

Preheat the oven to 350°F (180°C).

Traditional Key lime pie has always had a crumb crust, and I have discovered recently that the addition of Grape-Nuts breakfast cereal gives the whole thing extra crunch. So begin by placing the butter in a pan over the lowest heat to melt, then crush the oat cookies. The easiest way to do this is to lay them out flat in a plastic bag and crush them with a rolling pin, rolling over using a lot of pressure. Now, empty the contents of the bag into a bowl and mix in the Grape-Nuts, then add the melted butter and mix well. Next, place the butter-crumb mixture into the flan pan and, using your hands, press it down evenly and firmly all over the bottom and up the sides of the pan. Then place it on the baking sheet and bake on the center shelf of the oven for 10-12 minutes, or until crisp and golden brown.

While that's happening, place the egg yolks and lime zest in a bowl, and using an electric hand mixer, beat them for about 2 minutes, or until the egg has thickened, then add the condensed milk and beat for another 4 minutes. Finally, add the lime juice and give it another quick whisk, then pour the whole lot on to the baked crust and return it to the oven for another 20 minutes, or until it feels just set when you lightly press the center with your little finger. Now, remove it from the oven, and when it's completely cold, cover it with plastic wrap, and chill until needed. Serve cut in slices with crème fraîche and a twist of lime for decoration.

19

Cheese in the kitchen

For a beginner, coming to terms with cheese as a universal subject can be a little intimidating. That said, though, cheese for me will always be one of nature's supreme culinary gifts, for the same magic ingredient the world over originally preserved the excess milk yields of four species (cows, goats, sheep, and, to a small degree, buffalo) and transformed them into such a vast eclectic miscellany of textures and flavors, national and regional.

All of these are governed by varying climatic conditions, the types of grazing or feeding, with mountain air, sea breezes, highlands, and marshlands all playing their part – not to be forgotten is the wealth of human skill and creativity that goes not just into the making of the cheese but into its careful ripening and maturing.

In a very short space of time – just 30 years – we have all moved into a vast new world of cheese. There are now countless excellent regional cheesemakers and a multiplicity of imported varieties. So to say we're spoiled for choice would be something of an understatement!

Cheese – the ultimate fast feast

What else can provide, all by itself, an instant but interesting, complete nourishing meal without any cooking? One 15th-century writer reverently described it as being part of the Trinity of the Table, along with good bread and fine wine. Another revered combination, equally sublime but perhaps more British, would be the partnership of good, sharp cheese with real ale, crusty home-baked bread, and homemade chutney (or the Irish version, with Guinness or Murphy's and home-baked soda bread).

Without bread, cheese has a wonderful affinity with crackers, oatcakes, or sweet oat cookies, the last adding a touch of sweetness to a sharp, assertive cheese. Or, as my Yorkshire grandparents taught me, the combination of the same with some rich, dark, brandied fruitcake makes a enticing sharp and sweet contrast – great at Christmas with a glass of port.

The milder, lactic cheeses, such as Cotherstone or Lancashire, are great with crisp, sharp apples, while blue cheeses seem to have an affinity with crunchy celery and fresh-shelled walnuts. In Italy, Pecorino Romano is often served with ripe, fragrant pears, and in Spain they serve thin slices of their famous Manchego with a sweet paste made of quince.

Cheese for eating (the five families)

For a beginner, the easiest way to get a knowledge of cheese is to place them into five groups, or families.

1) Soft and creamy

These soft cheeses are distinctive in that they have floury, unwashed rinds. The most famous of these are Camembert, Brie, and Coulommiers, all from Normandy. Now there is strong competition from Scotland in their version, called Bonchester, and another beautiful cheese called Cooleeney from Ireland. Other popular textured creamy cheeses are Brie de Meaux, Reblochon, Emlett (sheep), and Tymsboro (goat).

2) Medium-soft

These are slightly firmer than the previous group, but still have a soft texture, and they undergo a washing process that keeps the rind moist and helps to encourage fermentation. Examples are Pont l'Evêque from Normandy, and Taleggio from Italy. Other cheeses I would include in this group include Livarot, also from Normandy, and Durrus and Milleen, both of which are Irish cheeses.

3) Hard and not so hard

This family includes pressed, uncooked cheeses, where the curds are drained and wrapped in cheese cloth, placed in molds, and then kept under pressure for up to 24 hours. The hardest of these are Pecorino Romano, Grana Padano, and the world-famous Parmesan (Parmigiano Reggiano). Pecorino is a sheep milk cheese very much like Parmesan, but has a coarser, sharper flavor.

Then comes the less-hard group, including Cheddar, Leicester, Double Gloucester, and Cheshire, as well as the hard but crumbly varieties, such as Lancashire, Cotherstone, and Feta.

Finally, there are the cheeses with holes, which have undergone a sort of cooking process before being put into molds and pressed as above. During the maturing period fermentation occurs internally, and this creates the little air pockets, or holes, that distinguish this type of cheese, of which the most famous are Gruyère and Emmenthal.

4) The blues

What happens here is the cheese is injected with a harmless penicillin mold while the cheese is being made. This lies quite dormant during the maturation process, but then later on needles are inserted to allow air in, activating the mold, which then spreads itself in tiny blueish-green veins throughout the cheese during the rest of the maturing period. Three countries claim to have the finest blue cheese: from France, Roquefort, from Italy, Gorgonzola, and from England, Stilton, all great cheeses indeed, although I add Cashel Blue from Ireland to the list of fine blues.

Other examples are Shropshire Blue, Bleu de Bresse, and Dolcelatte (a milder Gorgonzola).

5) Goat cheese

These can be like any of the groups above, from a soft, spreadable young cheese with a mild flavor, to a well-matured, strong, zesty, very goaty-flavored one. For eating I like the strong-flavored French Crottins de Chavignol, the English Chabis, or Mine Gabhar, which is Welsh. The log-shaped Chèvre, dusted in ashes, is a medium-matured softer goat cheese. For a fresh farmhouse goat cheese with a milder flavor that also broils very well, Perroche is superb. Because the quantity of goat cheese made on farms fluctuates with the seasons, it is often in short supply. Many farm-made soft-rind goat cheeses are fine for cooking.

Fresh soft curd cheeses

This is the unfermented fresh cheese collection – all are made from skim, semi-skim, whole milk, or cream. These are not strictly in the same cheese class as those just mentioned, being more similar to cream cheese but with a lower fat content.

How to serve a good cheese board

Keep it simple is my philosophy in this case. What I would do is choose one cheese from each of the following groups: one soft cheese (Camembert, for example), one hard cheese (unpasteurized Cheddar), one blue cheese (Cashel Blue), one medium-soft (Taleggio) and one goat cheese (Crottin). A cheese board sample is photographed left. Simply pick any five cheeses, using the lists to guide you as to what you would prefer.

Pasteurized or unpasteurized?

Pasteurized is a word that causes much debate both within the world of cheesemaking and among consumers and cheese lovers everywhere. In cheesemaking the skill is directed towards the flavor and aroma of the finished cheese. This is derived from the animal that has given its milk and the plant oils it has digested. We have all experienced that particular taste and smell, which we are at a loss to describe other than it's like tasting the farm or the countryside. Every good cheese, like every fine wine, has its own unique and special earthiness, which is linked to its equally unique and special environment.

If raw, untreated milk is used to make the cheese, all that's described above is left intact and unimpaired. What pasteurization (heat-treating the milk) does is destroy any harmful micro-organisms which may be a good thing if the traditional careful attention and skill of the cheesemaker has not been adhered to, the bad thing is that during the process much of the flavor-enriching micro-organisms are destroyed at the same time. So it is often argued that pasteurized cheese can never have the distinctive and unique flavor that will satisfy a true cheese lover. I would say that in my own experience I have found this to be absolutely true, and I would always go that extra mile for an unpasteurized Camembert or Cheddar. In the US, some states allow cheese to be made from unpasturized milk. There is, however, a new generation of skillful and clever cheesemakers who are making excellent cheeses with pasteurized milk, so in the end, let your palate be your guide.

Cheese for cooking

Some cheeses are best simply for eating as they are; others are good to eat and also respond extremely well for use in cooking; others are best kept only for cooking. Below I have put cooking cheeses into three categories.

Strong and assertive

Stilton
Gorgonzola
Pecorino
Roquefort

Strong unpasteurized Cheddar
Parmesan (Parmigiano Reggiano)
Crottin

Cheesy but subtle

Gruyère
Feta
Fontina
Medium goat cheese

Medium Cheddar
Lancashire
Brie

Subtle and creamy

Mozzarella
Ricotta

Taleggio
Mild goat cheese

Good melting cheeses

This group melts in a flash, so is excellent for cooking, and includes Fontina, Gruyère, Mozzarella, and smoked Mozzarella (Scamorza).

How to store cheese

This is a question with no absolute definitive answer to. I have heard of suitable cool places: a spare bedroom (no heating on), garages, garden sheds, and even car trunks, but it all depends on the weather. I was once storing and ripening a Camembert in my garage, but the weather turned warm when I was away and my mother was looking after the house. I got a call from her saying, "I think there's something dead in your garage."

Storing cheese in the refrigerator at too low a temperature means the flavor can be impaired, but if the weather is hot, sweaty cheese is hardly preferable.

The real answer to this question is to buy your cheese from a reliable supplier (see Suppliers, pages 481-2). You will then receive it in good condition so it's ready to eat. The very best thing to do is eat it a.s.a.p., otherwise store the cheese, wrapped carefully and completely in either waxed paper or parchment paper, sealed with adhesive tape or a rubber band. If the weather is cool, any of the places mentioned above is suitable, if not then place it in the lowest part of the refrigerator. Plastic wrap is not recommended, but I do keep my Parmesan in a plastic storage bag tied at the top in a cheese box in the refrigerator, and it keeps very well.

Welsh Rabbit with Sage and Onions

Rarebit or rabbit? I like the latter, because (so the story goes) the hunter had to eat cheese for his supper when the rabbits had escaped his gun.

Serves 4 for lunch or as an appetizer or 2 as a main course

4 large, thick slices from a good-quality white sandwich loaf
2 teaspoons chopped fresh sage
2 teaspoons grated onion
8 oz (225 g) sharp Cheddar, grated
1¼ teaspoons mustard powder
4 tablespoons brown ale
1 large egg, beaten
1 teaspoon Worcestershire sauce
a pinch cayenne pepper

You will also need a broiler pan or shallow baking pan lined with foil.

Preheat the broiler to its highest setting.

Begin by mixing all the ingredients together, apart from the bread and cayenne pepper. Now, place the bread under the broiler and toast it on both sides until crisp and golden; then remove it to a toast rack for 3 minutes to get really crisp. After that, divide the cheese mixture into 4 servings, spread each over a piece of toast – right to the edges so they don't get burned – then sprinkle each one with a light dusting of cayenne pepper. Then, back they go under the broiler, 3 inches (7.5 cm) from the heat, until the cheese is golden brown and bubbling, which will take 4-5 minutes. Serve it just as it is or with some salad greens and a sharp dressing.

Mini Pizzas

These are quick and easy to make and are perfect for a delicious snack. And because crumpets and English muffins are quite small, the fillings get piled up very high and it all becomes very inviting.

All you do is lightly toast the crumpets or English muffins on each side (they can be very close to the heat at this stage) – they need to be lightly golden, which takes about 1 minute on each side. Then remove them to a baking sheet and all you do is pile up the Gorgonzola and Mozzarella on each crumpet or muffin, then sprinkle with the chopped walnuts, and finally, place the sage leaves – first dipped in the olive oil – on top. Now, back they go under the hot broiler, but this time 5 inches (13 cm) from the heat source, for 5 minutes, by which time the cheeses will have melted, the walnuts toasted, and the sage will have become crisp. Then you can serve them immediately.

You can get really creative and make up loads more ideas of your own. Obviously the whole thing can be very easily adapted to whatever happens to be available.

Serves 4 as a snack or 2 as a main course
4 crumpets or English muffins
6 oz (175 g) Gorgonzola, cubed
2 oz (50 g) Mozzarella, cubed
2 oz (50 g) chopped walnuts
12 medium-sized fresh sage leaves
1 tablespoon olive oil

Preheat the broiler to its highest setting.

Mexican Enchiladas with Cheese

Tortillas are delicious made into enchiladas which can be spread with some spicy salsa and stuffed with almost anything you have handy – in this case cheese – and then baked. They make an excellent light lunch dish served with a salad.

Serves 4 for lunch or as an appetizer or 2 as a main course
For the salsa:
1 x 14 oz (1 x 400 g) can chopped tomatoes
1 medium green chili (the fat, squat variety that isn't too fiery)
1 medium red onion, peeled and finely chopped
3 tablespoons chopped cilantro, plus a little extra to garnish
juice 1 lime
salt and freshly ground black pepper

For the enchiladas:
4 large flour tortillas
4 oz (110 g) Wensleydale or Cheddar, grated
5 oz (150 g) Mozzarella, grated (a block of Mozzarella is best for this)
¾ cup (200 ml) crème fraîche

You will also need an ovenproof baking dish measuring 9 inches (23 cm) square and 2 inches (5 cm) deep, lightly oiled, and a frying pan.

Preheat the oven to 350°F (180°C).

Begin by making the salsa: first drop the tomatoes into a sieve over a bowl to let the excess liquid drain away. Next, remove the stem from the chili, cut it in half, remove and discard the seeds, chop the flesh very finely, and place it in a bowl. Then add half the chopped onion, the drained tomatoes, chopped cilantro and lime juice, and season well with salt and pepper. Now, give everything a thorough mixing.

Meanwhile, mix the two cheeses together in a bowl. Next, put the frying pan over a high flame to preheat, and when it's hot, dry-fry each of the tortillas for 6 seconds on each side. Place one tortilla on a flat surface and spread a tablespoon of salsa over it, but not quite to the edges, sprinkle 1½ tablespoons of the cheese mixture, then follow this with a tablespoon of the crème fraîche. Then roll the tortilla up and place it in the baking dish with the sealed-side down. Repeat this with the others, then spread the remaining crème fraîche on top of the tortillas in the dish and sprinkle the rest of the salsa over the top followed by the remaining cheeses and red onion. Now, place the dish on a high shelf of the oven for 25-30 minutes, garnish with the extra cilantro, and serve immediately – if you keep them waiting they can become soggy.

Toasted Goat Cheese with Blackened Sherry-Vinegar Onions

Toasted goat cheese became very fashionable in the 1990s, and not surprisingly since it's a supremely good way to enjoy good goat cheese just on the point of melting. The blackened onions make a great accompaniment — lots of lovely gutsy flavor.

Serves 4

2 x 4 oz (100 g) soft-rind goat cheese
⅓ cup (75 ml) sherry vinegar
1 lb (450 g) large, mild Spanish onions (about 3)
4 tablespoons (25 g) dark muscovado sugar or dark brown sugar
2 tablespoons extra virgin olive oil
1 small Boston lettuce
2 oz (50 g) arugula, stems removed
salt and freshly ground black pepper

For the vinaigrette:

1 clove garlic, peeled
1¼ teaspoons sea salt
1¼ teaspoons mustard powder
2 teaspoons balsamic vinegar
2 teaspoons sherry vinegar
5 tablespoons extra virgin olive oil
freshly ground black pepper

You will also need a shallow baking pan measuring approximately 10 x 14 inches (25.5 x 35 cm) for the onions, and a smaller shallow baking pan, lightly oiled, for the goat cheese.

Preheat the oven to 450°F (230°C).

Begin this by roasting the onions: first you need to mix the sugar and vinegar together in a large bowl and give it a good stir; then set it to one side for 10 minutes or so for the sugar to dissolve. Meanwhile, peel the onions, then leaving the root intact, cut each one into 8 sections through the root (in half first and then each half into 4). Then add the onions and oil to the vinegar and sugar mixture and toss them around so they get a good coating. After that, spread them out on the baking pan, pouring the rest of the dressing over them, and season well. Now, place them on the top shelf of the oven and bake for 15 minutes; after that, turn them over and give them another 15 minutes. Toward the end of the cooking time, check them and remove and take out and set aside any of them that are in danger of over-blackening. Continue to cook the rest until they are all fairly dark, then remove them from the oven and set aside—they're not meant to be served hot.

When you are ready to serve the salad, preheat the broiler to its highest setting for at least 10 minutes. Then make the vinaigrette dressing by first crushing the garlic and salt to a creamy paste using a mortar and pestle; then work in the mustard. Now, switch to a whisk and add the vinegars and oil, then season with freshly ground black pepper. Next, slice each goat cheese in half so that you have four rounds and season these with freshly ground black pepper. Now, place the cheese slices in the oiled baking pan and broil them 3 inches (7.5 cm) from the heat for 5-7 minutes, until they are brown on top and soft.

While they're broiling, arrange some lettuce leaves on each serving plate and divide and scatter the arugula among them. Then, when the cheese is ready, place one in the middle of each plate, scatter the onion all around, and finally, drizzle the vinaigrette dressing over each salad. Needless to say, lots of crusty bread should be served with this dish.

Pasta with Four Cheeses

I know you can see only three cheeses in the smaller picture below, but there is a hidden one, because Torta Gorgonzola is in fact made from layers of two cheeses, Gorgonzola and Mascarpone, as you can see from the main picture. Add to that Ricotta and some Pecorino and you have a five-star recipe – including the best-quality pasta, of course!

Serves 2

8 oz (225 g) dried pasta (penne, for example)

¼ cup (50 g) Ricotta

3 oz (75 g) Torta Gorgonzola, Torta di Dolcelatte, or creamy Gorgonzola, diced

1 oz (25 g) Pecorino Romano, finely grated, plus a little extra to serve

2 tablespoons snipped fresh chives

Sea salt

You need to start this by measuring out the cheeses on a plate to have them ready to use, then cook the pasta in plenty of boiling salted water for 1 minute less than the full cooking time (if you're using Martelli or other good-quality pasta this would be 11 minutes cooking time) – but you need to know your pasta, so see pages 219-20. As soon as it's ready, drain the pasta in a colander and immediately return it to the saucepan so that it still has quite a bit of moisture clinging to it. Now, quickly add the chives, Ricotta, Torta Gorgonzola, and Pecorino, and stir until the cheese begins to melt. Serve it in hot bowls with the extra Pecorino on the table to sprinkle on top.

Cauliflower Soup with Roquefort

This is a truly sublime soup because the cauliflower and Roquefort seem to meld together so well, but I have also tried it with sharp Cheddar, and I'm sure it would be good with any cheese you happen to have handy. More good news – it takes little more than 40 minutes to make.

The stock for this is very simply made with all the cauliflower trimmings. All you do is trim the cauliflower into small florets and then take the stalk bits, including the green stems, and place these trimmings in a medium-sized saucepan. Then add the water, bay leaves, and some salt; bring it up to a boil and simmer for 20 minutes covered with a lid.

Meanwhile, take another large saucepan with a well-fitting lid, melt the butter in it over a gentle heat, then add the onion, celery, leek, and potato; cover the pan and let the vegetables gently sweat for 15 minutes. Keep the heat very low. Then, when the stock is ready, strain it into the pan to join the vegetables, adding the bay leaves as well but throwing out the rest. Now, add the cauliflower florets, bring it all back up to the simmering point and simmer very gently for 20-25 minutes until the cauliflower is completely tender, this time without a lid.

After that, remove the bay leaves, then place the contents of the saucepan in a food processor or blender and process until the soup is smooth and creamy. Next, return it to the saucepan, stir in the crème fraîche and cheese, and keep stirring until the cheese has melted and the soup is hot but not boiling. Check the seasoning, then serve in hot bowls, garnished with the chives.

Serves 4-6

1 medium, good-sized cauliflower (about 1 lb 4 oz/570 g)
2 oz (50 g) Roquefort, crumbled into small pieces
1½ quarts (1.5 liters) water
2 bay leaves
2 tablespoons (25 g) butter
1 medium onion, peeled and chopped
2 sticks celery, chopped
1 large leek, trimmed, washed and chopped
4 oz (110 g) potato, peeled and chopped into dice
2 tablespoons crème fraîche
salt and freshly ground black pepper

To serve:
1 tablespoon snipped fresh chives

Caramelized Balsamic and Red-Onion Tarts with Goat Cheese

The long, slow cooking of red onions and balsamic vinegar gives a lovely sweet, concentrated, caramel consistency. These are then spooned into crispy cheese-pastry cases and topped with goat cheese and thyme. Serve as a special appetizer with some balsamic-dressed salad greens.

Makes 8

For the pastry:
6 tablespoons (75 g) butter, at room temperature
1¼ cups (175 g) all-purpose flour, plus a little extra for rolling
2 oz (50 g) sharp Cheddar, grated
½ teaspoon mustard powder
a pinch cayenne pepper
a little cold water
1 large egg, beaten, for brushing

For the filling:
6 tablespoons balsamic vinegar
2 lb (900 g) red onions, peeled and very finely sliced
2 x 4 oz (2 x 100 g) soft-rind goat cheeses, top and bottom rinds removed and discarded, each sliced into 4 rounds
2 tablespoons (1 oz) butter
2 teaspoons chopped fresh thyme
8 sprigs fresh thyme
a little olive oil
cayenne pepper, for sprinkling
salt and freshly ground black pepper

You will also need 8 mini flan pans, each with a bottom diameter of 4¼ inches (11 cm), ¾ inches (2 cm) deep, greased, and a 6 inch (15 cm) plate to cut around.

Preheat the oven to 350°F (180°C).

First, make the pastry by rubbing the butter lightly into the flour, then add the cheese, mustard, and cayenne, plus just enough cold water to make a smooth dough – 1-2 tablespoons. Then place the dough in a plastic bag to rest in the refrigerator for 20 minutes. After that, roll it out as thinly as possible and use the plate as a guide to cut out 8 rounds. Line the greased flan pans with the pastry and lightly prick the bottoms with a fork, then place on a baking sheet, and bake on the center shelf of the oven for 15-20 minutes, or until the pastry is cooked through but not colored. Then allow the pastry cases to cool on a wire rack and store them in an airtight container until they are needed.

To make the filling, melt the butter in a heavy-bottomed medium-sized saucepan, stir in the onions, balsamic vinegar, and chopped thyme, season and let everything cook very gently without a lid, stirring often, for about 30 minutes, until the mixture has reduced down, taken on a lovely glazed appearance and all the excess liquid has evaporated. Then let the mixture cool until you are ready to make the tarts.

To bake the tarts, brush a little beaten egg over each pastry case and place them back into the oven – same temperature as before – for 5 minutes: this helps to provide a seal for the pastry and stops it from becoming soggy. Now spoon the onion mixture into the cases and top each one with a slice of goat cheese and a sprig of thyme that has first been dipped in the olive oil. Finally, sprinkle with a little cayenne pepper and bake for 20 minutes.

Cheese and Herb Fritters with Sweet-Pepper Marmalade

If you want to serve a meal without meat or fish, this is just the thing. It's also a great recipe for using up bits of cheese, which can be varied as long as the total amount ends up being 12 oz (350 g) for four people or 6 oz (175 g) for two. The sweet-pepper marmalade is an amazingly good accompaniment and keeps well, so can be made in advance.

Begin this by sifting the ⅓ cup plus one tablespoon (50 g) of flour and cayenne pepper into a large bowl and season with salt and black pepper, then make a well in the center and break the eggs into it. Now, gradually whisk in the eggs, incorporating any bits of flour from the edge of the bowl as you do so. Next, whisk in the milk until you have a smooth batter, then gently stir in the grated cheeses and herbs. Now, cover the bowl and let it stand in a cool place for about an hour, as this allows all the flavors to develop.

While that's happening, you can make the sweet-pepper marmalade. First, heat the oil in a saucepan over a medium heat and, when it's hot, add the onion and peppers. Cook them, tossing them around from time to time until golden and tinged brown – about 10 minutes – then add the garlic and cook for another minute. Now, add the sugar, cider vinegar, and cider, stir and bring everything back to simmering. Then season with salt and freshly ground black pepper, turn the heat down to its lowest setting, and simmer gently, uncovered, for 1¼ hours, or until the liquid has almost evaporated and you have a thick, marmalade consistency.

When you're ready to cook the fritters, take 1 tablespoon of the mixture at a time and make 12 rounds, flatten them gently to about 2½ inches (6 cm) in diameter, then lightly dust each one with the seasoned flour. Next, heat the oil over a highish heat in the frying pan, and when it's shimmering hot, cook half the fritters over a medium heat for 45-60 seconds each side, or until golden brown and crispy. Then carefully lift them out of the pan to drain on crumpled paper towels. Keep the first batch warm while you cook the second, then serve with the sweet-pepper marmalade. A green salad would make a good accompaniment.

Serves 4
4 oz (110 g) Feta, finely grated
4 oz (110 g) Gruyère, finely grated
4 oz (110 g) sharp Cheddar,
finely grated
5 tablespoons chopped
mixed herbs (basil, thyme, oregano
and parsley, for example)
⅓ cup plus 1 tablespoon (2 oz)
all-purpose flour, plus 1 tablespoon
seasoned flour
2 good pinches cayenne pepper
2 large eggs
2 tablespoons milk
3 tablespoons olive oil
salt and freshly ground black pepper

For the sweet-pepper marmalade:
2 large red bell peppers, seeded, thinly
sliced into lengths, then cut into
1 inch (2.5 cm) pieces
1 tablespoon olive oil
1 medium onion, peeled and
finely chopped
2 cloves garlic, peeled and crushed
2 tablespoons dark brown sugar
3 tablespoons cider vinegar
1 cup (250 ml) medium hard cider
salt and freshly ground black pepper

You will also need a frying pan with a
diameter of 10 inches (25.5 cm).

Semolina Gnocchi with Gorgonzola

On page 192 we made potato gnocchi, but this is another quite different version, made with semolina instead of potato. They are equally charming, with crisp, baked edges, and are light and fluffy on the inside. Remember, though, that the mixture needs to be prepared the day before you want to serve the gnocchi.

Serves 3-4

¾ cup plus 1 tablespoon (150 g) coarse semolina
2 oz (50 g) Gorgonzola Piccante, chopped into small dice
1⅓ cups (275 ml) milk
1⅓ cups (275 ml) water
freshly grated nutmeg
2½ oz (60 g) Parmesan (Parmigiano Reggiano), finely grated
2 large eggs
¼ cup (2 oz) Ricotta
salt and freshly ground black pepper

You will also need a non-stick shallow baking pan measuring 6 x 10 inches (15 x 25.5 cm), 1 inch (2.5 cm) deep, lined with parchment paper, a 2 inch (5 cm) cookie cutter and an ovenproof baking dish measuring 8 inches (20 cm) square and 2 inches (5 cm) deep, lightly buttered.

First of all, you'll need a large saucepan, and into that put the milk and water along with a good grating of nutmeg, 1 teaspoon of salt, and some freshly ground black pepper. Then sprinkle in the semolina, and over a medium heat and stirring constantly with a wooden spoon, bring it all up to a boil. Let the mixture simmer gently for about 4 minutes, still stirring, until it is thick enough to stand the spoon up in, then remove the pan from the heat and beat in 2 oz (50 g) of the Parmesan and the eggs. Now, adjust the seasoning, then pour the mixture into the prepared pan and spread it out evenly with a spatula. When it's absolutely cold, cover the pan with plastic wrap and leave it in the refrigerator overnight to firm up.

When you are ready to cook the gnocchi, preheat the oven to 400°F (200°C). Turn the cheese and semolina mixture out on to a board and peel away the parchment paper, then cut the mixture into 2 inch (5 cm) rounds with the cookie cutter, reshape the trimmings, and cut out more rounds until the mixture is all used up. I prefer to make rounds, but if you like you can cut out squares or triangles – it makes no difference. Place them slightly overlapping in the baking dish, then dot with the Ricotta and sprinkle with the Gorgonzola followed by the rest of the Parmesan. Bake on a high shelf of the oven for 30 minutes, until the gnocchi are golden brown and the cheese is bubbling.

Begin by adding the semolina to the milk and water mixture in the pan

Bring to the boil, then simmer until you can stand the spoon upright in the mixture

Next beat in the grated Parmesan and eggs, then taste to check the seasoning

Spread the mixture out in the pan and, once cold, cover and refrigerate overnight

Turn the mixture out, peel the bottom paper away and stamp the gnocchi out

Lay them in the dish, add the remaining cheeses and bake until golden brown

Cheesecake with Greek Yogurt, Honey, and Pistachios

Well, the title says it all, and you can imagine what a brilliant combination of flavors and textures this is. It's quite simply one of the best cheesecakes ever, and perfect for parties, since it's quite large. It's also extremely good topped with summer fruits, in which case add ¼ cup (50 g) of superfine sugar to the cheese mixture and top with 1 lb (450 g) of any mixture of berries, then dust with confectioners sugar before serving. Don't forget that cheesecakes are best left in the warmth of the oven to get cold since this stops them from cracking, so you need to think ahead.

Serves 10-12
1⅓ cups (265 g) ricotta cheese
1⅓ cups (280 g) fromage blanc
½ cup (50 g) shelled unsalted pistachios, roughly chopped
6 tablespoons (75 g) butter
6 oz (175 g) sweet oat cookies, ie Digestives
4 tablespoons (25 g) Grape-Nuts cereal
3 large eggs, beaten
2 teaspoons vanilla extract

To finish:
¾ cup (200 g) Greek yogurt
3 tablespoons Greek or other honey, plus a little extra to serve
about 1 oz (25 g) shelled unsalted pistachios, roughly chopped

You will also need a springform pan with a diameter of 9 inches (23 cm), and a solid baking sheet.

Preheat the oven to 300°F (150°C).

First of all, make the cheesecake base: first melt the butter in a saucepan over a very low heat, then spread the oat cookies out flat in a plastic bag and crush them firmly with a rolling pin. Next, drop the crumbs into a bowl, along with the chopped pistachios. Now, add the Grape-Nuts and melted butter and mix everything together, then spread the mixture over the bottom of the pan, pressing it down very firmly, and place it on the baking sheet and into the oven for 20 minutes.

Now, in another bowl, combine the ricotta and fromage blanc, eggs, and vanilla and beat with an electric hand mixer until the mixture is smooth and velvety. Then pour this into the pan on top of the crumbs, smooth the top, and place it back on the baking sheet on the center shelf of the oven for 30 minutes, then turn the oven off and let the cheesecake become cold in the oven. After that, it should be covered and chilled for at least 2 hours, or preferably overnight.

To serve, unmold the cheesecake, spread the surface with the yogurt first, then drizzle with the honey, and scatter the pistachios on top. Serve extra honey at the table to spoon over it.

20
Proper chocolate

Evocations of the chocolate of my childhood have flooded my mind while pondering this introduction. Even when I was very small, I much preferred the dark, sophisticated, "grown up" chocolate to the over-sweet milky version. I had a favorite brand, no longer available, unfortunately, called Nestlé Superfine, which was always given to me on birthdays.

Sometimes it was a straight chocolate bar; sometimes it contained clusters of dark-roasted almonds. Either way it was always an enormous treat, not only to be anticipated but to be savored right down to the very last square. Those were the days of sugar rationing in the early years after the war, and I sometimes think it's sad that the specialness of chocolate has faded. Now it's available everywhere from news stands, drugstores, and vending machines and so has become just an ordinary everyday item. Worse than that, the mass marketing of chocolate has brought an inevitable downgrade in quality. An increasing addiction to sugar and sugar substitutes has meant that chocolate is not always eaten for itself but as a backdrop, more to satisfy a craving for sweetness – so much so that if you're addicted to sweet substances, like diet cola, the true glory of chocolate will probably escape you. What, then, is the true glory of chocolate? To discover it we need to consider how much *actual* chocolate is in a bar. It is a moot point. Close examination reveals that it can be as high as 70 or as low as 20 percent. For chocolate lovers – and particularly for the cook – these variations need explaining.

What is chocolate?

Chocolate comes from the cocoa bean, the fruit of the cacao tree, which grows in Africa, South America, and the West Indies. The beans vary in quality and flavor. After roasting and crushing, the beans become a thick paste called chocolate mass, and this is composed of cocoa solids and cocoa butter, which is chocolate's natural oil. Cocoa solids, after being crushed again and sifted, become cocoa powder. For chocolate, however, cocoa butter is essential, since this is what gives it its melting qualities; the higher the proportion of cocoa butter the better the chocolate. We need not concern ourselves here with the complexities of how the beans are transformed into the silky-textured ingredient known as chocolate; what we do need to know is how much actual cocoa the chocolate contains. My advice is not to worry about technical words such as cocoa mass, cocoa butter, or cocoa solids, but to look at the word "cocoa" on the package. How much does it have? Manufacturers usually use the words "cocoa solids;" we need 70 percent if we want an intensely chocolatey flavor, and if we are cooking with it and adding it to other ingredients (which will dilute it somewhat), the highest-possible cocoa-solid content is essential.

What is *not* chocolate?

If only 20 percent of the essential component, cocoa solids, is present in a chocolate bar, this means 80 percent of it comprises something else. This can be vegetable fat or butterfat, emulsifiers, milk solids, flavorings, and worst of all, sugar – so much of it that the flavor of the small quantity of cocoa solid is killed. The reason for this is that mass marketing is always about price. Real chocolate costs more money, so the higher the cocoa content, the higher the price. But here we are concerned with how to cook with chocolate and that means getting the best you can afford.

How to buy chocolate

Thankfully people are rediscovering real chocolate, and for eating, it is even possible for the connoisseur to buy chocolate made from single-estate cocoa plantations, each with their own distinctive characteristics. These will be clearly marked 70 or 75 percent cocoa solids, and you will find just three ingredients listed: cocoa, sugar, and cocoa butter. For cooking it's now easy to buy 70 percent cocoa-solid chocolate, which will contain an emulsifier called lecithin and sometimes a flavoring such as vanilla.

Milk and white chocolate

With milk chocolate, the intense flavor of chocolate is purposely diluted to produce a creamier taste. This is achieved by adding whole milk solids, sometimes in equal quantity to the cocoa solids. White chocolate is not actually chocolate at all; it is made from milk solids, sugar, and fat, with cocoa butter added, and it has a bland, over-sweet taste. Neither are ideal for cooking as such, but are useful for coating or topping (see page 478).

Listen to the snap

We had great fun, while filming the television series, demonstrating how to tell good chocolate from not-so-good. The secret is in the snap. When you break off a piece of good-quality chocolate it makes a sharp, quite definite "snap." With a lesser chocolate the sound is just a dull break – if you hear anything at all. We found the sensitive microphone picked up the snap superbly, so that none of us could be in any doubt ever again.

Cooking with chocolate

I have learned how to deal with chocolate the hard way, having, more often than I care to remember, ended up with a lump fit only for the garbage can. The outcome of these disasters is that I now know the solution to the problem of melting chocolate. Follow the instructions below to the letter and never rush it! I know this is a bore, but believe me, you have to wait.

How to melt chocolate

Here you'll need a large heatproof bowl to place over a saucepan containing a couple of inches of barely simmering water, making sure the bottom of the bowl doesn't touch the water. Break up the chocolate, add the pieces to the bowl, and keeping the heat at its lowest, let them melt – it will take 5-10 minutes to become smooth and glossy (though the time will vary depending on the amount of chocolate – individual timings are given in each recipe). Then remove the chocolate from the heat, give it a good stir, and it's ready.

A Very Chocolatey Mousse

This was the chocolate recipe of the 1960s, but it has now, sadly, been eclipsed by other eras and their equally fashionable recipes. So time for a revival, I think, because this is certainly one of the simplest but nicest chocolate desserts of all.

Serves 6
7 oz (200 g) bittersweet chocolate, broken into pieces
½ cup (120 ml) warm water
3 large eggs, separated
3 tablespoons (40 g) superfine sugar

To serve:
a little whipped cream (optional)

You will also need 6 ramekins, each with a capacity of ⅔ cup (150 ml), or 6 individual serving dishes.

First of all, place the broken-up chocolate pieces and warm water in a large heatproof bowl, which should be placed over a saucepan of barely simmering water, making sure the bowl doesn't touch the water. Then, keeping the heat at its lowest, allow the chocolate to melt slowly – it should take about 6 minutes. Now, remove it from the heat and stir it until it is smooth and glossy; let the chocolate cool for 2-3 minutes before stirring in the egg yolks. Mix it well with a wooden spoon.

Next, in a clean bowl, beat the egg whites to the soft-peak stage, then beat in the sugar, about a third at a time; beat again until the whites are glossy. Now, using a metal spoon, fold a tablespoon of the egg whites into the chocolate mixture to loosen it, then carefully fold in the rest. You need to have patience here – it needs gentle folding and cutting movements so that you retain all the precious air, which makes the mousse light. Next, divide the mousse among the ramekins or other serving dishes and chill for at least 2 hours, covered with plastic wrap. I think it's also good to serve the mousse with a dollop of softly whipped cream on top.

Note: this recipe contains raw eggs.

Chocolate-Crunch Torte with Pistachios and Sour Cherries

This is the easiest chocolate recipe ever invented – I first made a more basic version on children's television. Since then it has become much more sophisticated, but the joy of its simplicity and the fact that no cooking is required make it a real winner for busy people.

Begin this the day before by soaking the dried cherries and raisins in the rum overnight. When you are ready to make the torte, place the broken-up chocolate and butter in a large heatproof bowl, which should be placed over a saucepan of barely simmering water, making sure the bowl doesn't touch the water. Keeping the heat at its lowest, allow the chocolate to melt – it will take about 6 minutes to become smooth and glossy. Now, remove the bowl from the pan, give the chocolate a good stir, and let it cool for 2-3 minutes. Next, fold in the whipped cream, followed by the fruit soaked in rum, the pistachios, and chopped oat cookies, and give it a good stir. Finally, spoon the mixture into the cake pan as evenly as possible, cover with plastic wrap, and chill for a minimum of 4 hours. To serve, dust the surface with a little cocoa powder, cut the torte into wedges, and serve with crème fraîche, whipped cream, or simply heavy cream.

Serves 12
8 oz (225 g) bittersweet chocolate, broken into pieces
1 cup (110 g) unsalted pistachio nuts, roughly chopped
½ cup (50 g) dried sour cherries or dried cranberries
½ cup (50 g) raisins
3 tablespoons rum
4 tablespoons (50 g) butter
⅔ cup (150 ml) heavy cream, lightly whipped
8 oz (225 g) sweet oat cookies, ie Digestives, roughly broken

To serve:
a little cocoa powder, to dust
crème fraîche, whipped cream or heavy cream

You will also need a spring form cake pan with a diameter of 8 inches (20 cm), 1½ inches (4 cm) deep, lightly greased with a flavorless oil.

Melting Chocolate Puddings

This, I suspect, could be the *chocolate recipe for the beginning of the 21st century – very light, very chocolatey individual baked desserts that have a melted fudge-chocolate sauce inside that oozes out as you dip in your spoon. My thanks to Galton Blackiston and everyone at Morston Hall in Norfolk, England, for giving me their recipe.*

Serves 8

7 oz (200 g) bittersweet chocolate, broken into pieces

14 tablespoons (200 g) butter, diced

2 tablespoons brandy

½ cup plus 2 tablespoons (110 g) superfine sugar

4 large eggs, plus 4 large egg yolks

1½ teaspoons vanilla extract

½ cup plus 1 tablespoon (60 g) all-purpose flour

To serve:

a little heavy cream or whipped cream

You will also need 8 mini dessert molds, each with a capacity of 3/4 cup (175 ml), generously brushed with melted butter.

First of all, place the broken-up chocolate, along with the butter and brandy, in a large heatproof bowl, which should be placed over a saucepan of barely simmering water, making sure the bowl doesn't touch the water. Then, keeping the heat at its lowest, allow the chocolate and butter to melt slowly; it should take 6-7 minutes. Then remove it from the heat and give it a good stir until it's smooth and glossy.

While the chocolate is melting, put the sugar, whole eggs, yolks, and vanilla extract in a large mixing bowl, and place it on a dish towel to steady it, then beat on a high speed with an electric hand mixer until the mixture has doubled in volume – this will take between 5 and 10 minutes, depending on the power of your mixer. What you need to end up with is a thick, mousse-like mixture that leaves a trail like a piece of ribbon when you stop the motor and lift the beaters, (*see below left*).

Now, you need to pour the melted-chocolate mixture around the edge of the bowl (it's easier to fold it in from the edges) and then sift the flour over the mixture. Using a large metal spoon, carefully but thoroughly fold everything together. Patience is needed here; don't be tempted to hurry it because careful folding and cutting movements are needed, and this will take 3-4 minutes.

Now, divide the mixture among the pudding molds (it should come to just below the top of each one) and line them up in a shallow baking pan. If you like, the puddings can now be covered with plastic wrap and kept in the refrigerator or freezer until you need them.

When you're ready to bake the puddings, preheat the oven to 400°F (200°C). Remove the plastic wrap and bake on the center shelf of the oven for 14 minutes if they have been chilled first, but only 12 if not; after that time the puddings should have risen and feel fairly firm to the touch, although the insides will still be almost liquid. Let them stand for 1 minute before sliding a spreading knife around each pudding and turning out onto individual serving plates. If you're cooking these puddings directly from the freezer, give them about 15 minutes' cooking time and allow them to stand for 2 minutes before turning out. Serve immediately, with some chilled cream to pour over them.

As the puddings cool, the melted chocolate inside continues to set, so they can be served cold instead, if you like, as a fudgey-centered chocolate cake with whipped cream.

Note: this recipe contains partially cooked eggs.

Quick Chocolate Trifle

This one is either for people who don't like to cook or for devoted cooks who nonetheless need something really quick to make. First, you need to hurry to the supermarket to collect the ingredients, then, after the cherries have soaked, the trifle can be made in minutes.

Serves 8

3 double-chocolate-chip muffins, each weighing about 2 oz (50 g)

7 oz (200 g) bittersweet chocolate

1 lb 8 oz (680 g) jar pitted morello cherries, drained and soaked overnight in ⅓ cup (75 ml) dark rum

2 tablespoons morello cherry jam or conserve

1 cup (250 g) Mascarpone

1⅓ cups (400 g) fresh custard

1⅓ cups (275 ml) heavy cream

You will also need a trifle bowl or serving dish with a capacity of 2½ quarts (2.25 liters).

You need to start this recipe the day before you plan to serve it. All you do at this stage is soak the drained cherries overnight in the rum. The next day, begin by slicing the muffins horizontally in half, then spreading each slice with some jam, and welding the slices back together to their original muffin shape. Now, cut each one vertically into 4 pieces approximately ¾ inch (2 cm) wide, and place these all around the bottom of the trifle bowl or serving dish. Now, take a skewer and stab them to make holes; then strain off the rum the cherries have been soaking in, and sprinkle it all over the muffins; scatter the cherries on top.

Now, reserving 2 oz (50 g) of the chocolate for decoration, break the rest up into squares. Place the broken-up chocolate in a large heatproof bowl, which should be placed over a saucepan of barely simmering water, making sure the bowl doesn't touch the water. Then, keeping the heat at its lowest, allow the chocolate to melt slowly – it should take about 5 minutes to become smooth and glossy. Remove the bowl from the pan and give the chocolate a good stir, then let it cool for 2-3 minutes.

While that's happening, put the Mascarpone in a bowl and beat to soften it, then add the custard and beat them together. Next, beat in the cooled melted chocolate, then pour the whole mixture over the soaked muffins and cherries. Now, whip the cream to the soft-peak stage, then carefully spoon this over the trifle, spreading it out with a knife. Last, chop the rest of the chocolate (using a piece of foil to protect it from the heat of your fingers as you steady it), shredding it very finely. Sprinkle the shreds over the surface of the trifle, cover with plastic wrap, and chill until needed.

Chocolate and Prune Brownies

I never much cared for the flavor of orange and chocolate or raspberries and chocolate, but prunes and chocolate are, for me, a heavenly partnership. Plus, this tastes even better if you soak the prunes in Armagnac for a special occasion. Brownies can be served warm as a dessert or just served at room temperature as they are.

Begin this the night before you are going to make the brownies by soaking the chopped prunes in the Armagnac. The next day, preheat the oven to 350°F (180°C), then chop the almonds roughly, place them on a baking sheet, and toast them in the oven for 8 minutes. Be sure to use a timer here, or you'll be throwing away burned nuts all day.

While the almonds toast, put the chocolate and butter into a heatproof bowl placed over a saucepan of barely simmering water, making sure the bowl doesn't touch the water. Allow the chocolate to melt – 4-5 minutes – remove it from the heat, then beat until smooth. Next, stir in the other ingredients, including the prunes and Armagnac, until well blended. Now, spread the mixture into the prepared pan and bake on the center shelf for 30 minutes, or until slightly springy in the center, then let it cool for 10 minutes before cutting into squares and transferring them to a wire rack.

Makes 15

2 oz (50 g) bittersweet chocolate, broken into pieces
2 oz (50 g) pitted soft prunes, (pruneaux d'Agen, if possible) chopped and soaked overnight in ¼ cup (55 ml) Armagnac
2 oz (50 g) skin-on almonds
8 tablespoons (110 g) butter
2 large eggs, beaten
1¼ cup (225 g) demerara or raw sugar
⅓ cup plus 1 tablespoon (50 g) all-purpose flour
1 teaspoon baking powder
¼ teaspoon salt

You will also need a non-stick baking pan measuring approximately 10 x 6 inches (25.5 x 15 cm) and 1 inch (2.5 cm) deep, lightly greased and lined with parchment paper.

473

Chocolate, Prune, and Armagnac Cake

This is the very lightest chocolate cake of all, the reason being that no flour is used – it's simply made with eggs and cocoa powder. It's very fragile, almost soufflé-like, and once you've tried it you'll never want any other kind. Don't forget to start this a couple of days ahead, if possible, by heating the prunes with the Armagnac and leaving them to soak up all the delicious flavor.

Serves 8

For the cakes:
6 large eggs, separated
¾ cup (150 g) superfine sugar
½ cup plus 3 tablespoons (50 g) cocoa powder, sifted

For the filling:
14 oz (400 g) pitted soft prunes (pruneaux d'Agen, if possible), soaked overnight (or longer if possible) in ½ cup (120 ml) Armagnac (see the introduction)
1 tablespoon crème fraîche

To finish:
5 oz (150 g) bittersweet chocolate, broken into pieces
1 tablespoon crème fraîche

You will also need 2 x 8 inch (20 cm) loose-bottomed cake pans, 1½ inches (4 cm) deep, the bottoms and sides well oiled and the bottoms lined with parchment paper.

Preheat the oven to 350°F (180°C).

Start off by, first, placing the egg whites in a large, clean, grease-free bowl. Put the yolks in another bowl, along with the sugar, and beat them until they just begin to turn pale and thicken – be careful not to thicken them too much; they need approximately 3 minutes' beating. After that, gently fold in the sifted cocoa powder.

Next, with a very clean whisk, beat the egg whites until stiff but not too dry. Now, using a metal spoon, fold a heaping tablespoon of the egg white into the chocolate mixture to loosen it up a little, then carefully and gently fold in the rest of the egg white, slowly and patiently trying not to lose any air. Now, divide the mixture equally between the prepared cake pans and bake near the center of the oven for 15 minutes. They won't appear to be cooked exactly, just set and slightly puffed and springy in the center; when they're taken out of the oven, they will shrink (but that's normal, so don't panic). Let the cakes cool in their pans, then slide a spreading knife around the edges, gently invert them onto a board, and carefully strip off the lining papers.

To make the filling for the cake, first of all set aside 10-12 of the largest prunes, then place the rest, plus any remaining soaking liquid, in a food processor, along with the crème fraîche, and whiz to a purée. After that, transfer the purée straight from the food processor onto one half of the cake, placed carefully onto a plate first, then spread the purée out and place the other half of the cake on top.

Now, all you need is the chocolate topping. For this, place the broken-up pieces of chocolate in a large heatproof bowl, which should be placed over a saucepan of barely simmering water, making sure the bowl doesn't touch the water. Then, keeping the heat at its lowest, allow the chocolate to melt slowly – it should take about 5 minutes to become smooth and glossy. Then, remove it from the heat and stir it, then let the chocolate cool for 2-3 minutes.

Now, dip each one of the reserved prunes into the melted chocolate so that half of each one gets covered. As you do this, place them on a sheet of parchment paper to set. Next, stir the crème fraîche into the chocolate, then use this mixture to cover the surface of the cake. Spread it over carefully with a spreading knife, making ridges with the knife as you go. Now, decorate the cake with the chocolate prunes. Cover the whole cake with an upturned, suitably sized bowl or a domed cake cover, and keep it in the refrigerator until about an hour before you want to serve it.

Chocolate Crème Brûlées

What chocolate mousse was to the 1960s, crème brûlée has been to the 1990s; for a while, it was on almost every restaurant menu. It's truly a classic that easily lends itself to variations like this one – a smooth, velvety chocolate custard topped with a very crunchy caramel. Because of the vagaries of domestic oven broilers, I've cheated a little with this version of the caramel topping. There's even an alternative using a cook's blow torch.

Serves 6

5 oz (150 g) bittersweet chocolate, broken into pieces
2½ cups (570 ml) heavy cream
6 large egg yolks
¼ cup (50 g) superfine sugar
1½ teaspoons cornstarch

For the caramel:
¾ cup (175 g) white granulated sugar

You will also need 6 ramekins, each with a bottom diameter of 2½ inches (6 cm), a top diameter of 3 inches (7.5 cm), and 2 inches (5 cm) deep.

Start the crème brûlées the day before you want to serve them. Place the broken-up chocolate, along with ⅔ cup (5 fl oz) of the cream, in a large heatproof bowl placed over a saucepan of barely simmering water, making sure the bowl doesn't touch the water. Then, keeping the heat at its lowest, allow the chocolate to melt slowly – it should take 5-6 minutes. Remove it from the heat and stir it until it's smooth and glossy, then remove the bowl from the pan and let the mixture cool for 2-3 minutes.

After that, beat the egg yolks, superfine sugar, and cornstarch together in a separate bowl for about 2 minutes, or until they are thick and creamy.

Now, in a separate pan, heat the remaining cream just to the simmering point and pour it over the egg-yolk mixture, beating as you pour. Return the whole mixture to the pan and continue to stir over a gentle heat until it thickens – this will take 2-3 minutes. Next, beat the melted chocolate and cream together until completely smooth, add a little of the custard mixture to it, and continue to beat it in. After that, add the remaining custard, beating until everything is really smooth. Then divide the custard among the ramekins, making sure you leave a ½ inch (1 cm) space at the top for the caramel. Now, let the ramekins cool, cover them with plastic wrap, and chill them overnight in the refrigerator.

A few hours before serving the brûlées, make the caramel. To do this, put the granulated sugar in a small saucepan, place it over a medium heat, and leave it like that, keeping an eye on it. When the sugar begins to melt around the edges, *opposite, top*, and just starts to turn liquid – which will take 4-6 minutes – give the pan a good shake and leave it again to melt until it's about a quarter melted. Now, using a wooden spoon, stir it gently, *opposite, center*, and then continue to cook until the sugar has transformed from crystals to liquid and is the right color – amber, *opposite, bottom*. Keep stirring gently until you're sure all the sugar has dissolved. The whole thing should take 10-15 minutes.

Now, remove the pan from the heat. Take the plastic wrap off the custards and pour the caramel over them. Tilt the ramekins gently from side to side to get an even, thin covering of caramel over all, then leave them for a few minutes for the caramel to harden. Cover them loosely with foil (plastic wrap might cause the moisture from the brûlées will soften the caramel). Return them to the refrigerator until needed.

These also freeze well, but do this before you add the caramel. Instead, pour the caramel over them after removing the custards from the freezer, but since the caramel will set almost immediately on the frozen custards, tilt the ramekins from side to side as soon as you've poured the caramel over each one to distribute it evenly. Allow them to soften in the refrigerator for 2 hours before serving.

Note: you can use a blow torch to get a much thinner layer of caramel if you prefer. Simply sprinkle 1¼ teaspoons of superfine sugar over each ramekin of custard, and using a water spray, mist the surface lightly – this will help the sugar to caramelize quickly without burning. Now, using sweeping movements, pass the flame of the blow torch across each brûlée until the sugar melts and caramelizes.

Miniature Choc Ices

This is an unashamedly fun recipe, great for special parties and at Christmas, or to serve instead of chocolates or mints at the end of a meal. But although it's fun, the choc ices are seriously good to eat, particularly if you buy the best-quality ice cream. I have used three different chocolate toppings here, but to make it simpler, you can use just one.

Makes 25-30

2 cups (500 ml) vanilla ice cream
5 oz (150 g) bittersweet chocolate, broken into pieces
5 oz (150 g) good-quality white chocolate, broken into pieces
5 oz (150 g) good-quality milk chocolate, broken into pieces
3 tablespoons shelled unsalted pistachio nuts, roughly chopped
3 tablespoons toasted chopped hazelnuts

You will also need 2 baking sheets, a shallow plastic storage container measuring 8 x 5 x 2½ inches (20 x 13 x 6 cm), with a lid, and a 1 inch (2.5 cm) melon scoop, parchment paper, and about 30 toothpicks.

You need to begin this recipe the night before, so as soon as you get the ice cream home, transfer it to the plastic storage container and spread it out in an even layer, then put the lid on and place it in the freezer overnight. At the same time, line the baking sheets with parchment paper, place these one on top of the other and put them in the freezer as well.

When you're ready to start making the choc ices, begin by putting a small saucepan of water on to boil. Remove the ice cream and one baking sheet from the freezer, then dip the melon scoop in boiling water before making each ice. Just draw the scoop all along the frozen ice cream to form little rounds, and quickly transfer each one to the baking sheet. You do need to work at high speed here, so no distractions if possible, but if you find the ice cream is getting too soft to work with, just place everything back into the freezer and continue later. (With no interruptions you should be able to do them all in one session.) Next, insert a toothpick into the center of each ice, then put them all back in the freezer for a minimum of 2 hours, because the ice-cream balls need to get hard again.

After the 2 hours, melt the chocolates separately. For this, first place the broken-up pieces of bittersweet chocolate in a large heatproof bowl sitting over a saucepan of barely simmering water, making sure the bowl doesn't touch the water. Then, keeping the heat at its lowest, allow the chocolate to melt slowly –it will take about 5 minutes to become smooth and glossy. Then remove the chocolate from the heat, give it a good stir, and let it cool while you repeat this process with the 2 other chocolates (the white and milk chocolates will take 3-4 minutes to melt). Next it's very important to allow each chocolate to cool completely to room temperature before coating the ices, or the ice cream will melt. So start off by coating a third of the ice-cream balls with the white chocolate: lift each ice cream up off the tray using the toothpick and, holding it over a plate, spoon the chocolate over to coat the ice cream completely. Now, scatter with a few chopped pistachios (but not over the bowl of chocolate!), then return to the baking sheet; you'll find the chocolate will harden around the ice cream immediately. Coat a third in milk chocolate, then the rest in the bittersweet chocolate, and scatter these with the toasted hazelnuts. Put them back into the freezer as soon as you can and serve straight from the freezer.

Other nuts can be used, or finely chop up 4 pieces of crystallized stem ginger and mix with one of the chocolates before coating the ice creams.

Note: if you want to make these a long time ahead, cover with freezer foil.

Chocolate Mini Muffins with Toasted Hazelnuts

This is a good recipe for children to make using chocolate chips for melting and cherries instead of nuts.

Makes 24

2 oz (50 g) bittersweet chocolate, roughly chopped
1 cup (150 g) all-purpose flour
2 tablespoons cocoa powder
2 teaspoons baking powder
¼ teaspoon salt
1 large egg, lightly beaten
¼ cup (40 g) superfine sugar
½ cup (120 ml) milk
4 tablespoons (50 g) butter, melted and cooled slightly

For the topping:

2 oz (50 g) hazelnuts, roughly chopped
3 oz (75 g) bittersweet chocolate, broken into pieces

You will also need deep 2 x 12-hole mini-muffin pans (1¼ inch bottom diameter, ¾ inch deep), well greased or lined with mini-muffin paper cases.

Preheat the oven to 400°F (200°C).

You need to begin this recipe by toasting the hazelnuts for the topping. To do this, place the chopped nuts on a baking sheet and toast them in the preheated oven for 5 minutes; it's important to use a timer here.

Next, for the muffins, start off by sifting the flour, cocoa powder, baking powder and salt into a large bowl. Then, in a separate bowl, mix together the egg, sugar, milk and melted butter. Now, return the dry ingredients to the sifter and sift them straight on to the egg mixture (this double sifting is essential because there won't be much mixing going on). What you need to do now is take a large spoon and fold the dry ingredients into the wet ones – quickly, in about 15 seconds. Don't be tempted to beat or stir, and don't be alarmed by the rather unattractive, uneven appearance of the mixture: this, in fact, is what will ensure that the muffins stay light. Now, fold the chopped chocolate into the mixture – again with a minimum of stirring; just a quick folding in.

Divide the mixture among the muffin cups, about 1½ teaspoons in each, and bake on a high shelf of the preheated oven for 10 minutes until well risen. Then remove the muffins from the oven and cool in the muffin pans for 5 minutes before transferring them to a cooling rack.

While they're cooling, make the topping. To do this, place the broken-up chocolate in a small heatproof bowl, which should be sitting over a saucepan of barely simmering water, making sure the bowl doesn't touch the water. Then, keeping the heat at its lowest, allow the chocolate to melt slowly – it should take about 3 minutes to melt and become smooth and glossy. Then remove it from the heat and give it a good stir, then let the chocolate cool for 2-3 minutes.

Then, when the muffins are cool enough to handle, spoon a little melted chocolate on to each one, then place it back on the cooling rack and scatter the hazelnuts over the top of each muffin.

Suppliers

Delia Smith's Website
www.deliaonline.com
Includes recipes, equipment advice,
and culinary techniques

Mail-order cookware and specialty
foods:

Balducci's
catalog available
800-225-3822
www.balducci.com
424 Sixth Avenue
New York, NY 10011
Gourmet and specialty foods

Belgravia Imports
catalog available
800-848-1127
662 Bellevue Avenue
Newport, RI 02840
Maldon crystal sea salt, Wiltshire
Tracklement sauces, Marigold

Bridge Kitchenware
catalog available
800-274-3435
212-838-6746
www.bridgekitchenware.com
214 E. 52nd Street
New York, NY 10022
Extensive cookware

Broadway Panhandler
866-COOKWARE or
212-966-3434
www.broadwaypanhandler.com
477 Broom Street
New York, NY 10013
Extensive cookware

Carrs Flourmills Ltd.
(44) 01697 331661
Solway Mills, Silloth
Wigton
Cumbria
CA7 4AJ
Supplier of sauce flour

Dean and Deluca
catalog available
877-826-9246
www.dean-deluca.com
8200 E. 34th Street Circle
North Building 2000
Witchita, KA 67226
Extensive selection of specialty
foods and gourmet groceries,
cookware

efoodpantry.com
Specialty groceries including
organic and all-natural sugars

Kalustyan's
212-685-3451
www.kalustyans.com
123 Lexington Avenue
New York, NY 10016
Good selection of dried herbs,

spices, grains, beans, and nuts.
Asian and Middle eastern foods
including Atiki Greek Honey

King Arthur Flour
catalog available
800-827-6836
www.KingArthurFlour.com
P.O. Box 876
Norwich, VT 05055
Supplier of a full range of baking
ingredients, including Maldon
sea salt

Mermaid
(44) 0121 554 2001
www.mermaidcookware.co.uk
Samuel Groves & Co Ltd
Norton Street
Hockley
Birmingham
B18 5RQ
British supplier of roasting pans,
sheets, and saucepans as used on
the How to Cook 1 television
series

Penzey's Spices
catalog available
262-679-7207
www.penzeys.com
P.O. Box 933
Muskego, WI 53150

Suppliers

Peppercorn Gourmet
303-449-5847
www.peppercorn.com
1235 Pearl Street
Boulder, CO 80302
Asian and gourmet cookware,
spices, foods

Spice Merchant
catalog available
307-733-7811
www.orientalcookingsecrets.com
P.O. Box 524
Jackson Hole, WY 83001

Sur La Table
catalog available
800-243-0852
www.surlatable.com
Cookware and gourmet foods

Tavolo
catalog available
800-700-7336
www.digitalchef.com
Cookware, world foods, and
gourmet goods

Williams-Sonoma
catalog available
877-812-6235
www.williams-sonoma.com
Good selection of cookware

Zabar's
catalog available
800-697-6301
www.zabars.com
2245 Broadway
New York, NY 10024
Cookware and specialty foods

Dairy Products and Cheese

The Cheese Store of Beverly Hills
800-547-1515
www.cheesestorebh.com

Feast.Com
www.feast.com
Quality cheeses among other
specialty foods

Ideal Cheese
catalog available
212-688-7579
1205 Second Avenue
New York, NY 10021

Murray's Cheese Shop
catalog available
888-692-4339
212-243-3289
www.murrayscheese.com
257 Bleecker Street
New York, NY 10014

Fresh Game, Poultry, and Fish

Browne Trading Co.
catalog available
800-944-7848
www.browne-trading.com
260 Commerical Street
Portland, ME 04101
Good selection of fresh and
smoked fish, including
Finnan Haddie

D'Artagnan
catalog available
www.dartagnan.com
280 Wilson Avenue
Newark, NJ 07105
800-327-8246
Specialist game and poultry
supplier, stocks

Index

Acknowledgments

"A huge thank you to Sarah Randell who was deeply involved with the television series and the book in the UK, but who also took on the mammoth task of 'Americanizing' this edition so that American cooks could follow the recipes with confidence.

Thanks also to Dawn Fozard who patiently checked and double-checked."